*Identity and Experience
in the New Testament*

Identity and Experience in the New Testament

KLAUS BERGER

Translated by Charles Muenchow

Fortress Press

Minneapolis

HISTORICAL PSYCHOLOGY OF IDENTITY AND EXPERIENCE
IN THE NEW TESTAMENT

First English language edition published by Fortress Press in 2003.

Translated by Charles Muenchow from *Historische Psychologie des Neuen Testaments,* published by Verlag Katholisches Bibelwerk, Stuttgart, Germany, ©1991.

Cover image: Dancers (fresco from Campania). Anonymous © Alinari / Art
    Resource, NY. Used with permission.
Cover design: Zan Ceeley
Book design: Mary Ellen Buscher

Library of Congress Cataloging-in-Publication Data

Berger, Klaus
    [Historische Psychologie des Neuen Testaments. English]
    Historical psychology of the New Testament / Klaus Berger ; translated
    by Charles Muenchow.
        p. cm.
    Includes bibliographical references and indexes.
        ISBN 0-8006-2779-2 (pbk. : alk. paper)
        1. Bible. N.T.—Psychology. I. Title.
BS2545.P9 B4713 2002
225.6'01'9—dc21   2002152639

Manufactured in the U.S.A.
08   07   06   05   04   03   1   2   3   4   5   6   7   8   9   10

Contents

Abbreviations

1 Clem.	*1 Clement*
1 En.	*1 Enoch*
1QH	Hymn Scroll (*Hodayoth*)
1QS	Community Rule (*Serek ha-Yahad*)
2 Bar.	*2 Baruch*
3 Bar.	*3 Baruch*
3 En.	*3 Enoch*
ABRL	Anchor Bible Reference Library
Alleg. Interp.	Philo, *Allegorical Interpretation*
AnBib	Analecta Biblica
ANRW	*Aufstieg und Niedergang der römischen Welt*
Apoc. Sedr.	*Apocalypse of Sedrach*
ARW	Archiv für Religionswissenschaft
b.	Babylonian Talmud (*Babli*)
Barn.	*Epistle of Barnabas*
BET	Beiträge zur evangelischen Theologie
Bib	*Biblica*
BZNW	Beihefte zur Zeitschrift für die neutestamentliche Wissenschaft
CD	Damascus Document
Did.	*Didache*
Ep. Barn.	*Epistle of Barnabas*
FRLANT	Forschungen zur Religion und Literatur des Alten und Neuen Testaments
FzB	Forschung zur Bibel
Herm. Mand.	*Shepherd of Hermas, Mandates*
Herm. Vis.	*Shepherd of Hermas, Visions*
HNT	Handbuch zum Neuen Testament
HTKNT	Herders theologischer Kommentar zum Neuen Testament
HTR	*Harvard Theological Review*
Hul.	*Hullin*
Jos. Asen.	*Joseph and Aseneth*
JRS	*Journal of Roman Studies*
Jub.	*Jubilees*
KEK	Kritisch-exegetischer Kommentar über das Neue Testament
L.A.B.	*Liber antiquitatum biblicarum* (Pseudo-Philo)

LXX	Septuagint
Mart. Asc. Isa.	*Maryrdom and Ascension of Isaiah*
MT	Masoretic text
NovT	*Novum Testamentum*
NTD	Das Neue Testament Deutsch
NTSR	New Testament for Spiritual Reading
NTS	*New Testament Studies*
NumR	*Numbers Rabbah*
NZSystTh	*Neue Zeitschrift für systematische Theologie*
OTP	*Old Testament Pseudepigrapha,* ed. James H. Charlesworth
par.	parallel/s
Par. Jer.	*Paraleipomena Jeremiou*
Pes.	*Pesaḥim*
QSGP	Quellen und Studien zur Geschichte der Philosophie
RAC	*Reallexikon für Antike und Christentum*
ROC	*Revue de l'Orient chrétien*
S	Syriac version
SBS	Suttgarter biblische Studien
Spec. Laws	Philo, *On the Special Laws*
SANT	Studien zum Alten und Neuen Testament
Shep. Herm.	*Shepherd of Hermas*
SJLA	Studies in Judaism in Late Antiquity
StPB	Studia Post-Biblica
Strom.	Clement, *Stromateis*
StTh	*Studia Theologica*
SUNT	Studien zur Umwelt des Neuen Testaments
Ta'an.	*Ta'anith*
TANZ	Texte und Arbeiten zum neutestamentlichen Zeitalter
ThLZ	*Theologische Literaturzeitung*
ThW	*Theologische Wissenschaft*
T. Dan	*Testament of Dan*
T. Isaac	*Testament of Isaac*
T. Levi	*Testament of Levi*
TNT	Texte zum Neuen Testament
TRE	*Theologische Realencyclopädie*
UTB	Uni-Taschenbücher
VigChr	*Vigiliae Christianae*
WMANT	Wissenschaftliche Monographien zum Alten und Neuen Testament
WUNT	Wissenschaftliche Untersuchungen zum Neuen Testament
ZDMG	*Zeitschrift der deutschen morganländischen Gesellschaft*
ZThK	*Zeitschrift für Theologie und Kirche*

1
Introduction

Historical Psychology

Psychology is the disciplined investigation of the interior life of the human being—of the psyche and its constraints, interactions, and outward manifestations. Psychology is a distinctly modern science. In applying a psychological perspective to New Testament texts, then, I will be raising questions those texts do not answer directly. Adding the qualifier "historical" to the basic term "psychology" draws attention to our assumption that both the inner life of the human being and the ways in which it has been understood have undergone far-reaching changes over the course of time.

Significance of the Inquiry

Biblical psychology investigates the way the reality of human existence is presented within the horizon of revelation. Such an issue can hardly be a matter of indifference to anyone who would understand divine revelation in its most immediate context or, expressed in theological terms, who would reflect on the Incarnation in all its dimensions. To be sure, in this study psychology is understood in a strictly historical sense, which means it will differ considerably from modern or contemporary modes of psychological understanding.

A brief illustration can suggest the importance of our inquiry. In ancient Greek there is no semantic differentiation between the notions of suffering and passion; both are designated by the term *pathos* (cf. the Latin *passio*). Modern English, however, recognizes only a distant relationship between them. This has substantive importance for our understanding of ancient

consciousness and psychology. A historical-psychological study is called
for by more than semantic peculiarities such as this, however. We must also
consider the current scholarly discussion, which is directly fruitful for the
question of application.

Status of the Scholarly Discussion

Two quite different ways of posing psychological questions in the interpretation of Scripture deserve mention in this context.

1. In his two-volume *Tiefenpsychologie und Exegese* (Depth Psychology and
Exegesis), Eugen Drewermann offers a consistently psychological interpretation of the Bible. Specifically, he operates from the standpoint that
the Bible presents an "archetypal hermeneutic of the human psyche."[1]
Drewermann focuses on the developmental stages in the so-called process
of individuation, drawing alternately on the work of Sigmund Freud and
Carl Jung.

Criticism of Drewermann has repeatedly noted how his approach
threatens to relativize actual history and blur the distinctiveness of external reality. For example, G. M. Martin comments that Drewermann directs
his gaze toward that which "is valid for all times and places." Martin justifiably goes on to say, "I often cannot escape the impression that, with
Drewermann, whatever is unique to a biblical pericope fades into archetypal generality. With his approach, the consumer-oriented mentality of
our postindustrial age encroaches on both religion and church."[2]

Unlike Drewermann, I intend under no circumstances to gloss over historical and cultural distinctiveness while raising questions of a psychological sort. At the same time, however, I also intend in no way to discount
the value of psychological questions. In fact, I will go so far as to emphasize the religious and theological significance of a psychological approach
to the Bible—but one that is at the same time historically sensitive. That is
to say, I regard it as wholly proper to inquire after the nature of human
experience as reflected in the Bible. Furthermore, such investigation holds
out the promise of fruitful application to the Christian life. We must also
be careful, however, to recognize that reflections of human experience differ from one historical epoch to the next. Psychological investigation of
the biblical text must therefore proceed with all the care and patience of
the attentive historian, of one trained to overhear distinctive nuances in
the voices of persons from the past.

2. In clear contrast to Drewermann, Gerd Theissen has examined the fruit-
fulness for exegesis of a broad array of modern, pragmatically oriented (i.e.,
not broadly theoretical) psychological perspectives.[3] These include models

drawn from learning theory, psychodynamics, and studies in cognition. In the excellent introduction to his *Psychological Aspects of Pauline Theology*, Theissen has also discussed the theoretical problems involved in such religio-psychological exegesis. As he sees it, the use of psychological categories in exegesis is a natural extension of the historical-critical method.

It is true that Theissen does not simply read the New Testament in terms of modern experience.[4] He nonetheless frequently opens up the possibility of comparison with modern psychological understanding.[5] In fact, Theissen's book ultimately rests upon the very same criteria that dominate the more obviously modernizing studies, such as the notion of the unconscious.[6] Thus we must conclude that the overall intention of Theissen's book is precisely to establish points of contact with modern forms of psychological understanding.[7] (In my opinion, it is hardly wrong to see here an analogy with Rudolph Bultmann's requisition of the philosophical anthropology of Martin Heidegger.) In sum, even though historical arguments are occasionally offered by Theissen, the net effect is still that the sharp historical contours are constantly being obscured.

In contrast to Drewermann, one must credit Theissen for linking his psychological analogies to traditio-historical investigations. At least he starts from points gained by rigorous historical investigation, as opposed to being lifted from prior theoretical constructs. Nonetheless—and as is all too often the case with efforts at New Testament exegesis informed by modern social sciences—the uniquely historical aspect of the material is ultimately pushed aside. In short, with studies carried out from *any* perspective provided by the modern sciences of human behavior, it appears that similar results are inevitable. The best one can say of such studies, it seems to me, is that consciously and deliberately adopting a *social*-psychological perspective, because of its greater sensitivity to the historical dimension, would be less open to objection.

Here, for heuristic reasons, quite a different starting point is chosen. It strikes me as much too risky to work within a framework provided by any modern science of human behavior, relying on its categories of interpretation. With such an approach, too much of the modern situation gets imposed on the text. As can be seen with Bultmann's reliance on Heidegger, it is all too easy to think in terms of some unchanging human nature or world of experience—and therefore also of some relatively stable, transhistorical understanding of the human situation (with its corresponding "psychology").[8]

I thus deliberately call into question the possibility of any atemporal approach. Beyond that I am also convinced that rejecting modern modes of shaping the investigator's questions provides the best starting point if the Bible is to have a genuine impact on our own age. It is the very strangeness of the text, and not its confirmation of what we already know, that forms the foundation for its critical function as a corrective to our naive views of God and the world.[9] Thus the (perhaps rather presumptuous) goal of this book is to maintain and even to intensify an inquisitive fascination with human experience as actually depicted in the biblical text. At the same time, I intend to avoid the sort of psychological interpretations which, to date, have all too often blurred the historical specificity of the text. So a double strategy is called for here. On the one hand, I assume that the New Testament's ways of viewing and experiencing the psyche are different from our own. On the other hand, I will try to bring precisely what is distinctive about the New Testament perspective into dialogue with our own views and expectations. Such a procedure demands careful posing of questions and explicit attention to method.

Posing Historical-Psychological Questions

One goal of this investigation is to develop a whole arsenal of questions that can appropriately be directed to New Testament texts. With such an arsenal at hand, it should be possible for any given text to be analyzed from a historical-psychological perspective. Thus I will proceed not so much with new hermeneutical models as with a precise and deliberate posing of questions. First the more systematic questions need to be raised; then the strictly exegetical ones can be considered.

UNDERSTANDING THE PAST

As I see it, historical psychology is an especially important way of genuinely understanding the distinctive otherness to be found in the biblical text. In the past, historical-critical exegesis was often disturbing in the way it simply piled up inert material. Because it was not understood in all its peculiar strangeness, the material was just laid out and left undigested. To criticize uncomprehending exegesis of this sort was the aim of Eugen Drewermann; it was also the concern of Rudolf Bultmann's hermeneutic and, beyond that, of the dialectical-theology movement in general. All of these approaches are characterized by the fact that they seek to blend exegesis and application. However, it is precisely this effort that strikes me as illegitimate—or, to put it more cautiously, unnecessary. In my opinion, exegesis and application must be kept methodologically separate. As I see it, even the more traditional forms of exegesis fail to separate these two domains adequately. Too often the task of reconstructing the distinctive world of the text is abandoned prematurely; the context and function of a biblical text in its early setting is not reconstructed in any real depth.

Glossed over are such questions as how people were able to appropriate a given text *back then* and just what sort of concrete meaning it had *for them*.

The fundamental issue at stake is clarity regarding what constitutes the historical significance of a text. In my judgment, the goal of interpretive work should not be to find some broadly valid theme reflected in the text. Rather, we should aim to grasp what is historically distinctive about the text. The issue of contemporary applicability rightly comes up only later, as a second step. The historical significance of a text, therefore, is neither its impact on later understanding nor its role in the grand sweep of human history. Rather, a text's historical significance is the function it plays at each distinctive stage of its reception. Historical psychology is one way among others of discerning the varying nature of that reception. Our goal is to reconstruct, with genuine understanding, the shape of a text's reception at specific points along the way.

INVESTIGATING EXPERIENCES

Historical psychology has obvious implications for the distinct, yet related, issue of human experience and its role within the horizon of divine revelation. In saying this, I have no illusion about being able to explain revelation, much less of being able to penetrate the mystery of God. Still, we are here talking about the experiential aspect of what one also calls revelation.

The undeniable predilection of modern hermeneutics for the category of experience is actually an outgrowth of a hermeneutical impasse.[10] In the wake of demythologizing, it became forbidden to speak about the otherworldly in terms of the worldly. In the current discussion about experience, however, this prohibition (and its associated emphasis on the rigid transcendence of God's word) is to some extent undercut. In the arena of human experience both the divine and the human dimensions are once again being, if not blended, at least brought into relationship. Through the category of experience, the absence of relationship between God and the human being is being overcome, even if only by means of carefully circumscribed analogies. This renewed attention to experience is associated with a more accepting attitude toward myth. In short, as something of the "other" is being seen as reflected in experience, pure transcendence is also being broken down.

ISSUES RESOLVED BY A HISTORICAL-PSYCHOLOGICAL APPROACH

The modern science of psychology arose in order to ameliorate problems that seem to be located in the inner life of the human being. *Historical* psychology, however, primarily works on a hermeneutical plane. That is to say, historical psychology investigates whether and in what respect New Testament texts can in their own way offer help for such problems. In view of the temporal specificity of these texts, the nature of such help can be determined only on a case-by-case basis. Moreover, whatever resources are uncovered can never be applied directly. One cannot leap over the barriers of time by simply swallowing the New Testament whole, as it were. Rather, New Testament texts offer help only on certain occasions, and even then only by virtue of some demonstrable similarities. Nonetheless, it is precisely in confronting issues of this sort that historical psychology holds its distinctive promise. Through this approach the indispensably critical, as opposed to merely confirmatory, function of New Testament texts can be actualized.

The promise of historical psychology is best demonstrated by means of examples. So, for instance, New Testament texts know nothing of a bifurcation of the human being into separate categories called "body" and "soul." This fact certainly must be of importance in our evaluation of what it means to be corporeal beings. Any number of other illustrations can also be adduced. Consider, for example, what is implied for our estimation of the human psyche when we realize the following:

- An incomparably closer affinity exists between the domain of the juridical and the sphere of the psyche in biblical thought than in our own.
- A significant number of the contrasting categories that shape the way we pose questions are either completely lacking or are formulated in quite different ways in the Scriptures. In addition to the one between body and soul, this applies to such alternatives as visible and invisible, knowledge and action, or faith and works.
- Reflective consciousness is widely lacking in the New Testament, while the concreteness of action is regularly emphasized (cf. the first part of chapter 7, below).
- According to all that we can determine, the New Testament's mode of experiencing reality is much less rigidly separated into distinct spheres than is our own, and the thresholds between the spheres that are recognized are much easier to cross. This facilitates ease of transition from one sphere to the next.
- According to the biblical perspective, external reality is not uniformly "out there" but rather confronts human beings in varying degrees of proximity and with differing manifestations of power (cf. "Mythic Events" in chapter 6, below).
- The New Testament regards as "present" more than just what in our understanding is visible or actual.

What Carsten Colpe has said with regard to the notion of spiritual beings in New Testament times applies also to historical psychology as a hermeneutical perspective: "The key to a proper understanding is found only when one resolutely transports oneself into a worldview or a conceptual order where the temporal distinctions of past, present, and future, and such differentiations as those between spiritual and material, visible and invisible, celestial bodies and powers, thoughts and visions, all blend together."[11] The constant concern of historical psychology is precisely to dissolve these arbitrary dichotomies that so often became formulated only during the Middle Ages but that since then have dominated our thought at every turn. Working from within a historical-psychological framework thus amounts to an ongoing struggle to overcome our own presuppositions about what must have been regarded as obvious in New Testament times.

In the final analysis, the most fundamental features of self-understanding are at issue here. As historical psychology is only now beginning to make clear, the basic categories by means of which we form our view of the world and our sense of who we are as human beings are by no means as self-evident as they might seem. Deliberate sensitivity to biblical modes of experiencing reality heightens awareness of our own categories of understanding, and from this confrontation we learn that our way of experiencing both the world and ourselves is hardly the only possible way.

To be sure, allowing oneself to be criticized by another way of experiencing reality is still quite different from being transformed by the call of the gospel and coming to place all one's trust in God. Perceiving matters in a new light hardly amounts to what the gospel means by *metanoia* (repentance). The task of historical psychology is thus rather modest. Historical psychology contributes to our understanding of the gospel, and it does so by paying particularly close attention to those human beings who were its first witnesses. In this way historical psychology opens up a path toward genuine ecumenical dialogue—with the past! (It also can have an impact on ecumenical dialogue of today, such as the one between the church and the so-called Third World, which is as remote from many of us as is the world of the New Testament.)

As in every genuine dialogue, the outcome cannot be determined beforehand. It is certainly possible that our conceptual categories and our patterns of perception, fruitful as they might have been in some ways, in other ways block our access to the gospel. It might also be that some of the New Testament's modes of perceiving reality continue to exist among us (perhaps in the field of art), but in such a marginalized way that they no longer command attention or respect. In sum, the real issue here is not just a better historical understanding of the New Testament. I am also trying to expand our own field of awareness by paying careful attention to the modes of perception that characterized the voices that spoke in the New Testament.

From this there results the following as the most important method of historical psychology: to inquire into all those aspects of self-understanding that we take for granted but which are missing in New Testament texts. Thus of each text it must be asked, With regard to what we take as normal experience, what is absent here? What is stated differently from the way we would put it?

SPECIFIC QUESTIONS TO BE POSED

Almost every text can be investigated by using one or more elements from a distinct set of questions.

Semantic Field

Exactly how can the processes of the psyche be described? How can we express joy, sorrow, or pain? How can particular experiences (e.g., suffering) be verbalized?

In dealing with texts the focus is on reconstructing the presuppositions and the associations (or semantic fields or metaphors) that accompany specific terms pertaining to the realm of the psyche. The basic issue is the exact nature of the vocabulary used when describing the inner life of the human being. For example, Paul recognizes only one significant aspect relating to the specifically interior dimension of the person, and he refers to this aspect by means of the only (quasi-) reflective concept at his disposal: conscience (*syneidesis*). Significantly, however, for Paul this term has nothing to do with feelings but with good and evil—and then only in extreme situations, not in the routine living of the Christian life. The upshot is that, for Paul, the "inner person" is not some stable and durable interiority but rather an invisible eschatological identity (2 Cor 4:16). Likewise the inner person under discussion in Romans 7 has nothing to do with feelings or, as we might say, with the "spiritual life." Instead, the issue here is again good and evil—and human will (Rom 7:18-21). In sum, it is highly doubtful that the "spiritual" or "soul" aspect of the human being, in anything like our familiar understanding, is ever directly thematized in the New Testament.

Associations and Responses

"Semantic connotation" basically corresponds to the psychological phenomenon known as association. When they read or hear a certain word, most people immediately associate it with some other word or respond to it with a specific emotion. Association often plays a decisive role in the appropriation of a text. The philological practice of more precisely determining meaning through consideration of parallels serves as a familiar demonstration of this principle. Revelation 12:1 provides an illustration. Here the sequence "sun—moon—stars" signifies overwhelming splendor. The reader is expected to pick this up through the power of association. In other places, however, "sun" can awaken notions of the hostile or the destructive. In that case, reference to a shadow, far from suggesting something negative, would be welcomed for the way it softens or ameliorates the implicit threat. The exegete must continuously test his or her suppositions regarding the appropriate associations by paying careful attention to the structural features of the text (e.g., oppositional devices) or by investigating parallel passages in which the surmised associations are made explicit.

The Function and Intended Effect of the Text

By means of various rhetorical devices, every text intends to elicit some sort of response on the part of its addressee. To be sure, there is nothing intrinsically psychological about the study of rhetoric. The question of the effect achieved by rhetoric, however, is fundamentally a psychological one, since that effect takes place within the psyche. Strictly speaking, then, the effect of rhetoric is what constitutes the psychological issue. Since in most cases the original historical effect of New Testament texts is no longer discernible, the question must instead be directed toward what appears to be the intended effect.

The Generating Conditions of the Text

Does a text allow retrospective conclusions to be drawn regarding any particular emotional or psychological disposition on the part of either author or readers? One might think here, for example, of disillusioned love in 2 Cor 3:1-3, or of anguish in Romans 9—i.e., texts that, unlike those mentioned above, do not expressly make inner states of being their theme. To carry out a comprehensive investigation of a historical situation it is especially important to determine the social-psychological milieu within which those who interact relate to one another. So it is necessary to ask such questions as the following: What sorts of experiences most probably underlie and are presupposed by texts that are worded in this fashion? Was there feigned suffering or genuine conflict? Precisely what is the background of the biblical text with regard to such features as mental state or emotional situation? Do aversions dominate or do sympathies? Are any of these states or situations worked through in the biblical text, for instance, by setting up of some sort of contrasting experience?

*The Causes of and Conditions for Specific Experiences
and Modes of Perception*

It is not enough merely to substantiate the experiences reflected in the
New Testament. One should instead seek out the historical bases of such
experiences to the extent possible. This especially holds true with regard
to perceptions that deviate widely from our own, such as when we must
deal with uncommon (to us) experiences such as miraculous manifestations of power, visions, speaking in tongues, or rapture. Of course, hardly
ever are the reports of such phenomena adequate, from our point of view.
Seeking to account for such experiences, however, does not mean providing some sort of rationalistic explanation. On the contrary, it means
attempting to locate them in a religious, social, or historical context such
that we can understand the function of such experiences within their total
cultural milieu. So, for example, just what sort of people claimed to experience rapture? How did such people relate this to their other experiences? Or did they even try to do so?

In pursuit of this fuller understanding, we must go beyond such historical labels as Pax Romana or "the first-century crisis." Even economic
and sociological insights are of limited utility. When it comes to exploring
religious expressions, by far the most important factor is traditional popular piety with its distinctive forms and conditions—especially as fostered
within the primary setting of the family.

How Experiences Get Assimilated

Texts often reflect ways in which people come to terms with something.
For example, the destruction of Jerusalem in 70 C.E. prompted an array of
efforts to assimilate what was a catastrophe of the highest magnitude and
import for Jews and Jewish-Christians alike. Similarly, the early Christians
came to terms with their persecutions and sufferings in a variety of ways.
What goes on in human beings as they do this? On one level, they regularly look to established older traditions as a way of overcoming such
tragedies. On a deeper level, however, our interest must lie not in the content of the traditions but rather in the reasons within the realm of human
experience that cause precisely certain traditions and not others to be
selected. So the question becomes one of how the catastrophe had the particular effect that it did. What did the catastrophe awaken in the people
such that they responded to it in precisely a given way, and not in some
other way?

Fundamental Categories of Experience

TIME

Noting carefully the statements offered by a text, just how is time experienced? Is a linear conception of time presupposed, such as the one which (supposedly) guides our own daily living? What constitutes remembering? Does hope have a temporal orientation?

IDENTITY

What constitutes personal identity? Are the boundaries between "I" and "you" as sharply drawn as they are with us? Does a different set of boundaries apply in relation to God? Who, in general, is regarded as a "person"?

POWER AND WEAKNESS

Do perceptions of power and weakness correspond to our own? Clearly, there are far-reaching differences here. For example, we ourselves are acutely aware of weakness in situations where religious texts largely take for granted that power resides with the pious and the righteous.

CAUSALITY

In the New Testament a word or a touch can accomplish great things. We are no longer able to experience such marvels, since we could not operate in our technological world without a distinct notion of causality. (The ancient world had its own distinctive sort of "technology.") Thus, when it comes to trying to understand the people of the New Testament, we must be prepared either to expand or to curtail some of the basic categories by means of which reality is perceived.

REALITY AND SIGN

In the biblical mode of perception, a special relationship exists between reality and sign. There it is possible, by means of a "sign," for the hidden "essence" of a person (especially insofar as that person has something to do with either God or Satan) to break forth from its normally concealed state and become manifest at a special time or in a specific place (e.g., atop a mountain). In other words, it is possible to experience an epiphany, a manifestation of that which is normally hidden from view. There are a number of important epiphanies of just this sort in the Bible. Take, for example, the transfiguration of Jesus. This unveiling of his divine sonship takes place on a mountaintop and at a determined time (see Mark 9:2). The same holds true with the revealing of the kingdom of God, or of Jesus as the Christ, or even of the deeds of human beings at the end of time. Everything now concealed will be made manifest at a specified time, at a terminal point (on the "day of the Lord").[12] Another example: In his walking on the water, Jesus is revealed as one who can do what only God can do. This revelatory event in turn establishes and legitimates Jesus as undoubtedly "Godlike," as one who can then feed the masses (John 6; Mark 6). With something like Mark's account of the transfiguration, then, we are hardly dealing with a refined literary fiction (as Wilhelm Wrede assumed). Instead, we have before us a particular mode of religious experience. Perhaps one can go so far as to speak of an experience-paradigm. One could think of this paradigm as structured around the following points:

At a certain "hour of truth" (a biblical expression to some extent synonymous with "day of the Lord"), "all is made manifest." Time is thus not always experienced in linear fashion; reality does not possess the same quality throughout. Above all, reality (what *is*, in itself) is not uniformly accessible. Instead, reality displays oddities of a personal, spatial, or temporal sort.[13] Thus, in confronting reality, one finds oneself constrained by an inscrutable, unfathomable, ultimately arbitrary will.

OTHERNESS

Distinctive of biblical mentality is a pronounced openness toward the dimension of the Other; indeed, manifestations of the Other are expected. In New Testament times the venerable notions of sacred time, holiness, and divine election were being expanded and thereby also given new life. They were again becoming structural elements of experience. This fact makes them of interest to historical psychology and something to be reckoned with. The Other is no longer sealed off in the past but rather has become a latent feature of the present, a possibility lying just under the surface. The same holds true of eschatological realities, wonders, visions, and new revelations. The formerly unapproachable has once again drawn near, and one can again let oneself be surprised by it.

TOKENS (SYMBOLS) OF REALITY

Characteristic of the early Christian structure of experience is also an orientation toward "tokens" of reality. Here I refer to how some empirically concrete (and in this sense "real") phenomenon gets taken up as a part (and hence as a "token") of some more broadly encompassing whole. The token indicates the whole in the way the tip of an iceberg indicates the hidden mass beneath the surface. In other words, the token is the visible aspect of a reality that is more complex but nonetheless of the same nature as the token. The psychological dimension lies in the way the reader or the hearer moves from perception of the visible component to apprehension of the totality of which the token is only a part. Instances of such a shift include the following:

- The Eucharistic bread is itself part of the life which Jesus gives.
- The physical proximity of Jesus to his disciples is itself an aspect of the new relationship between human beings and God that becomes available through Jesus (cf., e.g., the incident related in John 6:19-21 and the ensuing discourse of Jesus).
- The miracles of healing are an aspect of the renewal of the whole person.
- The expulsion of the money changers from the Temple is an element in the messianic renewal of Israel.
- The coming together of the community in worship is itself a manifestation of its fundamental identity as the gathered people of God.

In each case—and this is the point—the empirically perceptible component is not just a sign, not just something ultimately superfluous over against the reality it points to. This stands in sharp contrast to the dominant Western way of thinking, with its Neoplatonic tendency to regard the visible sign as, at most, the precursor of that which it designates. Where such an understanding predominates, the sign itself becomes dispensable. Illustrations of this modern way of "misunderstanding" the New Testament are available for all of the examples given above.[14]

A large part of the demythologizing agenda—indeed, of the whole pattern of thinking deemed normal in the established churches since the Enlightenment—converges precisely on this point: The physical or corporeal dimension of reality is devalued over against some underlying feature that is regarded as truly essential, albeit highly elusive. I contend that this modern tendency leads to a serious misunderstanding of the way signs are perceived in the New Testament. Signs there hardly have just a didactic function; they do not become insignificant when set against the reality to which they point; they do not just disclose some deeper meaning elsewhere; they do not extinguish themselves in the process of making the invisible perceptible. Thus, for example, the New Testament does not view miracles as some ultimately inadequate way of speaking about God. Miracles are instead an actual component of some new reality that, while it certainly stretches beyond the miracle itself, nonetheless finds its starting point precisely in the miracle.

In the Gospel of John this relationship between incarnate wonder and subsequent discourse has become a key structural feature (e.g., John 5–6 and 9–11). The concrete event becomes the indispensable starting point for a chain of consequences—as is, indeed, the earthly Jesus himself. It appears that the Gospel of John as a whole served precisely the same function in its own day, namely, to present and narratively to advance that which had its concrete beginning in the event called Jesus Christ.

The Resurrection of Lazarus (John 11) is an illustration of the New Testament understanding of miracles as tokens of reality. John 11 contains two especially provocative statements. In 11:25, Jesus proclaims himself "the resurrection and the life"; in 11:39 Lazarus is restored to life even though he has been dead for four days and his body has begun to suffer decomposition. Both statements are "incredible," and in much the same way. Because of their tangible specificity (Jesus corporeally stands before us as "the resurrection"; Lazarus is physically restored to life), both call upon us to respond, not with an "if" or a "however" but with either a "yes" or a "no." No space is granted for getting around the challenge. Nonetheless, we can find in exegetical history two common ways of trying to avoid the challenge here posed. On the one hand, there is a simple-minded fundamentalism which, in effect, prunes away the thorny parts by simply accepting everything at face value. All the provocative features of the story are removed through a forced act of acceptance. The other way is to impose a "spiritual" mode of interpretation upon the narrative so that one sees in this story, above all, a statement about the essence of faith; the real miracle becomes the act of faith, while the resurrection itself is pushed into the background. With such a maneuver the distinctiveness of the story is not interpreted but interpreted away. A third possibility, however, could start from a deliberate refusal either simply to believe the story (to "swallow it whole") or forthrightly to deny its dual claim to facticity (the resurrection of a dead body; Jesus as himself the resurrection). In following this third possibility, we allow ourselves to be transported by the story into a process of ongoing reflection wherein we know from the outset that the provocative features of the text will not be overcome or eliminated. In this way the text would be taken neither as a straightforward empirical account nor as a purely spiritual story but would remain as an irritant to our understanding.

This sort of approach to the text can be defended from a form-critical perspective. Many texts in the Gospel of John present themselves as puzzling and enigmatic. Both the "Jews" and the disciples are often said to "misunderstand." The same feature appears outside the Gospel of John as well, particularly in the parables. As is shown by the summons, "Let the one who has ears hear," parables are enigmatic utterances that must be reworked and applied by the hearer. This is precisely what keeps them forever fresh; this is why they are so well-suited to an ongoing tradition. Just like the parables in the Synoptic Gospels and the sayings of Jesus in the *Gospel of Thomas*, the Gospel of John as a whole is to be taken as perpetual challenge. The challenge directed to the (not just ancient) reader is to enter repeatedly into confrontation with the incomprehensible "scandal" of the gospel. Such reflective confrontation is an ongoing process. The reason why exegetic efforts to tame the Gospel of John have remained diverse, contradictory, and largely unsuccessful lies precisely in this Gospel's literary character as enigmatic speech. Given its nature, a textually appropriate understanding of "faith" is to allow oneself to be astonished by the claims made in this Gospel. It means confronting the text head on, letting oneself be led by its provocations. Faith, in other words, is hardly a matter of calmly piling up items of belief. (If it were, the Gospel of John would soon become tedious.) On the contrary, faith is a way of plunging forward, of being prodded onward by the possibility of ever new application. To one who has set out upon such a path of intense but open-ended confrontation with the gospel, the message of John 11 is starkly clear. In the confrontation with Jesus, one is dealing with life-and-death issues.

Now we are in a better position to appreciate the scandalous quality of the concrete facticity in John 11. Spiritualized generalities and ethereal abstractions impose no demands. Time and again, however, the Gospel of John issues the summons to choose between light and darkness, and to do so now! This summons is congruent with the Gospel's Christology, which focuses on the abrupt and radical nature of Jesus' claims as well as with its conception of miracles. In the strict sense of the word, miracles are incredible signs (tokens of reality).

Historical-psychological observations of this sort also have consequences when it comes to applying the gospel to life. Two features especially trouble us about the story in John 11, features that we cannot get around. One is the blunt and outrageous claim by Jesus of Nazareth, a flesh-and-blood human being, that he is himself the resurrection. The second is that Lazarus was really dead! In the understanding of antiquity, after four days all possibility was gone that the soul could still be in the body. Lazarus did not just appear to be dead; he was beyond all doubt dead. Every rational explanation is excluded. Moreover, Jesus says nothing about the hereafter, nothing about the souls of the dead, and nothing at all about the process of resurrection. Only one question is really important here. When we come to the horizon of our earthly existence, must we sink into oblivion? The Greco-Roman world compared death to the sea. Is being at the threshold of death like standing on a seashore late on a stormy evening, as everything sinks into thick darkness? Is there some point of light? Jesus affirms that there is indeed a beacon of light. He himself is that beacon of light, and when you hold this light before your eyes, you find that anxiety and fear and uncertainty melt away.

FACTICITY

John 11 makes it clear that people of the New Testament era had a very different understanding of facticity from what we have.[15] We frequently pass off as naïveté or as a mythopoeic thinking—or, in fundamentalism's misunderstanding, as objective account—what is actually a different way of perceiving reality, one in which our basic dichotomies simply do not apply. We can draw closer to a historically accurate understanding of the New Testament perspective when we recognize that in its pages the facticity of an event is functionally dependent on the power or might of the one about whom the event is reported (cf. chapter 6, below). That is to say, in the New Testament the features of facticity or historicity are strongly tied to personal reputations. Accordingly, when something marvelous is reported about a worthy person (not: someone about whom it might merely be expected), then indeed the reported event "happened." Conversely, every act of the Adversary (Satan) is but a lie and a deception, a nonexistent illusion.

One further observation pushes to the limit the matter of differing judgments about what is "true." It is clear that Paul shapes his discussion of the *parousia* to match the situation of his readers. For example, he puts a damper on the theme in 1 Thess 5:2-9, but he stokes it up in Rom 13:11-14. One might well ask if the apostle is here being manipulative. Does Paul "bend" the "truth" according to his audience? If so, then just what does he "really" believe about the *parousia*? For Paul, unlike for us, not every true statement is "true" in the same way. Paul works with a hierarchical understanding of truth; the truth of any statement is measured by its ability to lead people to Christ. The more a statement is able to do this, the "truer" it is.

For us, on the contrary, truth is thought to be essentially uniform in nature. Our religious conviction is that all eras and peoples stand equally close to God ("equidistance"). The New Testament does not see things this way. The notions of "equiveracity" (that everything is "true" to the same degree) and equidistance are a legacy of the Enlightenment, according to which reality is a uniform continuum, uniformly accessible and unvaryingly constraining. Following the Enlightenment, all people are thought to stand in the same relationship to truth as to the Law—all are equal before it. From the perspective of the New Testament, such equality will come about only at the end of time. (There is an obvious parallel between the eschatological vision of the New Testament and the political agenda of the Enlightenment.) Our fundamental assumption that reality is a uniform continuum, then, is simply not shared by the New Testament. Paul is not engaging in equivocation. The culmination of time is determined not by a calendar but by proximity to Christ and to God.

Methods of Historical Psychology

Historical psychology employs no new methods of inquiry. Among the usual ones, however, the following emerge as especially important features to note for historical-psychological exegesis:

- *Turning point.* Not only parables but texts in general containing elements of traditional material lead up to some distinctive turning point—some feature that runs counter to expectation. Such deviations from the expected aim at a psychological impact.

- *Conventional piety.* The various associations that appear in a text or that a text allows also reflect the conventional religious beliefs and practices of its hearers and readers.

- *Associated worldview.* As has been demonstrated especially by G. Röhser,[16] one important task of exegesis is to investigate the model of reality that underlies the material in certain texts. (This is a fascinating and necessary task that especially needs to be carried out with regard to the sayings of Jesus.) Awareness of the associated worldview is a prerequisite for understanding how people of the New Testament would have perceived or understood something.

- *Rhetorical devices.* The exegete must also note the rhetorical features of a text in order to appreciate the range of possibilities being presented to the reader for identifying with the material.

- *Missing elements.* Most important is sensitivity to what in the text differentiates it from how a parallel situation would be presented in our own day. In other words, we must always ask the question, "What is missing?" (i.e., compared to how one of our contemporaries might speak). This sort of awareness is often rendered difficult because of translations that conceal alien elements in the text.

- *Terminology relating to the psyche.* In deliberate contrast to both Eugen Drewermann and Gerd Theissen, I will here intentionally employ colloquial terms in the area of the psyche (as in the catchwords for the chapters of this book). My course of action will be to fill out these colloquial terms with material garnered by historical-psychological research in order thereby to be able to delineate the contours of New Testament experience. Reliance on psychological expertise in any of its current manifestations or on any leading psychologists would be a mistake. I have intentionally avoided efforts to bother with any special efforts of this kind.[17]

- *The "psychology" of antiquity.* The ancient world itself generated a number of important "scientific" suggestions regarding the psyche that deserve attention because of their proximity to the New Testament. Such suggestions, however, must be used with caution precisely because of their more reflective nature. The psychology of antiquity is not the same thing as immediate awareness of psychological processes, and it is the latter that we tend to encounter in the New Testament. Still, antiquity's

own inquiries into the nature of consciousness can help us bridge gaps
in our understanding of biblical psychology.

- *Diversity.* There is no such thing as *the* historical psychology of *the* Bible.
- *Constants.* I believe that the existence of anthropological constants has
not been demonstrated and therefore none will be presupposed here.[18]

Exegesis and the Unconscious Mind

In recent discussion between the disciplines of psychology and history,
the issue of the unconscious mind has become a central point of conflict.
For the historian this issue is already the critical threshold; around this
issue cluster a number of key questions. Is there really no alternative to
the model of a mind bifurcated into "conscious" and "unconscious"? Is
this model actually suited to the task of illuminating ancient texts whose
authors are no longer alive? Of what value is the question whether
ancient authors were familiar with the unconscious mind—or at least
with something remotely similar to what we understand by the unconscious mind? Of what significance are images and metaphors in "psychological" inquiry? What about dreams and visions, to say nothing of
reports about journeys to heaven or the underworld? Are there aspects of
historical research where the notion of an unconscious mind would be
inappropriate and others where it would be suitable? Is there some work-
able middle ground in the controversy between historians and psychologists?

In modern understanding the "unconscious" has several noteworthy
characteristics. Negatively defined, it is precisely that which cannot come
to consciousness. I cannot become directly aware of my own unconscious
mind; it is something that can only be determined indirectly, from without. An added complication is that "repression" is a regular feature of the
unconscious mind. In any case, some distinctions would be helpful in
speaking about the unconscious:

- Can an author be unaware of something he has expressed in a text?
- If an author is indeed not consciously aware of something he is saying,
then from what source does he derive it?
- Can an author consciously speak about something that had previously
been buried in his unconscious but about which he subsequently gained
clarity?
- Can an author speak about matters that are not (or were not) features in
the conscious awareness of others, but which nonetheless appear in their
remarks?

Reflection on such questions leads to the following theses:

1. The "conscious/unconscious" model must not be the only possible one. For the historian this model is burdened with significant difficulties. The crux of the problem is the way this model draws attention away from objective interaction between subjects, which is constitutive of historical-critical investigation.

In the broader methodological discussion affecting religiohistorical comparison, the alternative between "conscious appropriation" and "unconscious appropriation" likewise sets up an irresolvable impasse. Given the temporal depths with which historians must deal, it is simply no longer possible to determine whether an author was making a specific allusion to some point or whether he merely had this point "in the back of the mind" (to use a commonplace psychologism). Even the much more modest claim that the author did not know (viz., in the sense of lacking knowledge, not in the sense of being unconsciously aware) the origin of a certain tradition cannot be established in specific instances.

In the final analysis, moreover, questions framed on the basis of the conscious/unconscious model of the mind are trivial. It is undoubtedly more important to investigate such features as catchword connections and semantic fields—i.e., features that yield insight into the normal connotations of words. Is it really helpful to use the psychologically suspect term "association" when in fact we know nothing about the intra-mental processes loosely categorized under this word? We are on much firmer ground when we deal with repetition of catchwords or the repeated juxtaposition of terms that belong to an actually used semantic field.

On the other hand, the category of "implicit understanding" could be of some significance. This notion, along with the one of a "horizon of expectation," is capable of some demonstration both philologically and historically.

In sum, let us stand by the motto *tantum valet, quantum probat* (demonstrate only that which you are able). Transposed into a critical question, Are there really cases where an interpretation of a text that employs the notion of the unconscious mind in its modern sense is really the most obvious, elegant, or convincing explanation?

2. The conscious/unconscious model of the mind is hardly applicable to persons long since dead. This is so because that model must in practice be applied on a trial-and-error basis; it needs biographical (even better, autobiographical) verification in order to be intersubjectively testable. Since the biography of someone like Paul is hardly known even in its broad contours, the model can generate no more than conjectures. To be sure, such conjectures are not illegitimate. At best, however, they are no more than weak hypotheses.

3. It remains an open question whether biblical writers knew of or reflected on anything like the unconscious in the modern sense in which this concept is employed as an interpretive category (cf. thesis 6, below).

With regard to both biblical and extrabiblical references to a "knowledge of the heart" (*kardiognosis*), Theissen has attempted to show that something like our notion of the unconscious is there being reflected.[19] To this claim one must raise the following objections:

    a. The texts make it clear that only God or a specially endowed representative of God possesses such "knowledge of the heart."[20] God displays it as creator or as judge. Ordinary human beings neither have this knowledge nor, of course, are they intrinsically creators or judges.[21]

    b. With this sort of "heart" one is not speaking about any latent or otherwise concealed mode of consciousness. One is dealing instead with someone's past deeds or with something that others cannot know about, because for them it is concealed in thought. On the basis of no text, however, is one justified in drawing the conclusion that these thoughts (or whatever) might be hidden from the doer as well.[22] We are by no means dealing, then, with the interior domain of the human being but rather with what a person has done in the past or with something that was not done in the open. That which the "heart" knows thus refers either to something that is no longer visible, to something that has vanished without a trace but which still is linked to the doer, or to some evil that the doer quite consciously schemed and plotted—only in secret, hidden from public gaze. At best, what the "heart" knows is the encompassing sphere of impending consequences that the doer attracts to himself or herself.[23]

    These observations warn us against any precipitous incorporation of the term "heart" into our inquiry into the psyche, or at least into that side of it that lies beneath consciousness. In texts of the sort noted here, "heart" stands for all that is invisible but nonetheless remains tied up with a person; the term does not refer to some particular component of the psyche.

4. An ancient theory concerning the "unconscious" would have to reflect some understanding of experience as outlined above. The texts to which reference has been made, however, argue more for reconstructing an ancient model than for simply utilizing some modern schema. The following reasons support this stance:

    a. The modern theory of the unconscious is stunning in its simplicity—a trait that also accounts for its ascendancy. All the same, it remains a characteristically nineteenth-century theory and as such is open to serious criticism. It reflects an understanding of experience that is distinctly nineteenth-century in its orientation.[24]

b. What we are inclined to lump together under the single rubric called the "unconscious" struck the ancients as more diverse and is properly to be parceled out among several different contexts. Here we can note that talk of an unconscious presupposes a conception of "soul" that was not characteristic of the Jewish-Christian writers of the New Testament. Because they did not connect the life of the "soul" with "consciousness," the concept of the unconscious was inconceivable to them as a corollary. This holds true even more with regard to the idea of the "collective unconscious" and similar notions. One cannot speak of the collective without also supposing individuality, but nothing resembling our notion of individuality is to be found in New Testament antiquity.

c. The situation in which antiquity simply did not perceive something that only recently came to be recognized or explained applies also to the particular concerns of "historical psychology." It is probable from the outset that the psyche has been variously understood, which includes being understood as more than a single reality.

d. Even if the theory of the unconscious does promise to give us a grip on the inner domain of the human being, we must first ask whether there really is such a distinct inner domain and whether it is really possible to speak of this inner region without regard to the external experiences of those affected. This holds true especially in the area of religion, which is all too readily stamped as an "inner" state of affairs. It seems to me that the demand for verifiability can better be satisfied if we work with such less dubious concepts as memory, association, connotation, and the theory of affects—concepts that either directly or indirectly were current also in ancient psychology.

5. Even modern theories about the figurative use of language do not have to draw on the notion of the unconscious. According to some such theories, of course, the unconscious is particularly active in the production and reception of pictorial art. But is the timeless element mediated through such productions necessarily to be ascribed to the unconscious?

Because in the New Testament we find many instances of figurative speech, we certainly must also ask about the applicability of some theory of unconscious images. But one must also ask whether the use of artistic images really needs to be explained by appeal to the unconscious. Are not deeply imprinted fundamental experiences, by and large mundane in nature, enough to explain the element of recognition in a metaphor? Does not the same frame of reference suffice to enlighten us about how metaphors in turn awaken new insights into the mundane? With metaphors is it really necessary to work with more than the assumption of a recollection and rearrangement of fundamental experiences?

6. The Bible's reports of dreams and visions as well as of journeys to heaven or to the underworld form a theme of particular interest to biblical psychology. The fact that those who attest to such phenomena do not regard them as events of the inner life should not be ignored, modern theories notwithstanding.

When it comes to evaluating such accounts, the biblical perspective is hardly insignificant. On the contrary, it is of the utmost importance whether one explains such experiences as rooted in one's own interiority or perceives in them some sort of transcendence. It is not uncommon to hear reports of experiences of "migration," of stepping beyond the boundaries of the immediate, even of passing out of this world into some celestial or infernal region. Modern psychology interprets such experiences as penetrations into the depths of the psyche. Where biblical texts are involved, the evaluations of "modernists" and of "fundamentalists" divide in curious fashion. Modernists can only regard as coming from the depths of the psyche what fundamentalists seize upon as evidence for actual zones of transcendence. A third stance is needed. From the perspective of historical psychology, the proper starting point is the determination not to equate premodern modes of experience with any contemporary concerns (see "Journeys to Heaven" in chapter 6, below).

7. There is something fundamentally problematic about reckoning with a dimension "deeper" than what texts (!) intend to say—a dimension that can be exposed only by reading "against the grain."

Certainly there is something impressive about a hermeneutical system that can lead one to make profound statements that run contrary to the apparent flow of a text—especially when as a result everything then seems to make good sense. Yet this is precisely where a note of caution is in order. As long as an interpretation "against the grain" does not really illumine the immediate historical and literary context, it remains no more than an interesting speculation.

It is precisely the current widespread tendency to search for signs of the unconscious that, I fear, threatens to lead New Testament interpretation into a dead end. For if in ancient texts the unconscious expresses itself only obliquely, as by definition it must, or if it finds articulation only outside the directly intelligible, then it must be sought "behind" or "alongside" the text. Such efforts, however, rapidly lead to allegorical or existential interpretations that lack compelling power. This is what happens with interpretations that try to uncover what lies buried in a text. The basic dilemma confronting efforts to expose the unconscious, then, consists precisely in the fact that the unconscious never expresses itself directly in the text; the best it can do is appear in disguise. In contrast, for example, to the involuntary movements that a person makes while speaking, which can be observed, a written text communicates with us in a single dimension only. We need to hold on to that single dimension. The search for traces of the unconscious becomes particularly problematic when even the context offers no points of reference.

An illustration of the problems here under discussion can be seen in 2 Corinthians. It is well known that the category of "law" plays no role in this letter. Nevertheless (or perhaps therefore!), in his psychological interpretation of this material Theissen pursues the notion that unconscious problems of Paul, rooted in his prior experience, are here coming to the surface. In particular, the problem is his relationship to the Torah. So the veil, of which Paul explicitly speaks, is to be taken as a "symbol of the boundary between the conscious and the unconscious" (*Psychological Aspects*, 129). The veil is said to conceal "the aggressive power of the Law" (ibid., 153). "The hidden aggressivity of the Law gets exposed"; its "shadow side" must be unmasked to the conscious mind (ibid., 149). When the veil falls away, then "that aspect of the superego, which had lain concealed to the conscious mind and had tormented and repressed humankind through its archaic power, breaks out into the light" (ibid.). Not the least of the difficulties attendant upon such comments is that they are by definition irrefutable.

8. Jungian theory, above all, relies heavily on results of early religiohistorical research that has in the meantime been methodologically superseded. This fact must not be overlooked in any discussion about the scientific foundation of observations employing Jungian theory.

Earlier religiohistorical research was inclined to operate in a methodologically uncontrolled fashion, and results of such research were uncritically taken up by psychology. This can be seen particularly where general types or abstract phenomena are used to explain particular features. An example of such use of secondary categories to explain primary features is the way the contested notion of the *theios aner* (divine man) has been employed in exegesis of the Gospels. Thus, for example, Judas's betrayal of Jesus can hardly be satisfactorily explained merely by saying that the "divine man" routinely has an opponent. In psychology in general, a specific instance of behavior is not to be explained by subsuming it under some general archetype or behavioral paradigm according to which the matter "had to be so."

9. Clarifying the relationship between psychology and historical research would require that due attention be paid to the following items:[25]

    a. Psychological research is already to some degree characterized by a historical point of view and thus is hardly averse to bringing a temporal dimension into the discussion. Thus, for example, psychology already speaks of an historical development of consciousness, distinguishing archaic from modern. Moreover, the notion of "regression" necessarily implies an element of temporality.

b. Following Carsten Colpe's suggestion, one way toward fruitful interchange between these two disciplines would involve careful distinction between archetype (an image rooted in the inner life) and prototype (an image whose genesis lies in intersubjective history). What the historian ascertains about an image as prototype could be interpreted by psychology as an archetype.[26] If such a bridge were to be constructed between the disciplines, it would be important to keep in mind that the creation of a prototype is already an interpretive process.

c. In any case, there must be genuine cooperation. Fundamental to such cooperation must be acknowledgment that the work of the historian precedes that of the psychologist, so that the latter can avoid making statements lacking historical foundation. The contribution of the psychologist would consist of interpreting what the historian finds.

All the considerations already established with regard to the application of modern humanistic disciplines to exegetical findings also apply here. It seems to me that too much contemporary biblical exegesis and hermeneutics still stands in the overwhelming shadow of Rudolf Bultmann and his like-minded successors. Considering all the (rather naive) effort that has gone into interpreting the historical deposit with the help of such theoretical constructs as the "scientific" anthropology of Martin Heidegger, precious little, it seems to me, has actually been learned. Replacing Heidegger's philosophical anthropology with psychology, however, would hardly amount to a hermeneutical advance.[27]

The best-case scenario would be some sort of interdisciplinary dialogue, but this dialogue would have to be characterized by mutual investigation carried out in a spirit of deliberate reserve and sensitivity. The urge to come up with some sort of generally applicable "method" must be resisted—a caveat that applies especially to theologians, with their penchant for reducing other disciplines to the level of preliminary concerns.

Summary and Preview

Historical psychology of the New Testament explores the dimension of human experience within the biblical witness. Historical psychology can thus be classified as a "scientific" (*wissenschaftlich*) response to contemporary theology's recognition of the hermeneutic significance of human experience. But it has been my concern that the discussion about such experience not fall back on platitudes and vagaries but rather that it uncover the actual structures of human experience as attested in the New Testament. This demands rigorous distinction between now and then, between today and formerly. Stated in the simplest terms, the issue here is the nature of the experiences of those people whose words form the basis of the biblical message. From this perspective, theological application of the biblical message comes down to a comparing of experiences.[28]

The relevant experiences are above all to be investigated through an analysis of texts directed toward discerning how established traditions were actualized or applied to new situations back then. At issue, in other words, is nothing less than careful reconstruction of an earlier mode of experiencing both self and world. The voices that speak in the Bible were directed toward other human beings of the same milieu, and therefore they had a different path of access to the message of the gospel than we do today.[29] Historical psychology can reopen their path of access.

Here at the outset we can anticipate that, compared to what we take for granted, experience as reflected in the Bible will be less "spiritual," less individualistic, less attentive to feelings, and not understood in terms of a body-soul dichotomy.

2

Identity and Person

Significance of the Issue

By the terms "identity" and "person" I refer to the bearer of the inner life—the element that remains constant amid the flow of experiences and expressions. In the New Testament this abiding point of reference is perceived quite differently than it is by us. Already the early church had great difficulty coming to terms with New Testament modes of thinking in this area, as can be seen in the development of christological and Trinitarian doctrines. Essentially, both of these doctrines developed as attempts to appropriate New Testament modes of thinking with the aid of Greco-Roman conceptual categories. These developments required centuries to complete. Only at the end of this lengthy process of appropriation did our characteristically Western notion of the self emerge. That is to say, our contemporary understanding of "person" is intricately tied up with earlier discussions about the nature of the Trinity.[1]

At the beginning of those discussions stand the biblical texts themselves, with their generally very brief formulations about Christ and about Christians. A caution: it would be a serious mistake simply to set New Testament statements on the same plane as those of the early church, assuming that the earlier statements were no more than an undeveloped version of the later ones or that the later ones were only a more carefully conceptualized continuation of the earlier ones. In fact, New Testament notions about identity and personhood, while thoroughly consistent with one another, are nonetheless fundamentally different from later constructions of these notions, including our own. This can be illustrated if one asks in a deliberately literal or naive way about the relationship between the pre-existent Logos (John 1:1; Col 1:15) and the earthly Jesus (John 1:14; Col 1:17). Was Jesus already present from the beginning, in the form of a soul or a spirit? Does one really take seriously the humanity of Jesus when one reckons with an already existent soul entering into a human body? With reference to Christians, how is one to understand Paul's language about "Christ in me"? Does this statement imply some suppression of personal identity, much like the Logos might have suppressed the personal identity of the earthly Jesus? The point of taking up such questions here is not to explore christological doctrines but rather to try to understand more adequately how, within the context of the New Testament revelation, human identity (personhood) is experienced.[2]

The initial impression one gets is that the biblical concept of personhood is not clearly stamped by sharp boundaries separating the outer from the inner. This stands in pronounced contrast to the concept of personhood current among us, which is that each person is a unique and clearly delineated individual.

Initial Questions

WHO IS A "PERSON"?

The question of just who is a bearer of a psyche ("soul") is answered differently in the New Testament than by us. We are inclined to think that only human beings have psyches, and hence that only human beings count as persons. Judaism at the time of the New Testament, however, saw all areas of creation as being administered by personlike beings.[3] The New Testament likewise reckons quite unabashedly with the personlike qualities of angels and demons, to say nothing of God or the devil (Satan). Clearly, different criteria than ours for determining what constitutes a person prevailed then. For us it has to do with biological (Homo sapiens) and biographical identity; these demonstrate that someone has "documentation" to verify identity as a person. For the New Testament and the Judaism contemporary with it, however, the following traits determine what constitutes a person:

- an ability to be summoned and addressed by words (angels carry out commands of God)
- an ability to speak and thus to be able to communicate with God or with human beings.[4]
- possession of a will and therefore, in a certain sense, independence (thus unpredictability) and responsibility
- possession of a name

The high premium placed on the ability to speak is particularly worthy of note.[5] The "Similitudes of Enoch" (*1 Enoch* 37–71) illustrate how the category "person" gets applied to any being that is human or more than human, that ranks above the human being in a hierarchy of creation. Thus, a sharply distinct concept of personhood is lacking here. The most important feature is the name, which can be ascribed to any being capable of satisfying the criteria listed above. But it is not just the experience of sheer power that leads to the ascription of personhood (in that case possession of will would alone be determinative). Personhood is also based on the ability to use power for the establishing of order, either by speaking or by carrying out a word of command.

In summary, a clearly defined concept of personhood is missing in biblical antiquity. The closest analogy with our understanding is the "name." The criteria necessary for possession of a name could fully be determined only after analysis of a number of parallel texts. We can say, however, that where we use the concept of person to mark boundaries, back then the corresponding concept served to indicate an ability, if not to create, then at least to reproduce order. I therefore henceforth distinguish between the "I" of the human being (the total person as he or she concretely existed at a given time and place) and the self as the reference point of all "I"-statements, as a reality that is in a sense transcendent over against the empirical "I."[6]

How Individualized Is a "Person"?

At least since the discussion about human rights during the Enlightenment, our concept of personhood has been accompanied by the notion of specific rights (the Constitution of the United States names some of them). These human rights guarantee something like an enclosure around each person, a protected minimum of civic space. Moreover, it is generally assumed that within this space free reign is given for the development of individuality, with all its distinctive properties, inclinations, and talents. Thus every individual's biography is unique, just as are his or her fingerprints and genetic makeup. These features especially are the basis for the individual "character."

Biblical thought does not share this concern about the individuality of each person; there one finds a much lower threshold separating one person from another. Matters such as individual character and unique life-history are presumed to apply only to important people—which is why the lives of only political and military leaders, prophets, and philosophers are recorded.[7]

One often gets the impression that in biblical antiquity the only "individual" aspect of a person that gets preserved is his or her name, along with the names of parents and siblings. But all these are extraneous factors that provide no foundation for any specific individuation. Be that as it may, it seems to me that the large role played in the New Testament by features extraneous to the uniqueness of individuals must be noted; also constitutive of individuals are various societal factors, in particular the everyday experiences within families. This issue will be dealt with below.

The Essence of a Person Can Return

Both Judaism and the New Testament exhibit formulations in which an earlier person returns in a later one. When this happens the point of emphasis lies on the impact being made by the later person. However, the very fact that an earlier person is brought into the formulation doubtless has considerable significance for the understanding of personal identity as conceived in the New Testament.

ILLUSTRATIVE TEXTS

a. Mark 9:13 (concerning Jesus or John the Baptist): "Elijah has come, and they did to him whatever they pleased"; cf. par. Matt 17:12-13: "Elijah has already come, and they did not recognize him. . . . Then the disciples understood that he was speaking to them about John the Baptist."

b. Mark 8:28 (about Jesus' question to his disciples, "Who do people say that I am?"): ". . . John the Baptist; and others, Elijah; and still others, one of the prophets"; cf. par. Matt 16:14: "John the Baptist, but others Elijah; and still others Jeremiah or one of the prophets."

c. Mark 6:14-15 (in reaction to the wondrous deeds performed by the disciples while carrying out the commission of Jesus): "Some were saying, 'John the baptizer has been raised from the dead'. . . . But others said, 'It is Elijah.' And others said, 'It is a prophet, like one of the prophets of old'"; cf. par. Matt 14:2: "This is John the Baptist; he has been raised from the dead, and it is for this reason these powers are at work in him."

d. Luke 1:17 (speaking of John the Baptist): "With the spirit and the power of Elijah he will go in before him [viz., God], to turn the hearts of parents to their children."

- Philo, *On the Life of Abraham* 113 (speaking of Sarah): ". . . yet another vision she received of the strangers who had appeared to her, a loftier one, namely, one of prophets or angels who had transformed themselves out of spiritual or soul-like beings into human form."

INTERPRETATION

In the texts cited above, some highly distinctive presuppositions are at work regarding the nature of personal identity.

1. In places there is simple equivalence of identity. Thus, John the Baptist (or also Jesus) *is* Elijah (texts *a* and *b*). The same holds true in John 1:21, where the Baptist is asked, "Are you Elijah?" "It is Elijah" in Mark 6:15 (*c*) likewise falls into this category (as does the reference to the appearance of Elijah in Luke 9:8). Apparently also fitting here are claims such as the one in Mark 13:6 ("Many will come in my name, saying, 'I am he'"). In this verse the possibility is being taken seriously not simply that Christ will return but that he might return as someone else.[8] Mark himself, on the other hand, entertains quite a different notion of Jesus' return; for Mark, Jesus will reappear as the Son of Man from heaven.

In all these texts we are dealing with the idea that a well-known and biographically distinct individual (Jesus of Nazareth, John the Baptist) is in reality someone else—someone who constitutes the theologically significant identity of that individual. This is apparently how the notion of a "return" was conceptualized.

2. Elsewhere, intrinsic association can replace equivalence of identity. In Luke 1:17 John the Baptist is not directly identified with Elijah, but he does go forth in the "spirit" and "power" of Elijah. Similarly, in 2 Kgs 2:9ff. the "spirit" of the departing Elijah passes over to his disciple and successor, Elisha. Note also Matt 14:2, where the powers effective in Jesus prompt the suspicion that he is the "resurrected" Baptist.

3. According to the text from Philo, prophets (or angels) have simply put on different bodies. Related to this is the motif of someone who, having been taken away for a time, returns under another name (cf. Pseudo-Philo, *L.A.B.* 48:1, where Phinehas returns as Elijah and then again at the end of time).

4. The notion of resurrection serves to bridge specific manifestations. So in Mark 6:14 one person (John the Baptist) is raised from the dead and returns as another person (Jesus of Nazareth). Note also Luke 9:8 (". . . one of the ancient prophets has arisen").

Thus the notion appears, nuanced in various ways in these texts, that one person can return in another person, the former person constituting the essence of the latter person. To be sure, in these cases one must be careful to distinguish between the underlying experience and the applied layer of interpretation. The underlying experience is best displayed in texts such as Mark 6:13-14, where what is experienced is a charisma (a "spirit" or a "power") made manifest in wondrous deeds. It is this uncanny feature, perceived as being at work in someone, that calls for an explanation. The explanation is arrived at through a course of re-identification; the one who works the wonders is actually someone else. In this vein, note how Luke 1:17 already engages in a sort of demythologizing. John the Baptist is not Elijah, but the powers of Elijah are at work in him. With this interpretive move Luke gives us the correct key for understanding all such texts. Where an uncanny power is experienced, ordinary identity undergoes theological re-identification. An experience of such power confronts one with a riddle: What is this power?

The riddle is not answered initially by the idea of "inspiration." Only later did this become customary, for example, in the sense that God had endowed someone with a measure of God's own power or spirit. In the texts cited above, there is no direct mention of God. (There is indirect reference to God in the passages that speak of resurrection, but these passages present a special set of circumstances.) Rather, these texts assume some sort of reemergence within history of the essence of Elijah or of John the Baptist or of Jesus. There is simply a renewed appearance, a return, of their power and their spirit. Thus the term "essence" must here be used in a way unencumbered by philosophical discussion. This "essence" is a potentiality or a power that can reside within different individuals, one that is not necessarily restricted to one person at a time (Mark 13:6), and one that is not always to be known by the name of its initial bearer (in *L.A.B.* 48:1 Elijah is not called a second Phinehas).

Worthy of note is also the precise wording of Mark 6:14. Because John the Baptist is resurrected, the powers are at work "in him." This can mean either that the powers are at work in John who has returned as Jesus or simply that the powers are at work in Jesus. When one recalls that no miracles are attributed to John the Baptist, the assumption lies close at hand that the resurrection of John opens up the possibility for wonders to be performed by others (cf. also John 14:12).

RESULTS

Prophetic figures have theological identities as well as their own socio-historical identities. A parade example: John the Baptist *is* Elijah. At its core, the notion here is one of a reappearing essence. Neither sort of identity obliterates the other, however. So we are led to ask what sort of experience of self must underlie the notion that one person (Elijah) can totally constitute another (John the Baptist). The answer lies in recognition of an experience of self that is not thought of individualistically. Precisely the opposite of our own mode of experience must be operative here. A very important person is not really that person at all (nor is he a divine being) but is some other significant person, one from the past. At the root of what is also called typology, then, is the sort of experience people have when they encounter charismatic individuals.[9] The more overwhelming such a charismatic individual is, the more intensely that individual will be experienced as someone else—as someone in whom the essence of an earlier prophetic figure lives again. In light of the prophetic identity that that person has acquired, his or her birth name and other features of sociohistorical uniqueness become marginal considerations at best.

Comparable cases of fluid identity appear today only as pathological conditions.[10] For us the general rule is that the more important someone is the more emphatically that person is a distinct individual. One who achieves sufficient greatness even deserves a monument *in memoriam*. A glance at Paul will show us what a contrasting situation holds in the New Testament, for also in his writings one finds anything but an egotistic experience of self.

"Christ Lives in Me"

What is said in the Gospels about the identity of John the Baptist and of Jesus is applied by Paul to the sense of self for Christians in general. While the basic motto of our own day might well be "My ego is my castle," for Paul the Christian is inherently someone totally taken over by Christ.

ON GALATIANS 2:20a

"It is no longer I who live, but it is Christ who lives in me." If we do not simply take this sentence purely as a pious formula, it raises some intriguing questions. How has Christ entered the Christian? What is the purpose of Christ's living in me? How does my own identity relate to his? Has it simply disappeared? How does the Christ who is "in" me speak "to" me? What sort of life experience underlies this kind of awareness? How does Paul's message relate to the fact that today we are inclined, at most, to sense some "it" at work within us, but hardly another "I"? Can Christ be at work as some sort of "it" within me? One suspects that a crucial issue is at stake here. Paul is talking not just about thinking or speaking as a Christian but about *being* a Christian.

". . . Lives in Me"

Life is the foundation of all else, the greatest value. Yet within me lives someone else. Life is the power to act, the impulse at the base of everything else. Yet Christ is the center of power within me; it is he who lives both for me and in me. Everything else, everything that constituted my former life, is now dead. While for us life is characterized above all else by motion (growth, etc.), for Paul being alive is being needful. To be alive is to desire and to strive; to be alive is to want and to try to get.[11] We who think of life especially in terms of breath would not naturally speak as strongly as does Paul of the snare of righteousness or of the dangers implicit in our actions.[12]

What Happens to the Human Self?

The self of a human being nonetheless persists. After all, Paul does continue to speak in the first person. Although the self is not extinguished, one does get the impression that it has been reduced to little more than a name. A good analogy is offered by the discussion of baptism in Rom 6:3-11. The one who is baptized has died; he has put off the old body. Here again, however, Paul continues to speak in first-person style; the self has therefore persisted beyond the death of the body. Moreover, the self that persists is hardly just some neutral point of reference. It is the "name" of Paul. The self is thus not dependent upon a specific body. On the other hand, neither can the self persist apart from any body, for a self without a body would be miserably naked, like a ghost (2 Cor 5:3b). But when a self acquires a new body, it maintains its former identity (1 Cor 15:52-53; 2 Cor 5:4).

In sum, the human self persists despite a person's "dying" in baptism or having Christ live within. It is even maintained across transformations of body. But this self can dissipate, as it were, to where it is essentially just a name, while in anticipation of being taken up in a new body.

Permeability of the Self

In contrast to our mode of experience, in biblical antiquity the self is thought to be immediately perceptible to the senses. (Thinking of the senses as "gateways to the soul" is an ancient notion.) Moreover, the self, not being sharply delimited, can be permeated by another "person." In effect, another person can become immanent within me.

Removing the Distinction between Person and Essence

One feature unintelligible to our way of thinking is that the distinction between a person and his or her "essence" can simply disappear. This was mentioned above, where we saw that the essence that returns (e.g., the spirit and the power of Elijah) is not some vague mana. Rather, it remains identifiable through its association with some particular person; the essence in question carries a name. Thus, it is specifically the power of Elijah or that of the resurrected Baptist that is at work (Mark 6:14). In the case of ordinary Christians, it is the spirit of Christ that is at work in them, a spirit that remains forever identifiable through its firm association with

Jesus. So the essence here under consideration is not some uncontrolled, impersonal substance. From this perspective one also sees how it is that the Holy Spirit acquires personal traits.[13] The same mode of thinking appears in Philo, who is able to ascribe to the Logos such names as "high priest" and "Israel."

This striking state of affairs leads to a situation where, in closely related verses, the theme of Christ's living "in me" can easily be replaced by that of the spirit's dwelling "in me." Romans 8:9 speaks of the Holy Spirit that "dwells within you," while Rom 8:10 directly ponders "if Christ is in you. . . ." Then, in Rom 8:11, this same reality is referred to as the Spirit of God. We must conclude that the expression "Christ in me" is not to be taken as just a metaphor and that reference to the indwelling spirit of Christ is not just an allusive way of speaking.

In our effort to understand how the distinction between person and essence can be elided like this, we must keep in mind that, as indicated above, the concept of a sharply delimited self is not to be found in these texts. It follows that a separation between concrete centers of effective action would not even be possible. Moreover, it appears that the nearer to God a being stands or the higher it is positioned in the hierarchy of the created order the less room there is for meaningful differentiation. In sum, these considerations compel us next to take a look at the New Testament's understanding of "power" (Greek: *dynamis*).

"Power" as the Basis of Christ Mysticism

According to our way of thinking, the aspect of Christ at work in us is especially his word, or perhaps his ideas. In thinking like this we are implicitly giving priority to our senses, and particularly to our sense of hearing. Should we have a feeling of something stirring us from within, something stronger than our own intentionality, we would most likely speak of it as some impersonal power, some "it." For Paul, on the other hand, Jesus himself can be called the "power of God" (1 Cor 1:18, 24).[14] This power is at the same time both substantive and personal, and therefore we can perceive it at work within us as the "power of Christ" (2 Cor 12:9). With this realization, however, our observations come full circle. As noted above, according to Luke 1:17 the "power" and the "spirit" of Elijah could so be understood that, in John the Baptist, Elijah himself had returned. The dynamic that held in the case of the Baptist holds also with Christians.

The upshot is that, from certain perspectives and in certain contexts, there is no significant difference between personhood and impersonal power. Jesus, the "power of God," is at the same time a vessel for God's self-communication to humankind, since this divine power becomes especially apparent in Jesus' (and our) resurrection (Rom 1:4; cf. 1 Cor 6:14 and 15:43; also Heb 11:19 and Mark 12:24). In the New Testament's remarks about "power" (*dynamis*),[15] therefore, an array of corresponding themes emerges. The close relationship between the Christ event and the nature of Christian existence (the kernel of every sort of Christ mysticism) is the first that could be mentioned. Also, the character of the whole Christ event as a powerful revelation of God might come to mind. At the same time, all sorts of experiences attested within Christianity, including such things as wonders perceived as acts of power and certain individuals being endowed with charisma, can be summarily grouped together by the contrast of power and weakness. This possibility even extends to the motif of overcoming death.

Jesus Christ appears as primal image and as point of beginning; the power of God that became visible in him spreads out through him to work a similar effect on all who believe in Christ. We find above all in "power," then, a singularly effective category under which to bind together God, Jesus Christ, and Christian existence, both now and in ages to come. Christ mysticism is to be understood within this horizon.[16] In this sort of mysticism, the power of God is the personal and also at the same time the substantive means by which a bond (or relationship) is established between God and humankind. This power of God is exclusively mediated through the ultimate act of divine self-revelation in Jesus Christ.

SUMMARY

For Paul, the person (or self) is experienced as a place where weakness and strength contest, an arena with permeable boundaries. Thus it is possible for the self to be reduced to no more than a name; in biblical language the name can be equivalent to the self. It likewise follows that the power (not the thoughts or the feelings) of another person can control me. The conceptual image directing the pattern of thinking here, then, is fundamentally different from the one that gives shape to the notion of "inspiration." (Inspiration as a concept is derived from the inhaling of unnatural air such as the mist at Delphi, which was thought to enable revelatory insights.)

Autonomy of the Self

The modern notion that each self enjoys a distinct "identity" is intrinsically connected to contemporary experiences with and assumptions about autonomy and freedom. Such experiences and assumptions are decisive for our understanding of "self" and the feeling we call "self-worth."

Again, however, the New Testament operates from quite a different set of assumptions.

A FUNDAMENTALLY DIFFERENT CONCEPT OF FREEDOM

A contemporary person thinks of the autonomy of self as having to do with self-determination, the human capacity for self-affirmation, or the shaping of one's own destiny. It is taken as obvious that freedom is to be highly valued and that freedom essentially consists in being allowed to do what one wants, without undue legal hindrance. Such an ethic has as its starting point the private will of each individual. Here the highest value is placed upon what each person individually wants and desires. In psychological investigation, then, the primary focus is the will and its dynamics.

As can be seen in Rom 6:15-23, Paul does not value a freedom that is tied up with the individual as such. Modern thought, with its distinctive notion of autonomy, regards freedom as centered in the individual. Freedom of this sort has negative value for Paul. According to Paul, the freedom of the Christian consists in no longer having to obey one's desires. Because this sort of freedom is tantamount to no longer having to transgress the Law, it is consequently and ultimately a freedom from death. Freedom, in other words, appears only as "freedom from. . . ." The ultimate freedom the human being can attain is freedom from transitoriness. Hence the proper human freedom is not the right of self-determination but especially an attaching of oneself to a liberator, which means entering into a new sort of bond. In short, Paul sees freedom as defined by factors "outside" the individual. In being set free from desire, sin, and death, the liberated person does not achieve a "neutral" freedom from everything but remains in tension between the alternatives of life and death. Because these two remain the only exits, there can be no neutral freedom located somewhere between them. A human being can only be dead or alive, and therefore one can be "free" (from death) only if one belongs to the giver of life. For psychological inquiry, then, the decisive insight is that the human being is always constrained in one way or another; one constantly finds oneself tied up in some fundamental way. (As Martin Luther once put it, "Whether by Satan or by God, one will nonetheless be ridden.") But there is a fundamental difference between the old bondage and the new bondage of the Christian. This difference appears in the final outcome. The Christian's new bondage leads not to destruction but to salvation. So the Christian's new status as servant hardly "protects" his or her freedom (as we might say) but offers the possibility of being at peace with oneself.[17]

If we were to look to the New Testament for a critique of the modern understanding of freedom, would we not be led to question the contemporary emphasis on individual autonomy? Is not the contemporary person also subject to differing modes of alienation, not the least of which is the blunt fact of death? As much as we rightly value our bedrock notion of freedom, it can never be more than partially realized in actual history. To express the same idea as a psychological question, can there really be such a thing as unrestricted freedom? Is it not rather an inescapable fact of life that certain restrictions always apply, restrictions imposed by history and by culture? Do not certain judgments and determinations precede any and all expressions of freedom? While freedom rightly holds an honored place in our scale of values, does not the Pauline mode of conceptualizing freedom actually offer a psychologically astute corrective to the modern fixation on autonomy?[18]

The New Testament emphasis on servitude, then, offers a corrective to the modern notion, popular in the churches as well as in the society as a whole, that each person should be allowed to do pretty much as he or she pleases. Quite apart from its questionable ethical implications, it seems to me that such a stance overlooks the positive psychological effects that can flow from attachments and connections. In this context it is perhaps helpful to remember that all effective forms of self-expression make use of predetermined symbols and gestures. One important function of festivals has always been to elicit public affirmation of established constraints, and in that sense they perpetuate a distinct other-directedness.

This means that, in contrast to modern individualism, Paul regards human beings as set within an inescapable network of relationships and interactions. As the more recent history of the church clearly shows, all sorts of tensions can arise between the modern commitment to freedom and the Pauline understanding of Christian bondedness. Such tensions, however, can prove fruitful. The task of historical psychology is to clarify the hermeneutical issue attendant on two such different notions of freedom and precisely thereby to make sure that the tensions do not get resolved from only one side.

Vicarious Acts

Early Christian texts mention different kinds of religious vicariousness[19] —the vicarious (atoning) death of Jesus, vicarious (intercessory) prayer and even vicarious (mediatory) fasting (*Did.* 1:3: "fast for those who persecute you"). A fundamental trait of religious vicariousness is that it proceeds quite apart from any formal consent on the part of those whom it is intended to benefit. Thus in the case of an intercessory prayer, those for whom the prayer is offered are not first consulted about the matter. Likewise in the case of a vicarious death, the consent (if one is permitted to speak in such a way) on the part of those who benefit comes only later.

The biblical understanding of vicarious substitution can be clarified by drawing some contrasts to modern thought. First, many today think of the human being's relationship to God as intrinsically a matter of the heart—a "personal relationship" with God. Everything else revolves around this central relationship. God looks directly into the heart of each individual; what lies outside the heart remains secondary. (For non-Christians, an ethical substitute for this sort of faith may perhaps be found as early as Matt 25:31-46.) A second contrast emerges from a consideration of the significance of corporal elements (e.g., blood) or physical acts (e.g., fasting) involved in vicarious substitution. Thus, for many an "enlightened" individual nurtured in the Protestant tradition, it is simply inconceivable that one person could stand in for another in the presence of God—with the sole exception of Jesus Christ, of course. Likewise, intercessory prayer (unsolicited prayer offered in behalf of someone else) strikes many as a contradictory notion. Even less is it possible in the eyes of many a modern person for "spiritual" benefits to be acquired by means of physical objects. (This is the root of modern difficulties with the notion of an atoning death.) The missing ingredient in all these instances is freely willed consent on the part of the beneficiaries, which in turn leads to the charge of "sorcery" and the reproach that all such acts are tainted by an *ex opere operato* mentality. In absolutizing the relationship of the human heart to God, the "enlightened" position on faith is also consequently tempted to regard itself as somehow prophetic in nature. The upshot is that in our modern way of thinking a dichotomy is often set up between sentiment and performance. From this position we tend to value those actions that flow out of a deeply felt personal relationship to God but disparage as "mere works" those that do not bear the marks of inner conviction. Where this is done, the biblical notion of vicarious substitution falls by the wayside, since it is not equivalent to the notion of heartfelt commitment nor is it just another way of speaking about works.

On the matter of vicarious mediation, the New Testament speaks in a distinctive way. There the relationship of the individual to God can indeed be affected—and decisively so—by the cultic acts (prayer, fasting, shedding of atoning blood) of someone else. Moreover, it is simply taken for granted that something concrete is to be offered to God (with prayer, time [cf. 1 Cor 7:5]; with fasting, abstaining from nourishment; with expiation, blood). These "externals" are in no way devalued. Where the modern perspective would emphasize the necessity of inner consent to the vicarious act on the part of the one who is to benefit, then, the biblical focus is decidedly on the "cultic" dimension. These concrete features are unquestioningly accepted as divinely established ground-rules for interaction with God. Consistent with the cultic dimension of vicarious substitution is also the theme that only one who is cultically qualified (and in that sense righteous) can play the role of mediator with God.

The precise extent to which the benefits of vicarious substitution extend is unclear. In any case, they apply only to the age of historical human existence. As was true already for the Judaism antecedent to the time of the New Testament, on judgment day no more intercessory prayer will be allowed (2 Esdras 7:102-105).[20] Matthew 10:33 par., and perhaps also Matt 7:23 and some other verses, reckon exclusively with a prosecutorial function for the Son of Man at the final judgment, though the possibility of some advocacy is not ruled out (Matt 10:32).[21] As a rule, the prospect for intercessory aid at such a late date is dim; at judgment day, no one else can be of help. This is the point at which the classic prophetic theme of rigorous personal responsibility for one's actions takes hold. With this particular theme, the judgment day scenario corresponds to the emphasis on retribution in the prophetic texts. One's time on earth prior to judgment, conversely, is not only a time for repentance but also a time when intercession can be made.

For historical psychology the important point is that, during one's earthly life, the relationship that is most significant soteriologically is not one between each individual and God. A relationship of soteriological significance will have a collective dimension. And this collective dimension is hardly confined to Christology alone; it is much more extensive. Vicarious substitution adds an enriching dimension to the whole array of cultic activities as it helps break down the barriers that separate one individual from another. A broader notion of vicarious substitution actually makes one's own participation in cultic activity more meaningful, since it helps to establish a unique and especially tight bond of solidarity between the worshiper and fellow human beings. Indeed, this bond is seen as being so tight that it affects also the other's relationship to God. Where the biblical notion of vicarious substitution holds sway, impermeable boundaries around the self break down. In sum, the piety of both Judaism and the New Testament is unintelligible apart from the dimension of vicarious substitution.

In the face of Protestant apprehensions with respect to cultic activities, I emphasize that, in the conceptual categories of the New Testament, such acts are hardly equivalent to deeds or "works" in any derogatory sense. Cultic acts such as prayer and fasting follow from a set of prescriptions quite different from the economic ones that inform the categories of work and wages. Cultic activity is not a matter of somehow compelling God to act in consonance with some sort of contractual obligation, as some seem to think.[22] In short, the activity carried out in a cultic setting is not some sort of "job" but an active recognition of the proper claim that God has on our praise. To be sure, something is being brought before God in acts of expiation, prayer, and fasting. However the conceptual framework that informs such acts is not one of economic exchange but of cultic thinking. In the strictest sense of the word, cultic activity follows its own set of rules (see chapter 5, below.)

In sum, at the heart of the notion of vicarious substitution is a sort of Edenic wholeness within which it is possible for one person to do something soteriologically significant for another in the presence of God. Such a possibility, however, is restricted to the context of earthly existence. When the Day of Judgment comes, the time for vicarious substitution will be past. Vicarious substitution is possible where the barricades which separate one person from another are easily scaled. One is tempted to advance the thesis that the notion of cultic solidarity is rooted in deep antiquity, perhaps in a family structure where children are to some degree interchangeable in the eyes of their parents.[23]

PUTTING ON ANOTHER PERSON AS A GARMENT

In various places the New Testament offers us the image of a new garment, the putting on of which transforms one into a new person. This garment can be described as a suit of armor, but the garment can also be identified as a person, namely, Jesus Christ. We are thus led to inquire into the psychological basis of this particular sort of "mysticism."

The Sociopsychological Role of Clothing

The basis of this mysticism obviously lies in a distinctive function of clothing or garments in the everyday life of antiquity (this function is obviously no longer current among us). In the milieu of the New Testament, something about the wearing of clothes enabled the construction of a metaphor about the putting on of a person. What are the distinctive sociopsychological factors at work here?

Galatians 3:27-29 speaks of "putting on Christ" in connection with the removal of what are normally imposing religious, ethnic, and sexual distinctions between people. Implied here is the notion that the social status of a person is to no small degree marked by the kind of clothing being worn. We encounter the same theme in a number of other New Testament texts. According to Matt 11:8 par., the personnel attached to the royal court are presented as people "clothed in soft raiment." According to Rev 7:14, those who have come out of the great tribulation have (metaphorically) "washed their robes and made them white in the blood of the Lamb"; v. 15 adds "For this reason they are before the throne of God. . . ." In both instances, the references to the garments serve primarily to indicate the social rank of those under consideration. Nowadays, apart from weddings and funerals, clothing marks social rank mainly with certain types of public officials. We normally rely on other means to indicate social status; the ancient practice of using clothing for this purpose is increasingly confined to special occasions or distinctive social settings.[24] In any case, one can certainly say that, at the time of the New Testament, clothing played an indispensable sociopsychological function, little of which remains among us today.

And so the following factors, listed in chronological sequence, have served to indicate social status from antiquity to our own age:

- clothing (dominant in antiquity, but today in the West operative only in isolated instances)
- place of origin and nature of occupation (the typical indicator during the Middle Ages and common in the West until fairly recently)
- various indicators of wealth (which one can either display or conceal, but which in either case are distinctive, compared with earlier indicators, in the way they are less governed by tradition or established practice)

Matthew 22:11-12 offers a good illustration of how much things have changed with regard to clothing as an indicator of social rank. Nowadays a guest who showed up at a wedding in street clothes would probably not even attract a disapproving glance—at least in a university town!

Clothing as Symbol of Reality

Regarding the sociopsychological function of clothing in antiquity, let us take one more look at Gal 3:27-29. The motif of "putting on Christ" here does not refer to a personal relationship with Christ in any sort of mystical or intimate sense. It has to do with a relationship between human beings, a relationship that gets transformed when the baptized individual "puts on Christ." If it is true that clothing indicates social role in antiquity, then the focus of attention here is hardly on the inner life of the baptized individual. One's garment announces what one is for another, not what one is in and for oneself. Through the close bond with Jesus Christ that baptism establishes, each baptized individual gets outfitted, as it were, with some quality of Jesus in a way that transforms all relationships; all the baptized in Christ become joint members of one new society. (In the context of Galatians 3, each comes to be clothed with the spirit of Christ and thus with the promised inheritance.) The effect of this "putting on Christ" is the disappearance of all distinctions between human beings, distinctions that had previously been expressed through differences in clothing. Thus their "old clothes" had served as insignia of their respective social roles.[25]

The way clothing can function as insignia also says something about the nature of the societal interactions of those involved.[26] As we have seen, in biblical antiquity the general significance that people have for one another is demonstrated by the garments they wear. This principle even holds true in the area of one's relationship with God. Thus, according to Eph 2:10, even our good works have been prepared in advance by God, so that we might wrap ourselves (as in garments) with these works. In a very real sense, then, our good works are to be understood as expressions of a righteousness that is realized in societal interactions.

Finally, according to 2 Cor 5:2-4 the Christian's eschatological fate is also oriented around the particular "garment" that God has bestowed. Indeed, one can go further and say that according to this text the nature of one's eschatological fate is largely determined by what (or whom) one will be found wearing on the Day of Judgment. It follows that being found naked on that day would be the most shameful and unfortunate fate of all!

Results

For people in the milieu of the New Testament, there is a much closer association between clothing and the self than there is among us. In the ancient context a person's fundamental relationships are rendered effective by the clothing that one wears, which in turn means that clothing shapes the quality of one's life. Thus, when it is said that someone "puts on Christ," what is meant is that a new role is accorded to that person, a role into which he or she is then expected to grow. The original "self" is maintained in such a situation, but only as the underlying carrier of the new role. The new role so bestowed upon one can be described by Paul as having a new garment. The underlying "self" is so deeply affected by this new garment that Paul can speak of a new person. In effect, the original self is covered over.

From this it is clear that:

1. In the New Testament, the clothing metaphor expresses the view that the human being is primarily other-oriented, which is to say that the human being is primarily a societal being.

2. This orientation toward the other can go so far that the garment is seen as transforming someone into a new person. (Here clothing really does "make the man"!)

3. When Jesus Christ is identified as the garment that one puts on, what is meant is that Jesus determines and defines what one represents in the eyes of one's contemporaries. This essentially says what one is. Conversely, it is possible to call Jesus Christ the garment that one puts on only because clothing can be seen as so radically transforming one's identity.

4. The radical reorientation of identity that the baptized experience when they "put on" Jesus Christ runs parallel to the societal function of clothing as experienced in biblical antiquity. Conversely, because the societal consequences of this garment that is Jesus Christ are so fundamental (the elimination of all societal distinctions), it subsequently becomes possible for this new "garment" itself, acquired in baptism, to call to awareness the prior function of clothing as a marker of societal differentiation.

In sum, attention to the metaphorical references to clothing in the New Testament helps us appreciate the significant degree to which in those texts the "self" is experienced as outer-directed, as shaped by its surrounding community.

3

Demonic Possession

The Problem

There are several excellent studies on demons and exorcism in the New Testament milieu,[1] which I here can do little more than acknowledge. When viewed from the perspective of historical psychology, however, these studies generally suffer from positivism in that they tend to take ancient traditions and notions too much at face value instead of locating such material more critically within its own conceptual horizons. I will here try to correct such absence of critical inquiry into the ancient categories of understanding. In what follows I will almost exclusively treat the phenomenon of demon possession, for it is especially in this area that problems emerge in historical psychology.

What happens in demonic possession is similar to the idea of the indwelling of Christ or the putting on of Christ as a garment (chapter 2, above). In both cases we are dealing with the notion of one or more personlike entities perceived as taking up residence within a person, suppressing that person's individual self in the process. The conceptual and experiential similarities are especially obvious in the following situations:

1. Sometimes it is not clear whether a good spirit or an evil spirit resides in someone (cf. Matt 4:1-11; Mark 3:22-27 par.; Acts 8:14-24).

2. Both kinds of spirit are designated by the Greek word *pneuma*—the same word used to refer to Jesus as dwelling within human beings. In fact, New Testament pneumatology almost always exhibits a dualistic orientation.[2] A good illustration is offered by the first chapter of the Gospel of Mark; in vv. 10 and 12 *pneuma* designates the spirit of God, but in vv. 24 and 26 the same term refers to an "unclean spirit."

The significance of demonology for the historical-psychological reading of the New Testament can be summarized in the following two points:

1. Demonic possession is the other side of inspiration, and both themes presuppose a permeable boundary around the person. In this regard the human being is comparable to a house; both can easily be entered (cf. Matt 12:43-45). In the ancient Near East a house was not usually locked.

2. In view of the mirrorlike similarity between demonic possession and inspiration, the hermeneutical problem in this area becomes rather complicated. Although we still speak of the indwelling Christ or more generally of the "spirit" of Christ, as well as of the Holy Spirit, we rarely speak any more of being possessed by demons. Much the same has happened with regard to Satan; Satan is now much less frequently thought of in personal categories than is God.

Observations on the Religio-Historical Context

AN UNNECESSARY APOLOGETIC

The New Testament accepts the reality of demons to a degree almost unprecedented even in its own milieu. Any attempt to gloss over that characteristic would be both untruthful and excessively apologetic. To put it mildly, the excision of references to demons (and angels) in modern liturgies and Eucharistic formulas is not biblical. In a sense, heaven and hell have been systematically depopulated. What a contrast is presented by something like the Gospel of Mark, where reference to demons is a constitutive feature![3] What is more, the central dynamics and themes of early Christianity were often developed around the exorcising of demons.[4] The absence of exorcism in the Pauline writings ought not mislead us into thinking of Paul as therefore more enlightened than the Evangelists. To be sure, Philo characterizes belief in demons as "superstition" (*deisidaimonia*; cf. *On Giants* 16), but then the charge of superstition could also be leveled against Paul, who in all seriousness speaks of being pummeled by Satan (2 Cor 12:7). It is undeniable that, on the topic of demons, the gap that separates the New Testament world from our own has become a chasm.[5]

THE IMPORTANCE OF DEMONS IN FIRST-CENTURY JUDAISM

At the time of the New Testament, demons were an important topic of discussion in Judaism, especially in the context of the following issues:

- theodicy (cf. *Jubilees* 10)
- soteriology (Writings attributed to Noah and believed to have been handed down by way of Levi served in the struggle against demons;[6] the Davidic Messiah, like Solomon, would be master of the demons.)
- eschatology (According to *Testament of Levi* 18, the eschatological high priest will be given power over the spirits.)
- apostasy (The tradition of the fallen angels, out of whose union with human beings the demons arose, was interpreted as a prefiguration of the Hellenistic apostasy of some Jews.)
- healing (As seen in the cults of Asklepios and Serapis, in the first century a close relationship was believed to exist between religion and healing. Writings such as the *Testament of Solomon* and the books of Noah arose in close proximity to Hellenistic magic.)
- Judaism's understanding of itself vis-à-vis other religions (The gods of other peoples are in fact only "demons"; they are all subservient to the one true God. For a Christian parallel, cf. 1 Corinthians 8 and 10.)

Demons in the New Testament Gospels and Epistles

On the topic of demons, close and instructive connections exist between the Synoptic Gospels and the Epistles of the New Testament. The "impure spirits" and "demons" of the Gospels are clearly associated with the "principalities," "powers," "thrones," and "dominions" of the Epistles. In each case, the sovereignty these realities have over human beings is abolished through Jesus Christ, because all of them have become subject to him. The precise manner in which this subjection takes place is variously described. According to the Synoptic Gospels, human beings are individually freed from the power of demons through exorcisms. Only Luke 10:18 offers anything like a summarizing principle; according to this saying, Jesus saw Satan fall from heaven like a bolt of lightning. Following the same course of logic as displayed in Rev 12:9-17, this fall would presage an intensive attack upon humankind by demons, to be followed by the subjection of the demons themselves. Mark, on the other hand, recognizes as the initial act of liberation effected through Jesus Christ only healing and exorcism—without, however, tying these to baptism.

In the Epistles, on the other hand, it is the resurrection or exaltation of Jesus that marks the beginning of the subjection of the powers (1 Cor 15:21-24; Heb 2:8-9) or even the completion of their subjection (Eph 1:20-21; 1 Pet 3:21-22). The resurrection or exaltation of Jesus accomplishes this subjection either because it serves to squelch angelic opposition to the divine partiality toward human beings or because in the resurrection of Jesus the power of God is uniquely and undeniably demonstrated (see also "Exorcisms and Power," below). The different perspectives of the Synoptic Gospels and the Epistles have less to do with the well-known shift from proclamations *of* Jesus to proclamations *about* Jesus than with the different geographical and sociopolitical situations of the addressees.[7]

F. E. Brenk has pointed out some of the distinctly "political" aspects of demonology.[8] In particular, Brenk is able to show how anti-Roman sentiments underlie Plutarch's report (in *De defectu oraculorum* 419b-e) about the death of a demon—specifically, the death of the "Great Pan," a central figure in Julio-Claudian symbolism.[9] In the same vein, according to the Augustinian imperial ideology certain demonic powers (viz., Jubo and Allecto) were restrained through the establishment of law and order as well as through the promotion of *pietas*. Such measures liberated the Roman state from demonic control. Finally, the New Testament thought-pattern could be compared to concepts underlying the story of the battle of Zeus/Jupiter against the Titans (gigantic beings that bring about disorder). The only major difference would be that, for the writers of the New Testament, all gods other than Yahweh belong to the realm of demonic beings.[10]

The political aspect of exorcism is also indicated by the fact that the "wondrous deeds" of Jesus are nowhere brought into direct relationship with the theme of the kingdom of God except in cases where he casts out demons, as at Matt 12:28 (par. Luke 11:20). Where demons are being cast out, the kingdom of God has to some extent already appeared; here, and here alone, the eschatological reign of God is partially realized. Another difference between accounts of exorcisms and other remarks of Jesus concerning the kingdom of God is that only in the former do we also find mention of a "counter-kingdom" that has been destroyed in the process. The kingdom of God is understood to be present in the aftermath of exorcisms because, after victory over the demonic powers, nothing is left that can really hinder its advent.[11] In short, in the New Testament exorcism is seen as a final and irreversible shift of power (see also "Exorcism and Political Power," below).

The New Testament thus does not aim at eradicating belief in demons but emphasizes that demons have been subdued or driven away. However, in the post-Pauline epistles the genuinely Pauline theme of conquering the "powers" and "dominions" has gotten somewhat intertwined with more distinctly Hellenistic views, so that here the demons are regarded as actually having been annihilated. Against this shift of perspective there arose a protest from the more distinctly Jewish Christians (e.g., in Jude and Revelation).

DEMONIC POSSESSION AND ILLNESS

Of central importance for historical psychology is the question of just what was experienced as "possession." It is extraordinarily difficult, indeed perhaps impossible, to describe these complex ancient experiences in modern pathological terms, especially since recent psychiatry deviates from the categories of mental illness established just a few decades ago, while it regards even older categories as just so many meaningless labels. In short, we simply cannot accurately reconstruct or "scientifically" describe ancient illnesses by using contemporary medical terms (even though many modern commentaries try to do just this). We would need to have the actual sufferers before us, which is an obvious impossibility. Nor does the New Testament transmit to us any first-hand reports by the demon-possessed. Instead of seeking to explore the inner experience of the possessed, then, we must content ourselves with analyzing New Testament texts that reflect the reactions toward the possessed on the part of those who were not possessed. In short, we cannot fruitfully ask what was really going on with the sick. We must instead content ourselves with asking how the healthy made sense of the sick among them. Only the notions and reactions of the former have been preserved.

While the question of the actual nature of illnesses mentioned in the texts must therefore remain open, it is still possible to advance some descriptive comments if we proceed cautiously. Thus, for example, in the Synoptic Gospels the boundaries separating demonic possession from illness per se are indistinct. If Mark 1:34a is taken as a thematic generalization and 1:34b as an expansion on the same theme, then the driving out of demons is an intrinsic aspect of the "healing of various diseases." The "mute spirit" of Mark 9:17 reappears in the Matthean parallel (Matt 17:15) as "one who is deranged and miserable." In Matt 17:18, however, the derangement is immediately described as demonic in nature ("and the demon went out of him"; contrast Mark 9:26, where a distinct identity is maintained for the demon). Luke 13:11 speaks of a woman who has a "spirit of infirmity."[12]

Demonic Possession in
Historical-Psychological Perspective

EXPERIENCING THE ALIEN

In demonic possession the repulsively alien, that with which one can in no way identify, is experienced as a hostile spirit; one encounters some threatening not-one's-own that can in no way be accepted as a part of one's genuine self. In a sense we are here dealing with the opposite of a concept already discussed in chapter 2, namely, the concept of a personhood that lacks firm boundaries. Precisely because one can come into such close contact with the spiritually alien, it can also be experienced as posing a serious threat. This sense of vulnerability that accompanies the encounter with the alien leads, for example, to the suspicion that Jesus, when suspected of being a Samaritan, must also be possessed by a demon (John 8:48).

EXPERIENCE OF VULNERABILITY

One would entrust oneself to an exorcist (or a miracle worker) only if all recourse to ordinary medicine had failed (Mark 5:26).[13] Because exorcism shares with cultic activity a certain aura of the uncanny, a person would be driven to this exceptional expedient only after one had exhausted all conventional remedies.

DEMONS AS PERSONS

Demons have names. That offers an advantage, because knowing the name of a demon also enables one to exercise power over it. Of course, knowledge of the demon's name alone rarely suffices. Such knowledge must be accompanied by various sorts of extraordinary, quasi-cultic measures.[14] Demons can also speak. They can converse and negotiate (Mark 5:12; *b. Pesachim* 112b-113) and, under the right circumstances, they must obey.[15] Above all, however, they are understood to be like persons. This is due to their essentially independent wills and the human inability to control them by strictly technical means. (In the modern world, we think of hurricanes in much the same way.)

A PREMORAL DOMAIN

Contrary to what we might suppose, in the New Testament and its surroundings demons are not regarded as morally evil; they are neither sinners nor transgressors of the Law. For this reason, concerns about moral malfeasance or moral improvement must be kept separate from considerations of demonic possession and exorcism. The issue at hand is actually one of premoral mischief. That is to say, one possessed by a demon is not thereby ipso facto to be regarded as previously having been "sinful." Here we are dealing with a totally different sphere, one with its own set of values. The issue of human responsibility recedes into the background.

EXORCISMS AND POWER

Jesus encounters the demons as their lord and master. The demons become subject to him, after having themselves previously dominated the sick. The core dynamic, then, is between power and weakness. In their illness the sick experience weakness; Jesus makes the demons experience a powerlessness of their own (cf. Matt 12:29). Even modern accounts of exorcism are regularly cast in terms of a power struggle. The one who is afflicted feels weak or powerless; the exorcist tries by all available means to break down what is perceived as an obstinate, resisting force.

When it comes to exorcising demons from the possessed, then, issues of morality give way to a struggle defined in terms of power—indeed, of power in all its naked purity (on the "purity" of power, see "Confrontation and Order," below). Here we can see why in each case the demon immediately perceives its "lord." That is, with lightning-fast speed the demon recognizes that the strength of its opponent is greater than its own (Mark 1:23-24; cf. Acts 19:15). Because of this feature of instantaneous recognition, I find unconvincing the supposed instances of demonic counter-magic.[16] As soon as the stronger one is ascertained, then this one can simply utter a word of command. The issue is resolved, in other words, by the pure use of undeniably superior power. All of this is clearly evident in Matt 12:29 (a strong man bound by someone yet stronger). Similarly, according to Luke 10:18 (cf. v. 17) it is Satan's loss of power that precipitates his fall from heaven.[17]

People of New Testament times experienced such deliberations about power primarily in the area of military affairs, as the parable of the king preparing for war illustrates (Luke 14:31-32). Thus it is hardly surprising that military metaphors dominate in descriptions of the casting out of demons. Such metaphors stretch from the name of the demon "Legion" (Mark 5:9) and the way the demons enter into negotiations resembling a military surrender (Mark 5:12f.; also b. Pesachim 112b-113, noted above) to the brusque commands and threats that are typical of the stronger combatant. The commands ordering demons to leave the possessed resemble the liberating of occupied territory.[18]

The resolution of struggle without combat thus runs strictly parallel to the previous experience of powerlessness. As so often elsewhere, so also here helplessness is balanced by wondrous power. Put another way, for every kind of powerlessness there corresponds a suitable (structurally corresponding) means of overcoming that powerlessness. Correspondingly, it is readily apparent how Jesus Christ, precisely as the resurrected one and thereby as the bearer of God's power (Mark 12:24), could so readily conquer the demonic forces (cf. 1 Cor 1:24 and 15:24b). In sum, exorcism in the New Testament gets played out in the experienced contrast between powerlessness and unquestionable, extraordinary power.

We should also note that demons were understood to be both spirits of the dead and at the same time the "other gods." That is to say, all those uncanny forces that threaten human beings were perceived as together constituting a power that leads toward death. This perception, reflected in the texts, can be described in the following way: Death itself is a power, and as long as death has power God must also have power if God is to establish and maintain "life." Exorcisms are a reflection of the struggle between these powers in the arena of illness. We moderns have unraveled the once tightly woven cord made up of the strands comprising life, illness, death, and God. In the process, the strand comprising religion has also become problematic.

The Inner Being of the Possessed Plays No Role

In contrast to modern assumptions about demonic possession, nowhere does the New Testament speak of the delusions of the possessed, or even of their anxieties. On the contrary, the demons are regarded as fundamentally reasonable and generally sane. Jesus can speak with them in a fully rational manner. In their encounters with Jesus, the demons may become mute, but they are never confused. This means that, beyond having been inwardly invaded and exhibiting certain physical symptoms of that invasion, the possessed have undergone no destruction of their personalities.

Dualistic Experience

Also in contrast to a contemporary understanding of illness as well as anything that might resemble exorcism in the modern world, the New Testament views demonic possession as but the negative side of a larger duality. Juxtaposed to possession by demons or impure spirits is the positive experience of inspiration. A pure *pneuma* is stronger than an impure one (cf. Mark 1:10 with 1:23), but otherwise both types produce fundamentally similar effects. So, for example, being driven out into the wilderness by a pure spirit (Mark 1:12) closely parallels being forced to live in a desolate cemetery by an impure spirit (Mark 5:2-5). Similarly, the loud voice of the expelled demon who recognizes Jesus in Mark 1:26 resembles the loud cry Jesus utters as he expires (Mark 15:37, 39—the loud voice is enough to prompt the centurion's reaction, "Son of God").

Mark 5 (the Gerasene demoniac), no less than Mark 15 (the crucifixion of Jesus), deals with a struggle centered on someone's body. Jesus is killed; the demons torment the demoniac nearly to the point of death. Jesus is raised from the dead; the demoniac regains control over his own body. We have here a good illustration of how ancient psychology envisioned demonic possession in a most corporal way. Clearly the indwelling presence of the spirit (or demon) is accorded much more importance than is any individualistic subjectivity on the part of the person involved.

CONFRONTATION AND ORDER

The extensive description of the Gerasene demoniac (Mark 5:3-5) suggests that demonic possession was perceived as a disruption of—or at least a threat to—proper order. No one is able to "bind" the demoniac, not even with chains! The one possessed is thus understood to be the bearer of an inimical power that threatens disruption, or at least condemns the bearer to a state of weakness. Our contemporary understanding runs in quite a different direction. Where the New Testament sees a threat to external order, we tend to see a threat to the order that lies within the psyche. In the same vein, when we speak of the effects of the Holy Spirit, we are inclined first of all to think of some inner certainty attached to our beliefs. (Contrast Paul's comments about the fruits of the Spirit and the transformation of the whole creation!) Obviously, where the external structures of order seem to be firmly in place, as in our own day, talk of demonic possession is likely to be interpreted as referring to some sort of inner turmoil. Conversely, where the external structures are thought to be unstable, demonic possession will be seen to threaten them. The converse also holds true. In biblical antiquity, the external structures that make for good order were regarded as a gift of the Spirit (Gal 5:22-23), whereas today those same structures are often perceived as intrinsically constraining. This brings us to the important point: The New Testament sees a close connection between possession and the experience of good order. Depending on the degree to which public order is thought to be either vulnerable or reliably stable, demonic possession is in turn experienced as either directly destructive of that order or as a chaotic revolt against it from within the person.[19]

Something similar holds true for the moment when the possessed and the exorcist meet. In the New Testament, an encounter with an exorcist is a sharp, concentrated clash between powers. Exorcist and demon share a deep affinity, in the sense that both are bearers of uncanny power. Today, on the contrary, someone who is ill would never be seen as the bearer of superhuman powers. Instead, such a person would be seen as weak, helpless, and pitiable. Nor is modern psychotherapy ever reduced to a single moment of confrontation. Rather, curative techniques of various sorts are employed. Physicians get involved, along with their pharmacopoeia, but so do ministers, psychologists, and—if necessary—even the police. Amid all this, there is rarely anything like a singular and decisive confrontation. In a strange sort of way, then, the mentally ill of today and those who treat them also share a deep affinity; the powers of each have been drastically reduced. Instead of the New Testament's shattering confrontation of powers, today we have the ministrations of the "helping professions."[20] Today only the most pathologically afflicted or the marginalized who live outside the bounds of "proper" society are still inclined to seek the help of an exorcist. Only on the fringes of psychotherapy, in other words, does there yet remain something of the ancient world's confrontation with uncanny powers.

In first-century Palestinian society, power was constantly experienced as monocratic in nature—concentrated rather than diffuse. This perspective finds close parallels in both the monotheistic view of God and also in the pattern of decisive confrontation characteristic of the exorcisms of the day. Has our modern concern that power be fragmented perhaps also contributed to the decline among us not only of the practice of exorcism but also of former certainties about God?

EXORCISM AND POLITICAL EXPERIENCE

Some time ago Peter Brown was able to establish that the exorcists of late antiquity filled a sociopolitical vacuum in their day, becoming in a special way the mediators between the rich and the poor.[21] Something similar holds true for the time of Jesus. Taking up a position outside the boundaries of ordinary politics, Jesus and his disciples demonstrate that there is no unconquerable power apart from God. The freedom they proclaim thus knows no territorial boundaries; it is available everywhere, for in the truest sense of the word it manifests itself wherever human power no longer avails. Their message is, in effect, that there can be a genuinely "para-political" experience of liberation.[22] Associated with this special sort of liberation is a distinctive kind of imperial universalism, involving, for example, the breaking down of boundaries between Jew and Gentile. A fruitful tension between participating in and yet remaining distant from the world of ordinary politics remains an enduring feature of the Christian legacy.

Questions of Application

PERSONAL METAPHORS

The prevalence of personal metaphors sets up a basic hermeneutical problem. The demoniac's experience of powerlessness is attributed to the workings of a personlike being. The demon's opponent, the exorcist, is also invariably a person. As a rule, the exorcist is the one who knows the name of the demon and deals with it as with a person. One could go so far as to say that the otherwise unnamed misfortune that had arbitrarily befallen a person immediately becomes intelligible and manageable once the exorcist gives it a name. This happens because the demon is then able correctly to estimate the exorcist's superior power. Having done so, the demon thereby also recognizes that it must obey the exorcist's commands. Identifying and correctly addressing the demon, then, is itself perhaps the essential achievement of the exorcist, for it is striking how often the naming of the demon is already the turning point. In sum, the New Testament mode of "therapy" (direct address, command, and dialogue between powers) is directly dependent upon the New Testament's distinctive concept of personhood.

In applying the New Testament's message to today, however, it is precisely this prevalence of personal metaphors that presents the greatest difficulties. So, for example, as soon as the notion of personlike demons ceases to be credible, so also is the New Testament's mode of therapy (direct address of the demon, etc.) no longer possible. To be sure, there was good reason why antiquity was compelled to regard demons as persons (cf. above). We still have experiences that suggest to us the influence of a personal God.[23] Yet, from a strictly methodological point of view, the same dynamics that shape our way of speaking about God should apply also to personifications of demons and the devil. In both cases certain experiences of overwhelming, uncanny power are interpreted by means of personal metaphors. God continues to be perceived as somewhat like a person.[24] So why aren't demons? In many a case of mental illness, the symptoms resemble an incursion by a second personality. The afflicted emit strange sounds and exhibit strange behavior—modes of expression that simply do not fit the person one formerly knew. Observing such strange behavior, people in the past were easily led to think of possession by some sort of personlike being. However, when one tries to explain the same symptoms now, in keeping with the tenor of modern psychiatry, the notion of being possessed by another being would hardly ever come up. This is primarily due to one of the most fundamental differences between ancient and contemporary thought, namely, that the ancient world grasped metaphorically what the modern world tries to grasp causally.[25]

Here it is important to keep in mind that talk of demons as persons also relies on an earlier and quite different notion of what constitutes a person. Between ourselves and the New Testament lies a major change in the understanding of the self, one shaped in no small part by Christian debate about the nature of the Triune God. The repercussions of that discussion reach also to the understanding of demons. One must also wonder about the extent to which various popular Christian traditions and practices regarding the mocking of Satan have themselves contributed to the fact that demons and the devil are not only no longer widely regarded as persons and are thought by many not to exist at all. As already noted, other factors account for why it has been easier to maintain personal metaphors for God and for at least some of the angels (e.g., Michael).

Experience and the metaphors one uses to make sense of experience form a unity. As the nature of one changes, so also must the nature of the other. To try to preserve the personal metaphors the Bible uses to speak about demons, simply because they are in the Bible, would amount to a naive biblicism. As I see it, this difficult hermeneutical situation can be confronted in several ways. The next section offers some suggestions.

DEMONOLOGY AND THE IMAGING OF GOD

When we take a close historical look at the course of the Western theological tradition, we can see that the demonology of early Judaism is an outgrowth of an earlier notion about a "demonic" aspect of Yahweh himself.[26] That is to say, the category of the demonic was used to understand experiences of the uncanny, the dreadful, the destructive, the fearsome, the hostile, or the threatening. Elements such as these are to be found in all layers of the Old Testament tradition, and such elements were apparently integrated into belief in Yahweh per se.[27] But we can also track a tendency in the later stages of Old Testament tradition to interpret the elements of the demonic in Yahweh dualistically. The best example of this is the way 1 Chr 21:1 recasts 2 Sam 24:1: In the account in 1 Samuel 24 Yahweh instigates the census of Israel and thereby also the subsequent disaster; that is, God entices David to order the census, and the punishment for having taken the census thus comes directly from God! In the account in 1 Chronicles 21, however, Satan becomes the instigator of the census. In other words, initially Yahweh himself was believed to have a destructive or at least a dangerous side. But this aspect of Yahweh's character was increasingly delegated to certain of his minions (cf. esp. *Jubilees* 10). In contrast to this tendency in early Judaism, the New Testament sets up a dualism along temporal lines. Contrasted with the merciful God of the present is the potentially terrifying God of future judgment (Matt 18:23-35; 25:14-30 par.). In the imagery of the thief who comes unexpectedly in the night, some of these frightening aspects of God are transferred to the eschatological Son of Man. Not until Marcion, however, does there emerge a split between the absolutely good God of Jesus Christ and a malicious counter-principle, a sort of anti-God. (From what I have seen of preaching during the past decades, the tendency is still very much alive to restrict theology to Marcion's benevolent God, so that God is often reduced to something like the principle of love.)

In the interest of taking seriously the biblical statements about demons, one might well try to trace this development back to its sources and, against such a background, interpret the texts about demons in light of the statements about a "demonic" aspect of Yahweh. Then one would no longer have to reckon with some spooky realm of ghosts. We could instead see these texts as speaking directly about aspects of God. The same goes for angels. Just like demons, they represent certain aspects of the divine totality, but in such a way that the unity of God is not compromised. It could be said that the angels represent the majesty of God in its myriad reflections.[28] The demons, on the other hand, represent the impenetrable and unfathomable aspects of the divine. From the standpoint of our historical-psychological perspective, all this would mean interpreting the reports of uncanny and threatening spirits, beings before which human beings are powerless, as ultimately having to do with an experiencing of Yahweh himself.

To be sure, the historical-psychological perspective raises new questions. One can wonder not only if such a perspective is helpful but also if it is theologically legitimate. What might ultimately be produced by such a hermeneutic? I offer a few tentative suggestions.

1. Since it is no longer possible to identify just what illnesses or conditions underlie New Testament accounts of demonic possession, we must renounce all efforts to treat such accounts as medical case-studies. Renouncing interpretations in terms of mental or metabolic imbalances, however, also opens up a new avenue of approach to the texts, one that at least has the advantage of corresponding to the biblical experience of the demonic.

2. Modern literature can also reflect human experiences aptly called "demonic" (see below).[29] In other words, the underlying experiential phenomenon continues.

3. Basically, then, what the New Testament describes as "demonic" can no longer justifiably be translated into the language of psychopathology. In the place of such an approach, we would urge the adoption of a consistently theological approach. That is, what we have labeled as demonic is to be approached not from the perspectives of modern psychology but in light of what the Bible has to say about God. To be sure, in a sense any experience can be interpreted theologically. But here we are dealing specifically with experiences of the overwhelmingly destructive seen as authentic encounters with God. Details aside, it seems to me that the insights already provided by historical psychology invalidate any further attempts to interpret such experiences along lines informed by psychology in its modern sense.

DEMONOLOGY AND POETRY

Within poetic genres of speech it is still quite legitimate to speak of angels or demons, as any number of examples could readily attest. No apologies are necessary for speaking of God, angels, or demons as personlike beings, provided the metaphoric character of one's language is clearly acknowledged. But all sorts of dogmatic and unreflective notions about the nature of "truth" tend to block the understanding of religious speech and religious acts as more akin to poetry than to journalistic reports. Often overlooked is the fact that a genuine seriousness of purpose can underlie playful (symbolic or metaphoric) use of language. Not every instance of such linguistic practice is only a game. On the contrary, poetic (metaphoric) speech is the only kind of speech adequate to treat many areas of human experience. Quite apart from speech about God, for example, poetic forms of speech are best suited to convey human experiences of love and intimate relationship.[30] In the same vein, theological dogmas are more easily grasped by the laity when they are embedded in hymns and liturgies. Put another way, it is clear that ecclesiastical pronouncements have a much greater impact upon people when they are communicated through prayers and hymns than when they are presented as official instructions.[31]

In sum, from an aesthetic perspective properly attuned to the role of metaphor there is no difficulty with speech about angels or demons. The difficulty surfaces when such language gets transformed into dogmatic prescriptions.[32]

DEMONOLOGY AND POSTMODERN OPENNESS
TO ALTERNATIVES

There is precedent for skepticism about the established sciences of modernity. Within the past few decades, there has emerged a postmodern crisis around the issue of rationality as such. Among its manifestations is a predilection for all sorts of irrationality, and in particular for parapsychology and faith healing. Traditional teachings of the church are being pushed aside, precisely on the grounds that they are too rationalistic. Obviously, traditional Christian theology does share with rationalism a commitment to precise statement, intelligible formulation, and intellectual rigor. To a significant degree, the attraction of irrationalist movements is due to a recognition that questions of ultimate truth cannot be answered on rational grounds. Many are thus drawn to what cannot be regulated and ordained by the so-called experts. The longing for freedom, or at least for more room to maneuver in significant areas of human experience, testifies to a yearning to embrace the not-yet-accepted, despite the caveats of both rationalist thinking and traditional theology. Mutatis mutandis, this yearning shows up even in professional theological circles, where all sorts of fashionable trends are accepted precisely on the ground that they are not obviously colored by Enlightenment modes of thinking.

With these tendencies in place, it would hardly be advisable simply to reaffirm the traditional teachings about angels, demons, or Satan. Although the outcome of such a move cannot be determined in advance, the result might well be even greater attraction to irrationality—precisely the opposite of the intended goal. The contemporary yearning for increased hermeneutical flexibility cannot be answered by renewed emphasis on systematic clarity. An instructive parallel is the way some of the contemporary and advanced forms of medicine, precisely in the name of progress, have entered into alliance with aspects of the premodern, essentially religious subculture that still exists in our midst.[33]

The newly invigorated irrationalism in our midst rightly directs our attention to oft-forgotten elements in the heritage of the Christian (and especially the Catholic) church. At the same time, one does not dishonor this legacy if one then allows the use of discursive, rational criteria in the ongoing discussion about it.[34] Thus, with regard to the hermeneutical problem of coming to terms with the demonism of biblical antiquity, the church finds itself in a dilemma. The biblical tradition offers answers to questions that these days are getting asked outside the church, in areas where the church is reluctant to speak a biblical answer. Some guidelines for entering into discussion with these areas would be helpful, not only for addressing the phenomenon of belief in demons but also to other areas accessible by means of historical psychology.[35]

Many phenomena in the New Testament that seem to invite interpretation through the notion of possession can also be interpreted under other rubrics. So, for example, in 1 Cor 12:9 (cf. v. 30) the power of healing is attributed to "charisma" rather than to possession.

SOME THEOLOGICAL CORRECTIVES PROVIDED
BY NEW TESTAMENT DEMONOLOGY

Apart from the importance of New Testament demonology as a corrective to any sort of unrestrained rationalism (see above), the following points also can be made:

1. The biblical understanding of God is sufficiently broad to encompass "demonic" elements. Put another way, biblical language about angels and demons has direct relevance also for the church's doctrine of God.

2. Biblical accounts of exorcisms are mythic in nature. As such, they function in a struggle against incomprehensibility and a sense of futility. These stories affirm that powerlessness too has its limits, and hence that we need not fear being swallowed up by it.

3. The destructive is conceived of as a totality (as having both physical and spiritual dimensions).

4. In the Bible emphasis is placed on what influences the human being from without. Accordingly, deliverance is thought of not as some transformation of the self from within but as a liberation from an occupying force. In this dynamic, neither moral guilt nor ethical improvement plays a part. None of these distinctively biblical elements really coincides with our own expectations, even with the modern relativizing of the notion of guilt (through increased attention to the influences of social milieu and arbitrary circumstances) or the increasing appreciation of factors beyond the moral dimension in religious experience.

5. Exorcism has to do with the experience of power in the area of religion. As such, political metaphors also get drawn into the picture. In this way, not only is another important domain of life connected to the reality of religious experience (experience that is partly cognitive, partly aesthetic, partly contemplative, and partly ethical—yet none of these exclusively) but a key is also provided to help us understand the broader array of power elements in both the Jewish and the Christian traditions. In other words, the political provenance of key metaphors illuminates such common Judaic-Christian religious themes as God the Lord of history, messianism, the providential directing of history, and the demand to shape a just society.

6. The psychosomatic totality of the human being must not be overlooked, neither in preaching nor in action.

7. The connection between demonology and the perception of order draws attention to the fact that our own desire to establish and maintain good order cannot help but be haunted by a deep sense of anxiety unless we also allow room for a certain amount of healthy disorder.

8. Christianity offers not so much a message as a mediator. His authority is effective as a center of good order.

4
Experience of the Body

The Problem

In Rudolf Bultmann's *Theology of the New Testament*, the section entitled "'Soma' (Body)" appears under the broader rubric "The Anthropological Concepts." In Bultmann's development of this topic, the primary issue is the relationship to one's self.[1] He attributes little significance to experience of the surrounding world, even going so far as to say of the surrounding world that it is "an outside power, which has seized from the self the power of control over itself. . . ."[2] The one-sidedness of this treatment, whose origin in Hegel and Kierkegaard cannot be denied, provides the starting point for our investigation. To be sure, the dimension of history is not altogether excluded by Bultmann, but he nonetheless accords it far too little significance. Above all, however, it is Bultmann's restriction of focus to the relationship between "self" and "body" that strikes me as inadequate to grasp the full dimension of "body" in both the writings of Paul and elsewhere in the New Testament. The texts actually suggest a constantly three-sided association of "self," "body," and "other/s" (or "world"). This three-sided association demands that we pay fuller attention to the historical-psychological dimension. When we do, there emerges in place of Bultmann's rather static duality of body and self the dynamics of an interaction involving also other human beings, the encompassing milieu, and God. Only when these additional dimensions are seen as indispensable features of corporeality—and not regarded as a mode of alienation or, at best, a preliminary stimulus to proper self-understanding[3]—can we adequately begin to grasp how "body" was experienced in the New Testament.

We can put the issue in the form of some questions. According to Paul, does not the Christian experience Christ (or the Holy Spirit) so directly (within one's own body) that there is simply no "room" left for the kind of self-critical reflection that Bultmann posits in his treatment of "body"? Can the body then adequately to be thought of as a self-subsisting reality? Is the reality called "body" not rather something determined in or by an experiencing of Jesus Christ and the Holy Spirit?

Relationship as Bodily Experience

For Paul, "body" is a term for the whole of the human being, though not in the self-contained sense in which we use the term today. Rather, "body" designates the point of contact for relationship, e.g., to other human beings, to God, or even to sin. The human being is therefore considered "body" also insofar as he or she submits to the rule of God. That is to say, from the Pauline perspective a person's body is never closed off to the outside; the body is not, to use a modern term, autonomous. Rather, the body is something to be ruled, either by God or by sin. Corporeality means experiencing dependence; bodily renewal comes from exchanging one mode of dependence for another. The Pauline "body" is thus not juxtaposed to any sort of "soul," nor is consciousness played off against a subconscious element. Familiar as they are to us, such categories of thought are alien to the New Testament.

BODY AND SELF

First a few exegetic observations:

1. Paul speaks of "body" or "members" in the same way he speaks of "self" (Rom 6:12-16).

2. In the same texts, however, Paul reckons with a responsible center that determines what is in the body (Rom 6:12). Therefore it is not the case that a human being simply "is" his or her body. Distinction between body and self is also important in 1 Cor 6:18, where the doer (the self) is said to be able to sin against his or her own body.

3. Paul thinks of being set free from this body of death (Rom 7:24). According to 2 Cor 5:2-5, he reckons with the dissolution of the visible body and the building up of a new, spiritual body—a process already underway in the present and increasing daily.

4. This new, spiritual body prevents the Christian from having to stand "naked" at the time of death or at the *parousia*, when "this tent" will fall away (2 Cor 5:3). To be "naked" in either situation would indicate damnation or annihilation.

5. The fate of the body and the fate of the self are tightly intertwined, for the quality of the body determines the nature of the self as well. Thus the self does not simply remain constant while only the body undergoes changes. With a new body, a different self also emerges.

In sum, the categories "being" and "having," which in modern times are frequently played off against each other, are equally unsuited as alternatives for describing the relationship between the body and the personal center. Use of the term "having" would make the body into an object, while use of the term "being" would lead to a false leveling of the distinction between self and body. Thus we must look for a paradigm that allows for the differentiation as conceived by Paul.

RENEWAL OF THE BODY

The most important exegetic findings are these:

1. According to Rom 6:4, 8, 11, the "death" of the body on the occasion of baptism leads to a renewal of the whole person. In all of this the "self" is maintained almost in a formal sense only, as a name or a stable point of reference. We already observed such stark reduction of the self to minimal bearer of experience in Gal 2:20 (where again little more is carried over than the name of the one who undergoes the experience).

The sort of experience that underlies these New Testament texts differs from the notions and experiences of moral renewal reflected in Greek philosophy. There the problem is generally conceived as pertaining to basic human nature; the defining issue is a struggle between body and soul, with victory in the struggle being perceived as conquest by the better (spiritual) side of the human being. Paul, however, frequently replaces this Greek notion of struggle between body and soul (a notion thoroughly familiar to him from his broader milieu) with the theme of a struggle between flesh and spirit.

2. According to Rom 6:6, the destruction of the sinful body is to be understood as a severing of all the established relationships of a person. Because in fact the same old skin and bones persist even after baptism, the "body" of which Paul is speaking is obviously not the overtly physical aspect of the person. Paul instead is here talking about all the relationships, the interlocking connections, the aspirations, and the orientations of the human being, both before and after the renewal that baptism effects. Thus the "death" and the renewal of the body actually amount to a reshaping of all external relationships. Obviously presupposed in all of this is that the dimension of "body" extends even so far as wherever dreams and desires are generated.

Decisive for the renewal of which Paul speaks is not the setting aside of corporeality but the establishment of a new kind of corporeality ("as though awakened from the dead"), one linked with a new freedom. This new corporeality results not in some interior attitude of certainty but in a new pattern of behavior.[4] In fact, it is quite likely that Paul's interest in corporeality is ultimately directed toward the realm of behavior. One can say this because, before baptism, the body was dominated by sin and served as the implement of sin. After baptism, however, the bodily members of Christians are to be implements of righteousness. For Paul the Pharisee, what really counts is action in accordance with the demands of the Law.

3. According to Paul, the body is not an end in itself but an instrument for behaving and acting. Thus the body is less a zone for relationship to one's "self" than it is a means for entering into relationship with God and the world.

THE BODY AND ONE'S FELLOW HUMAN BEINGS

In 1 Corinthians, both the body of the individual (6:19) and the body that is the community (3:16) are referred to as the temple of the Holy Spirit. Likewise, according to 10:17 "we are all one body." As expressed in 12:12-13, the body that is the community has been established through baptism in the one Spirit; according to 10:16, the same is effected by "participation . . . in Christ" in the Eucharist. However, if the Holy Spirit dwells in each individual Christian as in a temple and yet at the same time and in the same way also dwells in the community as a whole (or, if each individual is a member of Christ and all taken together are his body), then obviously the corporeality of each Christian has a constitutive relationship to the "body" that is the community as a whole. The totality that constitutes the Christian community is built up of many parts, analogous to the way the physical body is composed of many cells.

The body of the individual Christian is thus located in the body that is the community. Each individual body is connected to the others, and together they constitute the body of the community. The body of each individual Christian is thus more like a bridge than a private estate. This connective function holds true regardless of whether the body belongs to sin or to Christ. The body is the means by which we are connected to one another. According to whether we are linked to sin or to Christ, this connection is deemed to be either unrighteous or righteous.

The Body as Transferable Property

THE BODY ALWAYS BELONGS TO SOMEONE ELSE

According to Paul, the body of the human being is not autonomous or self-contained; an essential aspect of bodily existence is that one's body does not belong to oneself. That is, Paul thinks of the body in terms of mutually exclusive claims of possession. Either one's body belongs to sin (Rom 6:6) or it belongs to Jesus Christ (Rom 7:4). From our point of view, in either case the self would be estranged from its own body.[5] To be sure, even for Paul the passion that reigns within a person's body (6:12) is in some sense under the control of a "you" (6:13), so that one's body can come to be guided "from the heart" (6:17). These are modest indications that the self can desire to go in a direction other than the one dictated to the body by an indwelling power of sin (cf. Rom 7:20). None of that, however, changes the fact that the new status of the Christian is still one of servitude.

The body is thus regarded as an object for possession, ownership of which can pass from one person to another. The same scenario applies in Paul's understanding of Christian marriage; reciprocity of property rights also prevails here, as husband and wife each have rights over the body of the partner (1 Cor 7:4). Paul does not hesitate to decree for Christians a state of affairs that can only be characterized as reciprocal heteronomy. What it all comes down to is that the underlying religious experience allows for no middle ground. Either the body belongs to God and to life or it is in the possession of sin and death.

THE OWNER OF THE BODY DWELLS IN IT

Paul employs the image of a temple in which the Holy Spirit dwells (cf. the similar imagery of the body as the sanctuary of the Holy Spirit in *T. Isaac* 4:16). The one who dwells in a house is its owner, but at times that owner may be someone other than one's self. It may be sin, or it may be Christ. From this religious perspective, then, the body is not tied to the self but is oriented toward an *extra nos*. In another image, the body of the human being is a field of battle between God and sin, which means that the body is also a place where either destruction or deliverance takes place. This follows from the view that the body itself is in a state of total dependence on either one or the other of the two powers struggling for mastery within it. In Rom 6:16-22 Paul refers to this state of affairs as "slavery." The notion of being owned by another is even more explicit in 1 Cor 6:19-20, with its imagery of slave-purchase. The motif of glorification (v. 20b) also belongs to the imagery of slavery, since one of the traditional tasks of the slave was to glorify the master.[6]

In sum, constitutive of the reality of being human according to the New Testament is that people do not belong to themselves. Corporeality entails dependency. For Paul, the "worth" of the body is not determined by reference to its visible physicality. (Paul also speaks of the spiritual "body" in corporeal terms.) The body's worth is determined instead by whether or not Christ lives within it. Since the Christian is not autonomous, Christian identity is determined by the way one has become (in one's body!) a point where experience of Christ and experience of the world intersect. In keeping with this perspective, Paul becomes the first to dare to set up as the foundation of his ethic for Gentile Christians not the Law but the controlling presence within the body of the indwelling Spirit.

CORPOREALITY AND PROPER SOCIAL ORDER

First Corinthians 6:12-20 prohibits the intercourse of a Christian with a prostitute, because that would mean that the two become one body. The Christian is already a part of the body of Christ. To be one with both Christ and a prostitute would constitute a fundamental incompatibility, so the choice is obvious: either Christ or the prostitute. Note, however, that intimate relations with one's own spouse are not forbidden, even though here as well the two become one body. (Verse 16 is in fact derived from the description of conjugal union in Gen 2:24.) The decisive difference consists in the fact that, with a prostitute, the relationship is not based on reciprocity but on exploitation. In Paul's understanding, it is the prostitute that does the exploiting (6:12b). Be that as it may, reciprocity is not in and of itself the primary determinant of righteousness in a relationship. (Note the similarity of vocabulary in 1 Cor 6:12 and 1 Cor 7:4.) Still, the body of Christ cannot persist in a situation of social unrighteousness.[7] When a man becomes one body with his wife, then the quality of their interaction (whether based on righteousness or on unrighteousness) has a direct effect on the body of Christ. In short, the body is the site where social righteousness or unrighteousness becomes manifest. Here too Paul's Pharisaic interests in the social behavior of human beings is evident.

With regard to the psychological issue of the experiencing of body, what the aforementioned means is that, for Paul, the body is an instrument for activity. This principle holds to such a degree that there can really be no activity that does not involve the body (2 Cor 5:10). In contrast to our mode of perception, feelings or moods are not an important feature of the body. Neither is the body something that can be denied; Paul is no enemy of physicality as such. Not only is the body an instrument of activity but it is also that which is affected by the activity of others. Thus the threat posed by sin, namely, the sentence of death, is directed toward the body

(Rom 7:24b). The goal, then, is not to reject the body but only to remove the death-directed dimension of the body.

Again in contrast to ourselves, Paul only rarely associates the body with emotionality. In his view, the dimension of action and behavior is far more important. In other words, with the body it is always a matter of life and death and never just of "feelings." All of this could serve as a valuable corrective for us, with our penchant for egocentric navel-gazing.

Sinning against One's Own Body

Literally, 1 Cor 6:18b reads as follows: "Every [other] sin that a man commits is outside the body, but the one who whores sins against his own body." This puzzling sentence must be seen in the light of the following features of human experience as reflected in the New Testament:

- Sexuality affects the body as a whole.
- No other transgressions affect the body as their "object" (except perhaps those involving the stomach [1 Cor 6:13]). Only sexuality directly affects the body.
- In the case of prostitution, the body is not the agent but the recipient of the action. Still, while it is not the instrument, it is inescapably a partner, a participant. To a certain degree, it too must suffer for what I do. Much like we today think of the environment in relation to ourselves, the body is implicated in all that I do. In effect, Paul has split the self into an acting part and an affected part.

The underlying experience can be described like this: One cannot sin against objects or instruments; one can sin only against higher authorities or institutions of authority. As the prodigal son of Luke 15:21 says, "Father, I have sinned against heaven. . . ."[8] In a sense, then, the body is something outside myself toward which I comport myself. I can either show too little respect to my body or I can treat it with appropriate esteem. So Paul wants to make clear to his hearers that the issue with prostitution is hardly superficial. He wants to clarify for his hearers the real nature of an experience with a prostitute.

But just how does it happen that, in trafficking with a prostitute, one devalues one's own body? What does the body have to do with God who, after all, is the One ultimately concerned with sin? Prostitution differs from other sins in that it is an extreme sort of self-disdain, a treatment of the body "beneath its dignity." But then how does the body acquire its dignity in the first place?

I propose the following response to these questions. The sin in consorting with a prostitute comes from the fact that one's body rightly belongs to God. To the mind of Paul, the other sins are not directed against the body, and as such they have a different sort of impact on God. (Of course they still have an effect on God; sins are, after all, sins!) Obviously, in the texts under consideration here, Paul wants to awaken in his hearers a new sensitivity toward this particular kind of activity. He wants to establish a change in how they experience their own bodies. His message is that the body is holy, and that it is so because it belongs to God. As I see it, in vv. 19-20a Paul is presenting the grounds for his argument about not "sinning against one's own body," for here he explains that the body is surely the temple of God. It is because of this that the body acquires its distinctive value. This is why, in sinning against the body, one also sins against a higher authority. So in all of this Paul is not just advancing a new ethical demand but offering a foundation upon which can be built a genuinely Christian experience of the body.

From a historical-psychological perspective this means that the holiness of the Christian is not a matter of inner conviction or of some sort of feeling-awareness. Holiness arises instead from the obligatory claim of God upon this body. In simplest terms, the motto of the Pauline psychology of the body is: "My body does not belong to me." This state of affairs in turn affects how all activity is evaluated. Not only those who have vowed to remain in a state of virginity (1 Cor 7:32-34), but all Christians stand under the proprietary claim of God upon their bodies. In the whole range of what pertains to the body (to use Pauline language: in all my activities and my dealings), I encounter God's presence and God's claim on me.

The Corporeality of Both Salvation and Damnation

The state of the body also provides symptoms of one's prospects for salvation or its opposite. Experience of the body is thus structured not only with reference to its owner (God or Satan) but also with reference to its soteriological destiny. Thus the focus of attention is by no means directed toward some intrinsic worth of the body but rather upon what will befall the body at the end: life or death. Whether for weal or for woe, a person's fate is intrinsically connected to his or her body. Thus the most terrifying prospect, to be avoided at all costs, seems to be that of nakedness, that is, to be found as bodiless as a ghost (2 Cor 5:3b).[9] To be sure, the Christian at present has a body doomed to die, but a new body is invisibly developing. Thus one awaits a transformed body in the future (1 Cor 15:51). In any case, whether the final outcome is salvation or damnation, life or death, one's "body" will be inextricably involved.

All of this means that the mere existence of the self is not the ultimate good. The decisive feature is quality of existence. Strictly speaking I neither "have" a body nor "am" a body. The crucial consideration is the quality of the existence that I experience "through" my body. The quality of one's existence is determined by how one lives. While for us existence as such ("naked" existence) is self-evidently valuable, for Paul the primary concern is how one lives (in the body!). Riding upon that "how" of the body is the final outcome: salvation or damnation. If being "naked" like a ghost (i.e., deprived of a body) is an indication of extreme misfortune, then Paul can hardly have had an intrinsically hostile attitude toward the body.

In sum, just as human activity requires the instrumentality of a body, so also the human condition is determined with reference to the body. The notion of a bodily resurrection corresponds to the significance attributed to corporeal activity. Paul was not the first to speak of either theme; both were already features of the Pharisaic tradition that Paul took over and rendered Christian. The quality of corporeal activity in the present determines the quality of corporeal existence hereafter. Both aspects of corporeality (existence and activity) are absolutely fundamental for what it means to be human.

Conclusions

1. The body is a dwelling place for its inhabitant—for the self as the nominal owner, but also for the Holy Spirit or Satan (or demons), either one of which dwells in the body as an occupying force. The orientation of the body toward an *extra nos* is therefore an intrinsic feature. This means that every self is dependent on or subservient to some other. Salvation therefore comes down to having the Holy Spirit as one's occupying power—not against but in concurrence with one's own will. Human corporeality thus means that no one lives for himself or herself. (In place of the metaphor of indwelling, one could perhaps use that of putting on a garment.[10])

2. Because the body is the locus of both action and determination of the human condition, there can be no solace that is restricted to the soul.

3. If corporeality means our being located within a network of binding relationships, then the promise of bodily resurrection must also refer to something other than the restoration of mere skin and bones. Moreover, the relationships involved here are hardly just conceptual; they are concrete acts within the context of a community.

4. If the expression "body of sin" (Rom 6:6) is considered in conjunction with the expression "body of Christ" (Rom 7:4), then the genitive phrase in each case designates that authority to which I am bound. Put another

way, at all times my body is controlled by that reality for which I live, which I serve, and to which I belong. My body is totally other-directed. This other provides the direction toward which I live and at whose disposal I always stand. Like a sponge that absorbs whatever fluid lies around it, so my body is filled by that toward which it is oriented. This situation is the complete opposite of what is suggested by slogans such as "my body belongs to me" (taking the slogan as a universal moral principle). From the biblical perspective, one always lives for another.

It can therefore be no accident that, with reference to the body and its members, Paul speaks of slavelike servitude and of obedience (Rom 6:6, 12). In biblical antiquity, the Greek term for "bodies" (*sōmata*—plural) also served as a technical term for "slaves." Paul draws on this semantic overlap in his elaborations on "body" (*sōma*—singular).

As a possible corrective to our own point of view, these observations mean that Paul thinks of the body neither physically nor individualistically. For Paul the body is instead something like a ganglion in a network of nerves. To continue with the metaphor, sensitivity and even sensuality are thus intrinsic to corporeality, and relatedness to things and persons outside is indispensable. The theme of fundamental dependence of our bodies upon outside elements is an important aspect of biblical realism. What is concurrently and always "out there" is sin, death, the devil, and God. It is with reference to experiences of corporeal dependence on these realities that Paul maps out his rigorous ethic.

5

Interior and Exterior

The Psychological Question

The question about the "inner" and the "outer" of human reality is not confined to investigations into human nature or worldview. There is also a historical-psychological issue here. Why do human beings experience an inner, invisible world of the "heart" and also an external one (other human beings)? Is the experience of these two everywhere and always the same? Or are they experienced differently in different times and places? Since the distinction between inner and outer touches on the matter of purity, this dichotomy also marks one of the important boundaries between Judaism and Christianity.

The main point to note at the outset is that quite different appraisals of what lies "inside" the human being and what "outside" stand in close proximity to one another in early Christianity. These differing appraisals are in turn rooted in differently appropriated experiences. I now turn to such matters.

Inner and Outer: Basic Determinations

When the New Testament speaks of the interior of a human being, the reference is not always to that zone that, strictly speaking, lies "within"—a person's feelings, desires (conscious or unconscious), intentions, or designs. Instead, the reference might be to any one of the following three types of phenomena: (a) something hidden from public view but by no means invisible in and of itself, (b) something a person desires, in contrast to something a person can do, and (c) something that lies in the eschatological future and hence is not yet visible to human beings. So, for example, according to Matt 23:25 the interior is invisible in the sense of not being accessible to public view.[1] It is not something invisible as such, however, but something that does not display itself openly. In this case, then, the notion of what lies inside has a social orientation; it is not focused on the individual person. Above all, the New Testament understands the interior of the human being as something quite apart from consciousness itself. Failure to appreciate this difference leads to a common misunderstanding in our era of emphasis on personal disposition, namely, that Jesus preached about a refined or purified state of mind rather than about deeds.

Along this line it is also helpful not completely to blur the distinction between the interior of the person and the "heart" (cf., e.g., Mark 7:21). The inner sphere is invisible and intangible, but it nonetheless has a structure that is connected to a person's acts. It is something like what we would call the "center" of the person. Necessarily corresponding to this center is the exterior, outer dimension. What is meant here is not the physical corporeality of the human being—embodiment as such—but all that a human being does to or through the body. (For example, one nurtures or adorns one's body, and by means of it one speaks and acts in the world.) Here the point of reference also includes what happens to the body—what affects it as an object. Thus, the exterior of the person is defined by interactions and relationships; it is a point of orientation within a wider dynamic. In a certain sense, even the interior of the person is understood dynamically—but differently than it is by us (cf. "The Interior as Wellspring," below).

Devaluing the External

DANGER OF SENSUOUSNESS

The exterior dimension of human experience is devalued in relation to the interior whenever the locus of temptation is seen to lie, not in the inclination of the heart, but in sensuousness itself—even though this is a relatively superficial ascription of cause. Thus, in the apocryphal Gospel text Papyrus Oxyrhyncus 840, concern about external purity leads to temptation by stirring up human desires.[2] Anti-Pharisaic criticism has here linked up with a devaluation of sensuousness that stems from both Hellenistic popular philosophy and the Jewish sapiental tradition.[3] In this view, external purity is not just worthless; it is itself a trap. The Qumran text against the prostitutes (4Q184) attests that especially learned scribes saw themselves endangered by this kind of distraction.

The Danger of Hypocrisy

The anti-Pharisaic speeches that come down to us from early Christian tradition are frequently shaped by a contrast between inner and outer, or
between "heart" and external deed.[4] The term "hypocrisy" is often used
where such a contrast is drawn. The use of such language is to be understood in light of the following factors.

Standpoint of a Marginal Group

There can be no doubt about the popularity of the Pharisees in the eyes of
the common people of their day. Anyone who would criticize them in
ways such as those indicated above would be turning against an admired
group enjoying broad-based popular support. Criticism of this sort must
therefore be coming from outsiders, people who do not accept the prevailing standards. Anyone who would turn against those accepted as a pious
elite must be speaking from the standpoint of a radical minority. Thus, in
the criticisms directed against the Pharisees we must presuppose an
underlying feeling of distance and an urge to protest. The tensions
between a marginal group and the dominant society are being experienced, at the level of the individual, in terms of contrast between "outer"
and "inner."

Experiential Dimensions of Ethics and Cult

We think we readily understand hypocrisy but in fact hypocrisy is a complicated phenomenon, encompassing presuppositions and experiences
that are no longer current. For example, we tend to contrast the terms
"ethics" and "cult," attributing less value to the ritual than to the moral.
The New Testament's polemical judgment has become for us an uncritical
prejudgment. Underlying this contrast between ethics and cult is a presupposition that we are here dealing with two distinct spheres.

1. Ethics (social ethics). Here we are supposedly dealing with something
that first comes "from the heart" and then reaches completion by means of
a risk-filled decision with regard to persons and situations and is thus not
completely calculable.[5]

2. The cultic, in the widest sense of the word. In this sphere, activity does
not proceed "from the heart," nor does carrying it out necessarily have
anything to do with the interior of a person. This idea is puzzling, however, because cultic activity is generally carried out conscientiously and
deliberately. But the experience that underlies cultic activity is of something being done in calculated fashion and carried out in a strongly rule-
bound environment. Instead of taking a personal risk, in cultic activity

one fits into an established rhythm, a rhythm that is in turn based upon some reliable structure.

At first glance, we would have to say that a positive experience of cult, as described in (2), is lacking among us. As a consequence, the psychological background to the contrast between the ethical and the cultic is also no longer apparent. The historical result of the New Testament's statements about hypocrisy was a general diminution of the cultic in Christian experience. The upshot is that, in the texts about hypocrisy, the contrasting categories of inner and outer, of the heart and the deed, are no longer immediately intelligible to us.

One can describe the resulting historical and hermeneutical problem thus: If the performance of cultic acts is not to be anchored in the heart, then where? What follows from placing such a high value on the heart? Are we really talking here about consciousness or are we dealing with the discovery of the individual over against the external ordering of society, as many have supposed?

In fact, we are probably dealing in this case with two quite different ways of experiencing the claim of God upon human beings. (1) In cultic activity the divine claim gets realized in a limited way, even though the particularized expression also symbolically makes evident the claim of God upon the whole. The danger perceived in particularizing the divine claim is that its relationship to the whole can become blurred. Thus the charge of hypocrisy always boils down to the accusation that cultic activity obscures the whole through excessive attention to the part.[6] (2) Ethical activity does not differentiate between the symbolic (which stands for the whole) and the rest of reality but instead relates to the whole. One can thus say that the interior of the person, the heart, is the arena toward which the radical preaching of Jesus is directed. The thrust of his preaching is that God places a total and undifferentiated claim upon all aspects of human existence. God demands the total holiness of the human being. Precisely this, and nothing less, is the "surpassing righteousness" (in relation to that of the Pharisees) that Jesus demands, according to Matt 5:20. If the whole of the human being is to be radically holy, then that can come about only at the cost of devaluing the cultic.

From a historical-psychological perspective, what we see here is not a process of spiritualization or interiorization, not an emphasis on "true" ("spiritual") worship in contrast to the base materiality of the cult,[7] but precisely the opposite. The extra-cultic domain of life, in all its tangible concreteness, is being taken every bit as seriously as meticulous performance of cultic rites. The underlying experience is thus one of the demanding presence of God (God as judge) and of the prospects for reward or punishment in the age to come.

The Path from Interior to Exterior

At the center of the reflections in this section are texts such as Luke 6:43-45:[8]

> [43]No good tree bears bad fruit, nor again does a bad tree bear good fruit; [44]for each tree is known by its own fruit. Figs are not gathered from thorns, nor are grapes picked from a bramble bush. [45]The good person out of the good treasure of the heart produces good, and the evil person out of evil treasure produces evil; for it is out of the abundance of the heart that the mouth speaks.

THE ESSENTIAL QUALITY IS FIXED

The above-cited words of Jesus are oriented toward a certain "essence" of the human being, one that is qualitatively determined by the heart as either good or evil. This underlying moral identity finds expression in deeds. In other words, people are known by what they do; who or what they are comes out in their acts or deeds.[9] Ultimately, to be sure, it is what lies within that determines a person's identity. Yet this identity can make itself known only in works, which thus also function as signs. Works are the only avenue to the interior. In the form of words or deeds the exterior, like the tip of an iceberg, suggests what lies underneath.

In contrast to Matt 7:21, where words are accorded no importance because deeds alone count, in Matt 12:34 (as the broader context makes clear) the emphasis lies on how words also serve as signs indicating the quality of the heart. In any case, in all of the relevant texts it is presupposed that the ethical identity of the person is established already in advance of the deed (as in John 3:20-21), and that such identity is, in the sense of a strict moral dualism, either good or evil.

THE INTERIOR AS WELLSPRING

According to Luke 6:45 (". . . for it is out of the abundance of the heart . . ."; par. Matt 12:34), the interior of a person is thought of as something that streams out toward the exterior much like an overflowing vessel. This holds true for good and evil people alike. In other words, the inner is thought of as a dynamic reality just as much as is the outer. The image of overflowing presupposes a distinctive experience of the inner. If the interior operates like an overflowing vessel, then for the most part it remains concealed. Put another way, the interior of the person is like a storehouse out of which something is brought, but never more than a single piece at a time. (In addition to Luke 6:45 and Matt 12:35, note Mark 7:15b.)

Paul's language about the overflowing of grace shows that he also makes use of this basic metaphor.[10] Indeed he even employs it in the same way, to describe good works going forth from within, as can be seen in 2 Cor 8:7 and especially in 2 Cor 9:8 ("that you might overflow [*perisseuéte*] into every good work"). Although formulated differently from the words of Jesus cited at the beginning of this section, Paul thinks of the relationship between God and human beings along the same lines. God's condescending to human beings is understood as an overflowing of divine grace. The same Greek word (*charis*) that describes divine grace also designates the loving act that one human being performs toward another (2 Cor 8:7, 9).

The grace of God is also spoken of as "flowing" in texts from the immediate milieu of the New Testament.[11] Obviously, the image of a spring lies at the base of this. Just as a spring gives forth water, so also grace and mercy gush forth from God, and works flow out from a human being. In no case is the "spring" depleted in a single work or a particular instance of divine grace. This underlying image of the wellspring has important consequences for the understanding of human acts.

THE TRANSITION FROM INNER TO OUTER

With the image of the overflowing spring, just as with the image of the fruit tree, the bearing of works is regarded as a natural process, a process that happens as automatically as water pours out of a spring or as naturally as fruit ripens. Passage from the interior to the exterior is no more problematic than bringing something out of a storehouse (Luke 6:45; Matt 12:35). This is so because, in every such case, what the works proceed from is regarded as an unfailing cornucopia, spilling forth its abundance. It is like a plant that never fails to put forth fruit since the fruit is already within it, much like Adam or Abraham already had their descendants in their loins (cf. Heb 7:9-10). If this is so, however, it means that neither the person of the doer nor the process of initiating the act plays any important role. If we stick to the controlling metaphor, the emphasis is rather on not interrupting a natural passage from the inner to the outer. Put another way, it is simply a matter of bringing individual items out of a well-stocked storeroom. In none of the cases at hand is it envisioned that the act itself (as opposed, for example, to intentionality; cf. Rom 7:19) might be at all problematic. On the contrary, inner nature and outer act are linked together, while the intervening phase of resolving to act is simply passed over. This happens because the goodness of the heart is simply being presupposed.

For historical psychology, the significance of the perspective just described is somewhat ambiguous:

1. It could be that the relationship between inner nature and outer act was experienced in just this way. The effortlessness of bringing forth the act would then be an aspect of a charismatic experience. Speaking in favor of this view is the fact that the early Christian missionaries obviously understood themselves as being swept forward by some sort of dynamic power. This power quelled all anxiety in the presence of impurity or paganism, to say nothing of sickness and death. One could try to explain this sort of experience along the lines of a proactive holiness or purity.[12] In other words, we would then here be dealing with a reflection of a missionary impulse experienced as a force capable of breaking down all barriers against the manifestation of God's reign. Thus there emerges, in the place of a (Pharisaic) withdrawal into a defensive holiness, an experiencing of a divine benefaction that breaks through all barriers. It is quite possible that the psychological counterpart to the sociohistorical phenomenon of such missionary activity lies precisely in the notion of something overflowing from within a person. The analogy could be worked out along these lines:

category	direction	result
psychological	from interior to exterior	overflowing, a storehouse, fruits, gifts
missionary	from Israel to the nations	proactive purity, lifting of barriers

2. But it could also be that these statements suggest how the gap separating intention from act can be bridged. It would then be a forceful call to action, an exhortation growing out of the assurance that appropriate action is easily initiated. The presupposed dualism would then function in quite the same fashion. One would be talking of a good or an evil heart (or corresponding sorts of trees, as in Luke 6:43-45) in order to get the hearer to respond with appropriate action. Whether the message is about the basis of action (a good or an evil heart) or the effortlessness (automatic!) way to action, the pedagogic element is the same: in place of an imperative stands an indicative, which precedes the completed act. In this way, the summons to participation gains intensity. When reference is made to a good or a bad tree (Luke 6:43; par. Matt 12:33), the hearer of course wants to be part of the good tree. The very mode of description aims to elicit the desired response.

In sum, the behavior of the Christian is presented in terms of a desired harmony between inner and outer so that, when the preconditions are positive, the actual behavior of the Christian is thought of and experienced simply as the external manifestation of what lies within. Like water from a spring, good works automatically gush forth from an inner reservoir. It could be that this conception relieves the hearer of a whole array of anxieties, such as how one might become righteous or how one might succeed in transforming a good intention into a good deed. Both of these goals are commonly thought of as attainable only after an arduous process. The logic of sayings such as the one at Luke 6:45 aims at removing the burden of such concerns. In a manner of speaking, what is otherwise a cause of concern or even anxiety is here turned on its head. One who might otherwise be facing an interminable struggle toward righteousness is simply informed that he or she is already righteous—or unrighteous.[13] Arduous effort dissolves into unhindered outpouring of what lies within. This, I think, is a most impressive way of speaking metaphorically about justification.

GIVING AS ALMS WHAT LIES WITHIN

Luke 11:41 reads, "So give for alms those things that are within; and see, everything will be clean for you." This puzzling sentence develops two already mentioned aspects of the thematic of interior and exterior.

1. Generally, impurity poses its threat from the outside. Luke 11:41 promises that such a threat has been lifted.

2. The threat of impurity is usually envisioned as involving some sort of movement from outer to inner. Here, attention is on movement from within toward the outside and specified as an act of giving.

3. In giving, the giver does something like distribute goods from an interior treasury (Luke 6:45). But in Luke 11:41 that treasury is understood literally, namely, as the source of a monetary (or at least economically facilitating) gift. The main point is how all the images coalesce. The motif of "bringing forth out of the treasury" corresponds to that of "the overflowing heart," and both in turn are equivalent to the bearing of fruit by trees and other plants. In every case, the quality of the deed that the person does "on the outside" corresponds precisely to what lies "inside" that person. The point of the remarks in Luke 6:43-46 (and parallels) is obvious: from the quality of the deeds one can also determine the quality of what lies within. Luke 11:41 works with the same basic themes, but here the point is somewhat different. It is no longer a matter of determining identical qualities but of determining the specific nature of that which is to be brought forth. No longer are "good" or "evil" to be identified, but alms are to be produced. With this shift of focus, the precise nature of the promise (". . . and see, everything is clean for you") attached to the performance of the deed must be reconsidered.

4. Because the giving of alms is clearly a good work (for Luke, the primary good work), it follows that one who gives alms is also, without doubt, "good" and "righteous." But if such a person is good and righteous within (a condition demonstrated precisely by the external giving of alms), then nothing from without (and therefore also no impurity) can any longer affect that person. In other words, deeds such as the giving of alms demonstrate that the interior of the person is undoubtedly good.

Unlike in the above-cited passage (Luke 6:43-45; cf. par.), in Luke 11:41 we are not dealing with the foundation but rather with a specific demand (renunciation of possessions) and a specific problem (impurity) rooted in the areas of inner and outer. Thus our present text is especially significant for what it contributes to the theme of a proactive purity.[14] Historical psychology is particularly interested in the strong emphasis on the flow of movement from inner to outer, given the fact that impurity usually is seen to pose its threat from the outside. The centrifugal nature of the movement here can once again be traced back to the dynamics of early Christian missionary activity.

Luke 11:41 also differs from Luke 6:43-45 par. in that it is formulated as an imperative with an attached promise (a conditional salvation-proclamation). Yet the validity of the promise rests in the fact that the one who gives the gift is already righteous, not that he or she becomes righteous in the giving of the gift. For one can give only insofar as one is already righteous.[15] What Luke 11:41 has to say about purity has some validity even today. Can we not also say that impurity comes from doing evil deeds because they ultimately have a weakening affect on a person?

The "Inner Person" according to Paul

THE EARLY CHRISTIAN EVIDENCE

The "inner person" is spoken of in quite a different way by Paul and in the Epistle to the Ephesians, as the following considerations illustrate.

1. According to Rom 7:22-23 ("I delight in the Law of God in my inmost self, but I see in my members another law at war with the Law of my mind . . ."), the inner person is the area of pure will (cf. Rom 7:15b, 18b, 19, 20a, 21). What issues forth from this will is not good intentions, however, but deeds. Juxtaposed to the "inmost self" is what the human being in fact accomplishes with his or her "members," and this in turn stands in close relationship to the "law." So the duality here envisioned is not one of body and soul but rather one of willing and doing.

2. According to 2 Cor 4:16 ("Even though our outer nature is wasting away, our inner nature is being renewed day by day"), the external person is the earthly one, the one whose whole existence is bound up with this life. The "inner nature," however, is the new, eschatological existence of the person; it is that which has a future and which must yet develop. In 2 Cor 4:18 Paul sets this person in conjunction with the unseen. This ties in with the theme of the words of Jesus discussed above ("Inner and Outer: Basic Determinations").

3. In Eph 3:16-17 (". . . that you may be strengthened in your inner being with power through his [viz., the Father's] Spirit, and that Christ may dwell in your hearts . . .") just as in the passage from 2 Corinthians, cited above (note how reference to the "Spirit" also occurs in 2 Cor 5), the "inner being" is the new, eschatological reality that the Christian becomes.

Evidence for the prehistory of this theme is found in Plato and in *Corpus Hermeticum* 13.[16] In Plato it is a conflict between the inner "lion" and the inner "man." *Corpus Hermeticum* contrasts the "inner" or "essential" person to the senses. That is, while Plato emphasizes a contrast between man and beast (both of which are inside the person), *Corpus Hermeticum* picks up on a contrast between the "inner person" and the "senses." Romans 7 bears the closest relationship to these Hellenistic analogies, for here as well one finds reference to the senses (v. 7, "covet"). Paul juxtaposes to the inner person the body's members, as instruments for action.

I conclude the following:

1. The inner person is consistently evaluated positively. In no case is the reference to anatomy or subjectivity.

2. Where the notion of the "inner person" is understood as referring to the essential core of the person, this concept is regularly juxtaposed to the chaotic, "beastly" feature of desire (Plato, *CH* XIII, and even Romans 7).

3. In 2 Corinthians 4 and in Ephesians 3, on the other hand, the mode of thinking about the "inner person" reflects a temporal rather than a spatial orientation; the "inner person" is the new and not yet visible goal of a process now underway.

4. Only in 2 Corinthians 4 is there a direct contrast between the "inner" and the "outer" person. Precisely because this passage does not refer to some dichotomy intrinsic to human nature, however, in this case every bit as much as in the others the interior is more than just the opposite of the exterior. Nowhere in these texts, in fact, do we find an essentialistic contrast between the interior and the exterior aspects of the human being. The "inner" person is never viewed as the fixed opposite of the "outer" person. The important point is that in these texts the interior aspect of the

human being is never privileged over the exterior aspect as somehow being the locus of the "true" person. Rather, "inner person" stands either for a distinctly rational potentiality (in contrast to an irrational one) or for something not yet visible because its full manifestation lies in the future.

In sum, Paul calls the eschatologically new person the "inner" person because such a person is "free" (in the distinctively Pauline notion of freedom) from the tyranny of the passions, of sin, and of death.

PSYCHOLOGICAL EVALUATION

1. According to texts such as Matt 23:25, the interior of the human being is the nonpublic area. It is that place where in both word and deed there is no dissimulation. Where one finds mention of the "inner" person, the reference is to a primary domain of social interaction—as opposed to a secondary one, in which one tries to appear as others expect. It is between these two areas that the decisive caesura lies, and not between the external and the internal aspects of individuals. Anyone who opts for the "inner" person, then, is clearly commited to social criticism.

2. With Paul, the expression "inner person" in each case refers to those who yearn for freedom from all forms of tyranny and who look forward to the future realization of that freedom. The same expression also refers to those who are enslaved by sin-producing desires at work in their members, as well as to those who will someday be freed from transience and death (2 Cor 4:16). The inner person suffers either as one who longs to be freed from present tyranny or as one who will be liberated from death. Despite their differences in other regards, the passages from Paul and the Epistle to the Ephesians are in accord on the notion of freedom. Paul experiences the bondage of the body to impulsive desire, to sin, and to death as a form of slavery. At the same time, however, there is something about or within the human being that registers a lively protest against this situation of enslavement and that seeks a life-affirming alternative. The "inner person" is thus the new person, the one already present despite the perception of being enslaved and the awareness of being headed toward death.[17] In 2 Cor 5:16-18, both the present reality and the coming into being of this new person are understood as freely given gifts; the notion of struggle, which shapes the comments of Plato as well as the remarks about suffering in *Corpus Hermeticum* 13 (cf. Romans 7), are completely absent here.

Despite the attention paid to the "inner person," it does not follow that Paul regards the "outer person" as unimportant, for it is the suffering and the pain borne by the "outer person" that defines what it is to be enslaved to sin (Romans 7) and death (2 Corinthians 4–5). In Rom 7:24 Paul cries out in his pain, and in 2 Cor 5:4 he speaks of sighing under his burden. Following the context, in both cases the fundamental issue is one of tension between the "inner" and the "outer" person.

Especially important in all this is how Christian salvation is not being described solely by means of statements about God. Attention is also being directed to the already existent "inner person" who is the bearer of this salvation. In other words, we are not here dealing with free-floating religious statements or even with the "effects" of theological affirmations at the human level. Our attention is being directed instead to the "content" of salvation itself, namely, the condition and the rights of the "new person." So the "inner person" is never understood simply in terms of interiority. On the contrary, the inner person is the new person, a reality not yet visible or tangible, but a reality that one can sense at those break points with the "outer person," the existing body, at dismay over the difficulty of completing the transition from will to act and in disillusionment rooted in awareness of physical mortality. Precisely because they elicit pain, these "fault lines" along which the inner (new) person breaks off from the outer person are at the same time an indicator that the inner person longs to break out from the domain of the invisible and to become totally and fully visible.

Paul, then, designates as "inner" something that is not visible but nonetheless already exists (2 Cor 4:18). Put another way, Paul is not concerned about the unique interiority of each human being. Paul speaks of the "inner person" more in the sense of an interior dimension to reality than an inner-directed mode of awareness. For Paul, the "interior" is the future, already ripening beneath the visible surface. Psychologically speaking, the underlying experience is one of contact with the hard edges of the existent, "outer" person and, to be sure, with a highly intensified level of emotionality. (Cf. Rom 7:24 and 2 Cor 5:4, two of the few passages in which Paul directly expresses emotions common to all persons, not just those tied to his own circumstances [as, e.g., in Rom 9:1]). Putting a higher value on the "inner" as opposed to the "outer" also means, however, a concomitant decrease in level of concern about general societal approval. What matters more is the eschatological hope of the believers.

6

Perceptions

Perceptions of Reality (Facticity)

What we would designate as "facts" were experienced quite differently by people in the milieu of the New Testament, especially if they were perceived to be "acts of God," or of God's eschatological envoy. Time itself was experienced as having a different quality when it was seen as standing in close relationship to God. The suspicion therefore lies close at hand that the perception of both facts and time stands in direct relationship to the experience of God. Put another way, those New Testament personages who perceive facts and time in ways that would strike a modern person as peculiar do so because, in their minds, such realities actually have to do with God.

ACTS OF GOD

The Eschatological Acts of God Have Already Occurred

Scholarly research has long been occupied with a distinctive feature of the so-called Magnificat (Luke 1:46-55), namely, the use of the aorist (past) tense of acts for God that have not yet occurred.[1] To be sure, God has already "shown regard" for the "low estate" of Mary, but the rest of the deeds attributed to God (vv. 51-55) still await their eschatological realization. Nonetheless, the aorist tense is used to speak of those acts. A similar state of affairs is found in the so-called hymns of the Revelation to John.[2] So, for example, in Rev 11:15-17 the reign of God is already established, but then its establishment is later announced in 19:6. Likewise, according to 15:4 the judgments of God have already been revealed, and according to

19:2 God has already avenged the blood of his servants, although in 19:17ff. that revenge is still envisioned as impending. At the time when Revelation was composed, none of these events had yet taken place in the realm of ordinary history. Still, they are spoken of as already belonging to the past. In sum, both the Magnificat and the hymns in Revelation exhibit a peculiar anticipatory character.

The same holds true for the throne-vision of Revelation as a whole, starting with chapter 4. This sweeping historical vision includes events that, from our perspective, have actually been realized, at best, only in part. The similarity here to the hymns in the book is hardly surprising, for those hymns accompany the primary vision much like the chorus in an ancient Greek play comments on the course of the action and hints at impending developments. The seer (John) can already behold everything, including the downfall of Rome and the advent of the New Jerusalem. Such events are already perceptible reality, even if only for him. Within this reality, even the heavenly identity of Christians can be recognized (cf. chapter 7).

If one were to analyze the experience mentioned above, the following would be starting points.

1. In every case, what is perceived in the hymn or the vision is not totally future but has an anchor or starting point in the present. Thus, in the Magnificat Mary's condition of impending motherhood is already quite real and in Revelation starting points are provided by the death and resurrection of the Lamb, the deaths of early Christian martyrs, and the prayers of their souls for revenge (Rev 6:9-10).

2. One observation is particularly obvious: the relevant facts have already been established because of a definitive decision about the issue of controlling power. All that is left to do is to reveal the outcome that has been determined. Both the singers of the hymns and the seer can do this because they are persons who have experienced the decisive power *in actu*.

While the "ecstatic" state of the visionary still seems somewhat intelligible to us, a similar state of mind on an occasion of hymn-singing does not. We still sing hymns, but we experience no particular revelations while doing so. In the New Testament, however, singers are often thought of as Spirit-filled as, for example, Zechariah in the Benedictus (Luke 1:68-79; "filled with the Holy Spirit . . . spoke this prophecy," v. 67) and the inspired singers of "spiritual songs" in Eph 5:18-19 and Col 3:16. The freely formulated prayers of the early Christian prophets (cf. *Did.* 10:7) also point in this direction.

These considerations shed light on the notion of revelation as encountered in both early Judaism and early Christianity. When the Targums speak of the revealing of the kingdom of God, the gist is that the rule of God that has been effective all along in heaven and has already been in place on earth *de jure* is now becoming visible.[3] In a certain sense, then, nothing new happens; what is revealed is what has always been. Issues touching on justice are clarified in similar fashion. As Lord, God has established justice from the beginning; in the eschatological future that justice is realized in its fullness.

3. That the issue of power has long since been decided finds expression in Rev 12:7-9, the myth about the battle between Satan and the archangel Michael. Here an event is presented to the reader that cannot be located on a time scale but that nonetheless lies before the time of the seer himself, that has already taken place "in heaven," and that fundamentally establishes the background for the situation in which the community finds itself.

4. Paul is speaking from a similar perspective with his notions of a "security deposit" (*arrabōn*; 2 Cor 1:22; 5:5) and "first fruits" (*aparché*; Rom 8:23). Here juridical images set the tone. Judgment has already been rendered in favor of human beings. The point to note here is that talk about a "security deposit" and about "first fruits" also refers to the theme of revelation. These juridical images have the effect of foreshortening the future. In other words, under these images Paul is primarily speaking about the unveiling of a state of affairs whose outcome has already been determined (Rom 8:19; 2 Cor 5:10).

We conclude: the perspective that God's eschatological works have all already taken place presupposes that issues of power and the right to rule have already been decided. Either they have been resolved from time immemorial (the notion of the kingly rule of God) or they were resolved in the wake of a more recent event (in the fate of the Messiah, Jesus Christ). Special significance is thus attached to comments about heaven.[4] Because the decisive issues regarding power and right to rule have already been decided in heaven, all the important works of God have also already taken place there (cf. the analogous thought expressed in Eph 2:9-10).

In these passages, then, "heaven" is equivalent to "the truth." What is experienced as true, enduring, and precious—in short, what is regarded as "really real"—is projected onto the vast plane of transcendent space, from whence it draws attention to itself. Since "the truth" in this case is invisible, it is perceived as an invisible world existing alongside the visible one. A close analogy to this mode of perception is to be found in New Testament miracle stories.

On the Facticity of Miracles

Difficulties regarding the historicity of New Testament miracles crop up especially in those cases where Old Testament accounts appear to have served as New Testament prototypes, such as with the stories of miraculous feeding or the raising of Jairus's daughter. Precisely these stories, however, could provide a key to understanding the way "miracles" were experienced.

In contrast to our contemporary, inductive way of perceiving things, in the Bible miracles are not simply observed events. Rather, they take place within something like a loop, or a reciprocal relationship involving both induction (experience) and deduction (conclusion). In practice this means that, because Jesus was able to work miracles, therefore he did indeed perform them. The idea that Jesus was able to work miracles, however, is not itself a deduction, since it has a distinct point of origin. It is grounded in a complex sort of experience, one that incorporates the following features: (1) The miracle worker is experienced as someone gifted with an uncanny charisma. This is an all-encompassing experience, and as such it is also an experience of power at work. (2) The miracle worker comes into conflict with the established authorities. In my opinion, one can show that all "miracles" have a detrimental impact upon the established authorities. (3) The one for whose benefit the miracle is performed is "at the end of his rope." No one can help him anymore; he is in a "no exit" situation. (4) Neither the worker of the miracle nor the recipient of the same entertains any reservations about the possibility of extraordinary manifestations of power. A measure of cultural determination enters into the picture here, since miracle stories are typically associated with a "magical" mode of perception (cf. "Mythic Events," below).

Other features could be named as well; they all form a cluster. Enough have been identified here, however, to make the relevant point: these features mark off a horizon within which it is meaningful to say that, because the wonder worker is able to perform such wonders, then he has indeed done so. In exploring the assumptions behind such an affirmation, we note the following:

1. There is an interesting mode of understanding that finds literary reflection in the genre known as the panegyric, historically related to the ancient encomium. This involves all-encompassing, unrestrained praise. Constitutive of such praise is the theme that the one being praised has done all sorts of marvelous things because he could do them (recall the hymns mentioned earlier). Nowadays we are inclined to regard such texts as exaggerated, even insincere. For the most part, they have to do with adulation directed toward rulers, which is to say that they are based on experiences with the exercise of sovereignty. But the experience of the

ancients in this regard differs from our own. A panegyric is hardly just a bunch of fawning lies voiced by a pack of sycophants. Antiquity knew nothing about constitutional limitations on the power at the top. Precisely the opposite holds true. When the bearer of power is really the only one who can help, the result is that he is extolled in the panegyric as the "highest" precisely because his power is unencumbered. It is by following this line of thinking that the Roman emperor, the elevated embodiment of power, could also work miracles—something no modern prime minister could ever hope to do! In the same vein, it was possible for the Messiah to do things that no mere scribe versed in the Law could do.[5]

2. The distinctly miraculous element of a miracle lies in the fact that the one with power grants a moment of time to the one in dire need, that the powerful one deigns personally to turn to the one in distress. In a certain sense, then, "love" is the real secret of a miracle—and vice versa.

3. The wonders attributed to the miracle worker occur because they are only "signs" of what is within him, of what he is "made of." According to the mode of thinking dominant in the New Testament milieu, what one truly is gets revealed only through one's works.[6] In the Jesus tradition this feature is especially clear in Luke 6:43-45: Works consist precisely of what overflows out of the substance of the heart (recall the previous chapter).

This leads to a further observation. In the experience of the early Christians, the threshold between the ability to act and the act itself is very low (because ability flows from fullness of power, from being endowed with charisma). We, of course, view this threshold as quite high. In the ancient way of thinking, the threshold in question lies between having been chosen and not having been chosen. In the thinking of antiquity and early Christianity, it is impossible to inquire more deeply into the experience of having being chosen or having being endowed with charisma. Such an astounding state of affairs is itself the starting point; works and deeds merely give external expression to this state of affairs. Therefore Christology, both actually and logically, is effectively the presupposition for the miracles of Jesus. Our "democratic" way of thinking clearly clashes with New Testament thinking here. That is to say, we like to think that a person can learn almost anything, that all sorts of skills can be acquired through courses of study and supervised training. With us, the big test always lies in whether our training can lead to successful performance of a task. From the perspective of the New Testament, actual performance of the task is never the crucial issue.

4. An expansion on the preceding theme is found in Eph 2:10. Here the deeds that human beings perform are seen as preexistent. God has "prepared beforehand" the good works in which Christians walk. Given their

origin, it is quite obvious that such deeds simply must come to pass. It is not the Christians themselves who produce or determine these works; they all flow from the initiative of God.

	The New Testament	Today
Acquisition of authority	Chosenness, grace	Training, study
Primary challenge	Being chosen, charisma	Accomplishments
Secondary challenge	Visible acts	Inner competence

5. The theme of miracles as signs of what lies within finds further confirmation in the account of the raising of Lazarus (John 11:38-44). The core of the account is the theme that God "always" hears Jesus (vv. 41-42). Jesus can work any wonder he wants. Facticity is not at issue; for Jesus performing any deed is an easy matter. Jesus does not offer his brief prayer of thanksgiving because of any doubt about his ability. Rather, he must pray openly so the onlookers can recognize that his underlying legitimation comes from God (and not, e.g., from Satan). In short, the discussion focuses not on the power to perform a miracle but on the origin of the charisma that enables it to be performed.

I conclude that miracles are perceived in the same way as other works, namely, as signs of what or who one is. Recognizing this helps us understand how some miracles are so readily passed over. The greater astonishment lies in the election and the empowerment of the doer; the deeds, perceived as signs, follow almost as a matter of course. In no case is there a problem regarding the transition from the intent to the deed. In other words, precisely that feature which presents difficulties for us is treated lightly in the New Testament. According to our way of thinking, a person slowly "matures" or "develops" in conjunction with what he or she does in life. In the New Testament the whole dynamic of doing is treated as a consequence of a previously existent reality. Psychologically, this amounts to an essentially different way of understanding the relationship between doing and being.

This has relevance for us yet today. (a) Miracles are not to be considered in isolation but seen as an expression of the one who works them. "Believing in miracles" is not in and of itself a relevant or appropriate response. (b) One should guide other human beings so as to help them overcome their sense of distance between themselves and what they do, so they can more readily perform their own good deeds. This applies especially to the furthering of Christian morality.

THE EXPERIENCE OF TIME

A Different Fundamental Understanding

In Mark 13:20 one finds the comment that God "cuts short the days." When we take this remark at face value, it is apparent that early Christians entertained a notion of time such that its very flow could be altered. Our contemporary view of time is fundamentally determined by technology; for us the flow of time is dictated by machinery. Time is thus thought of as linear in nature and physically measurable. The flow of time itself is of little interest, however, since it always flows at the same pace. The situation was different for early Christians. For them, time's tempo could be accelerated; God could "shorten the days."[7]

This phenomenon is illustrated in an especially striking fashion in *2 Bar.* 20:1-2:

> Therefore, behold, the days will come and the times will hasten, more than the former, and the periods will hasten more than those which are gone, and the years will pass more quickly than the present ones. Therefore, I now took away Zion to visit the world in its own time more speedily.[8]

According to Pseudo-Philo (*L.A.B.* 19:13), this acceleration is brought about through an increase in the velocity of the stars. Along the same lines, the moon is envisioned as changing its "order" in *1 En.* 80:2ff. In other words, a change in the rate at which time flows involves the whole cosmos. The religiohistorical background to this theme, in its aspect both as a mode of punishment and as a mode of salvation, has already been investigated.[9] The significant point is simply that the rate of time's flow can be altered because time itself is obedient to God.

These theological or cosmological statements rest on the perception that time is not uniform. On the contrary, as is clearly recognizable in the longings being expressed, times of distress are experienced as unbearably long and one would gladly see a hastening of deliverance.

The Expectation of the Imminent End as an
Expression of the Experience of Time

Expectation of an imminent end is evident within the pages of the New Testament. So too are indications of a realization, already by the end of the first century, that such would not soon come to pass. Interestingly enough, however, neither the hope of an imminent end nor disillusionment regarding the same appears to have been of central importance for early Christianity. To be sure, an early Christianity without eschatological expectation would be unimaginable; each century of Christian history has exhibited some sort of expectation of an imminent end. The following observations are pertinent:

1. Expectation of an imminent end was not the determinative feature of earliest Christianity.[10] To speak more precisely, Jesus proclaimed the nearness of God—a theme that could be appropriated on at least three planes. (a) On a personal plane, such a proclamation opens up a new, childlike relationship of trust in God. (b) Regarding one's dealings with the world, it elicits an awareness of direct contact with divine power. (c) On a temporal plane, it intensifies expectation of the end of time. Although these three planes intersect, each has its unique and distinctive features.[11] Eschatological expectation might have potential for a helpful critique of existing power relations.

2. There are several reasons why expectations of an imminent end repeatedly surface across the centuries. Here we are actually dealing with a syndrome, of which the following aspects are constitutive for people who harbor such expectations:

They belong to marginalized groups; they stand on society's sidelines, disestablished, having hardly any part in the economy or culture of their day.

- They experience or expect catastrophes.
- They have distinctive genres of speech (particularly obvious in the case of the New Testament; imminent expectation of the end has a distinctive role in the basis for the exhortation in Romans 13).
- Subject to persecution or at least social rejection, such groups feel that they cannot hold out much longer. Their persecution is often politically motivated.
- For support such groups turn to the "classic" apocalyptic tradition, which they regard as an essentially unbroken stream reaching right up to their own time, albeit appearing in different forms. The tradition is transmitted in both oral and literary form.

Only rarely do all of these aspects occur together, but not all need be present to activate the syndrome. Only the last-named aspect is indispensable. Conversely, abandonment of the expectation of an imminent end follows less from frustrated awaiting of the *parousia* or accommodation to the status quo (thus F. Overbeck and A. Schweitzer) than from an alteration in the above-mentioned factors. Moreover, expectations of an imminent end are never simply given up in the way one might abandon a theory or forsake a teaching. Instead, in a certain milieu or under a particular set of circumstances, expectations of this sort simply do not arise. These observations lead to a new appreciation of the fact that, before as well as after the death of Jesus, both his message and his person attracted people holding a variety of notions about time. No single mode of experiencing time was primary; all were components of complex and fluctuating relationships to Jesus. The only constant element is orientation toward Jesus.

From the perspective of historical psychology, several important conclusions follow.

1. With regard to the expectation of an imminent end, what happened is that Jesus' announcement of the nearness of God, and the experiences bound up with response to that announcement, were projected onto a temporal plane. Such a move would follow as a matter of course because, as mentioned above, religious experience of the sort reflected in the New Testament regards the flow of time as standing at the disposal of God.

2. The particular experiences bound up with response to the message of Jesus include the following: (a) Existing political (and, later, ecclesiastical) power is perceived as doomed to destruction, and that because it is seen as riddled with lies and injustices. (b) Although the future is something over which we have no control, nothing lies beyond the control of God. Hence announcements about the future comprise one particular set of statements about God. The more intensely God is experienced as summoning human beings, the more likely this experience will find expression as expectation of an impending end. (c) There is a close connection between martyrdom and the expectation that the end is imminent or, more generally, between the divine demand for justice and the expectation that divine intervention will soon set things right. Especially this connection is accompanied by strong emotions.[12] Crying out through the relevant texts here is the victim who, pushed to the limits of patience, refuses to accept that injustice might triumph. No, injustice must be brought to an end in the quickest manner possible. Certainly God, who is just, cannot long leave unanswered such pleas as, "When will you finally make things right for us?" or "How much longer until you establish your rule?" The emotional distress of the speakers is often revealed by the fact that the prayers are calls upon God for vengeance. One would hardly call prayers like these stoic, but they are certainly honest! They recognize God as the only true defender of justice.

3. Expectation of an imminent end is, above all, an affective/emotional phenomenon. Because for us time is so firmly fixed, it is difficult for us to reconstruct the "loose" way in which time gets experienced in the New Testament. But certain features of that alien (to us) perception of time are suggested by some slogans still common among us: "Love can't wait"; "The game is as good as over"; "Time flows quicker the closer one gets to the end"; "The mission was finished even before it began."

To be sure, this emotionally based expectation of an imminent end also led to the fixing of calendric calculations—a process that appears to us erroneous. Early Christianity, however, was not a solidified whole but somewhat like a geologically young planet, still quite fluid beneath its surface, with its notion of a chronologically determined end resembling a chunk of still-solidifying crust. Much "cooling" would still need to take place before contesting "plates" could collide with one another. Indeed, it could be that those of earlier times who awaited the end did not so much err as that we, along with them, actually stand within an event of whose totality we can see no more than Isaiah could see of God in the Temple (viz., the hem of the Holy One's robe [Isa 6:1]). In that case the expectation of an imminent end could in fact be articulating something about an otherwise hidden side to reality.

In sum, the expectation of an imminent end provides one kind of answer to experiences of unjust and unchecked worldly power: God will soon draw near. The early Christian communities lived in the anticipation that, since there is a righteous God, those who must suffer on account of their faith in that God will not have to suffer long. Soon God would intervene on behalf of those being victimized for their faith. Moreover, evil as such can have no staying power; faced with the fact that God is indeed the Lord, injustice cannot long prevail. Not only will good eventually win out over evil but God will directly intervene to assure the victory.

Statements about Preexistence as the Experience of Time

In a certain sense, statements about preexistence are the other side to statements about an imminent end.[13] Here too we see reflected a mode of perceiving time that is bound to strike us as decidedly strange. While the expectation of an imminent end has to do especially with the rapidly approaching end of momentarily triumphant evil, the theme of preexistence refers to the righteous elect, chosen already before time began. To be "of" God is expressed as having been "before" the world.

Merely recognizing that preexisting persons or realities are important and "necessary to the process of salvation" is hardly enough.[14] Neither do such platitudes suffice as that God had salvation in mind from the beginning, that God had a distinct goal and its realization in view already at the creation, or that through the primal ordering of things God has set up one standard of values above all others.[15] All that is true enough, but it does not yet say much about the implicit understanding of time in all this. For that, it is important to observe such distinctions as whether something or someone was created "before all creation" or as "the first of the works of creation," and whether God is specifically identified as the creator of the reality in question.

In any case, for the implicit understanding of time several features stand out. (a) Age is not experienced as something negative. (b) In contrast to the eschatologically qualified category of "newness" (as in the notions of a "new creation" or a "new covenant"), here the eschatological validity is that which has already always been. (c) When the material is viewed from a sociological perspective, one can see that the "Golden Age" principle is operative here, which goes hand-in-glove with the workings of a patriarchal society. In the same vein, one frequently comes across the well-known metaphor of the firstborn.[16] Such high esteem applied to the older does not thoroughly dominate in the New Testament or its milieu, however. Recall the words of Jesus regarding children, or note how *Jubilees* 23 has youths—in contrast to their elders—beginning to seek after the Law. (d) For us, statements about preexistence resemble those about an impending end, in that they both have a "mythic" quality that does not sit easily with our linear notion of time. Just why should "former things" be more valuable than "latter things"? Is it not often the case that the things made first are inferior in quality to the things manufactured later? One can see that the statement "before all time" expresses the nearness (closeness, immediacy, primacy) of God, but the reason for the "pre-temporal" orientation is by no means obvious. The later things are made, the farther they are from God. Underlying this notion seems to be some peculiar (to us) fusion of spatial and temporal conceptions. From such a perspective, it would appear that each additional "new" thing God creates at the same time increases the "distance" between God and the created order, as though the "space" between God and the world were having to expand to accommodate the new realities. (e) In any case, that which preexists is neither a person nor a thing nor even some pure idea but rather a "self" (in the sense described in chapter 2). Here again we encounter notions about identity that are alien to us.

For a historical psychology of the New Testament, the point is that time can be experienced as flowing at different rates and as carrying variable significance. That is, not all moments are equally "near" to God. Time, especially the beginning, is highly qualified. Ultimately, only realities already present and established at the beginning will matter. Undoubtedly we are here catching reflections of the significance of time, especially of the beginning, for human life. For antiquity, the "beginning" is an especially risky zone.

In this context brief note should also be taken of "proleptic" curses or blessings, those formulated before their corresponding events take place in the world. Both the Old Testament (2 Kgs 4:29) and the New (Luke 10:4) know of blessings that can "wear out" if spoken too soon; persons commissioned to work wonders must greet no one while en route, lest the power of the commissioning word dissipate. The creative word of God is thus most powerful at the beginning; at that moment the fullness of God's creative power is still present. By the same logic, a patriarch can successfully bless his child only once (recall Isaac's blessings upon Jacob and Esau).

A Shifting of Perceptions

Borders Partially Removed

The New Testament participates in a worldview and a mode of perception in which there is no rigid opposition between natural and supernatural, individual and collective, body and soul, visible and invisible, present and future, or even person and thing.[17] Even though these realities hold up as general categories, the borders between them are flexible. Conversely, other oppositions appear in the New Testament which we would define less sharply than it does, such as that between good and evil (hardly unambiguous terms for us!), the godly and the ungodly, or the strong and the weak. In the religious worldview of the New Testament, it is precisely these latter oppositions that stand in the foreground; they identify the fundamental differences separating the domain of God from everything else. In sum, while we still operate with dualities of perception, the polarities that permeate the New Testament have been disarranged in our world.

For the New Testament the result of the dualistic separation between the realm of God and everything outside it is that no antitheses can still exist for those who enter God's domain. When Christians, through receiving the spirit of God, enter the domain of God, then oppositions such as those between Jew and Gentile, free person and slave, or male and female all necessarily disappear (Gal 3:27-28). In 1 Cor 12:13 as well, the setting aside of differences is directly related to the reception of the Spirit.

Two conclusions are obvious. (a) The perception of oppositions on the part of early Christians followed an interior logic. Because everything else turns upon a primary either-or (either of God and God's domain or not of God), it necessarily follows that oppositions are no longer possible within the domain of God. The experience of the lifting of oppositions within the domain where the Spirit of God is operative also implies, however, that such oppositions were perceived as all the more blatant outside the domain of God. To experience redemption specifically as a removal of boundaries also implies that one had previously experienced such boundaries as particularly trenchant indicators of an unredeemed state of affairs. For Paul it is especially social antagonism that has been eliminated. (b) The opening up of missionary endeavors among the Gentiles, free from the demand for circumcision, certainly was not an outgrowth of theological calculation. Rather, it was an extension of the experience of collapsed boundaries.

Historical psychology asks about the boundaries that were initially present and about how their removal was experienced. The experience of unity in Christ presupposes a prior experience of harsh social dualism. In such a setting, "conversion" and baptism stand at one end of a bipolar contrast. The wondrous experience of the removal of boundaries that had necessitated painful separations now becomes a mode of the very experiencing of God. This amounts to a distinctive way of experiencing "community."

Magical Messianism

One of the characteristics of early Christianity is the experience of disproportionality between cause and effect—more precisely, of perceiving an extraordinary power concentrated in the person of the Messiah and in those who could work wonders in his name. A simple word, a mere touch, the grasping of a hand, or even undiluted faith (no larger than a mustard seed) sufficed to accomplish mighty deeds, indeed such as had never been accomplished before. Similar are the expectations regarding the effect of blessings or curses; a mere word brings astonishing events to pass.

Basic to all these actions is a paradisal relationship between act and consequence, one that contrasts sharply with the endless toil of the ordinary and the everyday. I noted in the previous section how social boundaries were perceived as a trademark of an unredeemed state of existence. A similar perception holds with regard to endless labor that yields only modest success. Here an experiencing of God means that the almost endless sequence of failure or of only modest success is shattered.

I call this phenomenon "magical messianism," and I do so for several reasons.

1. The word "magic" does not have to be taken in a negative sense, as though it always denoted something disreputable. On the contrary, the term can be employed to designate anything that appears to take place ex opere operato. Textual warrant for this attitude toward magic can be found in Matthew 2. When the Magi bow down before the infant Jesus, magic itself is "taken up" into and by Jesus, the Son of David and the eschatological Solomon.[18]

2. The sources that testify to the daily lives of Christians up to the fourth century strongly suggest that they were much more attuned to wonders, to demonstrative responses to prayer, and to the effective utilization of blessings and curses than we might have imagined. The practical piety of those early Christians was out-and-out "magical" in nature, based espe-

cially on the formulaic use of the name of Jesus (and God). This much has long been recognized in studies dealing with the history of baptism and the other sacraments.[19]

3. Early on it became the practice to designate as "magic" those forms of piety that were regarded with suspicion. This charge was directed especially against cultic activities practiced by unauthorized persons, primarily laity. Although some differences are discernible,[20] by and large the kinds of such activities were not different from those referred to in the previous paragraph. There was also a comparable confidence in the effectiveness of such activities.

4. As the "Son of David" Jesus is the eschatological counterpart to Solomon and thereby, above all, an exorcist and a worker of wonders. Thus the "magic" that Jesus performs is "messianic" in nature; it is more or less tied up with the very person of the Messiah.

In the milieu of the New Testament, the decisive factor in determining who is capable of performing wonders (working *ex opere operato*) always has to do with the cultic integrity of the person in question. The requisite integrity is achieved through "faith" or "peacemaking" in the name of Jesus. So, for example, purification of interpersonal relationships is mentioned as a prerequisite for having one's prayers answered in positive fashion (Mark 11:25), as is forgiveness (Matt 5:23), reconciliation with one's brother (*Gospel of Thomas* 48), peace (*Gospel of Thomas* 106), and unity (1 Pet 3:7, referring to husband and wife). "Faith" is emphasized as prerequisite for the successful hearing of prayer in Matt 17:20-21 par. In any case, the outcome is that one can "move mountains" (with a "magical" word of command) or even topple them because all of one's prayers will be answered. In the Gospel of John the "magical" power latent in the use of the name of Jesus is, if anything, even more explicit (John 14:13-14; 15:16).

Faith is frequently mentioned in conjunction in reports of miracles (e.g., Matt 17:20 par.). In such situations "faith" is not so much an inner state of the person as it is a magical power acquired through trust in the worker of wonders. Thus it can be said that faith "saves," and even that it is capable of quantitative enhancement (Luke 17:5).

A historical-psychological perspective clarifies certain features of these texts. Thus, the normal state of affairs is for the sick not to be healed, the dead not to be raised, and prayers not to be answered. Jesus, however, through himself (through his name) or through conditions he specifies, opens up access to what had formerly and otherwise been inconceivable. The conditions Jesus stipulates may seem to be small matters, but they receive notable emphasis. In fact, they may even be what matters the most. They are such things as two people in one household making peace with each another, one person forgiving another, a husband genuinely honoring his wife, and the effective presence of a small amount of trust (faith). As is characteristic of magical thought, we are here dealing with an array of little things, things that pertain to the ordinary and the everyday. The prerequisite for wonders to occur is not some exotic power but seemingly little things like these. What we see here, in other words, is something like a transfer of magical modes of thought into the area of everyday interaction. It is what we see in passages such as Matt 10:42 (giving someone a cup of water brings with it a heavenly reward [cf. vv. 40-41]). The disproportionality between effort and result—the trademark of magic—is here carried over into the area of prescribed activities that are very important for the community. The concern for the "little ones" expressed elsewhere in Matthew (e.g., 18:5-6) lies in the same trajectory. In sum, it is not by grand words but by small deeds that the fate of this community is decided.

Two impressions emerge here—two that can be seen as mutually conditioning each other. One has to do with the proximity of the paradisal, the other with the significance of forgiveness, of peaceableness, and of small acts of kindness performed in behalf of one's fellow. The latter might appear to be insignificant matters, but they have in common the fact that in such kinds of encounter with one's neighbors something of great importance transpires. One also encounters God!

Visions

THEORETICAL CONSIDERATIONS REGARDING VISIONS IN NEW TESTAMENT TIMES

Vision and Metaphor

I have already indicated elsewhere some of the substantive and traditiohistorical connections between vision and metaphor.[21] With regard to such central features as the metaphors attached to the king and the royal throne or the use of "lamb" as an image in Christology, and even in smaller matters such as statements about the word of God as a sword that divides (Heb 4:12-13; Rev 1:16), it is obvious that a close relationship exists between visionary experience and metaphoric mode of expression. More specifically:

1. In contrast to a metaphor, a vision constitutes an event seen as a formative occurrence. Thus it would be more accurate to say that a vision resembles a parable, or that visions and parables have an analogous relationship to metaphor. The New Testament writers were aware of this, because they treated both parables and visions as pictorial language in need of interpretation—as can be seen, among other things, in the common employ-

ment of the interpretive triad of (a) the image as such, (b) reference to failure to understand, and (c) an "allegorical" explanation of the image.[22]

2. In all three (metaphor, vision, parable) we are dealing with communication of experiences through picture language. Exactly what sort of experience precedes each such concretization in language, however, can hardly
be reduced to a simple, abstract proposition. Moreover, one cannot detach
the "message" from the surface of the text as though the "essence" somehow lay beneath the actual wording. Strictly speaking, the image as presented is the only attainable stage of the process that produced it.
Nevertheless, one both can and must try to replicate the content of the
image, though not necessarily in abstract language. (One might, for example, try to describe the impact of an image on an audience.)

3. While the casting of metaphors is an aspect of ordinary speech, the
telling of parables requires considerable artistry. The seer's vision, on the
other hand, is tied up with specific sociocultural conditions.[23]

Visions as a Mode of Human Perception

In my opinion there neither is nor must be anything intrinsically "supernatural" about visionary perception. (The New Testament knows next to
nothing of any transcendent dimension to reality; it actually has no concept of the "supernatural.") Visions instead are but one mode of perception among others. To be sure, visions (including those related in the New
Testament) must be seen as a peculiar mode of perception, enabled by distinctive sorts of preparation and exercises. More often, visionary perception is linked to specific situations, such as stage of life, dietary practices,
or a nocturnal setting.[24] None of these peculiarities, however, alters the
likelihood that, in cases of visionary perception, we are dealing with one
mode of human perception among others.

Along with metaphors and parables, visions constitute an eidetic mode
of perception. As such, they stand at one end of a spectrum the opposite
end of which is conceptually abstract ways of assimilating experiences.
Visions can thus be regarded as extremely concentrated experiences. We
are accustomed to incorporating our experiences as temporally measured
sequences. In visions, on the other hand, all aspects of the experience get
lumped together. The same thing happens in dreams, and it is hardly an
accident that visions as well as dreams usually occur at night. The main
difference with the vision is simply that the visionary is not sleeping at
the time of the experience.

In the case of visions, then, we are dealing with "para-abstract" (not
paranormal!) constructions comprised of a number of experiential
elements, or with concentrated perceptions triggered by a physical

experience. So, by the term para-abstract I mean a mode of perception that is certainly not abstract but that in a distinctive way runs parallel to the abstract mode.[25] More precisely, we are dealing here with a capacity for bundling experiences together, a mental activity related to the constructing of metaphors and quite distinct from the forming of abstract concepts. The para-abstract mode of perception is especially evident in Revelation, where a whole cluster of experiences, shaped by various historical and sociocultural factors, are pulled together in visionary fashion.

The difference between abstract and eidetic perception is certainly conditioned by differences in cultural milieu. Let us grant for a moment the possibility of a certain analogy between our (Western, postindustrialized) relationship to lands on the fringes of the so-called Third World and our relationship to the world of the New Testament. If this analogy holds, we might better understand certain otherwise peculiar phenomena. So, for example, in parts of Sicily and in some of the monasteries in Ethiopia, both miracles and visions are not infrequently experienced yet today. Closer to home are instances of visionary abilities among the sick—for us, a clear sign of intellectual or social disorientation. (Visions, like daydreams, simply don't belong to the normal course of activities for most of us.) It follows that the capacity for visionary perception is quite possibly just being stunted or repressed in our "modern" culture. In the case of certain illnesses, however, this capacity resurfaces, and in "developing" countries it still flourishes unhindered.

These observations are not to be taken as an effort to contribute to modern psychology. My intent is otherwise. (1) I wish to demonstrate just how difficult it is for someone trained in an abstract, non-eidetic mode of perception to appreciate how visions are an alternate mode of human perception. Our own compulsion to "get to the heart of the matter" largely explains why we have difficulty gaining access to the visionary mode of perception. That is a way of seeing things we no longer understand. (2) Nonetheless, visions are a culture-specific way of experiencing reality. (3) Eidetic perception is not to be taken as specifically religious in nature.[26] To be sure, visionary perception has played an indispensable role in both Judaism and Christianity. Visions summarize complex experiences; their indispensability lies primarily in their summarizing function. The transfiguration of Jesus, for example, sums up his activities as a wonder-worker.

A kind of link to abstract perception can be seen in the New Testament's use of names as a means of classification, for example, christological titles. On the one hand, these titles are a nonpictorial summary but, on the other hand, each title carries with it an implicit Christology, and together they serve, right up to the present day, as a stimulus for christological teachings of an abstract sort. Note how in Mark 8–9 christological title and visionary experience are juxtaposed. The community formulates its understanding of Jesus by means of a title (Peter's confession, Mark 8:27-33) but also makes a corresponding confession in the form of a vision-narrative (the transfiguration of Jesus, Mark 9:2-8).

In sum, the eidetic mode contrasts significantly with the abstract mode as a way of perceiving and speaking about reality. Nevertheless, a connection between them can be established. (a) The eidetic mode of perception employs metaphor, parable, and vision. (b) The abstract mode of perception utilizes concepts, structures and patterns, and rule-bound logic. (c) Between these two lies the use of names (titles) and narratives to grasp and speak of reality. For hermeneutical purposes, it might well prove helpful to associate vision-reports with metaphors and indeed with aggregate forms of experience in general. Then it could become possible to regard visions not as supernatural oddities but rather as another distinctive form of human experience.[27]

OBSERVATIONS REGARDING VISIONS OF THE RESURRECTED

Sociopsychological Presuppositions

The Judaism of New Testament times is familiar with the reappearing of deceased or enraptured persons (prophets, especially Elijah).[28] In *Martyrdom of Pionius* 14 the appearing of Jesus is explicitly compared to that of Samuel. Notable agreement exists between the description of the manifestation of Samuel in *L.A.B.* and what is envisioned by both Zechariah (before the birth of John the Baptist) and Stephen (at his martyrdom).[29] Priestly figures occasionally replace prophetic ones, in keeping with the theme of heaven as a sanctuary. In *1 En.* 106 the enraptured patriarch ("at the ends of the earth") is implored to grant a revelation.[30] Here, as in *L.A.B.*, one can describe the situation as necromancy.

In the case of *1 En.* 106:8ff., four features stand out. (1) The deceased/exalted one is still addressed as father (n.b.: Enoch is enraptured, glorified in paradise). (2) The information he provides is revelation. (3) The revelation is granted to his sons, descendants in the line of authority. (4) The revelation is given from a transcendent locus, "the ends of the earth." One could just as well be speaking here of a vision.

In sum, the Judaism of the New Testament era also knows of the reappearing of the deceased. The Old Testament already nowhere denies that the dead could venture forth from their "region." As a rule, when one of them does come forth, it is to speak some revelatory word. The conflict with authentic Yahwism has primarily to do with the revelatory word, not with the actual reappearing of a deceased person. In our own times the subculture of the occult has rediscovered this proscribed realm; it has stumbled upon a whole "world" whose reality is taken for granted by the Bible. What we call the occult is actually but the latest way of participating in experiences that were widely familiar to antiquity. Resurrection visions are not, therefore, uncanny phenomena. When confronted by them, we should first ask in all seriousness about the conceptual horizons of such phenomena. In doing so, attempts to find a "rational explanation" must be abandoned at the outset. So-called rational explanations tend to interfere with careful historical reconstruction and in fact often amount to little more than an imposition of a simplistic modern schema upon an ancient situation.[31]

Experiences of "Presence"

Was the presence or the absence of the deceased experienced in antiquity just as it is today? Was death in every case thought to mean the utter absence of the deceased? Two factors are relevant. (1) The need for sociopsychological reconstruction is basic. How is the death of a family member experienced in the context of the small family of today in contrast to the similar experience in the context of the large family of antiquity or the Middle Ages? The transition from large to small families, which has occurred only during the past century, is certainly a significant sociopsychological development. What effect does this transformation have on the response to a death? (2) Evidence abounds for ways of perceiving death not as annihilation but as the transition to an alternate state of being.[32]

In the reports of Easter visions in the Gospels, the experience of presence comes out most strongly in Matt 28:20. Here Jesus not only appears to his disciples but also announces that he will always be with them. In notable contrast to the usual form of appearance accounts, no mention is made of his going away after this encounter.[33] Also in Mark 16:20, with its reference to the Lord's working "with" his followers, the dynamic and continuing presence of the risen Lord is affirmed. Again, the Emmaus story (Luke 24:13-32) expresses what was probably a typical experience of those early pairs of wandering missionaries, namely, that the Lord never abandons them (cf. Mark 6:7). They can meet him at any time, perhaps in the form of a mysterious stranger. Finally, the post-Easter community finds its understanding of Scripture legitimated by the instruction it receives from its living Lord.[34]

The Experience of Continuity

The experience of the deceased as present is often connected to succession (the model for this is the father-son relationship). As attested in New Testament vision accounts, those to whom the Lord appears are his "successors" the prime example of which is Peter (cf. 1 Cor 15:5, 7-8; John 21; Luke 24:34, etc.).[35]

In my opinion the origin for this kind of presence of the "dead" is to be found in the sociopsychological dynamics of the large family. This is also a way to account for the close association between visions and the handing on of tradition in Judaism. For example, the *Book of Jubilees* regards the preservation of continuity in tradition as tied up with the transmission of material from father to son, or even more so of grandfather to grandson. In keeping with this, the handing on of tradition to the son/grandson (the passing on of a "testament") is sometimes even structured so that the recipient sleeps near his father or grandfather, receiving in a dream what is to be handed on. "The motif of sleeping next to the grandfather intends to say that the younger party, in the process of learning the tradition, also shares in the grandfather's vision. . . . In such sleep both the ancestors and the subsequent bearers of the tradition receive the promise of blessing."[36]

Likewise in the case of Paul, there is no obvious difference between the taking over of tradition and the experiencing of a vision. This is especially clear in 1 Cor 15:3 ("what I also received" [*parelabon*—a Rabbinic technical term for transmitting tradition] and Gal 1:12 (acquiring tradition by means of revelation). To set tradition and vision against each other would thus be misguided. The elements here under discussion all converge in the passage from *1 Enoch* (106:8ff.) to which reference was made at the beginning of this section.

Resurrection Visions and Historical Psychology

The Easter visions can be reconstructed as

- experiences of the presence of Jesus
- experiences of continuity ("being with" and the continuity of tradition)
- legitimation of successors in authority
- experiences of revelation (of momentous speech by the Exalted One).

To me it seems legitimate to link questions about the appearances of the Risen One with the material treated immediately above. After all, the announcement of the resurrection of Jesus as such was communicated only to the women at the tomb. The appearances to the disciples have other functions, centering instead on the emergence of the living Lord (out of the invisible domain of God) in order to make living contact (commissioning, elucidating the Scripture, etc.).

Although the appearance visions present special problems, they nonetheless gain intelligibility by paying attention, on the one hand, to their ecclesiological dimension (emphasis on continuity) and, on the other hand, to what has been ascertained about the function of visions in general. An Easter vision is a concretized summation of what Jesus truly "is." Also, Jesus' exaltation by God is the experience of what Jesus is "in totality." Moreover, precisely because the one who so appears is present as a dynamic actuality, anyone who witnesses such a vision can properly take up an "official" role in the line of succession. One who experiences an Easter vision experiences the Lord as concentrated power, as it were.

What is going on with experiences of the presence of the deceased, then, is not what we so often think, namely, an encounter with a reality from "beyond." We are dealing instead with an emergence out of invisibility. The Lord who appears in the visions is not from afar but is near us and with us, only invisible. The New Testament's appearance accounts are thus a critical challenge to our usual habit of granting significance only to the visible. Here the invisible is the more real, and this serves as an analogy also today for human relationships.

Moreover, the linking of the visions with the theme of continuity (via the successors) has obvious implications. The vision establishes a certain connection with the one whose follower the visionary has become. In this sense the vision deals with the issue of religious priority; priority goes to those who have experienced living contact with the Lord (cf. 1 John 1:1-4).

To be sure, in the Easter visions Jesus appears "from heaven," not from the underworld. He is thus not simply one who has returned from the dead but one filled with life from God. (The rapture of Enoch presents an intermediate case.) Nonetheless, these visions actualize features that are functionally related to other accounts of appearances by deceased persons.

TRUTH AND APPARITION

The history of the Greek word *phantasma* suggests the following. First, the appearance designated by this word is consistently evaluated negatively. In contrast to our practice, however, no distinction was made between a purely imagined perception (a hallucination) brought on by a condition of illness or distress (cf. Wis 17:15), and which is thus not really "there" at all, and a more "substantial" deception of diabolical origin (e.g., Mark 6:49; one can see something, but what one sees only simulates reality; because it has no "substance," it is taken to stem from Satan).[37] Ancient (Epicurean) psychology already discussed these matters.[38]

For historical psychology, this means:

1. No distinction is drawn between "subjective" and "objective" apparitions. In other words, there is not even a hint of reflection about whether something appears out of the depths of the (sick) soul or through Satanic influence. Both possibilities are designated by the same term.[39] This lack

of a distinction between the inner/psychic and the outer/transcendent dimensions is certainly noteworthy.

2. Even more significant is the fact that a "phantasm" does not come from God but is regarded as a lie and a deception, as a sort of nonreality upon which nothing can be based or in which no one can believe. The controlling notion is thus that all merely feigned realities (which includes even Satan, who is capable of bringing into being only deceptive imitations) are void of significance. Ersatz realities dangle enticements before a person only to snatch them away again. On the other hand, if some manifestation does come from God, it is certainly not a counterfeit reality; it is "really real." On the whole, however, the one sort of apparition is not distinguished from the other. It is apparent that we are here entering a struggle for legitimacy that is being waged by competing claimants to revelation. In the final analysis, the criteria that decide the issue are firmly empirical (e.g., moral transformation in the life of the recipient of revelation, repeated revelatory experiences). So the duality with regard to apparitions is not whether they originate from within the psyche or from some transcendent realm but whether they work for good.

Mythical Events

The mythical statements of the New Testament have both a worldview and a psychological aspect. Here I take up the latter. Previous discussion of myth has primarily focused on worldview. To be sure, existential interpreters of the New Testament's mythic statements at least intended to deal with their implications about human existence, but this was generally expressed formally and abstractly. A historical-psychological approach holds out the promise of greater specificity. In the following I take as exemplars John 6 (Jesus walking on the water) and Revelation 12 (the cosmic battle between the archangel Michael and the dragon/Satan).

NEARNESS AND DISTANCE

The distinctive feature of nearly all mythic statements in the New Testament is that they are connected to a historical person, Jesus of Nazareth. (Admittedly, the archangel Michael's overthrowing of the dragon [Revelation 12] has only indirect ties to the historical Jesus.) This linking together of the historical and the mythical raises a number of important hermeneutical issues. Above all, however, it forces the question of what it means to experience the mythic itself.

An initial important aspect is that of nearness and distance. This follows from the fact that Jesus was a human being like us and yet at the same time that in him one encounters God. Therefore the question of salvation that this God has bestowed is directly connected to that of nearness or distance to Jesus. This finds dramatic statement in the narrative about Jesus' walking on the water. In John 6:19 Jesus is "drawing near," and yet the disciples become frightened (cf. v. 20). In 6:21a they want to take him aboard; according to 6:21b, the very effort to take Jesus aboard immediately produces beneficial results. Similar themes surface in the Markan parallel. According to Mark 6:48-49, the disciples are initially afraid, and Jesus at first intends to pass them by. According to v. 51, however, Jesus' presence in the boat with the disciples immediately stills the storm.

Only God can walk on water. When the one who has power like God's is close to the disciples, then in him the saving power of God has come near indeed. This closeness finds its realization in discipleship—in following after Jesus and in imitating him. Similarly, the issue of nearness or distance is at the crux of statements about the kingdom of God. If the kingdom has drawn near, or perhaps is already present, then it is of utmost importance not to remain at a distance (cf. Mark 12:34). So also the mere physical presence of Jesus can heal, whether he directly touches the one to be healed or is simply a guest in such a person's house. These "magical" features are a direct consequence of the overwhelming power of God's being "mythically" encountered in a human being.[40] The decisive feature is the element of touch; the mythic and the magical here converge in unique fashion.

THE MYTHICAL AND THE MUNDANE

The mythic statements of the New Testament concern such everyday realities as hunger, storms, illness, death—and also persecution of the community (Revelation 12). In other words, the mythic statements do not deal with the great issues of humanity but with profound, common exigencies. Perhaps that is why, in these stories, women play a heightened role.

These distressful situations are not resolved by being absorbed into some generic cosmic myth but find their resolution through the agency of a concrete historical person, Jesus Christ. The story of Jesus' walking on the water can serve as an illustration. When Jesus strides over the sea, the point is not his ability to perform a marvelous feat. The sea is more than a body of water; it signifies both death and the abyss of the underworld. Jesus can do what he does because he has total freedom in relation to both anxiety and death. Jesus is liberation from death; he is resurrection.[41] God, who alone can pass over the water, is not far away or beyond the clouds but has become tangible in Jesus, right in the midst of the ordinary experiences of Galilean fishermen. Put another way, God is present in a personal way in Jesus; God is not confined to any particular locale, such as the Temple in Jerusalem. Thus the appropriate way for disciples to participate in this salvation being offered by God is through personal attachment to the Lord.

In the process, however, at least a tangential relationship to mythic reality is opened up for later disciples. They too encounter complete freedom during a moment of epiphany, or at least insofar as they stand together with those first disciples in the ongoing chain of witnesses.[42]

NOT PRAISED HIGHLY ENOUGH

It has frequently been noted how many of the distinctly "high" christological predicates applied to Jesus in the New Testament are also very old.[43] There is thus no solid ground in the New Testament itself for the still widely accepted notion that New Testament Christology starts from a clear subordination of Jesus to God and then progresses toward a view of Jesus as ever more prominently seated at the right hand of God.

The basic reason for the antiquity of the high christological predicates in the New Testament seems to be that both mythic and hymnic (in the widest sense of the word) statements tend in a certain way to converge. A common motif of hymnic speech is the impossibility of praising highly enough the one who is being lauded.[44] Put another way, both the hymnic and the mythic statements of the New Testament are responses to the way in which human beings have encountered God in Jesus. They are answers rooted in experiences of awe and wonder, of amazement and of astonishment. The choruslike conclusions to the miracle stories, which typically bring the theme of amazement to the fore, are thus of all aspects of these stories the least to be doubted.[45]

On the basis of such form-critical observations, it should be clear that the mythic statements of the New Testament did not arise as illustrations of the kerygma but through a sort of spiraling effect, propelled by the expectation of constantly renewed experiences of Jesus.[46] The mythic statements of the New Testament are, in short, acclamations rooted in experiences of awe, and as such they are never to be dismissed as groundless concepts.

EXPERIENCES THAT CONSTITUTE MYTHS

The mythic mode of understanding and representation brings to expression not what is intelligible but what is incomprehensible about a complex event. Bultmann's reproach that myth inappropriately tries to speak of God in worldly terms thus misses the mark. On the contrary, the frequently surrealistic mythic images (such as those in Revelation 12) offer up all sorts of conceptual gaps and novelties. In other words, the surrealistic mode of presentation hardly flows into a compact, focused picture—precisely the opposite. Mythic surrealism affirms that every apparent uniformity of history can be shattered by an unexpected intervention on the part of God. The overpowering intensity that accompanies experiences of God's saving intervention also finds expression in the multiplicity of mythic *dramatis personae*. The believer encounters not only God but the whole *familia dei* of the heavenly court, a family that at the same time represents the faithful new community of believers.

Because the mythic features of the New Testament are not set in some timeless realm but rather are tied to a concrete historical person, the time of Jesus becomes a mythic time. That is to say, time is not a uniform continuum. The time of Jesus is a uniquely foundational time and functions as the norm for all later Christian time. While we today tend to experience time as uniform in its course, the time of Jesus can assume normative significance because, in the New Testament's mode of perception, an era acquires distinctive character depending on whatever power is dominant in it.[47] This mode of perception also opens up the possibility for a certain amount of conceptual flexibility, such as that certain times can be repeated. Repetition of time occurs in the cultic sphere (e.g., in the Eucharist or in homiletic recounting of stories about Jesus) as well as in the ethical dimension of life (e.g., in post-Easter discipleship and imitation of Christ).

THE MYTHIC STRUCTURE OF FAITH AND PRAYER

Faith has a mythic structure insofar as it is one's persistent engagement in the efficacious reality of God, in a certain sense the psychological realization of it (e.g., Rom 4:17-20; Matt 17:20). One could thus think of faith along the lines of an imaginative power. Prayer goes yet one step further. The word, voiced in confidence of being heard, paradisally brings to pass within the divine-human relationship that of which it speaks. The powerful words of Jesus are effective in a similar way.

Neither with faith nor with powerful words of this sort is it necessary to think that some remote, counterfactual "world" is being postulated. The perception of some more encompassing reality does not originate arbitrarily but relates to the experience of being surrounded by a supportive community—a community in which the most powerful member remains, to be sure, invisibly concealed but who nonetheless both wants to be and can be addressed. The experience, which still happens today, that prayer flows most easily in the context of a community could well be a remnant of the foundational experience in question here, namely, that the one who prays is especially aware of not being alone. Going along with the communal character of prayer is also an awareness of a stable underlying structure.[48] The "we-feeling" as the experience of structure is the psychic, tangible element of a "covenant" with the extraordinary—and that means "mythical"—concentration of power in the hands of God.

"CRAZY" ACTS AS RESPONSE

Mythic events call not just for verbal responses on the part of human beings but also for actions. Such actions usually fall outside the range of the ordinary and can be justified only with difficulty, if at all. So, for example, the poor widow's offering was disproportionately large by conventional standards; it was "irrational" (Mark 12:41-44).[49] Even more so must this judgment apply to the extravagant act of the woman who anointed Jesus (Mark 14:3-9). Undoubtedly the evangelists themselves already had to struggle with this scandalous story. Luke places it outside the Passion Narrative (7:36-50) and transforms it into an account of the forgiving of sins (v. 50); Mark had already interpreted the act as an anointing in anticipation of Jesus' death, and so he presents it as an act of love in line with the giving of alms. John tells the story in such a way as to discredit Judas (John 12:1-8). Yet the fact remains that the kernel of this particular piece of tradition is a "crazy" act, one that has (in its Lukan version) unmistakable sexual overtones as well as being totally out of line with normal expectations regarding the giving of alms (cf. Mark 10:17-22).[50] The heart of the matter is that, in the presence of Jesus, human beings act "beside themselves." They forget the bounds of everyday propriety and render their all unto Jesus. This is analogous to the behavior of the woman with the issue of blood who put all her hope in Jesus (Mark 5:25-34). In both cases such hope is tied with the theme of direct physical contact.

Risking all in order to touch Jesus is the antithesis of reasonable, ordinary behavior. The women long to touch Jesus physically, while the disciples follow at a respectable distance.[51] Luke hardly goes wrong, then, when he refers to the woman's touch as one of "love" (Luke 7:47).[52] It is on the basis of such love that the woman who anointed Jesus belongs in the Gospel tradition (Mark 14:9).[53] She herself is so "touched" that she acts in "crazy" fashion, ready to give to Jesus all that she has. Along the same line, it is thus hardly an accident that an element of extravagant response characterizes so many of the parables of Jesus. Frequently one finds there instances of shocking behavior meant to drive home a point. No father in his right mind, for example, would actually run out to greet a prodigal son (Luke 15:20).

In sum, amazement or fear are not the only reactions to epiphanic manifestations of the mythic presence of God in the person of Jesus. We also
find instances of behavior so irregular that we can understand them only
as exuberant displays of genuine love. In any case, the only way such
behavior can seem familiar to us is by means of the category of "love."

Journeys to Heaven

THE PSYCHOLOGICAL PROBLEM

Many stories of journeys to God's heavenly throne, or to places where the
righteous are rewarded, have been handed down.[54] The same holds true of
journeys to the underworld, to places of punishment. Are these stories not
reflections of unconsciously experienced inner processes? At least since
the time of Baudelaire it has also been customary to unlock the inner life
by means of pharmacological aids. If one adds to the traditional stories of
journeys to heavenly or subterranean realms some consideration of
accounts of drug-induced "trips" into the depths of the psyche, a series of
common features emerges.

- There is a sensation of wandering through open spaces.
- The experience has a sharply dualistic quality, shaped by either blissful-
  ness or a sense of impending doom.
- Especially significant are perceptions of bright light and brilliant colors.
- Certain preparatory techniques (ascetic practices, especially fasting) reg-
  ularly precede perceptions of this sort.
- Although not always, the experience is often structured in climactic
  fashion, that is, it progresses by stages until it reaches some high point.
- The experiences related are associated with specific individuals. That is,
  in antiquity experiences of this sort did not involve entire communities.

The methodological problem is how to deal with the obvious similarities
between accounts of spiritual journeys and drug-induced "trips," regardless of the considerable differences one could also point out. In what follows, I investigate the similarities in more detail.

THE PROBLEM OF EXTERIORITY AND INTERIORITY

Did antiquity experience as exterior space what we would normally experience as inner space?

1. What appears to us as the "depth" of the soul appeared both in antiquity
and in the Middle Ages as a multiplicity of different zones and spaces—

to say nothing of persons that one might meet in those zones or spaces. In other words, they experienced diversification where we experience depth.

2. This difference in perception is possibly related to the general mobility of persons. Might there not in fact be some connections here, especially by way of opposites? Specifically, might not a lack of mobility in exterior space correspond to a heightened inner "mobility" of the soul, and vice versa? Following this line of thought, one could say that in our era of heightened personal mobility the soul is correspondingly thought of as fixed to some undifferentiated interior space. The opposite would then hold for antiquity: with restricted personal mobility, the soul is correspondingly capable of journeying to celestial or subterranean realms. Might it not thus be the case that, for example, the monastic ideal of *stabilitas loci* (monks not allowed to move from one monastery to another) served to heighten "mystical" awareness?

Early Christianity, carrying on the older prophetic tradition, also exhibits a peculiar sort of relationship between personal mobility and psychic experience. I have in mind here instances in which the Spirit carries a charismatic wonder-worker from place to place.[55] In such an experience the Spirit is perceived as bypassing the hindrances imposed by slow travel on foot—a foretaste of how the Spirit is also experienced as guarantor of the removal of the final boundary, namely, the one between death and life. In other words, the Spirit is the power that can remove boundaries as such, including social boundaries (e.g., those that separate the circumcised from the uncircumcised). Even banished spirits have a distinct relationship to place. They are consigned to wander in desolate places, restless and ever eager to return to more habitable regions. They are the truly homeless. (The still-attested belief in spirits of the wilderness here finds its point of origin.)

3. In any case, for the ancients the soul could without difficulty leave the body for a time, as Paul suggests in the second option mentioned in 2 Cor 12:2. According to *Par. Jer.* 9:7-13 and *Mart. Asc. Isa.* 6:10-12 [=2:1-3 G], the souls of these prophets abandoned their bodies for three days in order to undertake journeys to heaven, leaving their bodies to lie in deathlike states. Here we see the complementary opposite of the concept of inspiration described above. Because the soul resides behind a low threshold, as it were, it is easy not only for another soul to enter but also for one's own soul to go "out." Perhaps this is also the context for the understanding of death as a mode of falling asleep; the soul withdraws from the body and returns to the realm of the dead, thereby presenting a specific instance of the soul's general ability to wander away from the body.

4. The three preceding observations suggest a dynamic relationship between spirit/soul and "house" (in the sense of suitable space). On the one hand, the soul/spirit can easily leave the body and reenter it. On the other hand, the soul/spirit endeavors to find a final resting place (*katapausis* in Greek texts). This is, in fact, a theme that still finds resonance in the Western cultural tradition, to no small degree under the influence of the Augustinian "restless heart" that longs to find its rest "in God." To the degree that the soul no longer wanders off but remains in place as "my inner self," the need for some ultimate place of repose naturally dissipates. One's soul might poetically still yearn to "take wings," but it is no longer looking for some other place in which to alight.

DISTINCTIVE FEATURES OF ANCIENT JOURNEYS TO HEAVEN

In addition to the above-mentioned affinities between journeys to heaven or to the underworld, on the one hand, and modern perceptions regarding the "depth" of the soul, on the other, there are considerable differences.

1. The ancient experiences are largely built up of reworkings of traditional material. This holds true both for the overall structure of the journey and the details, including persons encountered along the way. So, for example, Revelation contains many allusions to features known from the Septuagint. Nothing comparable occurs in corresponding modern experiences.

2. The ancient experiences are presented in thoroughly intelligible fashion. Thus, the separate phases of the experience are precisely distinguished (cf. the "third" heaven of 2 Cor 12:2). This follows from the fact that we are here dealing with experiences of an underlying orderliness. This in turn leads to the way the literary composition as a whole is structured; the intelligible segmentation into phases reflects the contours of the experience itself. It is hardly accidental that no other New Testament writing is more coherently put together than Revelation. Its compiler is also an author attentive to the literary architectonic of the whole.

3. Ancient accounts of journeys to heaven focus on encounters with various personages; the regions through which the visionary wanders are densely populated. This personalistic orientation is obvious from the outset, when the visionary is met by an angelic guide or is summoned by angels to serve as a witness, and it typically culminates in a vision of the throne of God. In the course of the journey, the visionary encounters other angelic beings or righteous worthies of the past. In the comparable accounts from our own day, such meetings are the exception rather than the norm.

4. The fundamental difference is that, from the modern point of view, the soul is something like a subterranean chamber buried deep within the human being. In contrast, for antiquity the "self" leaves the body behind. I say "self" here because it is only our modern interpretation that starts out from the assumption that we must be dealing in such cases with elements of the "soul" or of the "unconscious." With this move toward privatization and interiorization, a decisive interpretive move is also carried out, one that goes even so far as to affect the content. A modern experience of this sort often appears to be "amorphous" in nature. Contrast with this the ancient perception of clearly recognized figures and of scenes intelligibly ordered.[56]

5. As far as ancient experience is concerned, no sharp contrast exists between a literarily contrived account of a heavenly journey and a "real" (genuine) one derived from an "actual" vision. A literary work generated at a writing desk can at the same time be derived from visionary ecstasy (see "The Authenticity of the Visions," below).

The distinctive qualities of the ancient mode of perception can indeed raise critical questions about the modern mode of experience. The key point is that, for the ancients, even these perceived journeys to heaven get drawn into the quest to serve God. This quest is so strong that this whole array of experiences is stamped by it—indeed, saturated by it. This is evident in the way the blessedness or unblessedness in which the seer to some extent participates is connected with moral concerns (blessedness = reward, unblessedness = punishment). This puts a distinctive stamp on the nature of such "religious" experiences. Note how, for example, the vision of the heavenly throne in Revelation is thoroughly tied in with history. The vision is not strictly "ethereal" in nature, playing itself out far above the plane of human struggles. Instead, the divine throne is the forum before which historical events are presented and evaluated. It becomes clear that even the forces of opposition to the divine will ultimately derive their power from that same throne. Modern counterparts lack comparable connection to the mundane world.

AN ATTEMPT AT PSYCHOLOGICAL COMPREHENSION

It would be a mistake from the outset to decide whether the dimension of reality here under consideration actually "exists," either "inside" or "outside" human beings. To make such a decision would require our somehow taking up a standpoint outside the various historical particularities that would enable either possibility and on which they would both be radically dependent. To choose either of the two as somehow "truer" to reality than the other is something only a meta-historical observer would be in a position to do. Neither would it be appropriate to "reduce" to contemporary neurophysiological categories the experiences of transcendence that are conveyed by these ancient accounts of visions. Those who gave us these apocalyptic visions clearly understood them to be "unveilings" of reality as it actually is. In its own way, however, modernity also looks upon the depth of the human psyche as a window upon "reality." This enables us to establish a thesis to guide our inquiry: both the ancient and the modern "journey" experiences are comprehensive symbolic reworkings of reality.

1. The key point is that, in these accounts of visionary journeys, we are dealing with a *reworking* of reality—of no other reality than the one, inseparable whole that confronts all human beings. We are not here dealing with an alternative reality, one that could somehow be separated from the first, "foreground" reality. In these accounts we are dealing with a creative, distinctively conditioned way of perceiving ordinary reality.

This particular way of evaluating the experiences does indeed call into question the usual transcendence-immanence schema. This particular dichotomy, however, is postbiblical; it is actually an offshoot of the medieval (Neoplatonic) separation between the natural and the supernatural. So, for example, the sharp distinction one sees in Revelation between heaven and earth (in the sense of two distinct settings) is something quite other than a separation of transcendence from immanence. (If that were not the case, then Satan could not suffer a fiery "fall" from heaven to earth.) So when we describe the phenomena here under discussion as a particular mode of perceiving reality, we are at least in accord with the self-understanding of the apocalyptic visionaries who desired to unveil reality "as it really is."[57]

2. Reality is reworked *symbolically*. That is, something gets perceived and represented (re-presented) pictorially. The fullness of reality is condensed into a representable image. In this mode of perception, however, what is envisioned is not at all unreal, phantasmal, or irrational. With specific reference to Revelation, one can say that the whole of history, right up to its end, gets apprehended "esthetically," somewhat like a mosaic constructed out of various components. Thus, for example, the various beasts are a symbolic appropriation of widely differing features of reality, aspects that appeared to the author in just this fashion, and not otherwise. (It is not the case, for example, that certain beasts only "stand for" certain historical realities; such a way of speaking would be much too rational.)

3. Reality is being reworked into a symbolic *totality*. In other words, these visions claim to have perceived the whole, in contrast to the particularities (the "little pieces") of ordinary, day-to-day perception. (If the visionary

perception is not of the whole, it is at least offered as the key that unlocks the meaning of the whole.) In this context one can also appreciate the significance of the frequent references to "the book" in these visions, for books were thought to have the ability to unlock the secrets of reality. It should also be obvious how different all of this is from modern notions of the unconscious or the subconscious, neither of which (by definition) mediates anything like an understanding of the whole. Apocalyptic visions satisfy in their own way the ancient longing of the philosophers to grasp primal origins and ultimate ends. This is what is going on here. To be sure, it does not happen along intellectual lines, but it does happen in an esthetic-dramatic way. "Totality" plays itself out as a grand drama on the stage of heaven and before the throne of God.

THE AUTHENTICITY OF THE VISIONS

It is an old question whether, in the texts here under consideration, we are dealing with scholarly fictions or with actual experiences. This alternative is more apparent than real. Naturally it can always be the case that a text of this sort is purely the product of the writing desk; the contrary can never be convincingly demonstrated. Yet the probability speaks against the hypothesis of any purely artificial provenance—and will continue to do so as long as no literary (in the strict sense) version of such a text is found. One can offer a variety of reasons why the distinction between "fictional" and "authentic" is forced in such cases.

1. Neither in the New Testament nor in the Judaism contemporary with it is there any substantive distinction between vision and appropriation of traditional material.[58] On the contrary, we appear to be dealing with two aspects of one and the same phenomenon. The best-known case is the way in which Paul received his understanding of the gospel—by means of a vision (Gal 1:11ff.), yet also by being exposed to and taking over a tradition (1 Cor 15:1ff.).

2. With Philo of Alexandria we have evidence for religious ecstasy that is to be taken with full seriousness despite its having occurred at the writing desk. While reading and studying the Scriptures (according to the principles of allegorical exegesis), Philo finds opening up for himself a wholly new, timely, and genuinely religious (i.e., soteriological) mode of insight into their meaning. There is nothing "irrational" going on here. We are seeing instead a sort of "enraptured rationality"—an experience not unknown even to modern exegetes, and especially to interpreters looking to apply the Scriptures to the present scene. What happens is that a new arrangement discloses itself, one in which all sorts of particulars suddenly

seem to fall into place. Out of this suddenly perceived new arrangement, a word also emerges that can be directed to the present.

To be sure, Philo does not embark on a visionary journey to heaven. One would never mistake the writings of Philo with the book of Revelation! Nonetheless, the sort of ecstatic rationality evident in Philo does provide insight into the close connection between mystical visions and intensified forms of rationality. Coming at the same issue from the other side, there is a certain analogy to Philo in the way Revelation, with its many allusions to the Septuagint, exhibits a considerable "writing desk" mentality.

3. Likewise in the case of Paul one must reckon with an ecstasy of a distinctly rational sort. Traces of ecstasy in Paul have nothing in common with any chaotic outburst of the subconscious. The overall intelligibility of his writings and the modest attention he pays to human emotionality show that Paul ties ecstasy to rationality. This warns us, at the least, to avoid jumping to conclusions about "ecstasy" on the basis of modern conceptions. The same note of caution applies to glossolalia and "speaking in the tongues of angels."

Conscience

Historical-psychological investigation of "conscience" is clearly significant for understanding the human experience of self. To be sure, there are recent exegetical and religiohistorical works in this area worth noting.[59] By and large, however, such studies pay little attention to the historical-psychological dimension. To carry out such a study, it is necessary to make a much sharper distinction between cultic and juridical metaphors than has usually been the case.

CULTIC METAPHORS

Cultic metaphors are in evidence whenever it is said that the conscience is dirty or defiled, or that it has been purified. In such cases we have an extension into a new domain of older modes of speech in which the same had been said of the "heart," the "mind," or the "spirit" in human beings. Initially this sort of language was describing the consequences of a sinful act, or of an act of atonement. Underlying such expressions is the notion that there is inside the human being some sacred space that can be either defiled or purified. Also noteworthy is the fact that, when a conscience is being described in such terms, nothing specific is ever said about how that conscience manifests itself psychologically. A conscience is simply said to be, or to become, either soiled or purified; in neither case does one "notice" anything specific going on "inside" oneself.

What seems to have happened here is that concepts properly at home in a cultic mode of thought have been transferred to another sphere, to a domain of speech having to do with the human psyche and its modes of perception. Constitutive of this transfer of metaphors, however, is the fact that now nothing explicit can be said about the psyche's modes of awareness. Rather, in keeping with the dynamics of language in the cultic-ritual domain (including metaphors attached to that domain), "objective" (dramatic or demonstrative) modes of speech prevail. This mode applies as much to the conditions as to the consequences of an act. Out of this matrix is thus generated the language that speaks of the conscience as contaminated or as capable of being purified. Any sort of language about interim anxiety or psychological distress would conflict with the force of the cultic metaphors, notwithstanding the fact that such language is "only" metaphor. (A metaphor that is itself treated as a metaphor would lose its impact.)

Cultic language is like cultic activity in that both reflect the divine-human relationship in a total and comprehensive fashion. Thus, when one encounters references to the soiling or the cleansing of the conscience, one should also note the "psychological" silence characteristic of the cultic way of thinking.

JURIDICAL METAPHORS

When juridical metaphors are used in speaking of conscience, in contrast to cultic metaphors, a great deal more is said about the associated experiences. Here one finds reference to accusation and bearing witness, to disputation before a bar of judgment, to being convicted and sentenced, and to being punished. The domain from which such metaphors are drawn has a highly developed vocabulary, and an entirely different situation therefore emerges in comparison to one where cultic metaphors control the language. In the latter case, the force of the language is to "objectify" such realities as defilement (encumbrance) and purification (release). Where language about accusation and condemnation sets the agenda, however, a much wider array of associated metaphors can be articulated. This in turn makes it possible to speak of inner tensions and anxieties, as can be seen, e.g., in the writings of Seneca[60] and Polybius.[61] For example, thanks to the use of an alternate set of metaphors it thus becomes possible to speak of a tortured conscience.

In short, two things are important to recognize from the outset if we are properly to evaluate New Testament comments about conscience. (1) Conscience is never the source of good or bad deeds; the most that can be said of conscience is that it "is" good/pure or evil/impure. (2) Conscience never tells one what to do; conscience only evaluates in retrospect what one has already done.

PSYCHOLOGICAL ANALYSIS

Differences in Perception

Although we moderns continue to speak of "conscience," many of us no longer believe in its autonomy. Instead, we reckon with developmental factors in its origin, and we think of it primarily as a subjective phenomenon. Frequently we speak of conscience in the context of opposition to some governing authority, a feature that is completely missing in antiquity. At the time of the New Testament, on such occasions as resisting institutions of authority, one would instead have referred to the Holy Spirit or to a wisdom directly vouchsafed by Jesus—in other words, to some inspiration from outside oneself. This is precisely why no one could have spoken of conscience in such a situation. Neither, however, was conscience thought of as God speaking directly to a person.

Psychological Microcosm and Macrocosm

For the time of the New Testament, conscience is in every case an entity notably independent of the subject or person that bears it. Either the conscience appears as an object being acted upon (in the cultic sense the conscience is soiled/cleansed) or the doer is the object upon which the conscience acts (in juridical metaphor one, e.g., is accused by one's conscience). Where cultic metaphor sets the tone, the conscience is something like the temple in an ancient city—the sacred place that can be defiled by the unrighteous behavior of the city's inhabitants. When this happens the sanctuary must be purified. All immoral behavior in the city works against the holiness of the temple. As a result, the temple requires periodic cleansing. The temple is, so to speak, the cultic synapse of the city. Where juridical metaphor sets the tone, however, the conscience is like the judicial forum of the city. Every illegal act is here brought up for discussion and judgment.

The common element for both the cultic and the juridical sense is that conscience functions as a microcosmic reflection of the social macrocosm that was the ancient city. The upshot is that what we are accustomed to call a troubled conscience (a "pang of conscience") was conceptualized and experienced quite differently by the people of the New Testament and its milieu, operating as they did under the influence of the metaphors then current. The self-understanding of the individual imitated and was shaped by the societal mechanisms of the larger society. For them the "self" functioned in ways congruent with their social experience.

This can also be demonstrated textually. With regard to cultic metaphor, a good illustration is offered by the direct parallel between the purifying of the heavenly sanctuary and the purifying of the conscience in Hebrews 9, especially vv. 14, 21-23. Both sorts of purification are accomplished through the high-priestly activity of Jesus. Up to now the connection between these two acts of purification has seemed merely associative, hardly causal. Our analysis, however, leads to the recognition that the relationship between microcosm and macrocosm is indeed the determinative factor. The heavenly sanctuary and the conscience directly correspond to each another. Put another way, the microcosm-macrocosm schema has been applied quite directly to the task of interpreting experiences involving the conscience.

Our thesis finds added confirmation in the close relationship between the baptismal theology of 1 Peter and the pattern of thought in Hebrews 9, for here again the two realms are causally linked. According to 1 Pet 3:21-22, baptism amounts to an appeal (or plea) directed to God for a clear conscience. Directly connected to this statement is an explanation that at first glance looks like little more than a rote formula: "through the resurrection of Jesus Christ, who has gone into heaven and is at the right hand of God, with angels, authorities, and powers, made subject to him." What is the relationship between the act of baptism and the christological event here? There are actually two scenarios at work here, and they need to be distinguished.

1. In the first scenario, the victor conquers powers that are hostile to human beings and raise accusations against them before God. They do this because they do not want human beings allowed into the presence of God. In this scenario, the victor's conquest reduces the accusers to silence in the heavenly court; the one who sits at the right hand of God is the advocate for human beings.[62]

2. In the baptismal event, the first scenario is sacramentally applied (by way of imitative magic, one might say) to the inner "tribunal" of the human being. The accusatory voice of the conscience is silenced by means of an automatically effective plea that invokes the accomplishment of Jesus outlined in the first scenario. In other words, in the sacrament the intercessory plea of the baptizer (or of the baptizing community) becomes identical with the intercessory plea spoken by Jesus.[63] Just as the word of Jesus binds the heavenly accusers, so also the intercessory plea effected by baptism silences the accusatory conscience.

In sum, our argument presupposes a close parallel or analogy between the heavenly court and the court of conscience. What has transpired before the heavenly tribunal also comes to pass on the human plane: the silencing of the accusers.

In 1 Peter the juridical mode of speech so predominates that no mention at all is made of purifying the conscience. Recognizing this, I must raise a criticism against the usual translation of *eperotema* in v. 21 as "appeal." All the linguistic indicators here point to a forensic force for this term—more precisely, in the sense of a juridical decision.[64] Baptism by water would then amount to visible confirmation of the divine "decree."

Conscience and Incongruence

In 1 Cor 8:7 Paul reports the interesting case in which the consciences of the "weak" (viz., those who feel anxious about participating in certain rituals) become defiled when, going against their own convictions, they imitate the "strong" (viz., those who have no corresponding anxieties) in enjoying meat from animals sacrificed to idols. Paul is convinced that, objectively speaking, the meat of such animals is no cause for anxiety. But that is not the decisive point. What really matters is whether the weak have violated their own internally held norms of appropriate behavior.

Paul speaks of conscience in the same way in 2 Cor 1:12; 4:2; 5:11, which enables us to frame a unified Pauline notion of conscience. When Paul lays himself open to the conscience of the Corinthians, he does so in order that they might effortlessly examine whether or not he is behaving in accord with their fundamental norms. Here as well the basic issue is behavior that might be incongruent with accepted norms—in this case, the norms of Paul's hearers. In other words, the conscience is obviously being experienced as some sort of indicator, or seismograph, tuned to pick up any incongruity, any deviation from the basic pattern of expected behavior, that might interfere with the goal of acceptance. In a modern idiom, the conscience is being invoked as a litmus test to detect any deviation from the civic statutes, standards, or customs on which the ongoing life of a city depends. From this it is also readily understandable why, for centuries, conscience has primarily been experienced "negatively" (i.e., as the monitor of inappropriate behavior). Actions by its citizens that are not in keeping with a city's basic statutes would lead to the destruction of that city. Similarly, it is said in 1 Cor 8:11 that a "weak" Christian who does not act in accord with his or her own basic standards will be destroyed. That the conscience gives voice to something like a civic code is also affirmed in Rom 2:15.

It is interesting to track how this perception of the conscience's accusatory function has become one of the ways of establishing individuality in Western culture.

- Insofar as one's conscience raises the question of conformity with the fundamental code by which one lives, it becomes something like a high court whose task is to oversee one's identity.
- In this sense, the pangs of a tormented conscience come to be perceived as symptomatic of threats directed against one's identity.
- This in turn makes directly palpable a connection between morality and the psyche (pangs of conscience can be explained in this way).
- While it may be the locus of discomfort, conscience is nevertheless also the point at which one can exercise some control, even if subjective maneuvering remains sharply limited. No ancient author could have imagined that conscience would ever go against the established moral or legal codes (cf. Rom 13:5). This stance is in keeping with the above-mentioned function of conscience as the interior microcosm that reflects the exterior macrocosm, the *polis*.[65]
- Identity is hardly being established in a positive way here. Instead, the individual appears as the accused—an influential starting point for Western individualism, because conscience becomes noticeable only to the extent that one perceives oneself as its object.

This personifying of conscience in the juridical metaphor is a remnant of archaic multipersonality, which can only paradoxically or through suppression lead to the shaping of the "self." Philo makes all of this quite obvious when he speaks of a "person within me."[66] That other person is the conscience in the form of a court of justice to which I am subject. The paradox lies in the fact that this same court of justice to which I am subject also keeps watch over my own identity.

A further observation easily follows. Today conscience is no longer perceived as functioning in this way. For us, conscience appears much more strongly stamped or colored by subjectivity. We would immediately object to the ancient notion of conscience, for the good reason that it fails to ask after the origin of the norms it defends. (For the ancients, the reality of conscience is just accepted; it is not even said that it comes from God.)

Conscience and Christian Experience

THE CULTIC METAPHOR: UNHINDERED ACCESS TO THE THRONE OF GRACE

Following the cultic metaphor as operative in the Epistle to the Hebrews, Jesus has "purified" the heavenly sanctuary and thereby simultaneously also "purified" the conscience of the Christian. Heavenly court and conscience are thereby "sacramentally" intertwined. We are not dealing here with a specifically cultic experience but with an awareness on the part of the Christian community of a special status: the recipients of the Epistle to the Hebrews enjoy unhindered access to the throne of grace (4:16). In keeping with the theme of "confidence," the author promises these people that they can come before the throne of God without anxiety, being allowed to feel at home there, like natives. This is the most that Hebrews allows us to say about the experiencing of the cultically purified conscience. (Expanding on what is said in Heb 4:16 by referring also to chapters 9–10 would be inappropriate.)

HARDLY ANY "CHRISTIAN" INFLUENCE ON THE PAULINE CONCEPT OF CONSCIENCE

Astonishingly, the Pauline concept of conscience reveals no distinctively Christian influence (especially not from the Pauline doctrine of sin and justification), nor does it reflect specifically Christian experience. Instead, Paul appeals for conduct "with good conscience" in the same way others do, and he unabashedly does this as a form of self-recommendation (2 Cor 1:12). Conscience is said to be effective in the same way even among pre-Christian pagans (Rom 2:15). Becoming a Christian changes nothing about the way conscience functions within the human being, namely, as a court of judgment whose decrees are in turn confirmed by the judgment of God (Rom 2:16).

New with Paul in a certain sense, but still not specifically Christian in content, is the tying of conscience to social awareness. To be sure, the conscience of the individual Christian is not subjected to the judgment of another's conscience—it still judges and passes sentence only for itself (cf. 1 Cor 10:29b).[67] With regard to what he or she actually does, however, the Christian must also consider the claims of another's conscience. This especially holds true in a case where the conscience of the other is bothered by what I do (even though my own conscience remains untroubled). In such a case I do not act "against" my conscience, but instead I change what I am doing in order that the other might not fall into difficulties on account of my behavior (e.g., that in imitating me he might be led to go against his own conscience). Paul discusses this sort of situation in 1 Corinthians 8 and 10. Through it all, however, the conscience remains a strictly individual court of judgment (1 Cor 10:29b makes this abundantly clear). My behavior should not be surrendered to another's judgment. Nonetheless, even when no negative impulse issues from my own conscience, I am to pay regard to the conscience of the other. This is what leads Paul in some cases to differentiate between the judgment of conscience and the modes of behavior suitable for a Christian. It is certainly possible that a clash might emerge between these two considerations.

Death

DEATH AS A PUBLIC AFFAIR

For antiquity, and into the Middle Ages,

> human beings lived . . . with a much stronger consciousness of death. They knew that each day could be their last; the threat of death, by illness or hunger, was always at hand. Death was therefore a common feature of everyday existence. . . . In the sources . . . one frequently comes across this natural familiarity with death. . . . One died in untroubled simplicity, and an important element in the ritual of dying was the presence of relatives. In fact, back then people often had less anxiety about dying per se than they did about dying alone. Dying was regarded as a public affair.[68]

There are many indications that the same could be said about death as perceived in the New Testament.

It goes without saying that lamentation for the dead is a public matter. In fact, it can even be something like a political gathering (Mark 5:38-39) as crowds of mourners (Luke 7:12) or consolers (John 11:19, 31) assemble. Even after four days many people might still be gathered around the tomb (John 11:42, cf. v. 45). Although the words of Jesus on the cross ("Why have you forsaken me?" Mark 15:34) lie on another plane, even here death is seen as having a social dimension; Jesus dies alone, isolated, separated even from God. That is to say, attention is focused not on the cessation of biological existence but on the elements of isolation and abandonment. The bitterness of Jesus' death lies in the fact that he feels cut off from communion even with God. One might also think in this context of the Gerasene demoniac who, according to Mark 5:2-5, endured a sort of living death, shunned by others and forced to live among the tombs. A final note: Precisely because God, as the Living One, is remote from death and the dead, the reembracing of Jesus by God in the resurrection is all the more striking.[69]

In sum, death is perceived in social categories. From the perspective of the deceased, death is a breach of communal ties; from the perspective of the survivors (kin and acquaintances), it is an occasion for reaffirmation of social bonds. As an item of experience, then, death also corresponds to the general psychological structure I have demonstrated; it is oriented more strongly toward the societal dimension than toward that of the isolated individual. The New Testament does not focus on death primarily as a biological or physiological event.

EXPERIENCING DEATH IN BAPTISM

In line with the preceding section, the death experienced in baptism is not some personal devolution or extinction but an event whose primary dimension is social (on this theme cf. Romans 6 and its language of "dying with Christ" and "being crucified with Christ"; note also the reference to death as baptism in Mark 10:38-39).

1. In keeping with Paul's understanding of the body, this sort of death entails a breaking off of all connections and relations with both oneself and others. Brought to the fore by Paul is the intervening isolation of the situation.

In the Hellenistic-Jewish popular tale *Joseph and Aseneth*, Aseneth plaintively laments the isolation she must endure as a new convert.[70] Her lengthy prayers of lamentation also serve nicely to illustrate the abandonment of the one "baptized into death" in Romans 6. At the same time one can see, on the basis of the metaphors for death employed in *Joseph and Aseneth*,[71] that the experiences of those converting to Judaism constitute, to some extent, an aspect of the prehistory of Christian baptism.

2. When Paul goes on to speak of being crucified with Christ, this death is understood not only in terms of social isolation but also as a paradigmatic shift in the ordering of values. This is so because "the cross" represents a revaluation of everything honorable and good. For Paul the cross effects an inversion in the pattern of who serves and who lords it over others, and it alters the mechanisms for self-limitation, self-definition, and self-evaluation (Romans 12f.).

3. Interestingly, two contrasting images are employed in the New Testament for describing the significance of baptism: dying and being born. The birth-metaphor is socially integrative in nature and forward-looking in orientation. The death-metaphor presupposes the notion of sin (death as the deserved outcome of sin) and operates as a socially disintegrative image. These two images are actually incompatible and are not brought into direct combination in the New Testament.

4. The "death" undergone in baptism has implications for the way one carries on afterwards. At the least, one can hardly go on living as though nothing had happened. In baptism a fundamental breach is opened up between what one had formerly regarded as normal in the way of living and how one subsequently regards oneself. Paul does not take on the whole issue of what had passed for normal in the prebaptized state. Rather, he focuses on how it would be naive for the baptized to continue to serve their passions (Rom 6:12).

5. The "death" undergone in baptism signifies above all a fundamental experience of freedom, a freedom that affects all aspects of the Christian life. In terms of its content, Christian freedom remains thoroughly oriented toward what the death of baptism negates. In other words, this freedom is always understood as a "freedom from." Fundamentally, the freedom achieved through baptismal death is freedom from transitoriness—ultimately, from death itself. Pauline freedom, then, amounts to liberation from the necessity of obeying the passions and violating the Law of God. It is thus a deliverance from estrangement vis-à-vis the letter of the Law and indeed of existence under the divine Law as such. The perceptible mark of this freedom is not just the (relative) self-determination of which Rom 6:13 speaks but also the liberating removal of anxiety that the gift of the spirit bestows on the Christian. Only a freedom that is no longer subject to threats can truly be called the "freedom of the glory of the children of God" (Rom 8:21).

6. Thus for Paul baptism "in the name of Jesus" is not something like a transfer of ownership but is rather an intensified experience of "dying" in the midst of life. It is an experience of isolation and radical transformation of lifestyle, of denial, and of firmly saying no. All of this follows from experiencing "death" in baptism. That is hardly all, however. Conversion and baptism were also deeply penetrating experiences with unavoidable consequences in the realm of social relationships. In other words, conversion and baptism cannot adequately be grasped under the rubric of "sacred initiation." They are instead the foundations of what, from every perspective, must be seen as a fundamental "life crisis." Just how deeply this crisis was experienced becomes apparent in the way Paul can offer assurance to those who are suffering by referring to them as the community of the crucified. Conversion and baptism are thus hardly just "moving experiences"; they amount to nothing less than being crucified with Christ.[72]

THE PRE-CHRISTIAN SINNER AS "DEAD"

There is also a distinctive understanding of death at work where the condition of the sinner before conversion or baptism is referred to as "death." Implicit in this metaphoric turn of speech is the notion that death amounts to being distant from God—to being cut off from effective relationship with God. Moreover, when "dead" works are accredited to the sinner, then the reference is to the experience of reduced effectiveness of action. (For a completely different understanding of dying and of death, namely, in the sense of nearness to the majesty and the Spirit of God, cf. "Ecstatic Joy amidst Suffering," chapter 7, below.)

Alienation

Under the rubric of alienation, sociopsychological and theological elements combine in a particularly interesting way. Typical already for the Old Testament is a strong rejection of alien religion and foreign gods along with a concern for the actual person of the outsider. Not only that, but wherever the topic of weakness—or solidarity with the weak—comes up, the metaphor of the alien can be applied to Israel as well, and even to God. This singular conjoining of the themes of rejection and acceptance finds its unity on the theological plane: God is always ready to show mercy to anyone. I now turn to the way the New Testament nuances the theme of alienation.

DEMONIZING THE OUTSIDER

Previously unrecognized consequences follow from the fact that neighboring outsiders were often identified as demonic (John 8:48—the Samaritans), alien gods understood and explained as demons (1 Cor 10:20), and the psychically peculiar interpreted along the lines of demonism (cf. chapter 3, above). This comprehensive demonizing of the alien is, above all, an expression of human helplessness. The Old Testament perception that the outsider is also defenseless here returns in a particularly striking reversal; one who is demonic is at the same time one who is helpless. With this move, however, the foundation is prepared for the view that an exorcist can be the Messiah, for as an exorcist the Messiah occupies a position of distinctive and necessary power.

DIVINE NULLIFICATION OF EVERY SORT OF ALIENATION

In Jesus' proclamation of the nearness of God, in Paul's talk about spiritual adoption, and in the message of Hebrews concerning bold and confident access to God, every sort of alienation between God and human beings is programmatically taken up and replaced by a special intimacy. This divine offer was early on perceived as applying also to the Gentiles (cf. Eph 2:19). The perception here is of a foregoing act on the part of God. Concretely put, the emphasis on the miraculous and the exorcistic, which is present already in the proclamation of Jesus himself, offered by its very nature a good point of contact with the syncretistic world of that day. The same holds true with charismatic displays of spiritual power. All of this made it easy to speak of boundaries as having been removed. Important consequences follow from experiencing salvation in this way.

GOD BECOMES ALIEN ONCE AGAIN

By and large, Judaism rejected the proclamation of salvation as articulated in the immediately preceding section. This led, in turn, to a familiar retort: "If you won't come along, others will take your place."[73] Theologically, the thought is that God has in a certain sense abrogated the divine prerogatives of Israel. In Romans 9, Paul dramatically lays out how God, who ends alienation (see above), in fact must now back off from the people of Israel—must become alien to them. This is so because Israel's own righteousness was never other than the righteousness ordained for her, up till then, by God (Rom 10:3). Now God has acted anew, but this has not been understood. God's new act has become a scandal to the earlier followers of God. In short, God has become alien to the formerly chosen people, and that because God has done something surprisingly new. As a consequence, those who were formerly outsiders now take precedence over those who from of old were the insiders. Those who had been on the inside are left asking, "Has God turned against us?"

I am particularly interested in the psychological side of these theological explications. What brings people to voice such statements as these? From a methodological perspective, I am inquiring into the experiential counterpart of theological statements. One who says that God has changed (has moved in a new direction, has become alien) is someone who is personally very confused. Such confusion is sparked above all with regard to the contrast between a most disgraceful punishment (death by crucifixion) and acquisition of the loftiest sort of title (Lord, Son of Man), or the contrast between expulsion from Israel and incorporation into a universal religion (both being contrasts that were forced on early Christians). Had God adopted a new means of communication or method of operation? Discovered in the face of such considerations was a profound doubt attached to the familiar mechanism of expectation and fulfillment. Such loss of certainty must have had a profound impact on religious presuppositions that had previously been accepted as valid—to say nothing of one's religious identity itself! God has here come to be seen as beyond all human expectation. When according to theological statements God has become "alien" to God's own people, that is an expression of fundamental crisis on the part of the people.

NEW SELF-BOUNDARIES

Those who, in the sense of the message of salvation, know themselves as the beloved of God respond by setting themselves apart from all that is alien—from sinners, from tax-collectors and Gentiles, even from the Pharisees, in comparison to whom one now possesses a superior righteousness.

Also in the earliest layers of the Jesus-tradition one finds rhetorical questions whose function is to establish boundaries: "Do not the Gentiles do likewise?" All who stand outside the community, thought of primarily in familial terms, count as foreigners. Their inability to participate in the Christian community quickly renders them alien. Moreover, the "death" experienced with conversion brings about a freedom with regard to all emotional attachments that must strike others as strange (cf. 1 Cor 7:29-31).

In turn, the Christian community also regards itself as alien, as composed of those who are strangers to the world. In this regard they view the wandering patriarchs of Israel as their own prototypes. This experience of one's own alienation is grounded in attachment to an alternate value system, but even more it has to do with a sense of security and citizenship in a "heavenly homeland." This is paralleled by the close communion of Christians with one another, within their homes and in the hospitality they show one another. The Christian sense of alienation in the world is thus powerfully correlated with contrasting feelings of a new sort of belonging.

In sum, the strongly felt sense of being part of something new produces a corresponding sense of separation from all who do not participate in it. From both sides of the divide, then, a feeling of "we—they" is engendered.

OUTSIDERS' BOUNDARIES

Consider here not just the experience of the early Christians but also that of the outsiders who had to deal with them. Those outsiders certainly regarded the early Christians as strange, precisely because of lack of solidarity in the fundamental arenas of everyday life. People who present themselves as being "above" sadness and joy, possession and acquisition, sexuality and the fear of death (1 Cor 7:29-31) are not just strange, but annoyingly so. This is especially the case with people who refuse to participate in the veneration of the emperor in Rome, the one upon whom peace and public order depends (the book of Revelation). Behind all the anti-Christian denunciations and persecutions stands an emotional barrier that has not often been sufficiently noted. This barrier rests on a perception of deficient participation in the ordinary, everyday necessities upon which the orderly continuation of life depends. Non-participation (or partial participation) in such areas of communal concern is bound to be more antagonizing than is any amount of talk about "divine grace" or a coming utopia.[74]

REACTIONS TO MUTUAL SEPARATION

Alienated groups rarely remain in a static relationship to each other. They more often make efforts to overcome one another in any number of ways, such as leveling (a denial of the other's religious identity) or verbal apologetic (an attempt to present the other as not so strange after all—as one can clearly see already in Tatian's *Oratio ad Graecos* 33.2). Warfare is also a possibility, however, ranging from the verbal warfare of polemic to outright military action (e.g., that directed against the Muslims in Spain). Missionary activity is yet another possibility, wherein the strangeness of the other is often reduced through partial appropriation of elements of the "conquered" religion. Of course, all such activity tends to prompt countermeasures, such as resistance to absorption by strengthening one's identity.

ALIENATION OF THE ORDINARY

The message of God's nearness to human beings has yet another consequence. The familiar and the close at hand is actually the unknown, for in matters that we customarily regard as routine and of little importance decisions affecting our heavenly reward are being made. So, for example, in dealing with the humblest stranger we are also dealing with the Lord himself. We can no longer rest content with platitudes about God loving the sojourner or that in giving to the poor we are giving to God. Rather, in the humblest stranger we encounter the Judge of this world. Not the ordinary in general, but especially the insignificant ordinary, the consistently unappreciated persons and things of the immediate environment—these suddenly become extraordinarily strange. That is to say, they are suddenly revealed in all their disconcerting relevance because precisely in them we encounter God (e.g., Matt 10:40-42). The God of heaven has drawn so close that our immediate surroundings come to feel like foreign territory. Here we have undoubtedly discovered one of the bridges between Pharisaism (i.e., a deep penetration of the everyday by the will of God) and the message of the kingdom of God. It is no longer just the will of God that is close at hand but God himself.

RESULTS

From its very beginning, the New Testament proclamation of the lifting of all barriers has actually led to the setting up of new barriers. A distinctive characteristic of early Christian experience is a strong cross-connection between alienation (or intimacy) in relation to God and intimacy (or alienation) in relation to human beings. In Christianity the experience of alienation acquires a new quality and new dimension—also as conflict.

7

Emotions

Paul on Feelings

CHRISTIANITY NOT A MODE OF CONSCIOUSNESS

For Paul, new creation (dying in baptism and subsequent new being—cf. Rom 6:4-6; 12:2) is not a matter of feelings, of inner experience or certainty. Pauline Christianity has nothing to do with psychology of this sort. Thus Paul is a firm opponent of the modern union between pietism and psychology.

There are some who seek from Christianity assurance regarding salvation, a new self-understanding, a transformation of inner awareness—in short, as a way of understanding and relating to the "self" within, a reflexive movement. Paul, by contrast, emphasizes concrete connections with and obligations to the new community of Christians (new "body," new connections; for Paul there is not even "Christianity" but a new community). In any case, there is no trace of "self-reflection" in Paul. Essentially, it was medieval mysticism that found here linguistic traces of the categories of inwardness. Another reason for the difference between Paul and ourselves is the fact that we must first convince ourselves, as it were, about many matters whose reality was taken for granted in Jewish antiquity (cultural accoutrements), such as God and Satan. We might say that when culturally mediated understandings of the self have gotten lost, self-understanding has become all the more important. In such a situation, our only recourse is to engage in some deliberate mental representation, forcing ourselves to become aware of distinctive nuances. In the few places where Paul does make comments on "self-understanding," these are largely irrelevant or, at best, tangential for modern inquiry into the nature of consciousness.

THE CATEGORIES OF HUMAN INTERIORITY
ACCORDING TO PAUL

Paul knows of only one significant feature of the specifically interior aspect of the human being, and he lays out this feature with the sole introspective term at his disposal: conscience (cf. chapter 6, above). The real issue here is good and evil, but attention is focused only on the tangential matter of making judgments.

For Paul the "inner being" is not some fixed point of self-awareness but an invisible eschatological identity (2 Cor 4:16). Likewise in Romans 7 the issue under discussion is not feeling but the human will (cf. vv. 18-21). In the same vein, Paul can have only negative regard for desire. Unlike us, for whom desire is basically a personal feeling, for Paul desire has to do with a perverted will, one aimed at violating the Law and engaging in criminal transgression. Similarly, Paul closely associates yearning with hopeful longing for the still-to-be-realized redemption of the body (cf. "Sorrow and Openness," below).

For Paul, only the "be of good courage" (*tharrein*) in 2 Cor 5:6, 8 describes anything like a feeling-based Christian existence. While this state is "always" in effect according to 5:6, in 5:8 the focus is once again oriented toward being "at home" with the Lord. *Tharrein* acquired its religious connotation in Hellenistic Judaism, above all through its use by Philo, who sets it in opposition to "be anxious/afraid."[1] He uses the term synonymously with "be bold" (*parrésiazomai*),[2] an expression employed with particular reference to speaking before kings (or corresponding authorities), appearing before a law court, or when about to go into battle. Rudolf Bultmann could well be correct that the issue at hand in these passages in 2 Corinthians 5 is fearlessness in the face of death (the topic under discussion in vv. 1-5). According to Bultmann, 2 Cor 5:8 can be freely rendered, "We confidently look death in the face; indeed, we even greet it."[3]

ECSTATIC RATIONALISM

In view of the preceding paragraphs, it can be said that Paul hardly ever brings the new existence of the Christian into positive relationship with feelings, with emotionality, or with inner longings. Indeed, he is deeply suspicious of all such notions. One can thus hazard the thesis that Paul in his anthropology and theology is a resolute rationalist, fully in accord with Hellenistic Judaism (the divine Law as congruent with human reason;[4] it was only such conceptions that made possible the political significance of reason—with effective results down to Spinoza). In the same vein an enlightened sort of rationality characterizes, for example, post-conversion moral exhortation (dualism, formerly/now, light/darkness, new community of the converted), a genre illustrated in, for example, Romans 12:1-2, 5, 10, 16.[5]

On the other hand—or perhaps one should say, in addition—Paul stands on common ground with the Stephen-circle and with Apollos in frequently connecting rationalism with enthusiasm (a state of ecstasy). I call this "ecstatic rationality" and describe it as follows.

The Missing Subjective Middle

Between reason, on the one hand, and ecstasy, on the other, there is "missing" (or so we would say) in Paul the subjective middle of feelings, uniquely private needs, positive perceptions, and direct awareness of one's own corporeality. With Paul, both the reasoning capacity and the state of ecstasy are characterized by absolute clarity and penetrating insight. Nothing here is diffuse; all is as clear as glass. Moreover, one finds with regard to both reason and ecstasy no mention of inner disposition or personal inclination. Echoes of a juridical mode of thinking are obvious. Consider, for example, the situation presented in 1 Cor 7:34: the woman who renounces marriage is thereby "holy [for God] in body and spirit," expressing with her whole existence a property relationship, for as "holy" she "belongs" entirely to the Lord. Put another way, in this case a religio-juridical mode of thinking radically and completely determines the way corporeality is realized.

A Programmatic Text

What we have found so far in the texts we have analyzed from the perspective of historical psychology finds striking confirmation in the personal testimony of Paul in 2 Cor 5:13 ("If we are in ecstasy, it is for God; if we are in our right mind, it is for you" [my trans.]). Again there is no subjective middle between the poles of God and community. In his ensuing remarks, Paul suggests that this state of affairs is due to the effect that the death of Jesus has had upon him. Under the impact of that event, Paul no longer lives "for himself" but now belongs to the one who has given him new life, whose love he passes on to the community (5:14). Paul himself, then, is nothing more than a go-between; in and for himself, he has died (5:15).[6] Paul is totally, and only, an apostle.

A Religiohistorical Parallel

Paul's ecstatic rationality probably finds its closest parallel in Philo of Alexandria. This holds true despite the difference of Christian messianism. Philo similarly sees no opposition between ecstasy and rationality, because divine reason overwhelms the ecstatic's natural reason, forcing it to drop below the horizon like the setting sun (*Heir* 265). The divine reason that has infused the ecstatic, however, does not express itself as chaotic irrationality but as insight into connections within Scripture. That is to say, for Philo ecstasy amounts to the ability to discover the "spirit" behind the letters of a text. As he himself writes, when in the ecstatic state he experiences not simply irrationality but rather "a sober drunkenness." By and large, his writings are themselves the result of this desktop ecstasy.

With Paul the focus is also on the Scriptures, but in an even more comprehensive fashion than with Philo. Paul's ecstatic rationality enables him to uncover the inescapable necessity of orientation toward Jesus Christ. Paul recasts almost the whole of the religious tradition of Israel in the direction of Jesus, in the process discovering new and deep connections, "secrets" that all point to Jesus. (To a certain degree, a historical link between Philo and Paul is formed by the Stephen-group, of whom we have reports of both spiritual ecstasy and interpretation of scripture.[7])

Ecstasy and Joy

Paul especially connects ecstasy with joy. Although we would not be inclined to speak this way, according to Paul joy can be commanded (1 Thess 5:16). The use of *chairete* (rejoice) in 2 Cor 13:11 suggests that Paul understands this "joy" to be an overall stance or mode of behavior. Since joy is a gift of the Spirit (from outside!), it is not seen as having a subjective point of origin. Rather, joy is the mode of human participation in the revelatory events and the salvation mediated through them—the overcoming of all hindrances to God-pleasing behavior. To be caught up by joy is somewhat like a child's being grasped by the arms and tossed into the air. Put another way, joy is manifested as agility of behavior. Joy, then, neither starts from within nor remains within; it comes from without (from "Spirit") and it flows outward once again (into "works"). In sum, joy is the experience of being granted the ability to satisfy divine commands.

The significance of all this for us is that joy is not to be equated with gaiety, cheerfulness, or good humor. Rather, the joy of which Paul speaks is calm, anxiety-free rationality that allows all that is necessary for righteousness to be done easily and without hindrance.

The Will to Live

The absence of intermediary feelings in the case of Paul can best be explained, in my opinion, if we start from the basic Pauline thematic of life and death. As is especially evident in Paul's use of military metaphors (Rom 13:12; cf. Rom 6:13), the decisive contrast is between the human being's absolute will to live and the radical threat to that will posed by death. Here, just as in the dualistic mentality of the wisdom tradition, we are dealing with the basics.

At this point the phenomenon of sin must also be considered. For Paul, sin by no means appears as a latent consciousness of guilt. Above all, sin is experienced as powerlessness, as inadequacy in the face of reality, as having to surrender to an occupying force despite one's best intentions. In other words, sin is tied up with the whole range of human activity; it is the experience of having one's hands tied. The consequence ("wages") of sin is death. From this perspective it is readily understandable why Paul so often describes redemption as being set free.

Likewise the wretchedness about which Paul complains in Rom 7:24 is not any feeling of frustration. It is awareness of the absolute threat posed by death. To this end it is crucial to note that Paul's "existential crisis" is answered—as is apparent in the thanks Paul voices to God (Rom 7:25). Here too the experience of liberation does not remain subjective but expresses itself through performance of obligatory acts.

SUMMARY

Missing in the thought of Paul is the world of neutral, diffuse, but also personal (religious) feelings. This shows the influence of the wisdom tradition with its life-death dualism, communal conceptions (people of God), ecclesial thought, and Torah orientation. Even Paul's notion of a supra-rational ecstasy avoids subjectivity. In the one case where Paul really does express a feeling (sadness; Rom 9:2), he does so for the sake of his people. But even here his language is enveloped in juridical metaphors (Rom 9:1, 3; cf. 11:1-2a). In other words, for Paul the decisive dimensions are reason, will, and shared participation in God's revelatory events or the realities (such as the church) that have grown out of those events.

When we ask about the critical relevance of these observations for today, two main points emerge. (1) Paul's pragmatic, other-directed mode of thinking exercises a corrective function against any sort of Christianity that would place heavy emphasis on self-reflection or direct primary attention to a quest for inner certainty. Bluntly stated, Paul would object to any and all forms of navel-gazing Christianity. (2) Paul's renunciation of "the wisdom of this world" (1 Corinthians 1) in no way amounts to a rejection of rational clarity or argumentative methods. Even when Paul's mode of thinking strikes us as convoluted (as is often the case with his "proofs" from Scripture), the very complexity of his thought shows that Paul operates from an unabashed rationality. The divine mystery is not irrational. To be sure, this mystery's point of disclosure is deep within the being of one who receives the spirit of God (1 Cor 2:10-11).[8] As Paul attests in his letters, however, what transpires deep within does not obliterate ordinary powers of understanding. Paul's "ecstatic rationality" thus ought to warn us against every arbitrary (or prescribed) obstacle in the path to understanding. Christian mysticism does not mean surrender to irrationality. After all, the unsearchable nature of the ways of God (Rom 11:33-35) hardly hinders Paul from speaking at length about precisely the same (Romans 9–11)!

Desire (Covetousness)

PAUL'S THEOLOGICAL-PSYCHOLOGICAL DOCTRINE

Paul develops an explicit doctrine of the Christian's inner life with regard to only a few specifics. One such doctrine relates to "desire," or the feelings traditionally associated with eating, drinking, and sexuality. "Sin, seizing an opportunity in the commandment, produced in me all kinds of covetousness" (Greek: *epithymia*, inordinate desire) (Rom 7:8). Of all the factors having a direct effect upon the human being, then, "desire" stands out as especially dangerous. Undoubtedly, the emphasis lies upon the multiplicity ("every kind") of the forms of desire. Sin's dominance finds expression in the multiplicity of desires.

Already before Paul, in Greek-speaking Judaism, the centrality of the final commandment of the Decalogue was recognized. (Philo of Alexandria, as well as other Hellenistic-Jewish writers, speak of covetousness as "chief among the sins.") A psychological dimension was attached to the strictly theological one by appending the notion that coveted property was destruction-prone: if one could not have the object of one's desires, then neither should anyone else be able to have it.

THE EXPERIENTIAL ASPECT

Since Paul so strongly emphasizes that human beings transgress the Law by what they do, it follows that covetousness cannot be thought of simply as a mood or an inner feeling but rather as an act. It might first appear as an idle thought or a yearning, but desire goes beyond being a mood. Desire is actually twisted behavior.[9] But the other side of the coin is that, despite their complexity, sinful human behaviors have a lowest common denominator; they are all so many kinds of desire. So while there is no such thing as a totally inactive mood or sentiment, Paul is certainly talking about something perceptible within that underlies the various forms of desire and makes it possible to identify them all as "impulsive" forms of behavior.

One can only suppose that Paul, like Hellenistic Judaism before him, placed such strong emphasis on desire not only because of the influence of Stoicism but also because of the conviction that desire is just as capable of taking over the soul as is the love of God (Deut 6:4-5). Where the love of God ought to reign supreme, desire, as the perverted mirror-image of love, can also take control. Speaking in favor of this supposition is the tendency of the Septuagint to refer to pagan deities as *enthymémata* (mere thoughts), with the further qualification that, as such, they are "objects of desire." From the perspective of Hellenistic Judaism, in other words, idolatry (apostasy from God) is to be found in close proximity to desire.

One can try to reconstruct the way the experience that underlies this understanding of desire is structured. (a) The impulsive yearnings of the human being are understood in a quasi-religious way; they appear in conjunction with behavior vis-à-vis God. (b) These yearnings take exclusive possession of the interior of the human being. (c) Particularly important and symptomatic is their multiplicity, in contrast to the unified nature of a proper relationship to God. Paul's thought can be better understood from this hypothetical reconstruction.

THE DOMINANCE OF DESIRE

The Pauline Teaching

The very fact that human beings are capable of desiring becomes, for Paul, the precondition that allows sin to make inroads into them. This follows from the fact that God—and this was certainly a stroke of luck for sin!—placed the commandment "You shall not covet" at the end of the Decalogue as its culmination. In this way it became only too easy for human beings, with their inclination to desire, to come into conflict with the demands of God. This turn enabled sin to achieve its real goal, which was to bring death (the mark of sin's universal dominion) to human beings, since by their breach of the divine Law human beings must necessarily be condemned.[10] In its striving for universal dominion, then, sin took aim at the Law, for here (and uniquely here) God's claim on human beings could be up for grabs.

Paul's Connections with the Experiences of Hellenistic Jews

As mentioned above, Paul was able to link up with the experiences of Hellenistic Jews and even to elaborate upon them. This elaboration ran along two main lines. (a) The reference to "every kind of" desire (Rom 7:8) emphasizes the multiplicity of the covetous impulses and stands in sharp contrast to the unity of God. (b) Desire is the instrument through which sin exerts its dominion, and so human beings have been handed over to sin as though to slavery. ("Do not let sin exercise dominion in your mortal bodies, to make you obey their passions" [Rom 6:12].) Here Israel's proper relationship to God (the Israelites as "slaves" of their God) is carried over, mutatis mutandis, as the image of the Christian's relationship to desire.

What this now means, however, is that submitting to desires is equivalent to being handed over to a host of despots, who then reign in the place of the one God. Obeying all these petty tyrants leaves one no longer with a single point of orientation. Rather, and in a very real sense, one is left running back and forth. (Paul does not say this explicitly, but one finds the thought in Philo of Alexandria and, later, in St. Augustine.) To be sure, Paul's emphasis tends to fall on the unity of a *quasi*-personified sin, but the theme of desire's multiplicity hovers in the background.

Some Misinterpretations of Paul

The most common misinterpretation of Paul takes the form of an arbitrary opposition. On one side are "understanding" and "clear principles," both of which Paul is seen as favoring. On the other side is everything that Paul opposes: desires, all the human urges (especially the sexual ones), the sensations and feelings basic to living beings, any breach of norms. The truth of the matter, as should be clear from Romans 12–13, is that Paul ties righteousness above all to the interpersonal realm. Even in the case of the "sin against one's own body," in 1 Cor 6:12-20, Paul is not really arguing against lust but speaking in terms of proprietary rights, as he clearly does toward the end with explicit regard to desire. So Paul is certainly not an enemy of the physical aspects of existence. His goal is not acorporeality but a new corporeality, one without anxiety about death or about mistreatment at the hands of one's neighbor. One can say much the same in another way. Specifically, against desire (against the urge to possess unlawfully) are set those "fruits of the Spirit" that (in Gal 5:22-23 and elsewhere) could be summed up as "gentility"—a loose translation, perhaps, but one nonetheless functionally equivalent and faithful to the original text.

Fundamentally, then, love of God is shown by devotion to the rule of God, which in turn is shown by satisfying an array of obligations through which the physical integrity of other human beings is protected. Conversely, to give oneself over to the tyranny of the passions amounts to flitting from one tyrant to another, recognizing no stable obligations and, finally, damaging the very corporeality of others.

The Theological and Psychological
Significance of Paul's Comments on Desire

1. By connecting desire with lordship ("obey"), Paul makes it into a theological theme. This is so because God is the one who claims lordship and demands obedience.

2. In the Pauline mode of speech, "desire" really has no positive connotation—or at least Paul does not make it easy to see how he might think of the corresponding experience in a positive way. There are several reasons for Paul's skeptical perspective on desire. (a) Desire is a notion that applies to individuals, or to the nature of individuals. In and of itself, desire is neither social nor antisocial in orientation. This alone is enough to bring desire into conflict with, say, "righteousness." (b) Since Paul regards desire as a form of action, all the "deeds of righteousness" or "fruits of the Spirit" come into view as opposing realities. (c) In Rom 6:17 Paul says of the proper obedience of Christians that it flows "from the heart"—a turn of phrase that once again seems to lack a negative equivalent. Might a deliberate contrast be intended between the "passions" in Rom 6:12 and the "from the heart" in Rom 6:17? (In each case the issue is obedience.) Be that as it may, for Paul the most fitting contrast to "desire" is probably "faith," or even more so "the obedience of faith."

3. In contrast to, e.g., 2 Esdras Paul does not simply trace human sinfulness back to the "evil heart" or the "evil impulse" of the human being—a move that is more of a displacement than a clarification. Paul instead starts with a concrete experience, namely, the experience of desiring or yearning. Initially, however, this is a morally neutral experience, both in general linguistic usage and to a large degree also with Paul. That is to say, one who speaks of desire the way Paul does initially takes up an experience that is in and of itself morally indifferent—genuinely neutral. This experience is then used to clarify an ethical or moral issue. The effect of such a move, however, is a psychological deepening of the issue at hand. In other words, with such a move "good" and "evil" are no longer to be understood simply in terms of decrees or solely with reference to outcomes (i.e., by invoking origins or yet-to-be-realized expectations). These were the two classic ways taken by Torah and Wisdom, but here something new is happening. An experience that frequently crops up, and which one can examine, becomes the focal point of attention. Raising the ethical question in this way, in the midst of ongoing activity, draws the psychological dimension into the explanation. The upshot is that desire is no longer just some sort of feeling but a deviant impulse.

The potential inherent in this intellectual tour de force can perhaps offset its weaknesses, which touch on the ability sharply to differentiate good from evil and which thus affect the evaluation and criteria of such "examination" (see above.). But the gain lies in the fact that the actual evidence for morality has been established.

Paul's method of approach raises the stakes, daring to bring under scrutiny the basic impulses of life.[11] The distinct radicalness of such a psychological deepening of the ethical question is readily apparent.[12] Starting from where Paul starts, there is a positive side to emotionality; being "obedient from the heart" (Rom 6:17) is not just coincidentally related to the chief commandment's theme of loving God "with the whole heart" (Deut 6:5).

4. Characteristic of Hellenistic thought regarding human nature is a contrast between the rational and the irrational. In place of this, Paul sets "spirit" against "flesh." But the similarity between reason and spirit, or between feelings and flesh, is only apparent. One properly understands Paul only if one does not gloss over the differences here. "Spirit" (Greek: *pneuma*) has nothing to do with intellectuality but designates a new mode of being that involves the whole person. Similarly, "flesh" (Greek: *sarks*) does not refer to emotionality but to the old state of being. Paul has transformed the atemporal Hellenistic contrast into a temporal duality. Where Hellenistic thought postulates a division running through human nature, Paul sets up a contrast between the old and the new. (To be sure, traces of the Hellenistic mode of thinking can still be found in Paul, but these can readily be identified and can be accounted for on a case-by-case basis.)

RESULTS

If we are correct in maintaining that, in a certain sense, faith is the positive correlate of desire, then it follows that: (a) Desire is the means by which sin rules over human beings. Conversely, faith is the means by which God—more precisely, the righteousness that God intends—manifests itself in human beings. (b) Only one who knows what desire is can rightly appreciate what faith is. In other words, if my thesis is valid, then it poses a critical challenge to any primarily intellectual understanding of faith. Only a faith that is itself "emotional" can be a counterweight to desire. Conversely, distinguishing faith from desire by equating the former with rationality amounts to one of the typical misunderstandings of Paul. Paul is not struggling against emotionality but against "the flesh"—the surrender of human beings to all forms of weakness and instability, which in turn results in their not being able to "stay the course."

Fear and Anxiety (Angst)

No Difference between Fear and Anxiety

Neither the Greek Bible nor its Hebrew precursor distinguishes between fear and anxiety. (In Greek, both are rendered by variants of *phobos* and *phobeisthai*). The practical consequence is that, where the terms "fear" and "anxiety" are both employed in biblical statements about relationship to God or God's representatives, no distinction—such as is natural for us—is possible.

Mixed Feelings

The following excerpt from the Jewish tale *Joseph and Aseneth* (first century c.e.?) illustrates for the time of the New Testament the possibilities for differentiation of feelings.

> [After she has received the blessing from Joseph, it is said of Aseneth, in 9:1] And Aseneth rejoiced exceedingly with great joy over Joseph's blessing, and hurried and went into the upper floor by herself, and fell on her bed exhausted, because in her there was joy (*chara*) and distress (*lupé*) and much fear (*phobos polus*) and trembling (*tromos*) and continuous sweating as she heard all these words of Joseph.[13]

Aseneth's emotional convulsion is described by referring to her conflicted state. Since none of the New Testament is written in the fanciful style of the Hellenistic popular romance, one would search it in vain for genuine analogies to this extended description of Aseneth's emotional state. Yet the association of weakness with fear in her case is important for a proper appraisal of references to "the weak" in Paul's letters. Similarly, the linkage of "fear" with "trembling" in the above-cited text is significant for a precisely nuanced reconstruction of the Pauline phrase "with fear and trembling." This follows especially from the fact that Aseneth is reacting to an epiphanic experience: Joseph has just confronted Aseneth as a "son of God."

Fear and Trembling

Linguistic History

One can trace the history of this expression through several distinct phases.

1. The first phase deals with reaction to a superior enemy. In both the Hebrew Bible and the Septuagint "fear and trembling" appears as a stock

phrase in descriptions of an encounter between enemies. The inferior combatant experiences fear and trembling over against the superior (cf. Exod 15:16; Deut 2:25; 11:25; Jud 2:28; 15:2; Ps 55:6 [Eng. v. 5]; Isa 19:16). In Gen 9:2 the same notion is applied to the reaction of animals to human beings. An analogous situation appears in the texts from Qumran in descriptions of people at prayer.[14] Even in cases where it is God who brings about "fear and trembling" in the presence of a powerful foe (Deut 2:25; 11:25; esp. Isa 19:16), we are not yet dealing with a detail from an epiphany or theophany.

2. In other cases we are in fact dealing with a standard feature of epiphanies or theophanies. In *4 Macc.* 4:10 military events still set the context, but now "fear and trembling" are triggered by the sight of angels with blazing weapons. The same sort of reaction, within the context of an epiphany, also occurs in the above-cited text from *Jos. Asen.*, as well as in *Jos. Asen.* 14:10.[15] The related expression in Mark 16:8 ("terror and amazement") is also tied to an epiphany.

3. The third stage is marked by a partial ethicizing of the expression. Thus in the later apocryphal writings, with Paul, and in the early Christian texts of the post-Pauline period, "fear and trembling" tends to disappear from the depiction of epiphanies. At the same time one cannot fail to notice that both of the constitutive features identified in (1) and (2) above continue to operate. For example, the *Apoc. Sedr.* 14:12 says of the sinners that "they do not prostrate themselves (before God) in fear and trembling, but rather speak long words." On the one hand, we are dealing with the position of inferiors but, on the other hand, the situation is one of petitioning God, which is characteristic of epiphanies. A comparable situation is found in Rom 11:20: "Do not become proud, but stand in awe." ("Becoming proud" corresponds to "speaking long words" of *Apoc. Sedr.*)

The ethical aspect dominates in the way the expression "obey (obedience) with fear and trembling" (not yet a firmly fixed turn of phrase) is found in Paul and the immediately post-Pauline texts. Note, for example, Phil 2:12-13 ("as you have always obeyed . . . with fear and trembling"); 2 Cor 7:15 ("the obedience of all of you, and how you have welcomed him with fear and trembling"); Eph 6:5 ("Slaves obey your earthly masters with fear and trembling"). At the same time, however, an epiphanic element is present in these texts. Thus Paul is an apostle of Jesus Christ, Titus is Paul's representative, and of the "masters" in Eph 6:5 it is expressly said that they are to be obeyed with fear and trembling "as you obey Christ." In other words, before those who only represent God (even indirectly), the theme holds that they ought to elicit "fear and trembling." Put another way, the features that hold true for an authentic epiphany also hold true in encounters with the representatives of God.

(This is one of the most noteworthy phenomena in the histories of both early Judaism and early Christianity.)

The syntax of Phil 2:12-13 is interesting. Emphasis falls on the expression "with fear and trembling" because this is the reaction that follows from the presence of God among people (Phil 2:13: ". . . for it is God who is at work in you"). In 1 Cor 2:3 Paul connects mention of fear and trembling with a statement about weakness—just as we saw in *Jos. Asen.* 9:1, above. Here the epiphanic element receives unmistakable emphasis; Paul comes to the community "in weakness and in fear and much trembling" precisely because God's power is at work in him, empowering what he does to be effective. Associated with Phil 2:12-13 is the thought that fear and trembling are appropriate reactions in the presence of those in whom and through whom God himself is at work. One might say that the issue is the behavior of those who bear the holy within themselves, or of behavior toward that which they bear and which is at work within them. In any case, in both 1 Cor 2:3 and Phil 2:12-13 the emphasis decidedly falls on the workings of God. The focal point is the presence of the divine, a presence capable of doing mighty things. In the presence of such, reactions appropriate to an epiphany are expected. (For comparative purposes, 1 Pet 1:17, "Live in reverent fear during the time of your exile . . ." shows our expression in a purely ethical dimension.)

In sum, the content of the expression "fear and trembling" remains oriented toward accounts of epiphany. In New Testament times, however, a strongly ethical nuance has been added. In Pauline circles, in any case, "fear and trembling" is transformed into a mode of interpersonal behavior, or becomes the basis for such. The intervening factor in this transformation is the way that God is perceived to be present—not directly but through a herald or a messenger. In contrast to the predominant way this expression gets used in the Old Testament, in New Testament times the military aspect drops out (at least up to the time of *4 Macc.* 4).

Psychological Significance

PAUL AND THE "CURE OF SOULS" IN PHIL 2:12-13

In this brief passage Paul addresses the themes of "anxiety" and "action." With reference to anxiety, he says that only God is of any use in counteracting it. He says the same with regard to action—God makes it effective. Our task here is to understand why Paul argues in just this way.

Quite possibly Paul is here pursuing a dual strategy, as he does in 2 Cor 5:13. There he directs attention away from himself, from his own ego, to God and to fellow human beings (in his own case, specifically to the Christian community).[16] For at least two reasons, I see essentially the same going on in Phil 2:12-13.[17] (a) Paul says you should have anxiety only before

God, not (so I complete the statement) about yourself or your own possibility of failure. Is Paul here presupposing the experience of feeling as though crippled by the prospect of failure? (All sorts of mental blocks arise through the fear that we will be unable to carry through on something.) The one who is anxious before God, however, has already managed to escape his or her own ivory tower. In Phil 2:12-13 this God-directed anxiety is being urged specifically upon a group of God's own representatives. Where the appropriate anxiety is in place, it manifests itself as bound obedience. (b) In a second step Paul lessens somewhat the anxiety that one has before God. This follows from the recognition that everything that really matters is effected by God as a gift. All one needs to do is let one's hand be guided by God. As a result of this happy message (viz., that God enables what is necessary), the anxiety we meet at the threshold of the act is overcome. Our own ability to approach an act with courage and to carry it through is no longer at the center of concern. Attention is directed toward God, who is both awesome and gracious. The Christian who succeeds in doing this can "work out your own salvation."

I assume that Paul is here talking about human activity. Accordingly, it seems to me that Paul remained a Pharisee even as a Christian. He is asking, "How is righteous behavior possible?" And he leaves his addressees with no escape. As Christians they encounter the demanding will of God in a direct way through the representatives of God, and the God they meet in such a way can only elicit fear and trembling in response. The same dynamic holds true with regard to the work of God manifested in other Christians as well. Seen from the divine side of the relationship, God guides the works of the Christian much as a mother guides the hand of a child learning to write. The upshot is that the Christian, caught between solicitude and dread, no longer has any means of escape.

BENEFICIAL ANXIETY

The theme that anxiety/fear before God is important for Christian behavior appears not only in Phil 2:12-13 but also in Rom 11:20-21 (faith and fear) and in 2 Cor 5:11 (fear of God as a factor regulating Paul's behavior). To be sure, these latter passages no longer employ the full expression "fear and trembling," but they still make use of the Greek root *phob-* ("fear"). In both Rom 11:20-21 and 2 Cor 5:11 (cf. v. 10) this fear occurs in view of judgmental activity by God. The same was the case in references to "fear and trembling." Far from being without ground or reason, such a reaction was always related to awareness of the possibility of punitive response on the part of the magisterial Other to one's wrongful behavior.

Paul makes only occasional use of the theme of anxiety, and never when laying out his soteriology. But when he does revert to this theme, it is in important contexts—contexts in which the central focus is human behavior.[18] Anxiety, as well as "fear and trembling," are reactions to the power of God, and they reflect the awareness that God can indeed punish. If on the human side the experience of sin is connected with an experience of the power of God, then terror is an appropriate response.

As a rule, neither here nor elsewhere in the Bible (but see "Anxiety and Love," below) is there opposition between anxiety before God, on the one hand, and love (either for or from God), on the other.[19] Rather, the presence of fear/anxiety before God is already and without doubt something positive. This is so because such anxiety is not directed toward other gods or powers but toward the One who can bring about something desirable from this anxiety—in Pauline language, can enable one to do God's will.

CONTEMPORARY RELEVANCE

In contrast to our assumption that fear but not anxiety is appropriate before God, the biblical view is that fear and anxiety belong together and that there is an outlet for all our anxieties.

From the standpoint of biblical experience, the decisive feature is to have anxiety before the right God—not any deity, or in the face of our own misguided acts. It is indeed both given and presupposed that there is a genuine potential for anxiety. The decisive consideration is the object. Toward whom will we let this anxiety be directed or before whom we will experience anxiety? If and insofar as modern theology and pastoral care would talk us out of being anxious before God, the result would be that our anxiety would once again become misdirected, seeking new arenas for expression (e.g., in necromancy).[20] From another angle, anxiety before God—an anxiety that is both necessary and genuine—can all too easily be manipulated by some power-hungry ecclesiastical hierarchy, thereby becoming an anxiety before that which is merely human. Anxiety before God—and only such anxiety—is nonetheless legitimate. This is the anxiety that frees one from all other sources of anxiety (cf. Matt 10:28; Luke 12:4-5).

Like a prayer that takes accusatory form or like doubt and other "negative" experiences, anxiety before God is not to be suppressed or covered up. Anxieties ought to be admitted, and admitted in undisguised fashion, before God. According to both Jewish and Christian understanding, the human relationship with God allows for complete honesty. In sum, the New Testament does not "make" one anxious. Rather, the New Testament uncovers already-existing anxiety, calls it what it is, and points to the one opportunity for finally conquering it.

Anxiety/Fear and Joy

The combination of anxiety/fear with joy occurs, apart from *Jos. Asen.* 9:1 (see above), also with reference to the women in Matt 28:8 ("with fear and great joy"). For us the two terms would cancel each other out. In contrast to our way of thinking, however, there appears here no sense of contradiction. The "mixed feelings" (C. Burchard) both here and in *Jos. Asen.* 9:1 are in need of explanation, however, since they could be a hermeneutically significant indication of a mode of experience quite different from our own. The element of "fear/anxiety" in Matt 28:8 is clearly drawn from theophany accounts, where it signals the perception of the stronger power (cf. above).[21] Unlike with us, therefore, fear/anxiety is not to be associated with something negative per se. It simply relates to the perception of a superior power (to be sure, also an ambivalent power). Only from such a perspective can fear/anxiety be enlarged or expanded so as to include joy. The same perspective also throws light on how fear/anxiety can be the reaction in Mark 9:32b to the proclamation in Mark 9:31 that the Son of Man will be raised from he dead. At the same time it is instructive that the mention of joy in Matt 28:8 scarcely finds analogy in theophany accounts.[22] We are thus dealing with a new motif in the Easter texts. "Joy" here stands in contrast to sadness over the death of Jesus. (Admittedly, the sadness of the disciples is mentioned in the Easter texts only in the secondary ending of Mark 16:10b, while only John 20 mentions the weeping of Mary Magdalene.) Luke 24:41 is also noteworthy in this context ("while in their joy they were disbelieving"), where "joy" stands for being so spontaneously overwhelmed that nothing specific can yet be conceptualized.[23]

ANXIETY AND LOVE

According to 1 John 4:17-18, fear/anxiety and love are incompatible.

> [17]Love has been perfected among us in this: that we may have boldness on the day of judgment, because as he is so are we in this world. [18]There is no fear in love, but perfect love casts out fear; for fear has to do with punishment, and whoever fears has not reached perfection in love.

The basic meaning here is that one who must expect accusation and punishment is also one who fears (K. Wengst); for such a person, fear/anxiety appears like a fixed landmark on the road ahead (R. Schnackenburg).

The central dynamic in 1 John 4:17-18 is the stress on "boldness" (Greek: *parrhesia*). The term basically designates speaking freely; and by extension it also means confidence, frankness in discourse, and freedom from anxiety. The notion of unabashed candor underlies this semantic development.[24] Experiencing such boldness is one of the gifts of the Spirit and a sign of having been adopted as a child of God (compare esp. 2 Cor 3:12 with 3:17). This boldness prevails even in the presence of the majesty of God—which is to say, in the face of every reality before which the human being rightly would suffer anxiety.[25] It therefore strikes me as significant that the ruling metaphors here all stem from the public domain (e.g., civic assembly, law court, audience before the king), not the domestic. First John 4 understands such boldness as a direct consequence of being loved by God.

With regard to the theme of the incompatibility of anxiety and love, this text also provides evidence for a broader development, one that is indicated in several texts from Hellenistic culture of the first century. (a) For Philo of Alexandria, only by means of love (and *not* fear/anxiety) is God venerated in a truly fitting way. One who reveres God directly loves God. Such a person attributes to God neither bodily parts nor passions; in short, such a person entertains no anthropomorphic notions about God. Conversely, the one who fears God is caught up in anthropomorphisms (*Unchangeable* 69). One who fears God is not yet in a position to love God (*Migration* 21). The point of *On Dreams* 1.163 is that one is not to fear God as a "lord" (*kyrios*) but rather to honor God in love as a benefactor. Since with Philo love is unambiguously the fuller way of turning toward God, I would translate *teleia agapé* in 1 John 4:18 not (as is customary) "perfect love," but rather "love—as that which has been perfected." (b) Seneca also emphasizes the incompatibility of fear and love when it comes to revering God.[26] The issue turns on the association of *colere* (to honor/revere) with *amare* (to love), the proper ordering of which is decisive for one's relationship to the gods. (c) For Pauline theology as well a crucial theme is the overcoming of juridical thinking through the experience of love appropriated through Jesus Christ. This can be seen repeatedly in Romans 8: "There is therefore now no condemnation for those who are in Christ Jesus" (v. 1); ". . . who is to condemn?" (v. 33b); "Who will separate us from the love of Christ?" (v. 35). Particularly in Rom 8:38-39 the "love of God in Christ Jesus" is juxtaposed against everything that one has to fear (although the word "fear" is not actually stated, it is clearly implied).

From the perspective of the history of religions, these texts exhibit a thoroughgoing shift of paradigm.[27] Three features are involved in this shift. (1) There is a recognition of the superiority and unique suitability of love in the area of religion. (Are there connections here to the notion of the *Pax Augustea*?) As the text from Seneca makes clear, social consequences directly follow from this shift. (2) "Fear" and "love" no longer necessarily appear as a fixed combination, whether conjoined or as antagonistic opposites. Love has "conquered," but in such a way that its rivals (fear and/or anxiety) need not be forgotten. (3) In all this the possibility for intimacy and tenderness in relation to God has been advanced at the expense of fear and anxiety.

For the specific history of this paradigm shift within early Christianity, three additional observations are worthwhile.

1. In the proclamation of Jesus there still exists an unmistakable tension between juridical thinking (as in many of the parables) and the intimacy of his own relationship to God. Put another way: Jesus himself appears as the Savior (cf. the "I have come that . . ." sayings) who proffers love in advance of God's judgment. Whenever the focus is on the person of Jesus, the opposition between a saving Christology and a judging eschatology is resolved in favor of the former. (The Mariology of later times has blurred this tension.[28])

2. In Eph 5:25 husbands are commanded to "love" their wives; conversely, according to Eph 5:33 the wife is to "fear" (Greek: *phobētai*) her husband. The difference here might well be connected with the preponderance of religious motivation vis-à-vis the behavior of the husband (whom it was obviously more necessary to admonish). But the husband's relationship to the wife is also open to critique from the direction of the dynamic suggested immediately above.

3. A series of early Christian texts shows that the tension between fear/anxiety and love was a sociological problem in the early church. The problem has to do with the church as a civic institution over against a "mystical elite." The tension generated in such a situation seeks its resolution along the following lines: anxiety/fear is psychologically necessary to motivate those whose attachment to the church is basically an attachment to a civic institution, whereas the message of pure love suffices for the spiritually elite in the church.[29] As awkward as this might seem, it at least shows that the contrast was perceived and remains active. On the whole, then, this paradigm shift of the first century c.e. looks like a daring new way of speaking, one that has seldom since been superseded.

Terror

TERROR AND DREAD

With reference to Rev 9:1-12 I will demonstrate how the writer of that book both represented and communicated the sense of terror or dread. I will also address the issue of the religious function of these feelings.

Disarray and Shattered Expectations

In these verses the reader is disabused of a number of expectations, especially such as have to do with the regularities of the natural world and the constancy of species. Thus beasts are described in fantastic ways that defy established patterns (vv. 7-10). Locusts do no damage to trees and plants, their usual fodder (v. 4), but act quite unlike ordinary locusts, which makes them even nastier creatures. Ordinary experience yields no clue as to how to dispose of these beasts. Creatures previously known only within fables here acquire new concretization. In short, these descriptions directly challenge the reader's inclination to pigeonhole the customary, to pass it off as familiar and known, to find in it confirmation of normal expectations. The intensity of the terror here expressed runs directly parallel to the degree that ordinary expectations are shattered.

Other features of the same passage exhibit distortions of the natural order. Smoke is ordinarily visible in the sky but usually does not come out of the ground (v. 2), except with volcanoes. Ordinarily a shaft into the earth yields life-giving water, but not here. Perhaps the greatest anomaly is that these locusts, which look somewhat like horses (v. 7), are wearing crowns. What a montage of strange creatures!

A Description of the Perverse

In vv. 7-9 human body parts or ornaments that in themselves are appropriate and fitting (crowns, faces, women's hair, breastplates) occur in unsuitable contexts. Elsewhere in this passage human traits appear only on victims (vv. 4, 5, 6, 10). For the ancients, it was considered "abominable" and "perverse" for something to be found where it does not properly fit. This amounts to a "mixing" (Greek: *mixis*) of things that ought not be together, and any such mixing is scandalous.

This is the sense in which Mark 13:14 speaks of the "desolating sacrilege," the abomination of which consists precisely in the fact that it "stands where it ought not to be" (viz., in the Temple). On the same basis God punishes the misdirected worship of the things that God has made. Here the element of perversity lies in the fact that worship is directed where it does not belong (Rom 1:22-23). God thus delivers human beings over to perversity, according to the rule of *lex talionis*; in failing to respect the proper boundaries, they themselves fall into disarray (Rom 1:24-27). According to the ancient way of perceiving things, in other words, one kind of perversity elicits another.

This in turn leads to the recognition that, in the experience of the early Christians, nothing is more abominable than mingling of things that should be kept separate. Where unwarranted mixing occurs, disorder arises—and disorder is terrifying and dreadful. Obviously this mode of perception is conditioned by sociocultural factors. Where disorder is experienced as highly disgusting and threatening, there also order is perceived as a gift, an act of beneficence. The underlying perception in such a case is that order is not solidly established but unstable and vulnerable. A comparison: It is not difficult to see political relations in today's Europe as orderly, especially when viewed in relationship to other historical eras. But this very orderliness in turn changes the perception of perversity, which is no longer perceived as the blurring of categories but rather in the multiplicity of the forms of authority. The upshot is that, for many, order is itself experienced as oppressive—especially where, through the state's monopoly on power, this order penetrates into even the minutest areas of life.[30]

Appealing to the Senses and the Emotions

In Revelation 9 almost all the senses are stimulated: seeing (v. 1), hearing (vv. 1, 9), smell (v. 2—smoke ordinarily smells), touch (pain; v. 5: torture; v. 10: sting). The description of the bodies in vv. 3a, 7-9a, and 10 is so graphic as to make them almost palpable.

Emotions are awakened as well in this passage. There is the dismay occasioned by disarray (cf. above), the terror one feels in the presence of a conquering army (vv. 7, 9), the yearning for death brought on by despair (v. 6), the horror of monsters (vv. 7-9), the misery that follows the devouring of the crops (vv. 3-4), the helplessness and hopelessness of being hemmed in (v. 6). The text reflects the experience of being trapped between heaven (v. 1) and the underworld (v. 11), and of finding no refuge anywhere on earth (vv. 3-10). Humankind is caught in an inescapable pincer movement, hemmed in by the angel of heaven (v. 1) and the angel of the abyss (v. 11). A sense of powerlessness suffuses the scene (vv. 5-6, 10), especially in view of the enormity of the opponents (v. 9). Smoldering anger over the sadistic treatment of the victims (v. 5) and alarm over the fallen star (v. 1) round out the scene.

Intensification

This text leads the reader to realize that the consequence of godlessness is far worse than previously thought. Everything will turn out even worse than expected, and the consequence will be cosmic in scope. So v. 1 mentions the abyss while v. 11 refers to the king of the abyss. Although this king's name is given, he is not further described; his appearance is left to the reader's imagination. This makes the image all the more terrifying and greatly intensifies the sense of dread.

Dread—Its Pastoral Dimension

READER-RESPONSE CRITIQUE

The reader of this passage will have to make connections among the various figures (whose very novelty challenges their comprehensibility) and fill in the agony (only sparsely described in the text).

The author of Revelation 9 describes the consequences of turning away from God and tries to awaken the emotions of his hearers. To that end he graphically develops images of dread, deliberately preventing any easy appropriation. Using formulaic descriptions here would have made it too easy for them simply to be glossed over. Even after repeated readings, the details of the dreadful images in Revelation 9 are difficult to remember— precisely because they are not hackneyed formulas. In all likelihood this is what the author intended. He wanted his message to avoid the fate suffered by so many exhortations, namely, that they lose their sharp edges as they get taken in. In this case any sort of recollection of earlier admonitions is literally torn to shreds. The dread awakened by this scenario goes beyond anything that can be softened by prior experience.

What of enduring value is to be found in this text? One point is that this text cautions against our all-too-frequent practice of coming up with meditations that harmonize conflicts. In this passage, disjunctions and disruptions prevail. The critical point is that disharmonies and the dread they produce must also be granted a place. Be that as it may, Revelation 9 is not likely to have much impact on us today. Is that because we "know" the text was not written for us?

THE IMAGE OF GOD

The author's intention was not to elicit anxiety. If it were, that intent would have remained unsatisfied. This indicates that his real intention lies elsewhere:

1. The dread that human beings have or can have is conjured up through patent images. Nothing is being suppressed here; Revelation in this regard is clearly an expressive text. The sufferings of the victims are not described; this aspect must be filled in by the recipients of the text. Attention focuses on the appearance of the torturers.

2. Every possible terror is awakened, in order to draw attention to the abysmal reality awaiting those who are alienated from God. The author, however, was not concerned about prophesying the future. His main interest lies in illuminating the depths of what already is. (Recall my earlier remarks about the "enlightening" characteristic of eschatological revelations.) Nothing distressful is covered up, but at the same time neither is

God's truth obscured. The scene being depicted here speaks equally to these two aspects.

3. For the writer, the dread here depicted reflects the side of God that is normally hidden, the side open to experience when human beings turn away from God. The consequence of turning away from God is an experiencing of hopelessness. In the case at hand, the hearer is confronted with hell. "Hell" is also a mode of experiencing God. God is also to be found in the dreadful, not just in its amelioration. Moreover, Revelation does not clearly define what is involved in being marked with the "seal of God" (v. 4). This is not necessarily a reference to baptism, and thus everything here depicted also stands as a threat to hearers who regard themselves as Christians.

4. The terror is rooted not in what readily manifests itself to human beings but in the psychically alien. Human beings are trapped between angels and monsters.

5. There is only one exit out of the cul-de-sac depicted, and that is by way of repentance before God (9:21). From this alone can the terror be confined and managed. Quite possibly the writer of Revelation embraced the apocalyptic style because its traditionally expressive speech and its openness to surreal forms of emotionality offered a chance to shake his readers out of their complacency, their addiction to the familiar.[31]

In sum, the intended effect (terror and dread) is achieved especially in the gruesome way the creatures who torment the human beings are depicted. Their distinctive loathsomeness grows out of the fact that they are composite beings, creatures made up of disconcertingly juxtaposed segments. Their appearance alone becomes an expression of the gruesome nature of torture, the reality of which does not then need to be further described. Their composition as unnatural "mixtures" therefore becomes the primary conveyance of the theme of dread. Such surrealistic scenery depicts the true face of godlessness. Also noteworthy is the fact that the condition of godlessness is depicted as a threat posed by agents working from without; personal feelings or mental agonies arise only in response to what comes from the outside.[32] This actually expands the basis on which members of the audience can identify with what is going on. One is tempted to find a parallel for this in the cathartic possibilities of viewing surrealistic art.

A WAY BEYOND FEAR AND SADNESS

When observed from the standpoint of reader-response critique, the so-called tale of the rich young man (Mark 10:17-31) shows a deliberate pastoral guiding of the reader. It is therefore not to be regarded only as a contribution to theological discussion about the proper way to live or, in biblical language, to enter the kingdom of God. However much the story might seem to be shaped as a historical narrative, it is better to read it from an historical-psychological point of view.[33] The methodological starting point for such a reading is the recognition that the action in this narrative runs parallel to a psychological process in the recipient. The reader of the narrative is actually the one to be transformed, through empathetic experience with the rich young man. The process of transformation has several clear stages.

Yearning for "Life"

The reader initially identifies with the rich young man.[34] He suspects that he is lacking something and asks the way to eternal life. He makes his inquiry because he has recognized the goal as valuable (Mark 10:17). The ensuing conversation confirms what the rich young man suspected at the outset; there is indeed something he is lacking (Mark 10:19-21).

Sadness

The demand of Jesus to give all possessions to the poor (10:21) prompts a noteworthy reaction on the part of the rich young man. He is downcast and goes away sadly. His reaction is not indignation or stubbornness or smug persistence in his own way. The young man is indeed sad, because he genuinely would like to follow Jesus and attain eternal life. But he cannot attain what initially mattered to him, because his ties to riches are too strong. The young man is incapable of freeing himself from these chains, despite the summons of Jesus. He has the insight to recognize that he must refuse the promise offered to him. He must do so because he is crippled by his attachment to his possessions; they hinder him from taking the most important step.

If this narrative is to have a "therapeutic" function, it is important that it move beyond the young man's sadness. The young man is now out of the scene; he goes away unconsoled. Hence it is necessary for the reader's point of identification to change. If the story is to go on, the focus must now shift to the dimension of discipleship.

Dismay

Immediately after the reference to the young man's sadness comes not a soothing word but a shocker. The saying about the camel and the eye of a needle makes the point that it is actually impossible for a rich person to enter the kingdom of heaven. That in turn serves to emphasize how difficult it is to enter the kingdom at all (v. 24b). The disciples react with extreme dismay. They pose what must be seen as a rhetorical question: "Then who can be saved?" The answer to this question would have to be "No one." This (10:26) is the only place in the Gospel of Mark where the writer gives us such a stark, double description of dismay. The dismay applies to the reader, the one who has the sense of being spoken to. Indeed, the impossibility described here rightly brings in its wake a sense of dismay.

Entrusted to God

After presenting the reader with yearning for eternal life, excessive attachment to riches, sadness and dismay, the text now (v. 27) directs attention to God. The decisive point is the contrast with human beings, a theme that harks back to its introduction in 10:18. Because human beings are so attached to their possessions, it must be left up to the creative power of God to transform the hearts of human beings. In the present context that means enabling human beings to renounce their possessions.[35]

The reference to God at this point does not amount to an instance of deus ex machina. Leaving matters in the hands of God shows itself to be the only way of escaping from excessive attachment to possessions. Unlike in Luke 16:13, however, the contrast is not between God and possessions but between God and human beings. This has important psychological implications for belief in God.

1. Attachment to God—and only this—enables one to be free of attachment to riches and possessions. As will be discussed in detail below (in chapter 9), this is so because faith is a total orientation of the human heart toward the reality of God. If faith so fills the human heart, then any other fixation must be eliminated, relativized, or softened. Obviously, any sort of desperate holding on to possessions would be ruled out by faith's total orientation to God. It has already been shown, moreover, how faith and freedom from worry are linked.

2. Neither self-help nor human assistance in general is strong enough effectively to help people overcome the attachments they themselves have made. This is where the "psychological" significance of God comes in, namely, that through God a whole new plane of possibility for human transformation is reached. No frontal assault, mounted by one's own will or by the will of another human being, can be strong enough to shatter the firm attachments that human beings make. In the place of such an assault, whether mounted alone or with the help of others, there must intrude the power of God the Creator. This is a power that works from within. This means that "conversion," the giving up of human attachments in favor of

reliance upon God, must be seen as a genuine miracle—as something that requires the creative power of God.

The element of "shock" described under "Dismay" above, now appears to be something like the trembling that occurs at the approach of God. The sadness and the terror jointly relate to the unchangeableness of the situation—at least as seen from the human side. In sum, this passage carries on the concern evident also in Mark 9, namely, that God is active in human affairs right down to the fundamental level, in the very real attachments—even fixations—that have a hold on people.

Positive Role Models

Undoubtedly the disciples are held up to the reader as examples of people who have successfully reached the desired goal (10:28-31). God has already transformed the disciples, and so the hope for God's intervention need not be focused on the distant future. It has already happened.

Promise

In 10:29-31, in a two-sided promise, the reader is told that the summons to give up all goods, and indeed all attachments, is not a goal in and of itself but is the way to establish a new community in the here and now and to gain eternal life in the hereafter.[36] This promise takes most seriously the human desire for a secure place within a community and also the longing for freedom from death. Because this promise is directed to flesh-and-blood disciples (10:28-31), it is not depicted as some ethereal vision but as a concrete goal.

In sum, the key point is not just that Jesus sharply contrasts the summons to follow him, on the one hand, with strong emotional attachment to riches, on the other. The main point is that such attachment can be overcome only through an encounter with God. Only a complete turning toward God yields contentment and freedom from worry.

Worry

The New Testament texts concerning freedom from worry are found above all in the so-called Q source (cf. Luke 12:22-34, par. Matt 6:25-33), in 1 Corinthians 7 (see v. 32), and in 1 Peter (see 5:7, citing Ps 55:23 [Eng. v. 22]).

"WORRY" IN COLLOQUIAL SPEECH

In everyday language, when we speak of worrying or of having something on our minds, we are referring to a vague, generalized sense of apprehension. The same cannot quite be said when we are worried about someone or something in particular.[37] Worry is thus durative; it is not for the moment but stretches over time. With worry one is dealing with a more or less continuous or at least repetitious emotion. One becomes a "worrier." Often worry is only a mood that accompanies other emotions. The amorphous object of worry is related to its future orientation. New Testament texts, on the other hand, offer quite a different picture of the phenomenon of worry.

CHARACTERISTICS OF WORRY IN THE NEW TESTAMENT

Deliberate Planning

Planning with regard to some outcome is an important feature of worry as depicted in the New Testament. This feature is particularly well exhibited when it is said of the rich farmer in Luke 12:17, "He thought to himself, what should I do?" In general, worrying here means planning to do something in order thereby to achieve a particular goal in the future. One similarly thinks about how to please one's sexual partner (1 Cor 7:33), about how one is going to get an adequate amount of food for nourishment (Luke 12:22; par. Matt 6:25), or about how to gain some physical advantage (Luke 12:25). The methodical nature of the process finds expression in the frequent reference to "treasure" in the context of speaking about "worry" (Luke 12:21, 34). This follows from the fact that a treasure must be deliberately and conscientiously amassed. Another intrinsic feature of worry, then, is that the goal in view is not easily attained. One has to spend a lot of time and effort focusing on the goal, knowing all the while that it will not easily be reached. Worry thus becomes an all-absorbing emotion. All the relevant biblical texts presuppose that worry occupies one totally. If it didn't, it would hardly be worth mentioning.

Basic Necessities of Life

The items that occupy the worrier's mind are hardly trivial in nature but have to do with the uncertain but nonetheless basic necessities of life. For the addressees of the sayings in Q, food and clothing are items to worry about. (For the rich farmer, of course, the concern is a little different—what to do with the rich harvest.) In 1 Cor 7:32 the concern is how to make the marriage partner happy. (In the corresponding parallel in the writings of Epictetus, worry is focused on young children.) So, while the specific content of the worry is tied to social status or station in life, it nonetheless always has to do with matters of vital interest. Worry is based on the realization that nothing can be taken for granted.

Differences from Our Understanding

In the modern world, worry is rarely totally absorbing. Our pluralistic and prosperous society imposes on us a whole host of new "necessities." The fundamental presupposition of the biblical understanding of worry is set by the experience that one can plan for only one thing at a time, that one can have only one goal in mind. In biblical understanding, worry is not an accompanying feeling or one that perhaps attacks a person periodically. For the New Testament worry is the intrapsychic side of the pursuit of that one thing that is central to one's life to the exclusion of other things. At the same time, for the New Testament worry is always focused on concrete matters (nourishment, clothing, sexuality). The problem is simply that the way to attain these objects of desire is unclear. Only when one is aware of this can one also catch the full impact of the summons to cease worrying.

THE NEW TESTAMENT DEMAND

New Testament texts consistently call for one to cease worrying about earthly things. Some differences occur in the reasons or motivations for renouncing one's worries:

God Cares

According to 1 Pet 5:7, one is simply to cast on the Lord all one's worries because "he cares for you." Just how God's care will become manifest, however, is not said; for the writer, obviously, the authority of Scripture is warrant enough (Ps 55:23 [Eng. v. 22]). The conclusion drawn in Matt 6:28-29 (par. Luke 12:28) follows the principle from the lesser to the greater: If God so clothes the grass of the field, then how much more will he care for you? In Matt 6:26 (par. Luke 12:24) God cares for the birds of the sky, and you are considerably more valuable than they. Elsewhere the same point is argued by reference to the fatherhood of God: the Father knows the needs of his children (Matt 6:32; Luke 12:30).

Uselessness of Worry

According to Matt 6:27 (par. Luke 12:25) worrying can accomplish nothing. Worrying about the size of your body, for example, certainly cannot increase it. Here, as in the preceding point, worry is argued against on rational grounds.

Worrying Works against Holiness

According to 1 Cor 7:32-34, worry interferes with the ability of married persons to show undivided concern for the Lord. This in turn keeps them from being "holy" in body and soul, i.e., of belonging totally to the Lord. Sexuality and service of God are not actually described as incompatible, but the Christian who is married must deal with a divided loyalty. Some important psychological presuppositions are attached to this perspective.

1. Holiness is no longer being understood from a cultic perspective, as a matter of bodily integrity; a psychological dimension has taken over. The notion of perfection has extended beyond being something that can be elevated by cultic means; now holiness has to do with the deepest striving of the soul. Thus all hindrances to holiness are to be driven out of the heart. In many ways 1 Cor 7:32 reminds one of the "higher righteousness" urged by the Antitheses in the Sermon on the Mount. For example, as with Matt 5:28 so also here the demand for holiness is carried over into the area of thoughts, even casual glances. No sort of cultic holiness is any longer demanded. The demand instead is for purity of thought and freedom from attachment. Regarding this comprehensive notion of holiness as "Pharisaic" is no reason for not also regarding it as authentic to Jesus himself.

2. Concern for God is not spiritualized nor can it play a role secondary to anything else. That is precisely why it becomes a genuine rival to sexuality. Concern for God is not only to be one's top priority but it is to exclude all other concerns. In this sense, concern for God is to be a complete radicalizing of the First Commandment.

3. In keeping with this same line of thought, marital union is no longer seen as something only conventional or juridical in nature, but rather as something that can demand everything from a person. The conflict between sexuality and service of God comes about not because the one might be superficial and the other "high" or "deep" but because both truly demand a person's all.

Recompense Already in This Age

The texts about freedom from worry belong to a larger group of texts according to which, astoundingly, abundant recompense is guaranteed already in this age for all that one has renounced. One thinks here, for example, of Mark 10:29-30 (see above) or of the "bonus" attached to righteousness in Matt 6:33. As is clear from *T. Job* 4:6ff., God responds to the prayers of the righteous with rewards that are not exclusively "heavenly."

In sum, according to the texts dealing with worry or concern, the demand is that one renounce one's most obvious vital interests.

Disappointed Love

Among the letters of Paul, 2 Corinthians stands out in the way the apostle repeatedly speaks of his love for the community he is addressing.[38] To this end he makes use of the verb *agapan* (to love—a term entirely missing in 1 Corinthians) and the noun *agapé* (love—used in the same way in 1 Corinthians only in 16:24, a noteworthy variation on Paul's usual closing words; it serves as a bridge to 2 Corinthians). In what follows, I will use this linguistic peculiarity of 2 Corinthians as an occasion for considering other passages as well in this very personal letter of Paul.

Simply stated, 2 Corinthians is about disappointed love. Already before an interim visit by Paul (a visit that did not turn out happily for him), other apostles had appeared who found favor with the community. In their response to those other apostles, Paul sees a considerable disruption of his own relationship with the Corinthians. He had regarded his relationship with them as that of father and child (1 Cor 4:14) or groomsman and bride (2 Cor 11:2)—in any case, an exclusive relationship. (To be sure, in 1 Cor 3:10 [cf. v. 6] he also grants a certain, albeit secondary, role to Apollos). The argumentation using the notion of measure (Greek: *kanon*) as well as the lack of any other specific indication of the teachings of the opponents in 2 Corinthians 10 leads us to suspect that it was hardly heretics with a distinctly different sort of Christianity (or even pagan Gnostics) who had penetrated the community.[39] Instead, these opponents of Paul must simply have been other Christian missionaries, ones who had been so favorably received by the community that they saw an opening for themselves to make disparaging remarks about Paul (2 Cor 7:12), taking advantage of some of Paul's less attractive traits (2 Cor 10:10).

WRITTEN ON THE HEART

According to 2 Cor 3:1-3, the community at Corinth has been "written on the heart" of Paul, and this is obvious to everyone ("known and read by all"). Paul's opponents can display written letters of recommendation (3:1), a completely normal state of affairs in early Christianity. Paul cannot do the same for himself. In this difficult situation he must simply point out that his letter of recommendation is his heart, which lies open to all. His heart is overflowing with love for the Corinthians and, as such, offers a testimony beyond compare.

In contrast to any merely formal credential, then, Paul directs attention to the area of personal relationship. On the one hand, there is his intimacy with the Corinthians, which is the private aspect of that relationship. On the other hand, this relationship also has a public aspect; it is apparent to everyone. Paul then strengthens his argument by comparing the two aspects of his relationship, the private and the public, to the Old Testament contrast between "tablets of stone" and "hearts of flesh." He is saying that his own relationship with the Corinthians stands on the higher (the human) plane, while that of his opponents is on the lower (the stonelike) plane. Because "heart" and "stone" are incommensurate, Paul is counting on the Corinthians to side with him. After all, who would be so without empathy or feelings as to choose stone over the heart? In all of this, the relationship to the community of Paul's opponents is supposed to come out looking merely external, a pure formality and thus the opposite of anything deeply human.

In order to be able to evaluate this text from a historical-psychological perspective, it is important to keep in view Paul's starting position and to consider what he makes of it. He assigns his own love for the Corinthians to the highest rank, while he disparages the relationship of his opponents to that community as purely external, a mere formality, indeed as less than fully human. Through this deprecating contrast, as well as in his rush to "open up" his own heart, Paul shows himself as someone who feels that his love has been violated, not taken seriously, or at the least inadequately appreciated. In this difficult competition to win the favor of his audience, Paul bases his appeal solely on the superiority of the personal to the material.

Precisely in the fact that he seizes upon this tactic, Paul lets us see to what a significant degree he has been emotionally affected by the news from Corinth. He responds to the offense in dual fashion. In 3:2 he confesses the openness of his feelings and thereby also gives indirect testimony to his vulnerability. In 3:3 he denigrates his opponents, attributing to them a cold formality in their relationship with the Corinthians. In contrast, Paul's own relationship with them is one of warmly human, albeit wounded, love. This depiction by Paul exaggerates the conflict, in effect putting it under a magnifying glass. Paul does this as a way of protecting his own injured heart.

In sum, the injured lover is here responding in such a way that his love is shown to be the only truly human love. The relationship of his opponents to the community is denigrated as cold and calculating. Along the way, the injured lover is operating within the context of a hierarchy of values whose validity is taken as obvious.

MUTUAL RESPECT

Second Corinthians 3 opens with the rhetorical question, "Are we beginning to commend ourselves again?" For the problem here being addressed, 2 Corinthians employs two synonymous expressions: "to commend (oneself)" and "to praise (oneself)." (At a certain remove stands "to boast [of

oneself]," which always carries the notion of being blameworthy.) Paul
reproaches his opponents for taking pride "in appearances" rather than in
what is "in the heart" (2 Cor 5:12). Immediately thereafter he speaks of the
love of Christ, which urges him on (5:14a).[40] With "those who boast in outward appearance" (5:12), Paul again refers to the letters of recommendation. Paul's own emphasis falls on the term "heart"; through this
catchword a close connection is established with the theme discussed in
the immediately preceding section. Above all, in 2 Corinthians 10–12, the
semantic field "praise/commendation" is activated. The primary issue in
all of this has to do with the respective grounds on which Paul and his
opponents are basing their reputations and prestige. Although this issue
has traditionally been treated under the rubric of legitimacy, it seems the
issue has more to do with the way respect is to be won in the eyes of the
Corinthians. The ongoing connection to the theme of love is evident in
both 5:12-14a and 3:1-3.

Of fundamental importance for psychological inquiry is the intense and
sensitive way in which Paul reflects upon mutual respect as the foundation
for communal life—and that not only in 2 Corinthians. In Paul's comments
on this theme we gain unique insights into the sociopsychological dimensions of his experience. Undoubtedly his situation as a Jew in the Hellenistic world (viz., as an often-despised outsider) is an important
background element in the fact that Paul observes from the outside, as it
were, the game of prestige and recognition. This social position makes his
penetrating analyses possible. (Note the variation on this theme in 1 Thess
2:14-16.)

It is hardly accidental that most of the texts dealing with the theme of
mutual respect occur in 2 Corinthians. After all, this is the epistle in which
Paul engages in the sharpest of his conflicts with his opponents. This is also
the epistle in which Paul constantly reacts in a direct and personal manner,
making almost no use of the conventions established by Scripture or
hallowed by tradition. The baroque stretching of language in 2 Corinthians
is one of the consequences of Paul's speaking so authentically.

More light can be shed on the above-mentioned connection between
the themes of love and "praising/commending [oneself]" by considering a
text in which both themes occur, 2 Cor 11:10-12.[41] Paul has accepted no
material support from the Corinthians, and he wants that state of affairs to
continue. He regards such an arrangement as a source of honor, one that he
is not willing to let anyone take away from him. Obviously, however, the
Corinthians have not been able to follow Paul on this point. Paul fears at
least that they could interpret his refusal of support from them as an indication that he wants to know nothing about them.[42] It is precisely at this
point that he affirms his love. All of this goes on in the presence of Paul's
opponents. Were Paul now to deviate from his line and demand support

from the Corinthian community, he would only be giving his opponents an occasion for triumph. Then they could boast that "they stand at the same level as do we." If one analyzes the text from our perspective, then, the outcome is clear: Paul and his opponents are contending with one another for prestige (respect, honor) in the eyes of the community.

Several features define the dynamic of the competition between Paul and his opponents. (a) Paul holds fast to his claim that not having taken anything from the Corinthians redounds to his credit. He sees this as an aspect of the selflessness which he elsewhere characterizes as the love of Christ (2 Cor 5:14), the love that urges him on. (b) Paul does not want to yield the prize of honor to his opponents, and so he simply cannot imitate them and now also accept support from the Corinthians. In that case he would have to retreat, since then they would have won. (c) The community is still undecided. What Paul regards as honorable must not automatically have been so regarded in the community. He recognizes the danger that his behavior could also be interpreted in a negative way. Were that to happen, however, the community would automatically turn favorably toward his opponents. Matters have thus reached a critical turning point. (d) At this juncture Paul can do no more than aver his love and call upon God as his witness: "God knows I do [love you]!" Undoubtedly Paul is acting in the hope that, in response to such an asseveration, the community will in turn bestow its love on him—or at least not deliberately withdraw it.

Paul sees the desired response to his love for the Corinthians (namely, their reciprocating love) endangered by differing value-judgments.[43] In these verses, Paul seeks to remove this danger. To appreciate how he does this, it is important to realize that the relationship between love and prestige is multifaceted.

1. With his reputation hanging in the balance, Paul appeals directly to his love for the Corinthians. Paul is similarly explicit about the ultimate grounds for his behavior in 2 Cor 3:1-3. In speaking this way, Paul is not just saying that his love bolsters (or should bolster) his prestige; he is saying that he regards love as of much greater value than prestige.

2. Paul fears that his love for the Corinthians, far from being evident, is actually being poorly perceived. Thus he makes an additional reference to the transparency of his heart before God (cf. 2 Cor 5:11). In this way Paul, to some degree, goes deeper than just laying his underlying motivation open to scrutiny.

3. With his prestige hanging in the balance, Paul expects to tip the scales in his favor by his reference to love. As Paul sees it, he is caught up in a very complicated situation, one in which reputation goes against reputation. Moreover, it is worth noting that Paul is by no means simply ready

(or does not see himself in a position of being able) to renounce all forms of boasting.[44] Paul is realistic enough to concede the necessity of this factor in social interaction. Since Paul well knows that, fundamentally, the issue here is one of competing claims for recognition, he is counting on the Corinthians to recognize his protestation of love as an indispensable extra factor that will prompt them to decide in his favor.

4. For all that, however, it is in the arena of reputation that Paul is doing battle, and he is unwilling to yield to his opponents. In this battle he recognizes that, if he is defeated (i.e., if he wins no more than the semblance of a following), then his affirmation of love is also no longer worth anything. Thus one can say that while, yes, the affirmation of love can settle the matter in Paul's favor, yet this can only happen if love is recognized as of equal value with reputation. This further means that, according to Paul, mutual respect is the indispensable basis for a genuine love-relationship. Without the dignity of each being maintained, without each one receiving recognition by the other, real love is impossible. The subtleties of experience both testify to this fact and bear it out.

SARCASTIC PROVOCATION

In 2 Cor 10–12 Paul repeatedly accuses the Corinthians of having evaluative criteria that are at odds with his own. His rather sarcastic tone in these chapters has often led to suggestions about differing sources. But this state of affairs is quite easily understandable as resulting from disappointed love, because in this section as well the theme is frequently Paul's love for the Corinthians. The especially striking feature is the way that Paul sets his own love in ironic contrast to the reproaches that were directed against him.[45] Paul also employs sarcasm as a stylistic device in 2 Cor 11:19 ("You gladly put up with fools, being wise yourselves!"). He does the same in 11:21; after enumerating the ways the Corinthians were mistreated by his opponents, he remarks, "I was too weak for that!" (In 11:21 we can see a passing reference to an actual charge leveled against Paul, namely, that in person he is "weak"; cf. 2 Cor 10:10). The same thing is going on in 12:16, where Paul obviously repeats the accusation of guile that had been raised against him—an accusation that he had already thrown back at his opponents in 4:2.

It seems to me that the link between 12:15 and 12:16 allows the root of the Pauline sarcasm to become clear. In the words of F. Lang, "Paul is not only ready to spare the Corinthians the cost of supporting him but even more to sacrifice himself for their souls' salvation (cf. Phil 2:17). For that, the apostle ought to be able to expect a corresponding response on the part of the community. If that doesn't happen, however, he at least deserves not to be loved any less for it. Paul here earnestly seeks to have his love for the community returned, but he is not certain of the outcome."[46] Against his willingness to go the extra mile for the community, Paul then sarcastically contrasts the reproach that had been directed against him, namely, that he had captured the community by guile. At this point the reader's expected response is, "How could that possibly be so?" The reverse situation is depicted in 11:20-21 (if someone exploits the community, they gladly put up with it—but the apostle does not!) Once again Paul contrasts his love with the behavior of his opponents. This is not done directly, but it is clearly the point lying behind the sarcasm (". . . we were too weak for that!").

When Paul does engage in the sort of self-praise usual in the community (evident from the side of the opponents), he does so in a way that is unmistakable. Then he immediately turns around and labels such behavior silly. It is as though he is playing a game, the intent of which is to make the opposite of his own behavior appear foolish. Paul takes his wounded love and tentatively insinuates that it is the opposite of what it really is, intending thereby to provoke an awareness of the fundamental difference in outlook between himself and his opponents. Yet he does all of this only because he is motivated by the desperate hope that the conflict will not persist, but rather that his provocative remarks will lead to a mutual understanding.

Finally, the sharpest attack on the opponents, in 10:12-18, is really oriented toward nothing other than confirming that the apostle was selected (by God) for just this community, that he must fulfill his commission (from God) precisely here, and that no one else is permitted to do what he is to do. What it finally comes down to, even here, is that the apostle can offer no other proof than the very relationship he has with this community.

In sum, the fundamental contrast of values that Paul sets in the foreground (boasting according to the flesh or in God) as well as the sarcastic tone of his presentation have as their purpose a defense of the apostle's love and also a demonstration of the deficiencies in the community's reciprocal "love," by showing to what absurd consequences it has led. The reasoning in chapters 10–12 is therefore essentially that of a reductio ad absurdum. Sarcasm, demonstration of absurdity, disqualifying of opponents—these are strong weapons. Paul brings them into the fray out of wounded love and in a desperate struggle to win reciprocating love from the Corinthians.[47]

Groaning and Longing

THE PAULINE MATERIAL

In 2 Corinthians 5 and Romans 8 Paul speaks of the groaning and longing of Christians with regard to their heavenly goal (longing to put on the heavenly dwelling; manifestation of sonship). The passages that specifically mention "groaning" (Rom 8:23; 2 Cor 5:2, 4) have important features in common. (a) Consistently the "groaning" refers to bodily existence.[48] This feature is extremely important when it comes to determining the religiohistorical context, knowledge of which in turn enables us to recognize and establish the distinctive (redactional) contribution of Paul himself. (b) In every case the "groaning" carries with it a strong sense of hopefulness, seen in the similar structuring of the sentences:

- "we groan . . . wait for adoption, the redemption of our bodies" (Rom 8:23)
- "we groan . . . longing to be clothed with our heavenly dwelling" (2 Cor 5:2)
- "we groan under our burden, because we wish not to be unclothed, but to be further clothed" (2 Cor 5:4)

This means that the groaning relates not only to painful existence in the present body but also and especially to the fact that the new, redeemed body is not yet present.

Paul thus does not merely go on about sufferings but uses physicality and illness as means for expressing his eschatological hope. The eschatological message thus penetrates a new hermeneutical medium, gaining a fresh and totally distinctive shape in the process. That is to say, the ability to speak of Christianity in this way gives it a new and unanticipated aspect. Now groaning about sufferings is not an end in itself but, Paul explains (in an indirect way), it is actually a way of lamenting the fact that we are not yet redeemed. Thus in Rom 8:22ff. he expands on a widely used image of pain in order to announce both a limitation on and a happy outcome for the present discomfort.

A look at some comparable texts from the New Testament milieu shows just where the theological contribution of Paul lies in this matter. Our focus must be the degree to which "groaning" is mentioned in conjunction with the concept of "the body," since it is here that Paul's central concern lies.

THE CORPUS HERMETICUM

In *Corpus Hermeticum* 23 (*Kore Kosmou*), chapter 33 speaks of souls embedded in bodies, where "they wailed and groaned" like wild animals in captivity. In contrast to Paul, here we are dealing with the relationship between body and soul in a dualistic understanding of human nature. Of major significance, however, is the fact that *Corp. Herm.* 23.33 makes lamentation for souls that are "no longer" free, while according to Paul Christians groan because they are "not yet" free (cf. Rom 8:22, where the mode of expression admittedly follows Hellenistic precedents). Paul has it that the whole creation will be liberated—a notion from the thinking of the *Corpus Hermeticum*. Nonetheless, the decisive feature in Paul, when viewed against the background of *Corpus Hermeticum*, is that the temporal dimension in the theme of groaning is reversed ("not yet" instead of "no longer"). This move also lets us see something of the power of hope, in the Pauline vision.

ANALOGIES WITH PHILO OF ALEXANDRIA

In Philo the groaning of Israel in Egypt (Exod 2:23) is repeatedly interpreted as referring to existence in the flesh; quite simply, "Egypt" is a metaphor for the body.

According to *On the Migration of Abraham* 14–15, the human power of understanding is "encumbered by bodily lusts" (cf. the imagery in 2 Cor 5:4). The "groaning" of Exod 2:23 is explained as follows: "Then they lamented and cried bitterly on account of the excess of physical endowments. . . ." Here again, in contrast to Paul, suffering is understood in terms of a dualistic human nature; the spiritual side of the human being is not able to blossom or develop. Paul, on the other hand, undoubtedly links the element of distress with actual physical pain.

The Pharaoh who lives "in us," according to *That the Worse Attacks the Better* 93f., is sensual desire. But those who groan about the old way of living (Exod 2:23), let the Pharaoh within them die, and turn imploringly toward God will not be rejected by God. Cain, who admitted no repentance, forms the contrast; "groaning" here stands for repentance. This nuance is missing in Paul—at least in the passages under immediate consideration.

Especially informative is the section dealing with groaning in the tractate *Allegorical Interpretation* (3.211-217).[49] This text, from the first century c.e., contains a detailed description of the significance of "groaning." As in Romans 8 so also here a connection is drawn between groaning and lamentation. Also resembling Paul is the way this text from Philo makes groaning an expression of the human condition, namely, that of sentient physical beings. According to Philo, groaning is either bad or good. It is bad when it is an expression of frustration over not having achieved some goal that would have satisfied human desires. It is good when it is an expression of remorse over something for which the gracious forgiveness of God is necessary. (In this case, groaning is a form of supplication.) Neither of these ways of speaking about groaning is to be found in Paul. To be sure, Paul also regards groaning as, among other things, a consequence of sin.[50] In Paul's case, however, groaning has no intrinsic connection with regret.

In sum, with both Philo and Paul groaning goes with the miseries of our existence as sentient physical beings. In Philo, groaning is always associated with agonized feelings in retrospect—much like a new convert groans over former wretchedness. With Paul, on the other hand, groaning is about distress in view of what is to come. This future orientation is distinctively Pauline.

THE WISDOM OF SOLOMON

"For the perishable body weighs down the soul, and the earthly tent burdens the thoughtful mind" (Wis 9:15, RSV). This text offers two verbal parallels to 2 Cor 5:4 ("weigh down" and "tent"), and a third could just as well be present ("groan"). Moreover, the passage from Wisdom is speaking about the difficulties of bodily existence. In contrast to Paul the focus of attention is only on the present reality of human existence, not on the eschatological future. No alternative to the present reality is envisioned.

With Paul, "groaning" receives a future orientation because, among other things, this theme stands in parallel with "yearning for" (*apokaradokia*[51] and *apekdechomai* in Rom 8:19; *epipothountes* in 2 Cor 5:2). This future orientation calls for a look at some parallels from apocalyptic writings.

APOCALYPTIC TEXTS

"Yearning" is a common topos in apocalyptic literature. For example, "There I wanted to dwell, and my spirit longed for that dwelling place; in that place my portion existed already before, for thus has it been allotted for me before the Lord of the Spirits" (*1 En.* 39:8). Note also Luke 17:22, where reference is made to the longing of the disciples to see even one of the days of the Son of Man. One possibility is that this passage is referring to the end of the disciples' own time of suffering.[52] But one could also relate this verse specifically to the question about signs of the end. In that case, we would have here a denial of the ability to recognize one of the final days for what it is (viz., one of the "days of the Son of Man"). The first of these two possibilities is the more likely. In the approaching days of distress, the disciples will be on the watch for the dawn of the new day. Taken this way, then, the text speaks to the theme of eschatological yearning in the days of the final distress. In contrast to Paul, this verse is not dealing with the miseries of a body stamped by sin but with agonies specific to the end of time. To be sure, the reader of Luke's Gospel might well identify his or her own time with the impending end. In sum, the Lukan text does not explicitly link the yearning for the end with the human condition or with the miseries of the body as such. This is different from Paul.

There is a whole series of texts according to which the eschatological distress has a distinctive effect on people whose physical condition or situation leaves them vulnerable: pregnant women (Mark 13:17a par.), nursing mothers (Mark 13:17b par.), the married in general (1 Cor 7:28b). In a sense, then, there is a tendency for the distress preceding the end to correspond to the physical condition or situation of the human being in view. It would only follow that one can find corresponding nuances to the yearning for the end.

RESULTS

As far as I can see, Paul is the only one who expounds the theme of "groaning" (over the circumstances of our embodied, mortal existence) with an eye toward hope, with reference to what is yet to come. He clothes his expectation concerning the coming redemption in the categories of physical affliction, no doubt because he himself is suffering and knows only too well what it is to "groan" (2 Cor 12:7-9). Thus, Paul latches on to apocalyptic language about yearning and specifically relates it to a renewed state of physicality at the end of time.

With both sorts of statements Paul, in the final analysis, is concerned with the overcoming of human transitoriness, of the deterioration unto death to which we are subject (Rom 8:20-21). His hope can transform our maladies by setting them in a new framework, a future-oriented perspective in terms of which we can see ourselves being liberated from our maladies. Paul takes very seriously the groaning and the yearning of humankind. He is not the enemy of the body that he is often made out to be. The real enemy is death.

Joy and Sorrow

Many texts speak of joy and sorrow in the same context. It therefore seems advisable to consider both of these in one section, with a glance at a few specific texts.

JOY

Joy in One Another

In 2 Cor 1:23—2:4 Paul speaks about reciprocal injuries in his relationship with the Corinthians, injuries that are still fresh in memory. He discusses this difficult situation with the help of the contrasting terms "joy" and "sorrow" (and their verbal equivalents). The section ends with mention of anguish and affliction, of tears, and of hearts inextricably intertwined. Then, suddenly, there falls from the lips of Paul a word that resembles a secret weapon: love. Paul sets his love for the community against all that has happened between them. With this move Paul hopes, at the very least, to avoid exacerbating the sadness that each side has caused the other. After all, the proclamation of the gospel ought quite clearly to be an occasion for joy ("We are workers with you for your joy, because you stand firm in the faith," 1:24).

If we read between the lines of this section, we can discern the following about this joy of which Paul speaks:

- Nowhere does the section 1:24—2:4 speak of God; God is neither the object nor the content of the joy.
- This joy is grounded instead in the reciprocal relationship between Paul and the community. Joy is the most precious aspect of the connection between them, and it is indivisible.[53] It is joy in one another and about one another. For Paul, the happy reciprocity in his relationship with the community is also a most valuable messianic blessing. In short, apostle and community each becomes grounds for the other to boast and take pride.
- Paul can speak in a quite unabashedly "egotistical" way about how he wants to feel joyous—indeed, *that* he will feel joyous (2:3). In speaking this way, Paul is referring quite directly to the reciprocal love he expects to receive from the community.[54] Nonetheless, a distinction between private feelings and public displays of joy applies to neither party here.
- According to 1:24, joy is the direct result of faith and is its basic form of expression. It is equivalent to what Paul elsewhere calls righteousness. Joy is thus more than just the emotional side of the experience of redemption, of being made anew. Joy also finds active expression within an interpersonal relationship—specifically, one in which each partner avoids causing pain or injury to the other.
- As the distinctive fruit of the gospel, then, joy serves as the measuring stick for each and every communicative act between Paul and the community. To be sure, instances of sorrow could also surface in this relationship, but such would never be the goal.
- To help others find joy is quite different from lording it over them (1:24). That is to say, joy is possible only within a truly reciprocal relationship; asymmetrical relationships based on power leave no room for joy. As

Paul writes this section of his letter, he renounces from the outset an authoritative position of power.[55] In so doing, he helps actualize the mutual joy of which he is speaking. In the way he addresses the community, Paul practices what he preaches.

In sum, joy in and for one another is nothing less than an aspect of the messianic vision. Here the reality of salvation consists in one's becoming a source of joy for another.[56] This is the shape of the experience of the new righteousness, which is to say, of faith. Particularly striking in this section is the way Paul maintains his sensitivity for interpersonal relationships by resisting any sort of pious, but nonetheless inopportune, tongue-lashing. Joy is known in social interaction or it is not known at all.

The Benefits Are Already Present

The durative aspect of faith—its connection with constancy and stability—is a particular focus of the Farewell Discourses of Jesus in the Gospel of John, where the term "abide" is a central motif. According to John 15:5-12, this "abiding" amounts to the maintaining of communion with Jesus and with one another. Such abiding is keeping the commandments, the ultimate one of which is the command to love, to be present for the other. Love of this sort, however, is not an end in itself. The final rationale and goal of this love, of this preservation of community, is formulated as follows: "I have said these things to you so that my joy might be in you, and that your joy may be complete" (15:11). The similarities to the Pauline statements in 2 Corinthians are very striking.[57] In both cases the joy of the one (Christ or the apostle) is also the joy of the others. This joy has its origin in love (of Christ, of the apostle), and from there it reaches out to bind each distinct partner into an inseparable union (Christ and the disciples, the apostle and the community), into something that both partners cherish. This is so because each so closely resembles the other in the things that matter most.

This joy, although an ultimate goal, is also a present possibility, even though it leaves room for perfection and completion (from the side of the disciples). Thus it is that, in contrast to Paul, John 15:11 qualifies the traditional eschatological aspect to some degree. In general, joy (like "grace") is a traditional feature of Jewish eschatological expectation. However, in the Gospel of John it is not necessary for the eschaton to be fully manifest before there can be a realization of the blessings of salvation (whether described as grace or as joy). Thus both "joy" and "grace" emerge as the preeminent firstfruits of Christian salvation.[58] Put another way, it is precisely the emotional features that characterize the fullness of salvation that are capable of being experienced here and now. Besides, what can one have that is greater than joy? Joy is the outcome of the way of God with human beings and, according to John 15, this joy is accessible even now. It is the fruit of the love that goes out from Jesus and is passed on to others. As with Paul, therefore, joy appears also here as the highest and final goal of the new, messianic community.

All those impatient questions about theodicy or the delay of the *parousia* appear of secondary importance when viewed in the light of this eschatology. The real goal is the joy to be found in one another. Following the texts from Paul and John here considered, one could perhaps also put it like this: God has deliberately restricted the divine work of salvation to the sending of a single man as Messiah in order to draw attention to what matters most of all—the immediate and continuing joy of fellowship.

Time of Sorrow and Time of Joy

While John 15:5-12 is oriented to the community itself, John 16:20-24 addresses the problematic relationship between the community and those who stand outside it (the "world"). The image of the woman in travail, for whom the grief and pain of birth is followed by joy over a new child, suggests both the connection between phases of a process and the idea of certainty concerning the onset of a time of joy. Although precisely when the disciples will again see Jesus remains unclear,[59] there can be little doubt that the "sorrow" of the disciples refers to the time when this Gospel was composed and to the relationship then existing between the Johannine community and the outsiders.

For our purposes, John 16:20-24 yields the following points:

1. Sorrow is like joy in that both are determined by social relationships. In the case of sorrow, the social dimension consists in relationship with other human beings; in the case of joy, it consists in once again seeing Jesus. The sorrow of which Jesus here speaks is thus determined neither by one's physical condition (e.g., mortal illness) nor by one's material status (e.g., impoverishment). The nature of one's relationship to another is the decisive factor. Concomitantly, as suggested by the metaphor of the birth of a new human being, joy is also to be realized within the milieu of social interaction. Only of such joy can it be said that it will never be taken away (16:22). But the threat of dissolution hovers over every joy that is based on material things.

2. The dynamic of relationship shapes even the joy that one experiences vis-à-vis the Father (16:23). The promise that every petition will be granted is associated with the image of the relationship the "children of the household" enjoy with their patriarch. Only "children of the household" are permitted to approach the father on such familiar terms, and only they can expect to have their wishes fulfilled. This notion of a special

intimacy between the head of a household and his children can be illustrated by the traditional Jewish tale of Honi the Circle-Drawer, who is permitted to ask God for everything, even when his requests are contradictory.[60] So it is hardly accidental that the "Father" is mentioned in John 16:23.

3. Joy is the mode in which the eschatological newness will be experienced when the persecution of the righteous (Jesus and his disciples) ceases. Although there is no mention here of heaven or of a new creation, the focus is on a joy that no one can take away. Even in the very different, apocalyptic description in Rev 21:1-4, joy is the culminating expression (". . . he will wipe every tear from their eyes"). The remark in Rev 21:4b that "the first things have passed away" corresponds to the comment in John 16:21 that "she no longer remembers the anguish." All memory of the old is simply extinguished.

4. Following three comments to the effect that the hearts of the disciples are sorrowful (John 14:1, 27; 16:6), one comes across the correspondingly positive remark ("your hearts will rejoice . . . ," John 16:22). The discourse thus leads the reader forward from sorrow to joy. The joy, whose completion (fulfillment) was proclaimed in 15:11, is now in 16:24 more precisely defined and hence brought closer to reality.

In every case joy is the fruit of peace with God and with one's fellow human beings. Even more, this joy is to be found within a close-knit community on the occasion of seeing Jesus once again and having all of one's prayers favorably answered by the Father. Joy is thus not a subjective feeling but to the highest degree a relational concept.

Ecstatic Joy amidst Suffering

Unlike John 16, in 1 Peter suffering and joy are not two consecutive phases of one process but are intertwined throughout. At the same time, no other New Testament writing emphasizes quite so intensively as 1 Peter the "ecstatic" character of this joy. Note the reference to joy in conjunction with glory (1:7-8; 4:13), with rejoicing (1:8; 4:13), and with "Spirit" (4:14). Even more striking is the way 1 Pet 1:8 describes this joy as "unspeakable."[61] Thus 1 Peter is not so much concerned to promise consolation for a community that is suffering persecution as it is to convince that community of the possibility, indeed the reality, of overcoming suffering through a joy that is already present.

A number of analogies can be found in the martyrological literature. So, for example, immediately before death the martyr beholds the glory of God (Acts 7:55a), sees the Lord directly (Acts 7:55b-56; *Martyrdom of Polycarp* 2:2), or even speaks with the Lord (*Martyrs of Lyon* 51). The glory of the Lord rests upon the suffering martyr;[62] the martyr is filled with the Holy Spirit;[63] the martyr is able to rejoice because the reward for martyrdom stands close at hand.[64] More distantly related are those texts according to which the witness and potential martyr can in some sense count on the support of the Holy Spirit while being interrogated (Mark 13:11; Matt 10:19-20; Luke 12:11-12). The only difference is that, in these cases, the situation is not explicitly one of execution but of judgment.[65] Be that as it may, the gift of the Spirit to martyrs, as well as their visions, are themes that can be traced back to traditional depictions of the hour of death of exceptionally endowed individuals.[66] Since the death of a martyr is a public event, when placed in such a context these traditional elements acquire a new significance; they become contemporized. First Peter thus utilizes features that properly belong to the traditional depiction of the death of the righteous witness whose sufferings already lie in the past—i.e., who did not have to endure the bloody death of a martyr. The occasion for the composition of 1 Peter did not involve actual martyrdoms, but the author of this letter nonetheless elucidated the situation of his community by blending traditional features of the death of the righteous witness with elements from the martyrological tradition.

Concerning the joy of which 1 Peter speaks, the following observations are pertinent:

1. First Peter understands death not as a somber finality but as a transition and the beginning of glorification. The author then applies this vision to a situation of Christian suffering. His theological and pastoral contribution lies in the way he understands the Christian life, with its suffering, from the perspective of an alternative understanding of death.

2. Common to all the texts is the almost physical nearness of the solicitous God when human beings are in extreme distress, suffering for their righteousness or for the sake of God. Ecstatic joy lies as close to suffering as laughter to weeping. Here the gap that separates suffering and joy has become very narrow indeed.

3. In early Christian accounts of martyrdom, the temporal proximity of heavenly blessedness is emphasized in precisely the same way. The culminating moment of the martyr's struggle is also the moment just before victory. The victory is close at hand; it is like the sun about to burst over the horizon; it will become manifest as joy. What has already been said about the visionary aspect of faith applies here as well: in a time of distress, precisely the one who suffers for his or her convictions actualizes the reality of God. The attacks from outside, which lead even to physical destruction, make the martyr ready to perceive an alternative "outside." It is not some personal suffering that the martyr must bear but rather one arbitrarily

imposed from without; the martyr does not suffer for a personal opinion, but for the Christian faith.[67] In both cases the martyr suffers because of the inworking of something "outside." In regard to the "outside," which is God, faith wins such a strong visionary power that death can be interpreted as the threshold to the reality of God. In such a context death appears weak, even as something that can be completely transformed.

Grieve Not the Holy Spirit

When one is admonished not to grieve the Holy Spirit, it is presupposed that the Spirit is manifest in joy, indeed is in some sense equivalent to the sensation of joy. As stated in Eph 4:30, "Do not grieve the Holy Spirit of God, with which you were marked with a seal for the day of redemption."[68] When viewed in the light of parallels in *Shepherd of Hermas*, Mand. 10:1-3, the significant features of this comment are the following:

1. Here is outlined an explicit psychology along the lines of the ancient understanding of the emotions. The strongest link is with Stoic theory, according to which sorrow is an important "passion" (Greek: *pathos*).[69] Conversely, the joyous character of virtue is emphasized.[70] The *pathos* of sorrow allows both doubt and impetuous anger to enter to soul.[71]

2. The doctrine of God, the rationale for cult, the understanding of "Spirit," ethics, soteriology—all these are here developed from a psychological base. Because of the juxtaposition of joy and sadness and the connection with a doctrine of spirits, one finds here a general dualistic view like the two-spirits teaching of the Qumran texts and the *Testaments of the Twelve Patriarchs*. As in the conceptual world of demonology and exorcism, so also here the driving of spirits out of the soul, and the entering of the same into the soul, plays a considerable role. Even the Holy Spirit is mentioned as being driven out by sorrow (*Herm. Mand.* 10:1, 2).

3. In contrast to Paul, it is clearly and unambiguously stated that the Spirit of God can be experienced as joy. Joy is not a fruit of the Spirit (thus Paul, e.g., Gal 5:22); the Spirit essentially *is* cheerfulness (*Herm. Mand.* 10:3).

This sharpening of the opposition between joy and sorrow is noteworthy.[72] Most likely there are three causal factors at work here: (a) a pastoral need to counteract sadness, dejection, lassitude, and the tendency toward doubt that follows in the wake of these feelings; (b) the inclination of some New Testament writers to regard joy as in fact the essence of Christianity (in addition to the above, cf. the centrally positioned imperatives in 2 Cor 1:24; 13:11; 1 Thess 5:16.); (c) last but not least, Stoic doctrines about emotion.

Doing Works of Joy

First Clement in chapters 31–33 exhibits a noteworthy conception of the justification of human beings, one in which joy plays a significant role. In an initial phase, the human being acquires righteousness in that God takes the initiative and calls the human being, reckoning as righteousness the faith of the human being. In a second phase, the priority of God appears in another form; now God becomes a model after which the righteous are to pattern themselves. Specifically, God performs works purely out of joy, as embellishment and ornamentation.[73] The decisive point is that God exults in his works, adorns himself with them, and rejoices over them. The human being, already justified, should proceed in the same way. To the extent that the ensuing works are understood as proceeding from joy or as leading to joy, their character as coerced acts (imposed from without) slips away. Instead, such activity takes on a certain aesthetic or playful character. Following this line of thinking, then, the basis for Christian behavior would be (to speak colloquially) "because it's fun."

One might object that the dimension of human sinfulness is not being taken seriously enough here. Yet, repetitious mention of sin loses the power to motivate. I think it would be worthwhile to pay more attention to the position adopted in *1 Clement*. This could have a certain corrective function, in that Christian joy over being redeemed would not so quickly and easily be dampened by the dourness of those who are inclined rather to ponder the bitterness of the unredeemed condition.

SORROW

Sorrow and Openness

In the world of the Bible, sorrow is not a private matter but in every case a public act.[74] This is indicated by the words typically found in association with "sorrow," words such as "dirge," "lament/lamentation,"[75] "cry/cry out," "plead," or "groan." Additional evidence for the public nature of sorrow is provided by the gestures, spontaneous or symbolic, by which one communicates one's disposition to bystanders.[76] Thus, for example, Ezra tears his garments, including the holy mantle, pulls out hair from his head and his beard, and sits down pensively (1 Esd 8:71 [LXX]). Second Sam 19:1 reports that David was visibly disturbed, that he withdrew and wept. According to Tob 3:1, Tobit wept and prayed in anguish or, in a textual variant, cried out while weeping and began to pray while groaning. Isaiah 15:2-3 describes the behavior considered appropriate to lamentation for the dead: the hair of the head is cropped close, beards are cut off, people go about in mourning garments, beating themselves on the chest and crying aloud while weeping—all this while "on their housetops and in their plazas." A similar scene is described in Sir 38:16-17, where people lament bitterly, wail fervently, get agitated, mourn, and carry out the expected funeral rites.

Likewise in New Testament times, sorrow has a strongly "active" nature; it hardly amounts to just an inner reflex, a more or less autonomous emotion that suffuses a person, an emotion that either is suppressed or that dangerously takes possession of a person. In customary and legally prescribed ritual, an external "objectivity" was imposed on the subjective interior of the person. This ensured that sorrow would never be just an emotion, but also an action outwardly directed. The carrying out of the ritual thus made possible an overcoming of subjective boundaries and permitted the isolated pain of an individual to be submerged in a formalized, customary form of expression. The tendency frequently arose, in all of this, to venerate the dead.[77] Through the ritual, finally, neighbors and distant relatives were drawn into the scene. The upshot is that sorrow never had to be experienced in isolation.

The communal character of ritual sorrow as well as its nature thus had the effect that everything lying outside the individual was brought into a much more immediate relationship with the mourner's psyche than is the case with us. One offshoot of this situation is that lamentation was made not just for "private" tragedies but also for such "public" events as political grievances and persecution of the community (John 16:20). In short, all situations of suffering, even political ones, could become occasions for rituals of lamentation. Our contemporary way of experiencing the sorrow that is coupled with loss, namely, as something exclusively subjective and widely regarded as "negative," stands in sharp contrast. Because sorrow is today regarded as hardly more than an indistinct pain, the sorrowful can no longer take control of this pain. Instead, one either passively yields to it or else tries to drive it away.

Healing of Sorrow

Biblical texts mention different types of healing for human sorrow.

1. First, there is a purely physical overcoming of sorrow. An illustration of this can be seen in Gen 25:29. According to Prov 31:6 wine and drunkenness must suffice for the overcoming of distress when the king does not stand up for righteousness.

2. There is a way of overcoming sorrow through social interaction. Here one thinks of the summons to let oneself be consoled (Sir 38:17) and also of the summons to leave off mourning after the time allotted for it has passed (Sir 38:20; cf. 30:23). One is also to pay heed to the elderly so that they are not unnecessarily troubled (Sir 3:12). In this same category

belong the overcoming of suffering through seeing again (John 16:22) and through forgiveness (2 Cor 2:7).

3. Religion offers the third way of overcoming suffering. In 1 Esd 9:52-53 (LXX) Ezra summons the people to grieve no longer, for the day is holy to the Lord, and the Lord will exalt the people. According to Tob 11:17-18 (LXX *B*, *A*), Sarah is encouraged by her mother to be confident, relying as she does on the grace of God. (Instead of the usual Greek term *charis* ["grace"], *S* offers in the same place the related term *chara* ["joy"].) Tobit 13:14 says that seeing the glory of God makes joyful those who must now suffer in sadness. In the Psalms the petitioner repeatedly summons his disquieted soul to hope in God, from whom salvation is expected (cf., e.g., Pss. 42:5, 11 [Heb. 6, 12]; 43:5). Wisdom 8:9 also belongs in this category; living in harmony with wisdom yields good counsel and encouragement amid cares and grief.

Nowadays languor, quietude, and curtailed involvement with others characterize occasions such as these. Against this background it is especially striking how taciturn withdrawal is ruled out by the sorts of reactions mentioned above, and especially under (3), the cultic (in which area the Psalms belong).

The Sorrow of the Disciples in the World

The Farewell Discourses of Jesus in the Gospel of John are structured, at least in part, as consolatory speech, elements of which appear in John 13:36—14:4. The same holds true with regard to John 14:28-29, which give the departure of Jesus a positive meaning. This is in keeping with the consolatory speeches of antiquity, which typically mentioned the good that could come out of death. John 16:33 is an especially clear instance of consolatory speech, in that here the reader is led to take yet another step; the departure of Jesus is not only something good in and of itself but it is also the means by which sorrow is transformed into joy.[78]

Several features of the Farewell Discourses in the Gospel of John are worthy of note.

1. There is no mention of sorrow on the part of Jesus himself, despite his imminent leave-taking and impending martyrdom.

2. Nowhere in the Farewell Discourses, apart from John 16:20, is any allowance made for the sorrow of the disciples. (The most accommodating remark in this direction occurs in John 14:27-28.) In fact, the implication of John 16:6-7 is that the followers of Jesus should not grieve at all. For ancient thought such a notion would be downright offensive, since "rites of lamentation counted as unconditional obligation."[79]

3. The disciples feel sorrow because they no longer see Jesus (John 14:27; 16:6). But the promise that they will see Jesus again is not the only feature that is to soothe their sorrow. In addition, Jesus' going to the Father already works a positive benefit in that Jesus thereby radically "shortens" the distance to the Father, not only for himself but also for those who are "in" him. Henceforth, like Jesus, the disciples belong no more merely to the earthly but also to the heavenly world (John 14:20-22).

4. Closely connected to this is the fact that the disciples must experience sorrow "in the world" because of the world's enmity (John 16:20; cf. 15:18-19).

It becomes apparent that the distinctive goal of Jesus' argumentation is to lead the disciples away from a "false" sorrow to "true" sorrow that can become joy. Sorrow as an experience of loss is thereby transformed into sorrow as affliction within a relationship; the former is to be seen as actually a sorrow of the latter type. The immediate sorrow over the death of Jesus is contained within and deepened by the sorrow that is tied to relationship with Jesus. Both sorts of sorrow are then soothed by directing attention to the experience of the continued presence of Jesus (with respect to the Paraclete, the image of the vine, the theme of remaining "within"). Everything points toward the overcoming of the sorrow.

In sum, the disciples are not simply forbidden to feel sorrowful; the negativities of their experience are taken seriously. Through a prudent differentiation of types of sorrow, however, their experience is transformed into a positive awareness of how to experience divine presence. With an overcoming of the pain of absence, the suffering attendant upon persecution is also relativized—although not removed. A circumscribed space is left for sorrow (John 16:16, 20); consolation does not follow immediately.

Our culture speaks almost exclusively of sorrow within the context of loss, and almost never of sorrow because of specific circumstances that affect a whole group or community. Such a move individualizes sorrow, rendering shapeless both its nature and its causes. The biblical treatment of sorrow gives us occasion critically to ponder our narrowing of the scope of sorrow.

The Anger and Sorrow of Jesus

Next to Mark 14:34, Mark 3:5 is the most explicit statement about emotions on the part of Jesus ("He looked around at them with anger; he was grieved at their hardness of heart . . ."). Here Mark alerts his readers to an important conflict, indeed to a turning point. (The parallel passages in Matthew and Luke do not offer—or have left out—any such reference to the emotions of Jesus.) The emphasis in Mark arises from the combining of sorrow with anger, a juxtaposition that would have been unsuitable for a sage in antiquity.[80] Ephesians 4:31 speaks in the same vein.

For Mark, the combination of sorrow and anger on the part of Jesus is relevant because Jesus is an authoritative personage and therefore one whose reactions are not inconsequential. In contrast to both Matthew and Luke, Mark stands within the tradition of the Old Testament and early Judaism. In this tradition "anger" and "sorrow" share a close semantic relationship; both terms appear in the Septuagint as renderings of the Hebrew root *qzf*. Moreover, the terms often appear in close conjunction, and both are attributed to God.[81] Noteworthy in Mark 3:5, however, is the fact that the sorrow follows the anger, and not the reverse. This is an indication of the way Jesus will respond to what develops as a consequence of the decision by the Pharisees to destroy him (3:6). Even more, however, it is a cue for the readers about how they should be ready to transform their own initial reactions to the scene.

Sorrow and Materiality

In this context some of what Irenaeus of Lyon reports concerning the Valentinians is of interest. Among the teachings of the Valentinians about what transpired outside the pleroma, Irenaeus recounts that they had the following to say regarding Achamoth (female offspring of Sophia):

> On account of that passion in which she had been involved, and because she alone had been left without, she then resigned herself to every sort of that manifold and varied state of passion to which she was subject; and thus she suffered grief, on the one hand, because she had not obtained the object of her desire, and fear, on the other hand, lest life itself should fail her, as light had already done, while, in addition, she was in the greatest perplexity. All these feelings were associated with ignorance. And this ignorance of hers was not like that of her mother, the first Sophia, an Aeon, due to degeneracy by means of passion, but to an [innate] opposition [of nature to knowledge]. Moreover, another kind of passion fell upon her (Achamoth), namely, that of desiring to return to him who gave her life. This collection [of passions] they declare was the substance of the matter from which this world was formed. For from [her desire of] returning [to him who gave her life], every soul belonging to this world, and that of the Demiurge himself, derived its origin. All other things owed their beginning to her terror and sorrow. For from her tears all that is of a liquid nature was formed; from her smile all that is lucent; and from her grief and perplexity all the corporeal elements of the world. For at one time, as they affirm, she would weep and lament on account of being left along in the midst of darkness and vacuity; while, at another time, reflecting on the light which had forsaken her, she would be filled with joy, and laugh; then, again, she would be struck with terror; or, at other times, would sink into consternation and bewilderment."[82]

In this remarkable text, the Stoic teaching about emotions has been expanded into a cosmogony, in the process making use of the form of myth (artificially, to be sure). The genesis of the macrocosm is explained in the form of anthropomorphisms, a move that allows for the emergence of a corresponding ethic on the microcosmic scale. Thus, if the heavier materials arose out of the sadness and the tears of a being imagined along the lines of a person, then that has immediate significance for tears, sadness, and fear on the part of human beings. These are things that allow human beings to be close to the material realm. Moreover, this whole world has arisen out of yearning for the highest Father, or out of sadness about the remoteness of God. Sadness both remains tied to perception of the absence of the highest Father and draws attention toward that parent. We see here one way in which God is experienced, taking "experience" in the broadest sense of the word.

Because Valentinus used the genre of myth, he also accepted the fundamental mythic postulate, namely, that no solid line of separation can be drawn between human beings and the world. The fate of both is determined by one and the same course. As a result, a genuine "sympathy" exists between human beings and the world, between the microcosm and the macrocosm. Precisely this communality of suffering contributes to the makeup of the poetic content of the myth cited above. If all water is, as it were, the tears of a woman—and if everything material is, as it were, sadness over the remoteness of God—then all things in this world are drawn together into a tight, sibling-like relationship. And, along the lines of what Paul says in Rom 8:19-23, a common yearning can speak in words infused with shared emotion.

8

Suffering

Setting the Historical-Psychological Question

The New Testament letters belong also to a genre well-attested in antiquity, namely the diatribe (written pastoral advice). It is thus advisable to approach a study of 1 Peter from several angles. For example, what experiences of suffering are being assumed in the letter? How or by what means were the addressees' interpreted and thereby dealt with? Paramount among the historical presuppositions, which here are important, is the realization that we are dealing with Christians who are suffering slanderous reproaches from their pagan neighbors because of their Christianity. The suffering presupposed here is not generic. The semantic range of the words "suffering" and "glory" is also significant.

Seriousness and Avoidance

The writer of the letter takes seriously and does not hesitate to speak of only one aspect of the addressees' particular experiences. In this context it is noteworthy that nothing is said about any experiencing of the risen Christ. Peter appears only as a witness to the suffering of Christ (5:1), not as one who has witnessed appearances of the risen Lord. Given the way the letter strives to advance the authority of Peter, that fact must be important. Similarly, the letter does not speak of Christ as directly accessible in his current state of glory but only of a future revealing of the glory of Christ (4:13). The writer does not try to direct the attention of the community to something they cannot see. Instead, the suffering Christ occupies the center of attention in this letter. The writer thus refrains from depicting Christ's "glory." Note how, in the important section 1:3-7, the recipients of the letter are held firmly to their current situation by the use of passive verb forms all the way up to v. 6a. The distressful situation of the addressees is kept in the forefront, which in turn keeps the central theme of the letter constantly in view. Only at the end of the letter do we find the words, "Cast all your anxieties on him" (5:7).

On the other hand, some thorny issues are treated very circumspectly. That the community genuinely "believes" is taken for granted (1:5, 7). The writer carefully avoids voicing any doubt about the faith of the community, despite the fact that the relatively short time that has elapsed since the community's conversion would presumably raise concerns of this sort.[1] Instead, he turns the issue around in such a way that it has to do with a trial of faith; all the suffering of the community is interpreted through the category of "testing" (1:7). The hardships of the community are discussed only obliquely, by means of metaphor (i.e., purification by fire).

Interpretation of Suffering

There are sound pastoral reasons why the writer of 1 Peter falls back on customary concepts as he comes to grips with the suffering of his addressees. It is hardly accidental that there are striking parallels between 1 Pet 1:6 and Jas 1:2-3, 12 (similarities also appear in Hellenistic-Jewish literature intended for new converts, such as the *Testament of Job*). The addressees in effect are given a diagnosis of their suffering, one that makes use of concepts familiar to them (e.g., faith being "tested," "examined," "tried," or "purified" as gold by fire).

It is striking that the writer does nothing to diminish the reality of the community's suffering. He seeks instead to demonstrate that the community's suffering is necessary and goes with their status. The addressees should come to a religious understanding of their isolation and thereby actually affirm it as inevitable from their having been chosen by God, as part of their new status as a holy people and a royal priesthood. In short, they are to regard their painfully experienced isolation from a religious perspective—as yet another instance of the world's reaction to God's elect.

Contrasting Experiences

The writer of 1 Peter does not directly address his recipients until 1:6, when he says in most stirring fashion, ". . . you rejoice." Prior to this the recipients had been referred to in the third person. Even for a time after the "you rejoice" of v. 6a, the verbs used are in the passive voice. The theme of joy predominates, setting the tone for all other specifications, and is taken up again in v. 8b ("you believe in him and rejoice with an indescribable and glorious joy"). In 4:14 the addressees are called blessed "because the spirit of glory, which is the Spirit of God, is resting on you," which might be a reference to ecstatic or charismatic experiences (cf. 4:10). In any case, the Christian faith of the addressees is interpreted in this direction—related to some unseen reality. The promise of blessing in 4:14 contains an unmistakably charismatic element. In all these cases, what is most striking is that the joy referred to is a sharp contrast to the present suffering (note how the two themes are intertwined in 1:6-8 and 4:13-15). In other words, it is as though the addressees are standing before a double set of doors. Through one set comes the abuse and the mistreatment they are experiencing, while through the other the divine Spirit of glory comes to them and rests on them. One thing they cannot do is find security through their own efforts. Neither, however, can they look only to the future for surcease of their sorrow. In their difficult bind, a certain sort of blessedness is nonetheless already theirs.

Experiencing Being Valued

The addressees of 1 Peter are not merely sorrowful but are being oppressed by others; they are experiencing considerable difficulty in social interaction with their neighbors. This letter lets us see that the issue at hand especially concerns public reputation in the face of social ostracism. This is why the letter is so strongly oriented toward being valued. Right at the beginning, the letter names a whole array of worthwhile and desirable features: mercy, living hope, resurrection, inheritance (imperishable, undefiled, unfading), power of God, faith, salvation (1:3-5). Although the community is now being afflicted, it also stands amid realities of another sort (a testing of faith, praise, glory, honor), highly valued realities that glitter like gold. Praise, glory, and honor are basically social values, and so the addressees are here being enabled to experience compensation for precisely that which is being denied to them. Implied as compensation for them is also the notion of righteousness, another social value.

Splendor and Glory

The theme of "glory" is also significant in 1 Peter. The Spirit of glory (comparable to the *Shekinah* in Jewish tradition) already rests on the community. The praise associated with glory is also to be understood with reference to the dynamics of social reputation. Praise is something one gives to another by way of recognition, which means that praise is a socially determined reality. So the praise the writer directs to the addressees, along with the stirring images from the Old Testament interspersed between 1:24 and 2:11 and in 4:17 and 5:8-9, is intended to awaken or arouse within them a positive religious experience, a firm sense of self-worth. Thus, although it is only to be expected that the addressees would feel self-pity, the writer intervenes, directing their attention to the glory of God and the applicability to them of powerful images from Scripture. This move on the part of the writer is all the more effective in that the theme of glory is not overly specified.

Suffering and Dualism

Especially noteworthy in this letter is how much the experience of suffering leads the community toward a dualistic perception of reality. In 1 Peter suffering is juxtaposed to glory, sadness to joy, the painful experience of being tested in a fiery furnace (1:7; 4:12) to the splendor of the glorified, the present to the future. Indeed, in New Testament times generally, the experience of being disdained or persecuted draws in its wake a dualistic experience of reality. For example, the question of the extent to which the execution of Jesus accelerated the tendency toward a Gnostic dualism among some of his followers cannot be ignored.[2] More germane here is the specific kind of dualism invoked by the writer of 1 Peter in responding to the painful experiences of those who had to endure this type of early Christian persecution.

Notice that the writer of 1 Peter does not separate humankind into opposing categories (good/evil, righteous/unrighteous). It is quite striking that those persecuting the Christian community are not labeled as evil, nor are the Christians automatically placed on the side of the angels! It would be an oversimplification, therefore, to say that the suffering of these Christians is the suffering of the righteous. The argument of the writer of 1 Peter instead starts like this: It would be good if you would suffer as do the righteous (3:17). Neither does the writer speak of any dualism between death and life; his primary distinction is between suffering and glory. Among other things, this indicates that the addressees are not actually facing death but are experiencing "only" social disdain. The "religious" sorts of consolations that are offered (esteem, glory, etc.) likewise correspond to the fact that the "persecution" of these Christians is largely a matter of social opprobrium.[3]

Suffering as Origin of the Exhortation

In responding to the community's suffering, the writer does not direct attention to the past, nor does he raise questions about this or that person's guilt with regard to the present state of affairs. Instead, he resolutely directs his gaze toward the future. (a) He tells the addressees that they can (not: should) expect the revealing of their salvation (1:5). This has already been prepared for them; it needs only to be unveiled. (b) He uses the community's sufferings as an occasion for exhortation, telling the addressees that if they must suffer they should strive to suffer as righteous, not as unrighteous persons. If they were to suffer as evildoers, that would only be a matter of getting what one deserved. But having to put up with undeserved suffering opens a window to the future.

The writer appears to know from personal experience that the fact of suffering in itself often prompts disdain and disrespect in the eyes of others. What really matters, however, is how a person bears up under suffering. To assist the addressees in bearing their burdens, the writer reminds them that suffering is not just a matter of fate but an occasion for exemplifying righteousness. This certainly includes renouncing any urge to take violent counter-measures. To be sure, suffering is not simply to be accepted passively. The author wants the addressees to transform the potential passivity of the persecuted and the oppressed into an active expression of Christian obedience. The "activity" of righteousness, in this case, begins with submissive obedience, and the writer's appeal for precisely such a response deflects any questions about the possible guilt of the community. Suffering presents a new opportunity to demonstrate what it is to be a Christian—to renounce force, in imitation of Jesus. In this sense, suffering is a particular sort of "grace" (2:20).

Solidarity and Discipleship

The Christian suffers not alone but in communion with Jesus Christ, whom the Christian imitates and follows. No other New Testament writing emphasizes these features as strongly as 1 Peter, which thoroughly "Christianizes" suffering. The imitation of Christ acquires a moral significance— adopting the attitude of Christ.

That is not the whole picture, however. Although the Christian participates in the suffering of Christ, in another sense the suffering of Christ is unique because it has significance for the sins of all—something that can hardly be said of the suffering of individual Christians. The letter to the Hebrews recognizes this same schema of similarity and dissimilarity of the suffering of the Christian and that of Christ.

The Christian's suffering in communion with other Christians does not receive much mention. Even Peter is not a fellow-suffering Christian but a witness of the sufferings of Christ (5:1). The main point the writer wants to get across is that the Christian's sole point of orientation is to be Christ himself.

For the experience of suffering on the part of Christians in our time, Jesus Christ only rarely has the function of co-sufferer. This is certainly related to the fact that in today's church as a whole Jesus is not seen as having become truly human.

Suffering and the Experience of Time

The sort of expectation associated with early Christian eschatology receives a distinctive stamp in 1 Peter, which tries to make its addressees see that their suffering will last only a short time. Clear indications of this are given at both the beginning (1:6) and the end (5:10).

In addition, the repeated association of "suffering" with "glory" makes it obvious to the reader that the time of suffering will be limited, and that a better time will follow. This notion of two subsequent phases renders unnecessary any docetic denial of suffering. Precisely the opposite of docetism is emphasized; any glossing over of suffering is both prohibited and rendered impossible by the contrast. Juxtaposed to the brevity of the suffering is the imperishability of what is awaited (1:4), of what has already been prepared and only awaits its final unveiling (1:5).

Suffering as Grace

The calumny and defamation to which they are subject leads the Christians to an authentic encounter with Jesus Christ himself. Precisely these afflictions become the means to enable them to experience what it is to be Christian. Through these afflictions they experience true communion with Jesus and realize why they have become Christians. This is what it all comes down to. This encounter with Christ in the midst of suffering is a form of divine grace (2:20). Here one can see the handwriting of God, as it were.

Of course, it is not just any kind of suffering that leads to an authentic encounter with divine grace. It does not have this outcome when people are afflicted on account of their own guilt, and it does not happen to those who have nothing to do with Christianity. The encounter with grace follows in the wake of suffering when Christians, through their communion with Christ, find themselves participating in the trajectory that runs from suffering to glory.

Historical-Psychological Interpretation

One can investigate how 1 Peter interprets or reworks the interpretation of suffering in both christological and eschatological directions by considering the concomitant experiences that are involved.

1. Relief. The writer systematically unburdens the addressees of the pressures under which they have been living. There can be no talk of their own guilt in the situation—precisely the contrary (2:24). This means they can cast their anxiety on the Lord (5:7a). Of crucial importance is the fact that the tense situation between addressees and persecutors is defused. No transformation is called for that simply turns the tables. The persecutors are not evildoers. In fact, they may even prove capable of praising God for the good works done by the Christian community (2:12). What brings relief, above all, is solidarity with Jesus Christ, the martyr. Such solidarity softens the oppressive situation (social isolation) and at the same time ameliorates anxiety about the future. The writer strongly emphasizes the christological dimension because it is only in communion with Jesus, and not with other people, that the opportunity for relief is to be found. The suffering of Jesus is similar to the suffering of the community, but it is also quite different. It is the latter dimension of Jesus' suffering that can provide a way out of the necessity for suffering itself.

2. Activation. The addressees are not just passively to hold on but are to practice an active sort of endurance, following in the footsteps of Christ. All should honor the king; husbands should honor their wives.

3. Affirmation of Identity. The persecuted should not buckle under, because the very reasons for their persecution are also the pathways that lead to an opening up of the future and its promises. A central concern of 1 Peter is to provide its addressees a measure of psychological stability, and it expresses this concern by countering any urge to give up and to accept the judgment of the persecutors.

4. Acceptance of Negativity. There is to be no glossing over of suffering. This can be so because suffering is not the final word but a preliminary phase of a larger process. Thus the burdens of the present can be lifted by directing attention to a different sort of future.

5. Joy in Suffering. The attention of the addressees is directed not only to the intangible and to what lies in the future. Among the psychologically interesting parts of the letter are the sections dealing with the blessedness and the joy that are already present. It is to these realities that the letter tries to direct attention. The writer maintains that the community already finds itself in a joyful state. Other early Christian witnesses likewise men-

tion the connection between persecution and joy (e.g., Matt 5:11-12 and Jas 1:2).[4] The genre of the beatitude also reflects a close connection to the theme of present joy, as is suggested by such passages as 1 Pet 4:14, Matt 5:11, and Jas 1:12. Apparently the reference in passages such as these is to experiences of unadulterated, ecstatic joy within groups of early Christians undergoing persecution. Following the clues given by the relevant texts, this joy has three main aspects, each grounded immanently.

- Because Christ is already glorified, joy has come near. It is a matter of experiencing the glorified Christ, through the "spirit of glory" (4:14). Also 1:8-9 leads us to believe that we are here dealing with experiences with the risen Christ. To be with Christ where he now is—that is our goal.
- It is precisely joyful acceptance of suffering in the present that determines one's participation in the coming glory. (The "so that" of 4:13 is to be taken most seriously.) The dualism involved here is psychological; future glory, instead of eternal misery and punishment, is determined by present joy in the midst of suffering. Just as in the case of finding freedom from worry (1 Pet 5:7), so also here the attitude that is demanded of the addressees reaches beyond intelligibility to the level of emotionality. At first glance it is outright nonsensical to demand of people that they find joy in the necessity of suffering. But consistently carrying out the dualism involved here makes no other option possible.
- A psychosociological argument is suggested by a glance at the Jewish apocalyptic text *2 Bar.* 52:6:[5] The pressure being applied from without is felt so strongly by the oppressed that they can no longer bear it directly. As a way of "venting," they are inclined toward ecstatic experiences. Put another way, being in the depths of affliction makes one receptive to the charismatic experience of joy that is no longer tied to anything earthly. It is well known that religious-charismatic experiences go hand in hand with belonging to an oppressed minority. When they find themselves in an otherwise hopeless situation, the oppressed latch on to the joy that they can still find in ecstatic experience, thereby in a certain sense appropriating the anticipated liberation. All these dynamics apply particularly well to the early Christian situation in which it was "known" that the glorified Lord could be present through the gift of the Spirit (1 Pet 4:14). Here one could go on to ask about the relationship, in general, of the experience of the "Spirit" in situations where people find themselves marginalized.[6]

9

Religion

Faith

The biggest barrier to an appropriate understanding of New Testament statements about faith is that, for us, the word "faith" often stands for Christianity as such. In the New Testament, however, the semantic range of the word is considerably narrower.

On the plane of experience, faith as presented in New Testament texts is like an ellipse. Faith is oriented around two foci. One I call the aspect of encounter, the other the aspect of power. The experience of faith is jointly related to these two foci. Crucial to the understanding of faith as here presented is the realization that it is a distinctive way of perceiving reality. One of the main consequences of faith is the overcoming of fear/anxiety.

THE ASPECT OF ENCOUNTER

This aspect of faith is actually a mode of reaction to persons or objects that one encounters. Faith begins as such a reaction.

Encounters with Persons

We begin with two observations. (a) In Luke 7:36-50, Jesus interprets the devotion of the prostitute as faith (v. 50). Specifically, she wets Jesus' feet with her tears, dries them with her hair, anoints them with oil, and kisses them (v. 45). In 7:47 this activity is also summarized as love. Such love is called faith because it is directed toward Jesus. (b) Similarly, the trust in Jesus shown by the woman with the bloody flow is called faith (Mark 5:28-34). In both cases we are dealing with blind, unhesitating trust. In other words, turning to Jesus without reserve is already faith; Jesus himself calls it such. In these two encounters physical contact is especially important. The latitude Jesus displays in response to having been touched by the women, however, is more than mere tolerance, and the women, for their part, are more than representatives of Christians in general. These women have turned to Jesus in great fervor. In Mark 5, Jesus is the woman's last hope (vv. 25-26); in Luke 7 the woman's actions can appropriately be called love. Faith here is not some half-hearted interest in Jesus but an intense cluster of concrete acts in which two persons lay open the deep concerns of their hearts.

Paul also speaks of the intensity that marks genuine faith, most extensively in Rom 4:18-21. The *plérophorétheis* of v. 21 literally means "to be filled up by something," or "to want something totally and completely." (The emphasis is on the aspect of totality or entirety). And yet faith here does not consist of a lifelong attitude or state of mind but the accepting of a promise, never deviating from the conviction that the promise will indeed be fulfilled.

The faith of which Hebrews 11 speaks also has clear personal aspects. In v. 11, faith amounts to regarding as trustworthy (credible) the one who had given the promise (concerning the birth of Isaac; cf. Rom 4:21); in v. 8 faith amounts to obedience. As a rule, the personal aspect of faith has a dual dimension. One does not immediately and directly encounter the God "in" whom one believes but "through" some mediator—for the most part, Jesus (in Jewish texts, Moses). Thus, faith moves through the mediator to the God who stands behind the mediator. The mediator is regarded as having been sent by God. As the outcome of a missionary encounter, then, faith is the confirmation that one is actually meeting God, in a disguised way, in the one (e.g., Jesus) with whom one actually has the encounter (cf., e.g., John 11:27; 20:27). In Acts, faith is also mediated through the church (8:5-13; 17:34). Between proclamation and faith stands the feature of clinging to or relying on the proclaimer.

The aim of this brief survey is to emphasize that, in the New Testament, faith is not some spontaneous act of assent but the culminating stage in a process of interaction between persons.

Faith as Experience of Conversion

Faith is a comprehensive concept in which different experiences having to do with conversion are brought together. Basically we are here dealing with threshold experiences, at whose end and at whose culmination one speaks of faith. The notion of threshold implies a transition from old to new, a transition that has religious, theological, ethical, and sociological elements. The new relationship that emerges from this transition can, in effect, be sealed by a confession of faith.[1] The expression "I believe" thus has a constative (in a sense, conclusive) character.

Faith in the sense of a readiness to suffer is directly tied to the experience of conversion. This is clearly the case in Heb 11:24-26. The same idea comes across in the Vulgate's rendition of Jdt 8:22-23 ("probatus . . . per multas tribulationes transierunt fideles"). Faith's summarizing character becomes apparent especially in the list of examples given in Hebrews 11. Belonging to the construct here called "faith" are such essentially emotional features as "looking forward to" (v. 10) and "desiring" (v. 16). Faith also has some specifically ethical qualities; Heb 11:5 mentions "pleasing God," and 11:8 speaks of "obedience" (to God). In each of these cases, we are dealing with behavior directed explicitly toward God.

It is noteworthy that all the experiences mentioned so far are especially (and in more than one way) related to Christian initiation. There is also an important area of overlap between faith and wonder (see "The Aspect of Power," below). It is also probably necessary, with regard to the experience we call faith, to allow for different phases—and to recognize the necessity for the same.[2]

Faith Present in the Psyche?

Apart from the experiences mentioned above, for New Testament Christians faith was probably not directly experienced in the psyche. That is to say, in most cases faith does not manifest itself as something known immediately, as a sense of certainty or spiritual feeling. Faith finds expression in other ways. I will be more specific about this regarding the "power" aspect of faith (see below). For now, however, should this thesis prove accurate, we have come up against an important borderline case for historical psychology. We find ourselves in the position of having to speak about something that is *not* present in the psyche. How can we do this? The following possibilities emerge.

1. If faith is not directly present in experience, it can become visible and an item of experience in the fruits that it bears. This is really how it should be.[3] Faith for the most part is not a feeling nor a persistent state of consciousness nor an intellectual attitude (*habitus*). Faith, as pictured in the New Testament, is not simply some element in the psyches of ordinary Christians as they go about their day-to-day lives.

2. The certainty of faith directs attention to the fruits of faith. At the experiential level, these alone satisfy. Faith is experienced in the doing of it, and not otherwise. (In this context the question of the relationship of faith to confession and acts of worship follows as a matter of course; on this see "Pastoral Care," below.)

3. In the Gospel of John the experiential aspect of Christian faith is aptly described as "abiding" (Greek: *menein*). In Paul, the notion corresponding to this is not actually called faith at all but "being in the Lord."

4. In most cases, faith as a feature of Christian existence is perhaps best conceptualized through the image of a root—something that must be there but that cannot in all cases be dug up.

5. Where faith is contrasted with fear, faith is seen not so much as an attitude of serene confidence as a kind of stability. The same applies to faith when it is contrasted with doubt (*distazō*). Faith makes confidence possible (Matt 14:31).

6. In the ordinary lives of Christians, no solid distinction exists between faith and works. From this a couple of important consequences follow. First, faith is not some sort of act of trust that could then be compared with other instances of "blind" action. Faith is not to be sublimated into some kind of intention. Every lack in works is eo ipso a lack of faith. Second, faith perfectly transforms itself into love/works. As so transformed, it does not then also linger behind as some sort of psychological state or as pious thoughts about God. On the contrary, faith then takes on the form of a token of belonging, a sign of being marked or determined (for someone else). Faith particularly expresses itself in crisis situations. In general, faith appears whenever confession is called for. The actions taken within such situations are cultic (i.e., symbolic) in nature; they mark out boundaries and make explicit the factors constitutive of the whole. In a sense, then, it is quite correct to say that faith should be expressed only in a "religious" context (in church, at prayer, etc.). The "discovery" of nonreligious everyday Christianity in the theology of the mystics (e.g., Meister Eckhart) and in the more recent past (e.g., Dietrich Bonhoeffer), is genuinely true to the New Testament only if and insofar as it preserves confessional symbolism. Any one-sided resolution of this tension would prove fatal.

7. If faith primarily becomes manifest through certain initiatory rites or practices (conversion, baptism) or symbolic gestures (confession, cultic practices)—that is to say, only through particular experiences associated with the ordinary course of a Christian's life—then it follows without saying that such gestures are to be evaluated positively.[4] In fact, they are to be seen as indications of spiritual maturity.

In contemporary understanding, such biographical or cultic gestures tend to be seen as operating on a preconscious level. The New Testament exegete cannot speak in precisely the same way, however. The New Testament actually speaks of the fruits of faith (using botanical imagery), or of the faithful as the sons and daughters of God (using genealogical imagery), or of the realization of faith through works, or of enduring in the faith and keeping the commandments. Even where the New Testament speaks of faith as an abiding quality (viz., as fidelity—the durative aspect of both the Hebrew and the Greek terms for "faith" is often overlooked), its distinguishing trait is simply calmness of demeanor or absence of agitation.

In sum, because faith is not a state of consciousness, the opposite of faith is not uncertainty or doubt with regard to particular truths. The opposite of faith is anxiety and sin.

Conclusions

1. Faith means relying totally upon another, expecting everything of the other. The "totally" is here to be understood in a religious sense (Deut 6:4-5). Structurally given in this sort of relationship is also the fact that there can be only one such "other." The faith-relationship can be described as "being fully convinced" (Rom 4:21).

2. As a direct consequence of its "total" quality, faith acquires unconditionality—one could even say blindness. Because of its unconditionality there can be as many forms of expression for faith as are described, e.g., in Hebrews 11.

3. There is also with faith the perception of a significant difference in power between oneself and the object of one's trust. This perception, however, leads neither to anxiety nor to envy but to positive acquiescence coupled with hopeful expectation on the part of the believer. In other words, faith is not an end in itself but involves the conviction that it is of some benefit for human beings. In this regard, faith is a kind of investment in a power that one trusts, and at the same time also a highly valued good. Corresponding to the abundant power in which one believes is trust from the side of the believer.

4. Faith is not just a feeling of dependence but the transformation of the perception of a complex relationship into a gesture (see section below, "Faith as Imaginative Power"). The gesture (symbol) of faith can be a verbal expression or can take another form.

5. The gesture of faith lays open the heart; it breaks through the reticence and reserve of daily living, the dullness of the ordinary. Along the same line, the "totality" (unconditionality) of faith sharply contrasts with the brokenness and divisiveness of so-called normal life. This totality, with respect to content, means that the believer can look forward to a restored reality.

6. A distinctive solidarity emerges between believers and the one in whom they believe (cf. Mark 9:42).

THE ASPECT OF POWER

Faith as Wondrous Power within Human Beings

When Goethe said, "Miracle is the favorite child of faith," he was speaking critically, even mockingly, of faith. If applied to the New Testament, however, this same statement would apply without any overtone of irony or sarcasm. In the New Testament, the faith of a person who beholds a miracle is, in a strict sense, fundamental to the occurrence of that miracle. In many New Testament miracle stories Jesus says, "Your faith has saved you." This comment should not be watered down by moralistic or pedagogical interpretations[5] but taken literally and seriously. Faith, in other words, is the power (of God) within a person that has a causal connection with the miracle. For the most part, this takes place within the context of an encounter with someone specially empowered by God (e.g., Jesus or an apostle), an encounter that has the character of an epiphany. Faith, then, is the manner or way in which a person is grasped and held fast by the presence of God within the miracle.

Two elements are noteworthy, (a) the power within the person and (b) the epiphanic encounter. With regard to (a): Statements such as the one at Mark 9:23 ("All things can be done for the one who believes") ascribe to the believer a power not inferior to that of God (". . . for God all things are possible," Mark 10:27b). The same applies for the well-known statements in Matt 17:20 and Luke 17:6 (faith that can move mountains or trees). In all these, the issue is the fullness of power and the volition of the believers themselves. Faith is therefore seen as a wondrous power within the believers, a power at their disposal. The possibilities for such faith are unlimited. With regard to (b): Faith's fullness of power is not simply dispersed by God haphazardly among human beings. Most of the relevant texts show it connected to encounters that people have with Jesus Christ or with his designated messengers (see section above, "The Aspect of Encounter"). The power associated with faith, however, is not restricted to such encounters; it has a certain autonomy that transcends them.

In 1 Cor 2:3-5 this same sort of experience is described for Paul. Already in the "fear and trembling" that he experienced in his missionary encounter with the community, we see an element constitutive of theophanies or epiphanies. The same applies to the Corinthians, who experienced "Spirit and power." But the actual goal of this missionary encounter is, in the words of Paul, "that your faith might rest not on human wisdom but on the power of God." The missionary encounter brings about among Christians a unity of faith and divine power, a unity that obviously is enduring.

In narrative sections of the Gospels, the connection to Jesus of this power in persons comes about either as they make direct physical contact with him (Mark 5:27-29) or as Jesus through his word makes it real and effective in the world (e.g., Matt 8:5-13). Only when Jesus says, "Let it be done for you according to your faith" (v. 13), does the miracle really take place; by this time the faith of the centurion had already been acknowledged (vv. 8, 10). In the Gospels Jesus thus appears not only as the one who indicates the possibility of faith and summons people to it (cf. "Have faith in God," Mark 11:22) but also as the one who confirms the priority of faith, thereby securing a point of entry for the power of faith into the realm of earthly reality. It goes without saying that this faith is in God and that it is characterized by participation in the power that is God's.[6]

The power-character of faith also finds expression in Heb 11:33-35: "Through faith [they] conquered kingdoms . . . shut the mouths of lions, quenched raging fire, escaped the edge of the sword, won strength out of weakness, became mighty in war, put foreign armies to flight. Women received their dead by resurrection. . . ." As is well known, in Hebrews 11 faith is closely linked to Christ. It is presented as something that can surmount all barriers. Its amazing power amounts to a direct transfer to human beings of the creative power of God. As a gift of God, faith's only limitations are those defined by the extent and reach of the power of the Creator. At the very least, this means that faith is not confined within the borders of Israel.[7]

From the same perspective we can understand why in 1 Cor 12:9 faith is listed as one of the spiritual gifts. While faith as encounter applies to all Christians, in this particular context the power-aspect of faith is emphasized. Faith, arrayed with the other spiritual gifts, is the power that brings wonders to pass. The "gifts of healing" (12:9b) and the "working of miracles" (12:10a) are to be understood as intrinsically tied to faith. Similarly, this understanding of faith allows us to make better sense of the difficult passage in Mark 6:5-6 ("And he could do no deed of power there. . . . And he was amazed at their unbelief"). Jesus himself is one factor in the performing of miracles. The deciding factor in the realization of divine power, which is what a miracle is, here, however, lies on the side of the recipients of the miracle, i.e., in their faith. Confronted by the fact of their unbelief, Jesus demurs and withdraws. At the conclusion of many miracle accounts, it is said that the people are amazed at what Jesus has done. Here Jesus is the one amazed; he is taken aback by the lack of belief on the part of the people. Faith's proper relationship to power has here been reversed.

According to Rom 4:20-21, faith has to do with the experience of power in two respects: Faith is the power of the believer to hold fast, and faith is what enables the power of God to perform what has been promised.

Faith as the Experience of Contrast

Faith has very little to do with mere doctrines or theories, but its true character becomes apparent as the power to withstand all sorts of threatening realities. One sees this especially in the miracle stories, where faith is intrinsically connected to restoration. And this aspect of faith fits in nicely with the view of conversion as reaction to an encounter. In the reaction, which is conversion, chaotic and life-threatening forces are overcome by faith. Conversely, the perception of faith as a conquering force presupposes that human beings are vulnerable and in need of help. All of this means that faith, eo ipso, is the overcoming of fear and anxiety; it is the power that gives "victory over the world" (1 John 5:4).

In sum, to have faith is to be caught up by the presence of the living God, and this makes faith a power for salvation in the fullest sense of the word. Indeed, faith is a power even greater than the power of death.

The Principle of Disproportionality

According to Matt 17:20, even a little faith is enough to move mountains.[8] Both here and in the parallel passage, Luke 17:6, where it is trees that are to be moved, faith need be no larger than a mustard seed in order to be highly effective. Other New Testament and early Christian texts speak in much the same fashion about peace, unanimity, and reconciliation between persons.[9] Faith, then, bears a structural resemblance to other manifestations of the marvelous presence of the creative power of God; it is not unique in its effectiveness. When compared to faith, for example, peacemaking stands out ethically. The same sort of relationship with regard to faith and peacemaking obtains when we consider the overcoming of anxiety/fear. This happens through faith, but similarly also through love (see below). Faith, then, is much like love, reconciliation, and peacemaking. Their similarity lies especially in the disproportionality between the reality itself and the results that follow from it. Here we touch upon one of the distinctly novel features of Christian "revelation."[10]

It is a common feature in texts about the effect of faith and peacemaking that disproportionally large consequences follow from small beginnings—or at least from beginnings that seem small. Seen from another angle, the scope of the consequences shows how important it is to satisfy the seemingly modest preconditions. It is thus hardly an accident that both faith and the peacemaking are such central elements in early Christianity.

FAITH AS IMAGINATIVE POWER

In Matt 8:13 Jesus says to the Gentile centurion, "Let it be done to you according to your faith." One must wonder how he believed, or in just what his belief consisted. In Matt 21:22 it is promised to believers, "Whatever you ask for in prayer with faith, you will receive." Here a similar question arises: What differentiates the petitioner who merely prays from one who prays and "believes"? Also with regard to such texts as Heb 11:33-35 (considered above) one is led to ask if there is some feature in the psyche that corresponds to the power aspect of faith.

At the outset we must identify some features that do not play a role here. First, in none of these passages does faith refer to the intensity with which the plea is voiced or to the submissive attitude adopted by the petitioner. Even less does it refer to a confession of error or sin on the part of the petitioner. There are, however, several indications of what actually is in the psyche of the believers: (a) In Matt 9:28 Jesus asks, "Do you believe that I am able to do this?" The import of the question in this case, as generally, is whether faith is directed toward God. Faith is total and unhesitating orientation toward God. The message of Matt 8:9 is similar; with regard to Jesus and the illness of the servant, the centurion thinks of things as though it were a military situation. A command is to be given, and it will be obeyed. Indeed, it must be obeyed, because Jesus has great authority.[11] (b) In Heb 11:27b it is said that Moses fled the wrath of the king of Egypt, but without fear, "for he persevered as though he saw him who is invisible." (c) In Matt 21:22 faith essentially consists in being able to "imagine" the petition as already received. (d) There can be no doubt that faith is just as much a gift of God as a human activity, despite the injunction, "Have faith in God" (Mark 11:22). Any distinction between divine gift and human act, here and elsewhere, amounts to inappropriate modernizing. (e) According to Matt 14:26-33 Peter, while walking on the sea, began to sink at the very moment he began to be afraid. It was this fear that Jesus called "little faith." Peter's fear had to do with the ominous power of the waves. But in just what did his faith consist? Notice the flow of the narrative: Peter's faith follows directly upon the Lord's summons, "Come."

These observations lead to several conclusions. Both the Peter who walks on the waves and the person who prays believing have a highly distinctive relationship to what we call reality. A threat is not perceived; what is not present is seen as being present, and vice versa. Reality itself is being perceived from the perspective of God's disposing power. As long as this perspective holds, wondrous results can follow. Mark 9:29 even indicates how one can appropriate such a perspective: through prayer and fasting. (Contrast Mark 9:18—the disciples are reproached for their lack of faith, which in turn makes them incapable of performing a powerful work.)

According to New Testament understanding, faith's particular way of viewing reality is neither a psychological projection nor a form of wishful thinking. It is to be described positively, and in several ways.

1. First, faith's way of viewing reality consists of two fundamental elements: complete trust in God (i.e., in the power of God; cf., e.g., Rom 4:20-21), and the envisioning of a contrary reality (but nonetheless established by the power of God).

2. Analogous to this understanding of faith is the early Christian renunciation of worry, which rests on the two features noted in (a), applied to the concerns intrinsic to human life.

3. Trust in God manifests itself in such a way that the reality perceived by faith is allowed to overflow into the present world, affecting the conditions of life here and now. This happens in the fulfillment of, or even in the expectation attached to, a command spoken by Jesus (or one of his messengers), or in his touch. Examples here are Peter's response to the command spoken to him by Jesus in Matt 14:28 and the centurion's expectation in Matt 8:8 (par. Luke 7:7). This connection to the present world, above all, distinguishes faith from mere psychological projection. By means of no more than a word of command, the imaginative power of faith can cut through present reality, transforming it.

4. In Heb 11:33 one reads that "through faith . . . they administered justice." From this remark one can see that the relationship between faith and ethics is determined in a new way. Is not the effecting of justice just as much a miracle as the performing of mighty deeds?

5. Along the same lines, the apocalyptic hymns discussed earlier offer a natural continuation of what the Gospels understand by "faith." Just as the wondrous manifestation of God's power is envisioned before it actually occurs, so also these hymns sing of judgment, namely, the demise of "Babylon," as though it had already taken place. Here the destruction of Rome corresponds to the miracles of the Gospels. The structure of faith is the same in both places; faith draws its vitality from the divine realm, where what is perceived has already taken place. Faith can therefore be said to have an eidetic nature with regard to the mighty deeds it envisions. In Revelation the crossover from the reality of the divine realm to that of the human is the victory of the Lamb, seen as already accomplished. Thus the Lamb is able, by opening the seal, to unleash that other reality upon this world, bringing about its end.

This eidetic character of faith also allows for a better estimation of the so-called cognitive elements of faith such as appear in the writings of Paul. A crucial feature is that the modern term "cognitive" has connotations that can lead to a considerable narrowing of what is actually meant here. The New Testament is not referring to recognitions based on some specific perception but about relying on an alternate reality, one that calls for more courage as the conflict between God and world becomes greater. Appropriate texts here are 2 Cor 4:4-6[12] and Heb 11:6. The issue is not just that faith posits a "nevertheless" but also and quite simply that faith envisions a reality greater—decidedly greater—than the present reality.

FAITH AND ANXIETY/FEAR

"Faith" and its synonyms often occur in the New Testament with reference to anxiety or fear.[13] Moreover, apart from one significant exception, these realities stand in opposition to one another; they are seen as incompatible. (As mentioned above, no significant difference exists between fear and anxiety in the New Testament.)

Distributed to Apostle and Community

First let us consider the exception to the rule that faith and fear/anxiety are treated as opposing realities. This is to be found in 1 Cor 2:3-5 ("I came to you in weakness and in fear and in much trembling . . . that your faith might rest . . ."). Here fear/anxiety is not set over against faith; Paul has not lost his faith when he feels fear/anxiety. In this case, fear/anxiety goes with Paul's role. Paul admits it—he has been anxious, he is not someone who had felt compelled heroically to overcome anxiety. He admits that he has felt fear/anxiety, and he says that this has happened to him precisely in his role as an apostle in the service of God. What is more, this phenomenon is an aspect of an epiphanic experience of God. A similar dynamic is at work in 2 Cor 4:11-12, where death on the side of the apostle is set over against life on the side of the community. Once again, however, the whole dynamic is bound up with the process of becoming Christian. Again, in 1 Cor 2:3-5 anxiety is indeed contrasted with faith, but not in a mutually exclusive way. Instead, each conditions the other in the interaction between the two parties. Paul does not shy away from admitting to weaknesses in other situations as well; cf. 1 Cor 9:22. Such admissions are and remain a part of the weakness/strength polarity in the theology of Paul, a polarity that forms a precondition for God's work in the world. There are other instances as well in the context of epiphanic occurrences where fear/anxiety is not regarded as incompatible with faith.

Faith as the Overcoming of False Fear

Faith can be the power that neutralizes fear/anxiety when confronting someone else (other than God). The more powerful and frightening that someone else is, the stronger and more salutary is the faith. According to Heb 11:23, the edict of the Egyptian king could have caused anxiety, but faith removed the anxiety. In Heb 11:27, the believing Moses had no fear in the presence of the increasing wrath of the same king. The fear mentioned in the story about the raising of the daughter of Jairus is the fear occasioned by death; what is being spoken about is the anxiety that encircles those who are doomed. Jesus speaks directly to this fear/anxiety when he tells Jairus, "Do not fear; only believe" (Mark 5:36; the parallel in Luke 8:50 adds "and she will be saved").

That which overcomes the fear/anxiety felt in the presence of the powerful, or the fear/anxiety that death brings, need not always be called faith. It can itself be called fear. This is evident, for example, in Luke 12:4-5 (have no fear of those who kill the body, but fear the one who can cast down into hell). The one toward whom fear ought really be directed is God. In Luke 12:4-5, that before which one feels fear has changed, but the phenomenon itself has remained. It is questionable, however, whether one should adopt the same perspective with regard to the believers mentioned in the preceding paragraph. Normally, faith is something quite other than anxiety.

The textual evidence supports two conclusions. (a) One who has faith is always one who places trust in someone stronger. God is the one power capable of protecting against all anxiety. (b) Out of the semantic field associated with the Greek term for "faith" (*pistis*), it is the element of stability—or of being stabilized—that is being actualized. In other words, the consequence of faith is a serenity that overpowers panic.

Peter Walking on the Water

In Matt 14:26-33 the relationship between anxiety and faith is made into the main theme, and in a most impressive fashion, as can be seen by the artistry of the narrative. According to 14:30 Peter becomes so anxious that he sees (!) the wind instead of keeping his eyes on the Lord (4:26). It thus follows as a matter of course that, falling into doubt, he also starts to sink. Already in 14:28 Peter's faith is not wholly firm, for he says, "Lord, if it is you. . . ." (The "It is I" that Jesus speaks in v. 27 was apparently less than totally convincing.) In v. 31 Peter's fear of the wind (v. 30) brings him the reproach of being of "little faith." Finally, one must ask whether it was really only the sight of the wind that made Peter anxious. Were those steps already taken upon the water such a small matter? Clearly the narrator is concerned to present Peter's anxiety as something that surfaced only in the second stage of a sequence, after he had already been able to venture a few steps on the sea. Within the narrative, then, two sets of synonymous relationships emerge. One appears in vv. 30 and 31: anxiety about the wind = doubt = little faith. The other appears in vv. 27, 28-29, 30, and 33: being brave = obeying the Lord's command to come = crying out to the Lord ("Lord, save me!") = confessing the Lord's divine sonship.

Jesus is the one who verifies the smallness of Peter's faith; in the corresponding place in other miracle stories he affirms, "Your faith has saved you." Important here is the effect of a lack of faith; it shows itself as weakness and loss of ability to perform miracles. Such is the case also in Mark 9:18-19 ("They could not . . ." / "You faithless generation . . ."). Contrast, however, what is said of even a small faith in Matt 17:20 (it can move mountains!).

But doesn't everyone know that even such a believer as Peter would never be able to walk on the sea, or that the disciples would never be able to displace mountains? What meaning can be attached to these seemingly absurd little narratives woven around the theme of the power of faith? First, in a mythic[14] and therefore (from a secular point of view) hyperbolic manner, these texts illustrate a christological affirmation. They underline the difference between Jesus and the disciples.[15] For it is indeed Jesus who walks on the water; it is Jesus who drives out demons. Second, these texts say something about the phenomenology of faith: faith is participating in Jesus and at the same time lives from holding fast to the vision of an alternative. Third, these texts say something about anxiety and its destructive impact on faith. It is not theoretical skepticism but natural anxiety that is the enemy of faith. Can there really be any doubt that this is the case? After all, what effectively stands up against anxiety in the presence of death is the eidetic power to see and to experience the world from the standpoint of the reality of God.

Holy Spirit and Charisma

THE STRIKING EMPHASIS ON THE SPIRIT IN EARLY CHRISTIANITY

Compared to the Targums, with their distinctive emphasis on the "spirit of prophecy," the Holy Spirit plays a very large role in the New Testament. The more fundamental the level at which one begins here, the more profitable ought to be considerations regarding just why the role of the Spirit is so emphasized. By no means is the theme of the Spirit necessarily attached to the term or concept of a Messiah. Indeed, it is striking how, during his lifetime, it is almost exclusively Jesus himself who is said to bear the Spirit—and he does not pass the Spirit on to others. Only after his exaltation do the disciples also receive the Spirit. Thus it is apparent that

"Spirit" stands for an experience of presence, namely, of God in Jesus Christ and of the presence of some reality that continues to connect the disciples to Jesus after Easter. In other respects as well, one cannot help but be struck by the breadth and the frequency of pneumatic experiences in early Christianity (see the next section).

There are several reasons why it might have become so important to speak about the Spirit of God. (a) In contrast to the deities of the pagans, the God of Israel was experienced as the Living One, and particularly in the sense of being one who not only has life but who also passes it on to others. A living relationship with this God is effected by the gift of the Spirit of God. (b) Jesus both experiences and proclaims the nearness of God. In the Holy Spirit this nearness becomes actual presence in the midst of life, right there where otherwise only powerlessness is experienced. In this power vacuum, far removed from all earthly lords, the true Lord of the world can be experienced, as genuine power. In other words, the "Spirit of God" is essentially an experience of power—of a driving, onward-pressing force. (c) At no point is the Holy Spirit simply a stand-in for spirit in general or for spirituality (it is also that, but hardly *only* that). "Spirit" is to be understood more in the sense of life spirit than a particular kind of experience.

THE VARIETY OF EARLY CHRISTIAN EXPERIENCES OF THE SPIRIT

For contemporary consciousness, just how the "Holy Spirit" can be experienced has become quite problematic. This problem is clearly tied up with the connection of the Holy Spirit to baptism (especially when one thinks of infant baptism). In early Christianity, however, there was a variety of perceptions of the Spirit:

1. Spirit and peace. It is striking how often peaceableness and gentleness are seen as consequences of being endowed with the Spirit. In other words, being endowed with the Spirit is not devoid of ethical consequences; the Spirit puts a clear stamp on one's character. The Spirit itself was experienced as a gift bestowing geniality and amicability (cf. *TRE* 12:186).

2. Spirit and praise. Praising God in various types of songs is also traced back to being endowed by the Spirit. This raises the theological problem of the human relationship with angels, who likewise sing praises before the throne of God. But a distinctive experience is here being attested, and the songs of early Christianity serve as another key to understanding the experience of the Spirit at that time.

3. Spirit and interpretation of Scripture. As with Philo of Alexandria, for whom insights into the allegorical meaning of Scripture amount to a sort of spiritual ecstasy (a "writing desk ecstasy"), so also for early Christians the unlocking of the Scriptures (the Old Testament) in a christological sense is experienced as a gift of the Spirit. And as in the case of the early Christian songs, this experience has two sides: it not only legitimates scriptural proofs but also is experienced as enlightenment by the Spirit. In all this, it is not the exegetic discoveries themselves that are found to be inspiring but rather the distinctive experience of Christ that is mediated through the Scriptures.

4. Spirit and joy. Joy is also a frequently mentioned gift of the Spirit, one that is frequently contrasted with sadness (cf. "Joy and Sorrow," in chapter 7, above). Manifested as joy, the Spirit is also the emotional counterpart to all sorts of desire (cf. Rom 14:17; Gal 5:19-23).

5. Spirit and power to resist. There is a widespread tradition to the effect that the Spirit, like wisdom, is experienced as a power that enables resistance—especially against powerful officials before whom Christians are summoned. Put another way, the Spirit opposes the reputed wisdom of worldly officials with a superior wisdom that comes from God (cf. , e.g., Luke 12:12; see *TRE* 12:182).

6. Spirit abolishes human differences. When the differences between the genders, between Jews and Gentiles, and between masters and slaves are perceived as annulled, this experience is also attributed to the Spirit. The experience of the Spirit is so unifying that all divisions seem to fade away under its impact. That the Spirit is experienced as breaking boundaries is intrinsically connected with the experience of being one of the children of God. The Spirit that appears in the Lukan account of Pentecost effects unity among human beings in a distinctive way: it enables understanding across linguistic boundaries.

7. Spirit and purity. According to the testimony of early Christianity, the Spirit (or the "charismatic power" of Jesus) removes the threat of impurity; everything that renders something impure is overcome. This applies across the board, from impure spirits to the impurity associated with Gentile ways to the impurity of death. The power emanating from Jesus breaks through all barriers created by prohibitions of impurity.

Why was the Spirit of God experienced in early Christianity as, among other things, a purifying force (a power effecting holiness)? What, if any, contemporary circumstances contributed to the nearness of God being so strongly experienced in just this way? It is quite possible that early Christianity was here offering a deliberate alternative, rooted in Jewish messianism, to the universalism of the Roman Empire, which by this time was clearly starting to deify its Caesars. Not Caesar but God's Messiah is the "king of peace." The future lies not with the universalism of the Roman Empire but with the universalism inherited from Deutero-Isaiah.

8. The groaning of the Spirit. Romans 8 speaks of the Spirit bestowed on Christians as expressing itself in "inexpressible cries of groaning" (see v. 26). These outcries (*stenagmoi,* traditionally rendered as "sighs") are not simply to be taken as ecstatic utterances. When Paul speaks of groaning, he means something quite different—the reaction to acute awareness of human imperfection (sin). All the relevant analogies indicate that this "groaning" is the fundamental expression of revulsion in the face of human imperfection. According to Romans 8, then, the Spirit of God is groaning over the necessity of human condemnation to death. (Rom 7:24 could well be reflecting what Paul is thinking on one such occasion of groaning.)

9. Overcoming the letter of the Law. With his alternative between "letter" and "spirit," Paul formulates a new experience regarding behavior with reference to the Law. To be free from the letter of the Law means that the radical love to which the Spirit drives a person superabundantly fulfills all individual commandments.

10. Spirit as giver of "charisms." Charisms are gifts that transcend normality. Wherever Christians are able to do something extraordinary, something that must be traced back to God as the heavenly giver, there one speaks of charisms. It was the accomplishment of Paul to connect all of the many charisms of early Christianity with the one Spirit of God.

THE UNITY OF EARLY CHRISTIAN EXPERIENCES OF THE SPIRIT

With respect to content, the experience of the Spirit of God clearly does not stay within hard and fast lines. Groaning differs considerably from joy; the experience of peace and fellowship, on the one hand, and of the ability to resist those in authority, on the other, are obvious contrasts.

Spirit and Opposition

Despite differences, however, one thing is noteworthy: the Spirit of God is never experienced alone, in and of itself, but always in community or, on an occasion of resistance, in contrast to some opposing reality. That is to say, the Spirit of God is regularly tied in with some new experience of an "other"—another human being or something that contrasts with the experience of Spirit. This means that, in experiencing the Spirit of God, one is always and at the same time also experiencing the world. This is a given, yet it is always differentiated from the world.

Thus the experience of the Spirit of God stands in contrast to the human subjection to death and, indeed, to all the burdens of earthly existence and to the failure to perform the will of God (as expressed in the Law). The Spirit groans in contrast to malice, but also to every sort of human frailty and decrepitude. In addition, the Spirit stands opposed to all sorts of barriers and discrimination, as well as every form of envy and dislike. When early Christian charismatics maintain that the Spirit impels them to the places where they do their missionary work, the burdens that weigh on life are being overcome. Lastly, the Spirit also overcomes separation from Jesus. In the legal trials of Christians, the Spirit grants the power necessary to withstand opposition.

In short, the Spirit conquers everything that stands in opposition; the Spirit is the conqueror par excellence. There is therefore a latent "dualism," in the widest sense, in the experience of the Spirit.

Spirit and Action

The experience of the Spirit is an experience of "driving power" for, as already shown, it is a manifestation of the living God in opposition to all idols. In this way God bestows life-enhancing power. Any interior spiritualizing of the experience of Spirit must therefore be avoided. The Spirit of God awakens the dead; it does not make the living feel better! According to Paul, what we must do—and all we need to do—is follow the Spirit of God, along with the associated impulse to love. The living law of the Spirit is substantively identical to the Torah.

PSYCHOLOGICAL INTERPRETATION

Avoiding False Alternatives

Even with careful exegesis of New Testament texts, it is difficult to arrive at an answer to our modern question about how the Spirit is actually experienced. For example, how does one experience the power that leads one to undertake a particular act? The painstaking, detailed search itself arouses suspicion that something is awry with our framing of the questions and should warn against having to choose between unfruitful alternatives. One such would be to assume that the reality of the Spirit must show itself as, on the one hand, an authoritative word of command or juridical dictum or, on the other hand, an emotional stirring within our consciousness. The Spirit is neither just the underlying cause of a particular emotional condition nor simply a factor making for proper behavior. Certainly the Spirit is both of these, and more. Yes, the Spirit awakens "joy," and is thus genuinely to be grasped by the emotions. And yes, according to 2 Corinthians 3 Christians live bound in a covenant of the

Spirit. But that cannot be the whole picture. The experience of the Spirit is reducible neither to joy nor to a sense of obligation.

Priority of the Via Negativa

NEGATION OF BOUNDARIES

The Spirit is experienced primarily in the removal of boundaries and the negating of limitations. That the Spirit appears as opposing established realities indicates that interpretation of the experience of the Spirit ought to proceed by way of a *via negativa*. Because boundaries and limitations are negated by the Spirit, the Spirit can better be known by paying attention to what is negated.

That the New Testament experience of the Spirit is focused on the removal of boundaries and limitations is already highly significant. With regard to its consequences for human beings, it is precisely here and in this way that people feel touched by God. There are also important implications for the way God is imaged in the mind; God is experienced as one who apportions ungrudgingly and is above and beyond all distinctions.

In order to draw out the implications of such experiences of the Spirit of God, it is important to note which barriers in particular are set aside and which limitations are felt to be especially oppressive. In 1 Corinthians 6 and 12, attention is clearly directed to the barriers that separate human beings. Consequently, the work of the Spirit here is to make one body out of all Christians. The boundary set by death is addressed in 1 Corinthians 15, as are the limitations of the body that is destined to perish. In this case the Spirit conquers by effecting transformation of the mortal body into a spiritual body. The concern in Romans and Galatians has to do with limitations in the ability of people to behave righteously. These same two letters take a special interest in the barriers that separate Jew from Gentile, barriers perceived to be especially incompatible with the early Christian experience of God.

In sum, the major difficulties facing New Testament Christians become evident in retrospect by pursuing the question of just how they experienced the Spirit of God. Put another way, Paul's remarks about the Spirit also serve to indicate those problems perceived to be especially grave and pressing for his community and for himself.

ANALOGIES TO THE CONCEPT OF FREEDOM

Paul's comments about the Spirit have considerable affinities with his concept of freedom. Freedom is frequently said to be a work of the Spirit (e.g., in Galatians). Particularly significant here is the fact that freedom can be defined only in negative terms; freedom is regularly spoken of as "freedom from. . . ." If God, by means of the gift of the Spirit, leads human beings across the barriers that confine them, then the result of this activity of God is freedom, when seen from the human side.

The predictable consequences of being liberated from such barriers doubtlessly lie in the being freed from senseless anxieties, especially such as have to do with personal limitations (weakness, death, inability to enter wholeheartedly into the life of a community). In saying this, however, we are generating our own reconstruction; Paul himself doesn't spell out the details. Perhaps his silence in this regard has something to do with the public nature of his writings.

Insights from Positive Statements

FOCUSING ON THE FACTUAL

For Paul the Spirit is most evident in the Christians' love of one another. The power that Christians have from God is as a rule perceptible neither as feeling nor as sentiment but in concrete deeds, especially in the realization of genuine community among Christians. Here, above all, is where the empirical dimension of Christianity is to be found. This is also why Paul gives such great attention to the works of Christians. The reality of faith for Paul is not primarily to be found in a subjective state of feelings but quite decisively in an experience that is distinct and verifiable. This experience consists in the fact that Christian communities, associations of persons bound together in love for one another, actually exist. This experience takes precedence over all others. Stated from the negative side, what is crucial is that no command of righteousness is any longer being violated in actual life. Stated from the positive side, what matters is that the body of Christ is being built up. The actual fulfilling of the commandment of love is the final goal of the imparting of the Spirit of God to human beings, and it is precisely this that is being experienced.

Around this essential point there also exist, however, great obstacles to the accurate reception of Paul's message. The cause of these obstacles is partly theological (a universalizing in the teachings about sin) and partly sociological (replacement of churchly piety by a supposedly wholly sufficient inwardness). The reticence to praise one's own works, while fully legitimate from one theological perspective, has led to an illegitimate (from another theological perspective) renunciation of works altogether. Such a concept amounts to a subsidizing of human weakness. Paul is a sober pragmatist. He would have quickly exposed as illegitimate every effort to lay down a smokescreen of human inwardness that conceals the great distance between human beings and God.

EXPERIENCES OF ORDER

There can be no doubt that for Paul the Torah is the instrument through which God establishes good order and brings about righteousness. Moreover, it is the Spirit of God that actively prods human beings toward participation in this orderliness. And so "spiritual songs" are hardly an expression of disordered spontaneity but, with all the applicable analogies, they were understood to be a mode of human participation in the angelic praise of the Lord. As such, these texts themselves serve to mediate an experience of order. The strict structure of these songs and the frequent repetitions found in them (whole songs were frequently repeated) serve to locate the "singer" within the established order that the songs manifest. Once again we find ourselves in a close connection between rationality and ecstasy, a link that is constitutive of Pauline Christianity.

EXPERIENCES OF PEACE

In Gal 5:22-23 the "fruits of the Spirit" are named: love, joy, peace, patience, kindness, goodness, faithfulness, gentleness, self-control. All these expressions of the Spirit are on a par with one another, and it is evident that there are also psychological phenomena involved here. Thus the question raised above about the relationship between actually exhibited love and the interior zone of the psyche needs to be taken up once again. First, it is obvious that the focus of attention here is "fruits," which is to say, deeds. But these deeds have an inner side to them, a side that almost makes it possible to recognize something like a unified character of the Spirit, a character that is imparted to human beings. This does not, however, contradict what was said above about the importance of the *via negativa* in understanding how the Spirit was experienced. Instead, it is the fundamental deficiencies in the relationships of "spiritless" people that become apparent, deficiencies of false and "godless" use of power. The question of power is thus intrinsically tied up with the question of how God is experienced. Where human beings exercise power, there more than anywhere else the issue also involves the right and the claim of God. (This is also the root of the political significance of both the Jewish and the Christian religions.) Stated positively: With the bestowal of the Spirit of God on human beings, humankind's propensity for the aggressive use of power is fundamentally altered. Paul expects the Spirit to bring forth a calm serenity. Several important psychological consequences follow.

1. Human works, on which everything depends theologically as the goal of what the Spirit does, come to be seen as a unity. They are no doubt works of the Spirit, but they stimulate a sort of inner continuity, to wit:

2. There can be no doubt that the fruits of the Spirit in Gal 5:22-23 presuppose some kind of unity, which can be described in several different ways. However described, the choice must lie somewhere between some constant but wholly inner-directed factor (one without external manifestations) and something that completely fragments itself into isolated, individual works. The unifying factor here must be some new foundation for action, some foundation whose character is not simply reducible to a dichotomy between good and evil. This foundation (or enduring mood, or action-determining disposition) would bear some sort of analogy to the later notion of the *habitus*.

As in the case of the Spirit itself, so also this foundational disposition or inclination is not experienced directly but only as a contrasting point of reference within some experience. As with awareness of the Spirit in general, so also these fruits of the Spirit are to be described negatively, which is to say as renunciation—depending upon the occasion—of the use of power or as rejection of the propensity to act in one's self-interest. In other words, the fruits of the Spirit become evident through *not* acting in certain ways. The underlying continuity we are here talking about thus emerges *through* or *within* what is actually evident. In Gal 5:22 Paul calls this element of continuity "faithfulness" (Greek: *pistis*).

The psychological (not just ethical) relevance of what we are talking about here lies in the presupposition of a certain kind of enduring mold that puts its imprint on each and every actual encounter with power. A part—though only a part—of the reality under discussion is the "joyous heart" that comes as a gift of the Spirit. As the basis for an "imprinted" mode of behavior toward the use of power or acting from self-interest, the Spirit shares in the usual dualistic structure of other modes of experience. Also here the Spirit remains "dualistically" oriented with respect to the distinction between God and world. Experience of the Spirit thus enables this sort of "bias" in one's dealings with the world.

3. Paul basically proceeds from the notion that one transmits what one has previously experienced. This is the rationale behind his statements in Romans 5 about accepting the love of God, in connection with experience of the Spirit. This acceptance of God's love works toward the final fulfillment of the Law. Considered psychologically, one should not here speak of some mode of being that precedes action but rather of first being loved. It is the relationship established by love that sets the condition within which and on the basis of which proper action becomes possible.

Sin

CONTRASTING POSITIONS

In modern discussion of the experience of sin or the psychological aspect of sin (especially in the Pauline sense), two positions stand in contrast. According to the first, sin is the defiant self-assertion of human beings over against God. According to the second, sin is to be understood as the experience of powerlessness.

The first position is oriented around the understanding of the human situation characteristic of the Renaissance and of nineteenth-century liberalism. From this perspective, "modern" human beings seek to affirm themselves apart from and even against God. This striving for autonomy is regarded as sin. To me it seems this position accurately grasped something essential about the human condition during the era of nineteenth-century capitalism, something to which Christianity saw itself as the antithesis. On the other hand, this position has not been demonstrated as dominant in the pages of the New Testament (especially in the writings of Paul). I hold this view despite that fact that in its more recent variants the focus of this first position has shifted away from self-aggrandizement toward experiences of powerlessness. (Sin is despair consequent upon experiences of powerlessness; faith is trust in the Almighty God.) Following the structure of the second position, sin is experience of powerlessness per se, and faith means participation in a power that bestows on the human being a new self and the capability of affirming the same.

The two positions are reflected in highly divergent interpretations of Romans 7. According to the first position, the sign of faith is precisely the ability to admit to the weakness, the internal disunity, of which Romans 7 speaks. In the second position, Rom 7:7—8:11 describes two different modes of being, of which only the second (8:1ff.) is properly to be characterized as Christian. I hold that the second of these positions is much closer to the understanding of Paul himself. This stance needs to be argued in the material that immediately follows, since our concern here is not with systematic theology but with what can be established exegetically.

THE EXPERIENCE OF POWERLESSNESS

According to Rom 7:17, sin is itself an actual agent at work in human transgressions. In a certain sense sin leads the sinner by the hand; what the sinner does is to some degree alien to the sinner's own person. Human beings would act quite differently than they do were they free to follow the dictates of their reason (Greek: *nous*). (I equate this understanding of *nous* with what people—but not Paul himself—later came to understand in a positive sense as the act-inciting conscience.) But they are not free; they are powerless in the face of the occupying force that acts within them but independently of them.

The ultimate explanation for the fact that something like an alternate person can take up residence within a human being is to be found not in the perverted will of human beings, but rather in their weakness.[16] To use Pauline language, it is due to the "fleshly" (Greek: *sarks*) aspect of human beings—their frailty, their insufficiency. Sin can thereby engender covetousness in them (Rom 7:8). Moreover, only by a fundamental alteration, in which a human being receives the spirit of God and so acquires a new ("spiritual") body, can a significant transformation of behavior come about. As long as human beings are governed by *sarks*, they can never take on the "spiritual" quality demanded by the Law.

If one asks why Paul here personifies sin to such a degree, the answer is certainly not that he wants to prove some point about human innocence. Paul is speaking from his own experience, and it is his experience that neither death nor life has been brought about independently. Rather, each has come about within a broad, supra-individual context. Death has been effected by the power of death, and life by the power of life. The "teaching" of Paul about these matters, sketched here, has psychological implications that must now be considered.

1. Paul speaks about the experience of powerlessness as linked above all to his body, and especially to its members. Paul's comments about experiencing the body are not primarily to be understood in an anatomical way; the focus is social in nature. This implies, in turn, that the powerlessness experienced in the body's members is also an absence of freedom with regard to social constraints. The "body of death" (Rom 7:24), a body that nonetheless itself dies in baptism (Rom 6:6), is above all unhealthy relationships that do not allow one to fulfill God's command and thereby also do not let one achieve self-fulfillment.

This means that the first-person style of Romans 7 should not deceive one into thinking that sin is a problem affecting individual human beings only. For Paul, sin is not tied to the individual's body but is an aspect of an overlapping, collective, indeed global connectedness. The "bodily" experience of sin thus encompasses much more than one's own body. The corresponding positive way of speaking is to say that righteousness is possible only within the context of a new connectedness. (It is hardly accidental that the "body of sin" in Rom 6:6 finds its corresponding point of reference in the "body of Christ" in Rom 7:4—an association with considerable ecclesiastical implications.)

2. Sin thus amounts to the experience of powerlessness, a fundamental incompetence in the face of reality. Experiences of sin are primal in nature;

they are not adequately summarized as consciousness of guilt. Experiences of sin are perceived as instances of being handed over to death (Rom 7:24), and thus they are occasions of utmost gravity.

3. Paul typically uses the singular form of the noun when he refers to sin. This is consonant with his experience of sin as involving a tightly compact interweaving of relationships, global in scope. It also corresponds with the modern view that finds it difficult to speak of individual acts as sins. (This is due, among other things, to the lack of absolute norms in our day.)

TWO WAYS

The two traditional interpretations of Rom 7:7-15, that it relates either to pre-Christian existence (the inner conflict of the unsaved) or to distinctly Christian existence (faith as admission of powerlessness), miss the mark. Starting already in Rom 6:1, Paul sets the discussion on an ethical footing. As is also apparent from Gal 5:17-18; 6:8, in the context of such discussions the Christian is envisioned as facing two different paths, and the decisive point is that the Christian need no longer be compelled to continue to follow the way of the flesh. The other way, the way of the Spirit, is more suitable for Christ and his followers, and it is also now a genuine possibility.[17] It thus seems to me that this section is neither a dogmatic exposition about soteriology (whether the Christian is a sinner or righteous or perhaps both at the same time) nor a bare appeal to hold fast to the Spirit (which would be a moralistic foreshortening) but something else. (If it were a dogmatic statement, it would relate solely to the being and status of the human being, making no mention of the sort of will or behavior expected or required of the person. This is how the Reformers understood this text—as a soteriological statement. From such a perspective, however, the continuation of the discussion into chapter 8 gets disrupted, given that here chapter 7 is understood to be a statement about the Christian as *simul iustus et peccator*. On the other hand, if the discussion were simply a call to moral behavior, it would have to presuppose an unhindered will. One could cite 8:12 in support of such a view. But that text is better read as drawing out the consequences of what had been said previously.)

The preferred option is to read this text as setting two ways before the Christian (!), two possibilities for orientation. On the one hand, the Christian can be oriented toward his or her presently given state of corporeality (in the broad sense of the word)—an orientation that ends up in hopelessness (7:24). On the other hand, the Christian can take up a hopeful perspective, one within which the power of the Spirit provides support. The function of the Law will depend on the way chosen by the Christian. (Paul is also here offering a defense of the Law.)

So in Rom 7:14ff. Paul is not complaining about the internal discord of the Christian[18] but is using this discord as a presupposition. His attention is actually directed elsewhere. The resurrection of Jesus and reliance on the Spirit bestowed through that event open the possibility for a new way, one that can now be realized. The brief prayer of thanks voiced at 7:25a stands on the threshold between the two ways. Two important consequences follow.

1. Acknowledging goodwill is not sufficient; referring to the goodness of intentions is not appropriate for Christians. Stated more directly: In no way is the interior dimension of the Christian (his or her goodwill) more important than what the Christian does. Precisely the opposite holds true. According to Rom 7:14-25, the whole of human misfortune, including consignment to mortality, rests on the fact that people are incapable of doing what is right. Having even the best of intentions does not suffice; all that counts is the act. It is precisely because the act alone counts that human beings are so hapless.

2. As shown by its cry of distress, the inner person of Rom 7:22 is just as miserable as the inner person of 2 Cor 4:17—5:4. (The inner person spoken of there also groans, because it has not been able to break through from the inside to the outside.) To use the language of 2 Cor 5:4, Rom 7:24 also amounts to a groan on the part of the unredeemed. To be sure, there is a difference between these two passages. In 2 Cor 4f. we are dealing with a soteriological statement about what human beings cannot change. De jure, the situation in Romans 7–8 is different (see Rom 8:12).

Paul presents both ways in summary fashion in Rom 8:12-13. In the final analysis, Christians must live according to the Spirit, because they have within themselves the spirit of the risen one, a spirit that brings life in place of death. By drawing in mention of the Law, the description of the two ways also serves to establish an independent foundation for a Christian ethic.

Psychologically, we can see how it is that after the description of internal discord in Rom 7:14-24 there follows in 8:1-11 a description of the beneficent effects of the Spirit. Here we need mention only the gifts of "life and peace" in 8:6, the sense of liberation in 8:2, and the setting aside of anxiety about judgment in 8:1.

As reflected in Rom 7:7-24, however, the experience of sin has even deeper dimensions.

SIN AS ADDICTION

The experience of sin can be elucidated by referring to several features of what we today perceive as addiction, or as being addicted.[19] Specifically:

- Death is the outcome. With addiction it comes more quickly, or more gruesomely, especially with sin, which makes death a certainty.
- Something stands in the way of one's better judgment, a puzzling kind of coercion that seems to come unbidden from without and rob one of one's freedom.
- This compulsion does not operate apart from one's own ability to act (a person remains responsible) but rather in consonance with it.
- What one desires appears to be good but in truth is an illusory good. In Rom 7:11, this feature is described as "deception."
- Compulsion comes across as repetitiveness. It is not the isolated act that matters but the behavioral syndrome.
- The "covetousness" of Rom 7:7 parallels the placement of addiction among the broader compulsions that drive human beings. At least we are dealing with the area of "vital interests"—vital in the sense of being tied in with the physical constitution of the human being.
- Addiction isolates the addict. Paul describes the structure of covetousness in the same way (cf. "Desire," in chapter 7, above).
- To be set free from addiction requires a sort of dying (agonies of withdrawal). This corresponds to Paul's language about "dying with Christ" in Rom 6:3-6.

The first feature, namely, the close relationship between addiction and death, is especially illuminating when we inquire about the intent behind certain Pauline statements. In Rom 7:7—8:12 Paul is concerned with nothing less than pointing out a way to be liberated from death. In other words, Paul's intent here is hardly to describe the existential discord of the human being, or some such thing. He wants instead to describe the inevitability with which bondage to the "flesh" (*sarks*) leads to death. The compulsive aspects of addiction should make it all the more obvious that the human being who follows the "way of the flesh" stands no chance of evading death.

Addiction was also known in antiquity. It was described with images employing the Greek root *anagk-* (compulsion or necessity). So, for example, we find reference to the compulsive eater, the *anagkositos*.[20] But I am not saying that Paul was speaking of the medical phenomenon. In order to reconstruct the presuppositions at work in Paul's comments, I have found it helpful to take some observations from another area, one not under discussion by Paul. It is only a partial, but perhaps helpful, analogy.

Prayer

Among the many and, for historical psychology, exceptionally instructive aspects of prayer I will examine three: self-abasement, experience of the Spirit, and expansion of purview to include the throne of God.

SELF-ABASEMENT

The prayer of Jesus in Mark 14:36 does not contain three parts, as is usually assumed,[21] but four. The fourth is the statement at the end, namely, where Jesus "subsumes his will under the will of God."[22] There is even a technical biblical expression for such self-abasement: *tapeinos*. In other words, Jesus is praying when he says, "Yet, not what I want, but what you want." In the prayer this statement signals complete submission of the human will to the will of God, with particular reference to the concern at hand. The parallels customarily cited from the Psalms are of limited applicability in this case.[23] The closest analogy is the relationship between Luke 1:38 ("Here I am, the servant of the Lord; let it be with me according to your word," following Mary's objection in v. 34) and Luke 1:48a, where Mary says, "For he has looked with favor on the lowliness of his servant."[24] The key term, introduced in 1:38, is "servant" (or "handmaid"); it is taken up again in v. 48 to emphasize that the Lord has indeed worked his will with Mary—she is now pregnant. The expression of self-abasement in v. 48 (*tapeinosis*) is thus not to be taken in the sense of acknowledging a distinction of social class. On the contrary, Mary's response is closely tied to the immediate context. In similar fashion, in Mark 14:36b, Jesus submits himself as would a slave.[25]

The Greek root *tapeino-* frequently occurs elsewhere as well in texts involving prayer. With this term, the one who prays customarily acknowledges that God will and should be the one to decide, since God is holy and powerful, while the petitioner is not. Several important New Testament texts regarding prayer can shed additional light on the semantic range of this term.

1. In Luke 18:9-14 the prayers of a Pharisee (a prayer of thanks, v. 11) and a tax collector (a petition, v. 13) are juxtaposed and commented on. In the summarizing words of Jesus, "For all who exalt themselves will be humbled (Greek root: *tapeino-*), but all who humble themselves will be exalted." The abasing of self is thus a kind of prayer. *First Clement* 38:2 allows us to see why the prayer of the Pharisee was not humble; whoever "testifies for himself" does not abase himself.

2. Several important features constitutive of this perspective are brought together in 1 Pet 5:6-9. That passage starts out by saying, "Humble your-

selves therefore under the mighty hand of God, so that he may exalt you in due time." This comment relates to prayer, because directly afterward comes the remark that one should cast all cares on the Lord. This is something that happens, concretely, in prayer, for example, in the petition for daily bread in the Lord's Prayer. Then follows the admonition to sobriety and watchfulness (v. 8), and finally come the remarks about resisting the temptations of the devil (although explicit mention of "temptation" is missing here). All of these features offer particularly close parallels to Mark 14:36 (self-abasement) and 14:38 (watching, praying, resisting temptation).

3. James 1:9-10, a notably difficult passage, here finds some clarity with regard to both its textual location and its content. The preceding verses, 5-8, offer exhortation about prayer, which suggests that we should see prayer being treated also in vv. 9-10. Thus, the one who is humble can boast, in that exaltation is applied to him (as with Mary in the *Magnificat;* cf. esp. Luke 1:48b-49). Similarly, the one who is rich can boast when he humbles himself—and his humility consists in that he admits he is as transient as a flower.[26]

4. Fasting is a particular mode of self-abasement. Thus it is that the combination "prayer and fasting" is often replaced by "fasting and humiliation."[27] In such cases fasting has the special meaning of driving out arrogant thoughts.[28]

5. According to *1 Clem.* 56:1, an attitude of humility is bestowed so that one "can give in to the will of God" (and not the will of human beings). This text also has obvious similarities to the content of Mark 14:36.

Results: It is a frequently attested tradition that prayer acceptable to God is tied up with renunciation by the petitioners of their own wills and with their acknowledgment of themselves as the servants of God. Even the Lord's Prayer invites interpretation from this angle ("Your will be done," Matt 6:10b).

Both the New Testament and Jewish texts, however, also attest to the opposite state of affairs: prayer is a struggle before and with God.[29] Philo also speaks of wrestling with God in prayer.[30] Apparently these statements are to be seen as prior to those about the surrender of the will; the surrender of one's own will stands at the end, not at the beginning, of a struggle with God. Even Mary presents objections (Luke 1:34), and Jesus starts out by stating what his own desire is. In a sense every petition is a sort of contest, even if they all end in the same way.

Finally a few comments about "temptation" (mentioned not only in Mark 14:38 but also several times in James 1 and, in substance if not explicitly, in 1 Pet 5:6-9). The biblical notion of temptation always consists in following one's own will, in pursuit of one's own advantage. The prayer in Mark 14:36c ("Not what I want . . .") is therefore the overcoming of temptation as such. Prayer helps overcome temptations (which come from within the petitioner) because, in the final analysis, prayer must always be submission, as by a slave, to the will of God. To this extent the prayer of Jesus in the Garden is paradigmatic.

Several features in all of this are interesting from a psychological perspective. (a) The feature of subjection to the will of God is consistently the final stage of a struggle (a wrestling match). (b) The words that express self-abasement (humiliation), as well as those of being exalted, at least to some extent have their usual original setting in the practice of prayer. (c) According to Mark 14:41, the outcome of just such subjection to the will of God is the strength to overcome anxiety. At this point Jesus can awaken his disciples and encourage them to go forth. He has once again been enabled to seize the initiative, and he has been enabled to do so precisely because he has committed himself totally to the initiative of God. This corresponds to the way in which, in other texts, submission to God is always followed by exaltation of the one who submits. (d) Relationship to the theme of not worrying (cf. 1 Pet 5:7) comes about through the fact that one's own will is primarily concerned about preserving one's own life. Indeed, this is precisely how temptations are often conceptualized (cf. the tempting of Jesus by bread in Matt 4:3-4 or by the assurance of protection in vv. 6-7). Mark 14:36 makes it clear that those who renounce their own wills are also prepared to risk their lives. They can do so because they now know that they are in the hands of God. (Note how it is said, in 1 Pet 5:6, that one should humble oneself "under the mighty hand of God.") (e) Self-abasement before God is therefore at the same time a realistic act of self-esteem; it is not just a passive giving up. It is thus full of hope and promise. (f) The association between petition and self-abasement remains an enduring feature, for they both are part of a whole. When the will of God is finally acknowledged as decisive, then the petitioner leaves himself or herself open for any outcome. It is as though the petitioner anticipates not being granted what is desired but indicates readiness, even willingness, to accept the refusal of the petition. Thus an old aphorism retains plausibility: prayer does not change the will of God but rather the will of the one who prays. This truth resides in the fact that the one who prays is no longer just a victim of blind fate, no longer just an object. The orderly parameters of an established relationship, that of a master and his servants, are put in the place of what might otherwise seem to be blind fate. Everything now is played out within the confines of this relationship, a relationship personally affirmed by the petitioner. Terror is thereby overcome, and a personal relationship is created in which the dignity of the petitioner finds expression. This dignity is derived from the petitioner's free consent to enter into a master-slave relationship with God.

This master-slave relationship is undoubtedly regarded by the writer of the text as a given, as an "objective" fact. As this relationship is taken up within the act of praying, however, it becomes something more than just a given. In subjectively embracing the relationship, the petitioner is put in the position of being able to accept whatever the Lord intends on the specific occasion of the prayer; whatever the response of the Master, it is now seen as only one instance within the context of the broader relationship.

The feature of self-abasement at the end of the prayer thus has a calming effect. The petitioner's concerns now assume only relative importance against the background of the ongoing master-servant relationship. And it is probably not too much to think that some advantage is to be found for master as well as slave in the relationship. Be that as it may, the relativizing of the petitioner's concerns at the end of the prayer plays an important role in view of the fact that adversity and not deliverance may well follow the completion of the prayer.

Prayer and Spirit

The intertwining of culturally conditioned metaphor and psychological perception offers especially fruitful grounds for inquiry here. The basic issue has to do with the effectiveness of human prayer, whether it can ascend to God. To be accepted, prayer must rise to God much as the aroma of a burnt offering rises to God.[31] That human prayer is rendered effective by the Spirit of God rests on the idea that only what has previously descended from heaven can ascend to heaven.[32] Everything else is encumbered by earthy heaviness and cannot ascend. From this perspective we can understand why prayer must first be made to the Spirit, out of whose power all else takes place.[33]

At the base of all this lies the particular experience of inadequacy in praying (Rom 8:26b). This is not just the failure to have one's petitions granted but also of inability for self-abasement (*tapeinosis*). The ability to pray is understood as a gift—but a gift with certain conditions attached to it. Thus one must make a sharp distinction between a prayer that requests the Spirit and a prayer that is actually Spirit-filled. It is by no means necessary to think of the latter in terms of ecstasy or aphasia. A "successful" prayer is one that is Spirit-inspired.

Prayer before the Throne of God

Typical for the New Testament conception of prayer is the notion that the distance between God and human beings (what we call transcendence) has been broken through. Theological language here speaks of free access to God or of the relationship of children to their father (e.g., Rom 8:14-15). From a psychological perspective, one would instead here speak of a loss of neutral feelings. A glance at the genres of hymn and prayer in biblical speech is illustrative. The lament, the giving of thanks, the cry of joy (e.g., "Hallelujah"), as well as sighs and the addressing of God as "Father" (cries of "*Abba*") are all expressive modes of speech. In each case we are dealing with emotional intensification, precisely the opposite of indifference to the heavenly realm of God. Put another way, what theologically or metaphorically would be described as entering into the domain of God has a clear psychological correlate, namely, the abandoning of any and all emotional indifference, with feelings intensifying even to the point of ecstasy. Speaking with God is an occasion for self-expression, in the literal sense of the word (*expressio*). "Entering the realm of transcendence" is accompanied by either an exposing or an intensification of emotions, depending on the situation of the one involved. The genres of prayer and hymn are the place for expressivity.

The relevance of these remarks should be obvious. Hymns and prayers are neither the place for restrictive moralizing nor for parading one's readiness to accept all that God has decreed. Lamentation and accusation also have a place here.

Pastoral Care

Historical psychology also needs to investigate the modes of interaction between, say, Paul and his addressees, as they get played out in the Pauline letters. At the least, we see displayed there a strategy intended to have a powerful effect on the addressees. The more strongly that rational argumentation dominates (e.g., in Romans 4), the less interesting are such texts for historical psychology. From another angle, however, precisely those texts are instructive in which the writer proceeds with all the weapons of persuasion at his disposal. As a prime example of Pauline epistolary pastoral care,[34] I consider 2 Cor 10:1-6, analyzing the verbal performance of Paul and evaluating its use of psychologically effective measures to influence and persuade his addressees.

THE INTERPLAY BETWEEN GENTLENESS AND THREAT

Paul starts at a disadvantage. He has the reputation of being humble in person—indeed, even obsequious (10:1b). When absent, however, and in his letters, he takes the risk of using strong language (10:1c). The judgment about his character to which Paul refers in 10:10 is similar. Paul reacts by making reference at the outset (10:10a) to the "gentleness and meekness" of Christ. Then he suggests that any display of boldness on his part will have to wait until he visits the community in person (10:2a). What is going on here is that Paul, with all the means at his disposal, attempts to refute the image that people in Corinth have of him, an image he regards as not only inaccurate but also, and more importantly, as deleterious to the gospel. He needs to show that precisely the opposite of their image is in fact the case. So he starts gently, setting aside for the time being any display of boldness. That will be displayed later, and then only in case his gentle admonition meets with no success. In the same vein he will later (in 10:8) emphasize that he has received his authority not for destroying the community but solely for building it up. At the same time, however, Paul tacitly allows the possibility of destruction to be recognized. All of these steps are part of his tactic of intimidation. Still, it is by no means clear whether, by the end of what Paul here writes, the effect has not been actually to reinforce the image that the Corinthians had of him at the outset. In other words, Paul may have actually achieved precisely the opposite of what he intended. One is tempted to think this because what he says in 10:3-6 is anything but meek and gentle. The kindliness attached to these words consists only in the fact that he himself is not at the same time traveling to Corinth to punish the recalcitrant.

This passage (2 Cor 10:1-6) thus shows Paul engaging in an interplay between gentleness and threat. But that is not the whole picture. It also shows the way Paul struggles against the image that the Corinthians have of him. For Paul, unconcealed threat has a place alongside of gentleness. Both features are part of the total "game" that an authority figure must play in opposing the reactions (feelings) of his addressees. Here Paul is making real what he elsewhere calls "persuasion" (2 Cor 5:11a; Gal 1:10). He fully knows the devices he is using, and he is quite open about this with his opponents. It is really up to the hearers to determine whether or not Paul can stick to the tactic of gentleness.

THE MEANING OF THE MILITARY METAPHORS

In 2 Cor 10:1-6 Paul uses the following military metaphors: engaging in warfare (v. 3), weapons (v. 4), demolishing (v. 4), strongholds (v. 4), fortress (v. 5), taking captive (v. 5), avenging disobedience (v. 6). Paul's comments here are completely framed by the imagery of warfare,[35] with the goal of punishing (avenging) all disobedience.

The obstacle Paul hopes to overcome in all this is comprised of (anti-Pauline) thoughts on the part of the Corinthians (v. 5), thoughts that interfere with proper knowledge of God. The Corinthians' thoughts are a form of disobedience, and as such they must be punished. Put in a more positive light, every thought should be compelled to be obedient to Christ (v. 5). Of particular significance in this context are Paul's weapons. Following v. 4, they are not of a worldly sort, but they acquire their power through God. As such, they are invincible.

Several implications follow from Paul's use of military metaphors here. (a) Paul looks upon himself as a field commander of a particular realm or kingdom. (b) In this realm, the alternative to obedience is annihilation. (c) Paul knows that he possesses the far superior weaponry, and merely mentioning it serves as a threat (the weaponry has deterrent value). (d) Within the context of a military campaign, no room is left for gentleness, mercy, or forbearance. (e) The kind of thoughts against which Paul is struggling are not abstract heresies but are of a mundane sort—personal objections to the claims of Paul and to shape of his message.

Paul uses military metaphors, then, for the following reasons:

- The radically imperative nature of the task leads to an abandoning of any and all consideration for individual hesitation or subjective notions.
- The competition is so serious that one must call on the strongest power at the time (indeed, as of all times), namely the military. This amounts to nothing less than a summons to total involvement. Just as in actual warfare, it is a matter of life or death,[36] one of the central themes of Pauline theology. Only against such a background can one understand the compassionless stringency of Paul. For Paul, when it is a matter of life or death there can be no bourgeois tolerance, no "freedom of religion." In such a case, scruples or objections are not to be disposed of through polite persuasion; they must simply be gotten rid of. Paul is behaving like a person who tries to yank someone back from the abyss into which he is about to fall. In such a situation, one does not engage in discussion or exchange ideas. One has to shout at the other!

The lesson in all of this for us today seems to be that we should not water down the sort of strategy Paul employs or interpret away all the sharp edges associated with these metaphors. In every attempt to modify this language, we should consider whether we adequately recognize Paul's seriousness about the life-or-death decision. This also indicates that hard decisions need to be made about how any sort of missionary activity is to be conducted.

10
Behavior

Mandated Hatred

A number of biblical texts and extracanonical parallels call for "hatred" of certain persons. This striking theme merits closer scrutiny.

LUKE 14:26 AND ITS CONTEXT

The verse in question reads as follows: "Whoever comes to me and does not hate father and mother, wife and children, brothers and sisters, yes, and even life itself, cannot be my disciple." The introduction to this passage (v. 25) mentions "large crowds" as those whom Jesus addresses. This makes all the more striking, by contrast, the fact that Jesus is addressing individuals in v. 26. The continuation in v. 27, a summary of conditions for discipleship, also addresses individuals: "Whoever does not carry the cross and follow me cannot be my disciple." The parable about the building of the tower and the one about the king plotting to go to war immediately follow. Both of these parables present discipleship as a risky matter, as something that requires careful prior thought. Because of its demands, choosing to become a follower of Jesus is a serious matter indeed.

Both the comment in v. 26 and the one in v. 27 place emphasis on actively seizing the initiative. In each case we are dealing with something that, for a reader of antiquity, would have been dismaying. Loyalty to family was the highest virtue, and crucifixion was the most shameful mode of execution. Yet to become a disciple of Jesus requires that one be ready to go against the highest virtue and to choose the path that leads to scandalous execution. In the broader context, Luke associates the stipulation to "hate" (v. 26) with the similarly formulated summons to "renounce" all that one has (v. 33). Thus Luke uses the notion of possessions as his unifying theme and provides examples from that perspective.

CLOSEST ANALOGIES

The Q parallel to Luke 14:26, Matt 10:37, is worded considerably more cautiously: "Whoever loves father or mother more than me is not worthy of me; and whoever loves son or daughter more than me is not worthy of me." There also follows in Matthew a comment about bearing the cross (v. 38), but here again the saying ends with the words ". . . is not worthy of me." Matthew's notion of degrees of love is hardly as strident as Luke's reference to hatred, and it is generally the Matthean version of this Q passage that is subsequently transmitted (see "Being a Disciple," below).

In the *Gospel of Thomas,* however, the more radical version is preserved. Thus, logion 55 reads, "Jesus said, 'Whoever does not hate father and mother cannot be my disciple, and whoever does not hate brothers and sisters, and carry the cross as I do, will not be worthy of me.'" Note also logion 101: "Whoever does not hate father and mother as I do cannot be my disciple, for my mother [. . .] but my true mother gave me life." No mention is made in logion 55 of spouse or children. In other words, it is presupposed that the disciples of Jesus have already renounced family ties of this sort. Also lacking is the culminating point of Luke 14:26, the motif of hating one's own "life" (Greek: *psyche*), but this results in the comment about bearing the cross (with the clarification "as I do") being directly connected to the main clause. The version in logion 101 coincides with the version in logion 55 only in its first half, with the reference to father and mother. But the father and the mother here intended are actually the "true" (i.e., heavenly) parents, with God being the "father" and wisdom (or something similar) being the "mother."

In its lament by Aseneth, the Judeo-Hellenistic writing *Joseph and Aseneth* offers an important analogy. Central to the matter at hand is 11:4-8:

> [4]All people have come to hate me,
> and on top of those my father and my mother,
> because I, too, have come to hate their gods and have destroyed them,
> and caused them to be trampled underfoot by men.
> [5]And therefore my father and my mother and my whole family
> have come to hate me and said, "Aseneth is not our daughter
> because she destroyed our gods."
> [6]And all people hate me,
> because I, too, have (come to) hate every man,
> and all who asked for my hand in marriage.
> And now, in this humiliation of mine, all have (come to) hate me,
> and gloat over this affliction of mine.
> [7]And the Lord the God of the powerful Joseph, the Most High,
> hates all those who worship idols,

because he is a jealous and terrible god
toward all those who worship strange gods.
[8]Therefore he has come to hate me, too,
because I worshiped dead and dumb idols. . . .[1]

In this context Aseneth voices a lament occasioned by her turning away
from both pagan gods and her family. In Luke 14:26 the hatred that is
demanded radiates from only one point, namely, outward from the disciples toward their relatives, or inward toward their own lives. In *Joseph and
Aseneth* the hatred described (not demanded) goes in multiple directions,
affecting various participants. Thus, Aseneth herself is hated by her father
and her mother, but she is also hated by the wider circle of her family and,
finally, by all people. Conversely, Aseneth herself hates all others. (Since
she is still unmarried, her statement functions similarly to the one about
hatred of spouse and children in Luke 14:26). Moreover, it is then said that
the God of Israel harbors hatred toward all worshipers of idols—and
therefore also toward Aseneth. In contrast to the structure of Luke 14:26,
then, the emphasis here is chiefly on Aseneth as the object of hatred. To
this she responds by directing her own hatred outward, indiscriminately
toward all persons.

The common point between Luke 14:26 and this passage from *Joseph
and Aseneth* lies especially in the way profound social tensions occasioned
by a radical conversion (to worshiping the God of Israel or to becoming a
disciple of Jesus) result in a particular psychological reaction, "hatred."
One thus finds reproduced in early Christianity certain experiences evident also in Hellenistic Judaism. In both contexts conversion takes place
under dramatically similar circumstances; in both it is experienced as
sharp rejection and thus is perceived as "hatred."

Basically the same theme, though without actual use of the term
"hatred," is found elsewhere as well in the Jesus tradition. In Matt 8:21-22
(par. Luke 9:59-60), a disciple of Jesus is reluctant to leave his parents, yet
he is not even permitted to carry out the sacred obligation of burying
them.[2] According to Luke 12:51-53 (par. Matt 10:34), Jesus has not come
to bring peace but rather division among those who are closely related.

Analogies to the theme of hating one's nearest relatives, in the form of
direct actions taken against them, are known from Old Testament tradition. In Exod 32:27-29 the Levites, enacting punishment at the command
of Moses, slay sons and brothers as well as friends and neighbors; in *Tar-
gum Onqelos* the list of victims comprises brothers, neighbors, and relatives.[3] When someone tries secretly to entice a faithful Israelite into
worshiping other gods, the faithful Israelite is to hand over the culprit for
capital punishment, even if the enticer is brother, son, daughter, wife, or
friend.[4] Finally, the theme of intra-family conflict plays a role in the scene

of the clash between the generations in *Jubilees* 23. (The younger generation does battle against the older for the sake of a pure interpretation of
the Law.)

DIFFICULTIES IN SUBSEQUENT INTERPRETATION

Matthew 10:37 already seems to have softened our theme. Clement of
Alexandria replaces the idea of hatred with "not regard as higher" (*Strom.*
6.100.2). Elsewhere Clement explains, "He (Jesus) does not command
hatred of one's own family . . . he means instead, Let yourself not be
diverted by irrational urges nor allow yourself to become dependent on
conventional habits . . . pleasing to the world" (*Strom.* 3.97.2). A similar
theme is voiced a little further on (*Strom.* 7.79.6): "For he hates the fleshly
inclinations, which include a powerful temptation to lust, and he holds in
low regard everything that contributes to building up and nourishing the
flesh, but he also aids in resisting the bodily soul in that he takes control
of the irrational spirit that would like to throw off its reins." In his writing
on riches (*Dives* 22.2), Clement directly addresses the reader concerning
Luke 14:26, saying that that verse "should not trouble you" since the God
of peace, who commands love even of enemies, "cannot command hatred
of and separation from those most dear to us." One should love one's enemies, yes, but all the more one's nearest relatives, for if one were expected
to hate one's kin, how much the more would one then have to hate one's
enemies? The issue is only that one should not honor one's parents more
than one honors Christ, nor show consideration for relatives if they block
one's path to salvation. In sum, with the help of the command to love one's
enemies (Matt 5:46 par.), Clement of Alexandria succeeds in taking the
edge off Luke 14:26; indeed, he even manages to transform it into its opposite. With such a systematic reworking of the directives of Jesus, then,
tradition exposes itself as incapable of preserving the sharply pointed
teaching in Luke 14:26.

INTERPRETATIONS TO BE EXCLUDED

It is obvious that Luke 14:26 is not dealing merely with one phase of
human development—a severing of immature ties to parents and family.
Just as obviously we are not dealing with hatred as an end in itself, as
though the "religion of love" had here been transposed into its opposite.
There is no blind urge for destruction lying behind this demand to break
off ties. Along the same line, we are not here dealing with a systematically
applicable principle; this demand hardly moves on the same plane as the
Ten Commandments, which constitute the core of the Law. Nothing like a
Kantian "categorical imperative" can be distilled out of this statement.

(Any attempt at such a move would only serve to illustrate the incompatibility between philosophical ethics and the pointed directives of the New Testament.)

More significant, biblical "hatred," just as biblical "love," is much less a feeling than a mode of activity. The orientation is not emotions but praxis, which can be illustrated by Lev 19:18, the command to love one's neighbor as oneself. According to the context, the specific issue at hand is how to deal with a neighbor's misdeeds. The command to love here appears in the form of a reprimand.[5] Nothing necessitates the understanding that to "love your neighbor as yourself" needs to involve sympathetic feelings. The command to love one's enemy does not mean somehow or other to have positive feelings for the enemy but rather to avoid trying to impede what good might come to the enemy. This would include such things as prayers spoken in behalf of the enemy, blessings directed toward the enemy, and both religious and secular deeds performed to benefit the enemy. What all of this means with regard to Luke 14:26 is that we are not talking about developing an emotional dislike of one's relatives but about giving up or breaking off contact with them, the severing of long-term relationships.

PROBLEMATIC RELATIONSHIP TO COMMANDMENTS

Unlike the comment about bearing one's cross (v. 27), Luke 14:26 not only goes against conventional moral notions but also directly contradicts one of the Ten Commandments, the one about honoring parents. Beyond that, it at least appears to contravene the command to love one's neighbor as oneself. And Matt 8:21-22 offends against a fundamental human obligation (burial of one's parents). These difficulties were noted by the church fathers, who tried to harmonize the oppositions.

Is this saying of Jesus really directed against all the commandments that demand the contrary? Note how no specific commandment is cited in these contexts. This suggests that we are here dealing with a summons that is not intended to be equated with the Law or to be directly compared with it. The Law, in other words, is by no means the standard against which this particular command of Jesus either can or should be measured; a focus on Law in Luke 14:26 is most unlikely. The concern is not with certain commandments but with fundamental social realities. Keeping both the closer and the broader contexts in view, it is even quite probable that the point of concern is precisely the fulfilling of the commandments and the will of God. It is just that this fulfillment will now depend on a new foundation, one that is being established in its social and its psychological aspects. That new foundation is discipleship.

HATRED ACTIVELY DIRECTED AGAINST FAMILIAL CONSTRAINTS

The hatred to which Jesus summons his followers is certainly not rooted in embittered resignation but grows out of his awareness that the social fabric of the family was tightly knit and therefore was an important factor making for inflexibility in social interactions or interpersonal relationships. What we have here is a breaking open of precisely that area whose strictures would normally be beyond question. The words in Luke 14:26 and Matt 8:21-22 penetrate like a sharp knife into that zone where social constraints (whether acknowledged or concealed) rule most strongly and where traditional piety determines just about everything.

When the Gospels speak biographically about Jesus (e.g., Mark 3:21, 31-35; 6:3-4), it is quite possible to see that he himself could have been affected by traumatic experiences of the sort rooted in family interactions. One can say this because, in these texts, the pressures for social and psychological conformity to the norms of family life are strikingly apparent. Obviously the greatest hindrance to the emergence of a discipleship oriented toward Jesus was to be found here, at the familial basis of society.

When Jesus summons his followers to "hate" their families, then, the issue really only has to do with the intensity with which Jesus perceived family constraints. What some understand and interpret as "love" can be considered by some family members as suffocating. It is against controlling "love," which hinders any sort of genuine renewal that Jesus directs his provocative command to hate. The connection of this command with the comment about bearing one's cross brings out just how closely the constraints of familial "love" tend to be linked to conventional social standards about what counts as valuable and what does not. Some indication of what would presumably come to pass is the most persuasive means of defending the ideological control that families impose on their members. ("What would people think?")

Jesus' unconstrained association with women could also illustrate the fact that he himself was positioned to shatter such social constraints. Moreover, there is a striking difference regarding family ties between some of the imagery Jesus uses and his explicit instructions. Family relationships are presented in a positive light in metaphors (e.g., brotherly love as a model for the relationship of Christians to each other) or in similes (e.g., the father-child relationship in Luke 11:11-13). The same is not the case, however, in sayings of Jesus that have no edifying function.[6] All of this leads to the following conclusion: One aspect of the content of Luke 14:26 is the fact that Jesus exposes as unabashed social oppression precisely those domestic relationships that are most frequently mislabeled "love." The command to hate members of one's own family thus aims at putting an end to this sort of rigidity.

In sum, the great difficulties the church has had in interpreting Luke 14:26 show that these statements of Jesus were generally not capable of being practiced. Nor is this difficult to understand. Since the New Testament so forcefully emphasizes love as the essence of the new relationship with God, there has always been a strong impulse to confirm the almost inescapable constraints of the family by invoking the theme of divine love. It must also be said, however, that churches have rarely withstood the temptation to make use of these stabilizing forces as a way of advancing their own power and influence. This has led in turn to a situation where a summons to Christianity has served to strengthen conformity rather than call family constraints into question. Given how it first gains meaning within the family circle, then, the notion of "love" has itself become a basic factor in the partnership of Christianity and bourgeois conventionality.

INDISPENSABLE CONDITION FOR NEWNESS

Jesus is certainly not talking about being consumed by persistent feelings of hatred but about a fundamental departure, a prompt and complete separation from all old ties. In designating such a break as hatred, Jesus is referring not only to the external act of a leave-taking but also, and even more, to a basic liberation—one that is also a fundamental purification.

The psyche is certainly also affected by such a clean break, such a complete extinction of old ties. "Hatred" thus designates the necessarily total stance to be taken in the face of threatened reincorporation into the old network of social relations. Put another way, "hatred" is the counterpart in the psyche of the fact that something genuinely new is being established in social relationships. Without this "hatred," no more than a partial transition would be possible, hardly sufficient to satisfy the summons to eschatological newness. Speaking of hatred is a way of demonstrating genuine newness, and as such is also an indication of the credibility of its proclamation.

BEING A DISCIPLE

The words of Jesus about necessary hatred presuppose that he regarded the old social relationships primarily as detrimental and that he could conceive of a genuinely new beginning only in the wake of a total and complete separation from such relationships. Seen in a positive light, the goal here is quite simply a new community gathered around the Messiah. For this reason, discipleship entails nothing less than a new communion with Jesus, which in turn entails the fullest possible separation from old entanglements.

The true messianic revolution thus here takes place as a transformation of social relationships realized in the arena of discipleship. It also becomes apparent why this Messiah gathers disciples around himself. They are not just bearers of his message but precisely as a community they are themselves the realization of the eschatological people of God. To effect this realization, Jesus requires no special christological title, no peculiar self-consciousness, or any novel program. All that is required is the distinctive mode of relationship that defines discipleship. This sort of relationship is built on "authority" and "lordship," not on "love." Reciprocating love is not the theme in pronouncements about discipleship but the radical freedom of this new community. Remarkably, the nature of this freedom is not specified at the outset; each of the four evangelists contributes to fill in the details.

The messianic aspect of these words of Jesus needs further specification. The God of the Old Testament demands the equivalent only in exceptional circumstances, and then only in the context of exemplary punishment (Exod 32:27-29). This is so because the God of the Old Testament was not materially present in a comparable way. Only the concept of God's immediate presence in Jesus enables such a new form of community, one that is structured around Jesus. Two features thus stand out as important with regard to this new revelation: (a) the presence of God in Jesus and (b) radical separation of the new community from older structures. Both features were unprecedented.[7]

Thus it is only under the condition of discipleship (imitation of Christ) that the new pattern of social relationships emerges, a pattern truly messianic and redemptive. This new pattern is unthinkable apart from its living center, Jesus. To this end the Gospels were written. Replacing the natural ties of family and kinship, discipleship has now become the messianic social structure. Since there is now a personally incarnate center, unconditional subordination becomes the expression of the quality of eschatological newness. Put another way, because God is now close at hand in Jesus, a new social ordering is possible. At the outset, it is hatred of the old structure that enables the radically new to emerge. From this perspective, then, Jesus is hardly to be thought of as a guru, pointing out the way to an altered inner state but the one who points to God. Only thus can the new really be a liberation from the old.

HATRED OF ONE'S OWN LIFE

According to Luke 14:26 one is to hate also one's own life. In addition to the basic social relationships, the natural attachment to one's own life also comes under consideration.

Most closely related to Luke 14:26 is John 12:25, "Those who love their life lose it, and those who hate their life in this world will keep it for eternal life." The other parallels are more remote. Mark 8:35 reads "would save/will lose," as do Matt 16:25 and Luke 9:24; Matt 10:39 speaks of "finding" and "losing"; Luke 17:33 contrasts "lose" with "seek to gain." Explicit mention of "hating" one's own life is thus found only in Luke 14:26 and John 12:25. This adds a psychological dimension lacking elsewhere; everywhere else the negative side of the formulation mentions only the losing of one's life.

Having the reference to one's "own life" in the concluding (climactic) position, as in Luke 14:26, has an informative parallel in Philo, *On the Virtues* 103: "To love as oneself is something essentially more than loving as friends or relatives."[8] Thus individual egoism (love of one's own life) functions as an intensification of collective egoism (communal conformity).

In all this it is important not to spiritualize the Greek term *psyche*. Although often rendered "soul," the term is better understood when translated in the concrete sense of "life." This also means excluding those interpretations that too strongly suggest the notion of inwardness. The issue here is not one of renouncing joy of living, for example, nor is it one of self-disparagement, as though one were no longer to pay any heed to oneself. There is also no indication that the theme of hatred refers to a negative evaluation of one's own past or that it refers to one's sins. As evident from both the context and the parallels, the theme of loving one's own life has an exclusively forward-looking orientation, with attention directed toward the things that promote vitality. (This is similar to what was said above on the theme of worry; cf. "Worry," chapter 7.) In other words, love of one's own *psyche* deals with everything having to do with preserving life in its physicality (nourishment, clothing, possessions, desire, power). The presupposition in effect here is that everyone clings to these vital concerns. Setting these concerns aside, then, amounts to taking the most extreme of risks but also of finding the greatest freedom. In short, any interpretation that focuses on feelings for oneself or on one's sins would be an exercise in navel-gazing and would have no direct, practical consequences.

The focus, then, is not on negative feelings toward the self or a yearning for extinction of the self but on a suspension of one's own vital interests. The goal of such suspension is that the one being summoned to follow Jesus might find, through "hatred" of this life, quite another life. The parallel passages say essentially the same thing.

In these words Jesus summons his disciples to win the greatest sort of freedom. Hateful feelings do not make this happen. It follows in the wake of a fundamental letting go of all that to which people most tightly cling. The goal is not simply rejection of everything but that sort of renunciation through which alone the genuinely new can emerge.

ASPECTS OF RECEPTION HISTORY

One of the few texts deemed worthy of mention in the Gnostic writing known as *The Exegesis on the Soul* is Luke 14:26—in particular, the climactic section about hating one's own life.[9] But the particular slant *Exeg. Soul* takes, namely, that the reference is to repentance, too strongly spiritualizes. The gnosticizing *Acts of John* finds hindrances to faith in the following: "worry, children, parents, splendor, poverty (!), flattery, youthful strength, beauty, boasting, envy, riches, anger, arrogance, frivolity, jealousy . . . money." Clement of Alexandria offers the following warrant for hatred directed against one's kindred: "For the Christian does not want to be warm through contact with war, nor shining through reflection of fire; the Christian wants to be actual light."[10] Here the positive aspect of hatred is not sought primarily in a new association with Jesus but in a spiritual self-reliance in which one has cut oneself free from all attachments. Thus the words of Jesus become, among other things, a contribution toward the discovery of individuality.

Necessary Self-Love

The question here involves a close interacting of psychological and ethical problems. As presented in Lev 19:18, the command to love the neighbor presupposes as its standard the love one has for oneself ("Love your neighbor . . . as yourself"). What has happened in post–New Testament times is not just that the reality of such self-love gets called into question. A remarkable intensification occurs. Specifically, alongside the command to love one's neighbor "as yourself" (e.g., Mark 12:31 par.; Rom 13:9) stands another, "You shall love your neighbor more than you love yourself/your soul/your life" (Greek: *psyche;* cf. *Epistle of Barnabas* 19:5, in contrast to its parallel in *Didache* 1:2). Doesn't the formulation in *Barnabas* alone correspond to the radical newness of the Christian proclamation? Notice, for example, how *Barn.* 19:5 is cast as a direct imperative, whereas Lev 19:18 is built upon a simple comparison. It would seem that *Barn.* 19:5 reflects a genuine continuation of the summons to hate one's own "life" (Greek: *psyche*) as found in Luke 14:26.

A UTOPIAN SOCIAL PROGRAM

In Lev 19:18 love of self, far from being erased, is treated as the criterion of righteousness. Here the writer presupposes that love of self, a very strong impulse, is not something to be suppressed but something on which to build. The agenda calls not for denial of self but for equivalence for the other. That is to say, the goal is a society in which the agent being addressed is still very much "there." It is clear, from the immediate context, that we are here dealing with sentiments, such as animosity and resentment, that arise on occasions of reprimand. The addressee is being challenged to think of his opponent's interests as analogous to his own, and then to show respect for the interests of both parties. Accordingly, the ethical directive in this case presupposes a psychological foundation.

CURTAILED SELF-LOVE?

The New Testament citations of the commandment in Lev 19:18 never associate the love of self with sinfulness. Moreover, sin is never characterized as self-love. Put quite simply, to define sin as self-love is to engage in an unbiblical form of thinking. In biblical understanding the sinner is characterized not by love of self but by disobedience. Sometimes the sinner's disobedience is even prompted by an apparent good (cf. the motif of deception in Rom 7:11).

In fact, a number of Jesus' sayings become intelligible only when we move beyond the category of self-love. So, for example, in the parable of the prodigal son (Luke 15:11-32), the turning point comes when the son recognizes that it is in his own interest to return to his father (vv. 17-18). The lost son ponders where things would go better for him. He recognizes that the day-laborers in his father's household have it better than he does. This leads to his resolve to make a change. In other words, he is hardly a model of remorse. He does what is advantageous for himself. Interpreting the parable in this way also enables a tighter connection with the material that immediately follows. In a formal sense, the dishonest steward of Luke 16:1-9 is a model for the Christian. He is a model not in his misdeeds but in his cleverness. In timely fashion, he watched out for his own future. This parable bases its message on an instinct for self-preservation which, it is assumed, is at work even in Christians. Just as the prodigal son, so also the dishonest steward simply strove to put himself in the most advantageous position possible. Finally, note the comments in Luke 12:42 and 19:17-19. The good and true servants are given authority over cities or over other servants. The desire of people to be in charge is thus accepted.

What it all comes down to is that the Lukan "way of peace" is hardly some leap into the dark but is based on sound and well-understood self-interest. The difference is simply that Christians are not oriented toward immediate material interests, toward what might be gained today or tomorrow. They take the long view. The message of Jesus has given them patience. To take the long view now seems credible, since God has shown Jesus to be the Lord of history, the one who lifts up the lowly, restores the dead to life, and lets the wealthy go away empty-handed. If God works such transformations as these, then certainly it is worth asking what it takes to be a part of this new state of affairs. Alternately expressed: this God is the guarantor of a worthwhile future. Insofar as Christians can keep their gaze on the future, it belongs to them; the future is where their investment lies. So the question for Christians becomes how best to enhance their holdings. According to Luke, the answer of Jesus is to make friends of the needy. In sum, with both the prodigal son (Luke 15) and the dishonest steward (Luke 16), a healthy egoism is being encouraged. This is the way to overcome fatalism, a blind acceptance of things as they currently are.

The Jesus of Luke's Gospel clearly knows how difficult it is effectively to motivate human beings. He directs his message to people who know something about the ways of the world. In a certain sense, Jesus comes at them from the "right." Basic human interests are maintained—if anything, more astutely than before. Now those interests can persevere even in the presence of a God who topples the mighty and brings down those in high places. So, for example, the Jesus of Luke 16:9 is not determined to do away with money. The decisive issue is what one does with one's money; the fate of money as such is insignificant. (It is presupposed that money comes, in any case, from unjust dealings.)

Christians, then, do not do good for its own sake but because, in the process, a certain new way of looking at things emerges. Luke is hardly testifying in favor of an ethic of world-denial that ends in frozen utopian formulas. The "radical" aspect of the sort of ethic to which Luke testifies lies in the ability, despite being in the world and participating in its ways, to be free from the constraints of the world—to be free for servitude to the will of God (Luke 16:13).

In sum, the New Testament does not merely take self-love for granted but goes beyond this and actually makes repeated appeal to self-interest. A basic starting point for the message of Jesus is precisely such an appeal. Even the summons to hatred of self (Luke 14:26) leads indirectly to the enhancement of life.

DIFFICULTIES IN APPROPRIATION

For several reasons, contemporary Christians might find it difficult to accept the position laid out in the preceding section. (a) A particular doctrine about sin, which gained ascendancy in the church particularly in the nineteenth century (because it seemed to presuppose no "supernaturalism"), led to a mistrust of everything that seemed to affirm the "natural human being," even in the smallest of matters. (b) The influence of Kantian ethics supported the notion of doing good simply for its own sake.[11] On this point, Idealism is characterized by self-denial. Brought into conjunction, these two aspects of nineteenth-century thought were mutually rein-forcing. (c) From another direction, some exponents of liberation theology emphasize that, for many people, the ability to develop self-oriented inter-ests (to see themselves as subjects of their own volition) has been extin-guished. With such people one must first instill the capacity for self-love. (Much the same was sometimes said about the "victims" of the manifesta-tions of sin as perceived from the perspective mentioned under point "a.") It is therefore at least questionable that one should now contribute to the erosion of the self through systematic emphasis of a particular under-standing of sinfulness.

FROM LOVE OF SELF TO LOVE OF NEIGHBOR

The big question at the heart of Kant's categorical imperative was how to achieve the transition from love of self to socially responsible behavior, from self-gratification to ethics. What his answer comes down to, in effect, is a transformation of self-love into "enthusiasm" for the univer-sal.[12] (This is also one of the reasons for the link between Kantian thought and patriotism.)

Biblical psychology, conversely, connects directly to the self-interest of the individual and can therefore be seen to continue the recognition, evi-dent in ancient Israel's wisdom tradition, of a degree of human autonomy. At least since Sirach, this limited autonomy of the individual has been connected to and interwoven with the heteronomy of the Torah. Much the same happens in the teachings of Jesus. This line of thinking does not speak of any transformation of self-love into love of neighbor but rather, as already in Lev 19:18, of the "being together" of siblings. This is cer-tainly also a reasonable principle for communal life. In its specifically New Testament form, however, this model goes much further. Here faith in God as the Lord of history leads to the conviction that any sacrifice can be meaningful, including the sacrifice of renouncing egoism for the sake of the other. This is so because a judicious ordering of affairs does not hap-pen on its own. The assumption of a self-regulating human reason is replaced by emphasis on Christian hope, a hope that in turn is grounded in the Christian image of God. After all, the Kantian categorical imperative becomes significant only if everyone acts according to it. Christian hope does not hang from such a thin thread.

Going beyond love of self presupposes a fundamental affirmation of individual self-interest. Even in an ideal community, individual agents are actually present. One's "neighbor" in the web of society, then, is to be seen as one's brother or one's sister. The point of orientation is the other in his or her concrete specificity. Justice follows from taking seriously the interests of others, not from pursuing some universal ideal.

Sexuality

Here it is instructive to proceed with a look 1 Corinthians 5–7. In order not to awaken false expectations, the first item of business is to set out the differences between the Pauline way of approaching the topic of sexuality and contemporary experiences. In this way the enduring significance of what Paul has to say can be highlighted.

SIGNIFICANT DIFFERENCES

Lack of a Personal Aspect

Paul places no particular value on sexuality as a mode of relationship between individuals. Nowhere does he speak of the emotional ties between sexual partners. He mentions only that they are "one flesh," never that they are joined together as "one heart and one soul." Even the aspect of friendship between husband and wife, which was known to Aristotle, is missing in Paul. With Paul, moreover, ways in which the sexual impulses might come up against one's relationship with God likewise fail to receive discussion.

In the poems of Catullus, notable exemplars of the ancient lyric of love, no particularly personal aspect is reflected. This suggests that we should probably not expect to see such in the writings of Paul either. The discourse of the time was apparently such that that aspect was not open to experience. The Western understanding of the person has continued to develop during the two thousand years since Paul, but at that time the notion of love as a form of personal relationship was hardly possible. Likewise, 1 Corinthians 13 does not speak of love in terms of personal relationship but as a divine gift that outlasts and surpasses all others.

Difference in Biographical Perception

That we experience sexuality differently now is in no small degree due to the fact that sexuality has become for us an important aspect of personal biography. Shared experiences over a span of time are important in our experience of sexuality. With love, we expect the emergence of a shared story built on joint memories and convergent hopes. That this aspect of sexuality was apparently not yet developed at the time of Paul can be inferred from the rudimentary stage of development of autobiography and biography in his day. There was not yet then any genre that we would truly label biography, nor was there any fixed form of autobiography. The *Confessions* of Augustine is the first autobiographical milestone—and that has to do with conflicts within a single heart. In sum, just as we think it takes experiencing the passing of time for personhood to develop, so also we regard the sharing of experiences over time to be important in the development of a love relationship. It was otherwise in the time of Paul.

Lack of Erotic Fascination

Because Paul does not think of love in terms of a personal relationship, there is also lacking in his writings any trace of erotic fascination between persons. Perhaps such fascination can arise only when love is seen as a complex phenomenon. In any case Paul did not so regard love.

In antiquity, erotic fascination had something of the preternaturally uncanny about it. An enraptured lover might feel that he or she was experiencing divinity.[13] Such a response would not have been conceivable for Paul. Since its beginnings, the religion of Israel had opposed the mythicizing of sexuality, and this certainly influenced Paul. Against this background it is worth emphasizing that "love" in 1 Corinthians 13 refers not to sexuality but to relationship with God. This is in keeping with the pattern of a significant transformation in discourse about love begun by Israel's prophets. Love ceased to be spoken of as sexual relations between gods and human beings; it came to describe the relationship between God and Israel. Within Israelite religion only this relationship (between God and Israel) counted as being similar to a marriage.

The way Paul speaks of sexuality, then, leaves no room for sentimentalizing this area of human experience. What is apt to move us most about sexuality is the way it promotes an openness to imaginative and sympathetic participation in the life of an other. We would see "true love" as blossoming only within such a context. Of all this Paul knows nothing. Consequently, it is somewhat distressing and odd that throughout the history of the church people have turned to Paul for advice about love. Paul in fact paid no attention to major aspects of what we today understand by "love."

Shameless Speech

Paul speaks of sexuality without granting it any sort of mystery. Thus he plunges into a description of an incestuous relationship at the very beginning of the portion of his letter dealing with specific issues (1 Cor 5:1-13).[14] Just as bluntly, he then speaks about becoming "one flesh" with a prostitute (6:12-20). More problems dealing with sexual relations are treated in 1 Corinthians 7—as matter-of-fact as a discussion about borrowing and lending. Whoever speaks so "objectively" about such personal issues is, so to speak, acting shamelessly. At least it is possible to take Paul's words in this way, especially if one thinks there is a close connection between the sense of personhood and feelings of shame. One (like Paul) who does not see the relationship between a man and a woman in terms of a blending of personalities can hardly avoid speaking of such a relationship indiscreetly (which is to say, without shame).

Conclusion

With regard to relationships between the sexes, there is in Paul not a trace of the personal element we regard as so important. He approaches sexuality primarily as a set of factual or objective problems. Because Paul sees sexuality as stripped of all its mythic possibilities, the aspect of love that we find especially charming—its insubstantiality—entirely escapes him. Paul has nothing to say about the "peak experience" of life that so many find in the act that passes on the germ of life. Instead, he talks about the living God, the One who can make the dead live again. Paul's interests are directed not toward the irretrievable preciousness of the moment but toward the whence and the whither, toward what is of lasting value, not toward the ephemerality of the contingent. And God is the only eternal value.

PAUL'S PERCEPTION OF SEXUALITY

Cases of Property Rights

Paul inclines toward a view of sexuality as a matter of property rights.

1. According to 1 Cor 6:12-20, Christians are to eschew relations with prostitutes because Christians do not belong to themselves (v. 19). They have been purchased (v. 20). Through the indwelling spirit of God they are now house and temple and henceforth the property of God. Given this state of affairs, any use of the property that goes against the will of the owner or proprietor must be seen as illicit. Relations with a prostitute constitute such a case, since control over the property is transferred to someone who is not the actual owner (6:16). According to Paul, the true owner is not at all inclined to allow his property to be misused in this way.

2. According to 1 Cor 7:4, husbands and wives have proprietary rights over each other's bodies. It is therefore possible to speak of a marital obligation (v. 3). Paul employs the same verb ("to rule") here as he does in his discussion of relations with a prostitute. The difference in the case of married persons is simply that the marital relationship is based on reciprocal rights. In relations with a prostitute, no such reciprocity exists. Reciprocal rights legitimizes sexual relations within marriage.

3. Paul even grounds his renunciation of marriage in terms of property rights. The unmarried woman (and the virgin) is "holy in body and spirit" (1 Cor 7:34). According to the understanding of holiness formulated in 1 Cor 6:19, to be holy in this context means nothing other than that such a

woman has been totally converted into the property of God, and that she is to actualize this proprietary relationship. Indeed, every Christian has the Holy Spirit within and so belongs to God. It is just that the unmarried are to express this status in and through their bodies.

4. Paul often speaks about the problems of sexual partnership between individuals through the use of genres characteristically employed for instructing and exhorting communities, especially juristic genres. This leaves the impression that Paul is concerned to have each person get what properly belongs to him or her.

Conflict between Sexuality and Religion

Many well-meaning Christians today think it possible without much trouble for sexuality and service to God to coexist. This would be unthinkable for Paul, for whom at least the cultic (symbolic) expression of veneration of God directly competes with the exercise of sexuality. (a) Prayer and sexual relations are mutually exclusive. Thus, for Paul (1 Cor 7:5), the only reason why a married couple might withdraw from one another (for only a limited time, to be followed by reunion) would be for the sake of prayer. (b) Concern for the Lord and concern about the well-being of one's sexual partner also come into direct conflict, according to Paul. Anyone who wants to combine the two as a married Christian faces a truly difficult task; such a person is genuinely "divided" (1 Cor 7:34). Concern for one's sexual partner rates as nothing less than concern "for the world." As such, it can hardly be good. At best, it must be seen as something dangerous. The underlying reason for this conflict undoubtedly lies in the fact that Paul equates service to God with marriage, both being understood as the unrestricted and physically expressed belonging to another.

Being Totally at Another's Disposal, as a Slave

Several times Paul lets his Jewish/Old Testament understanding of the relationship between God and human beings come to the fore. In this understanding, human beings are "slaves" of God. Paul also carries this understanding into the interpersonal realm. (a) According to Rom 6:16-23, the metaphor of slavery is applicable to the Christian's new relationship with God. Indeed, Paul expressly states that he is using a metaphor to depict this situation (v. 19). But in 1 Cor 6:20 one can also see Paul directly describe becoming a Christian in terms of a transfer of masters, such as would happen at a slave market. (b) Describing the relationship between a married couple in terms of each person's "rule" over the body of the other (1 Cor 7:4) appears to be unique. Reference to the desire to "please" (Greek: *areskō*) the spouse (1 Cor 7:32-34), however, uses language typically employed to the relation of slaves to masters. (c) In Rom 13:1 Paul uses the same metaphor to describe the Christian's relationship to governing authorities ("be subject to"). The Greek word rendered "authorities" is *exousia*, which is something of a catch-all term in discussions of power relations.

For the Greek-speaking Christians of Corinth, hearing the relationship with God depicted by the metaphor of slavery would have been, at the very least, unusual. In the Jewish-Hellenistic milieu of the New Testament, however, it is not unusual to find the conjugal relationship described with the metaphor of slavery, as attested in the widespread use of *hypotassesthai* (to be subject to). In any case, it is evident that Paul used his estimation of the primary social bond of marriage to communicate his understanding of God and of the human being's relationship to God. Metaphors of slavery are applied in both areas.

The metaphor of slavery might still be meaningful as an aid in understanding our relationship with God; it emphasizes how totally one's being is involved in this relationship. Thus we might still find plausible precisely that feature that must have struck the first-century Corinthians as very strange. With regard to social relationships, however, the notion of being "subject" hardly seems a suitable metaphor any longer. While the actual words may not be there, the sort of reciprocity described by Paul in 1 Cor 7:4 amounts to saying that each partner is to be subject to the other. I have no other explanation for this striking way of looking at things than that a Jewish-Hellenistic model of the divine-human relationship has been carried over into the area of social relationships.[15] No double standard is to be applied here.

From a distinctly historical-psychological point of view, several conclusions follow. (a) Relationship with God has moved to the center; it has become the absolute standard. Further indications of this can be found in the oft-repeated formula about the importance of being subject "as (was) the Lord." At the same time we are here dealing with a remnant of Paul's Pharisaic heritage, namely, the penetration of the sacred into the everyday and the ordinary. (b) The lowest rung of social relationships, that occupied by slaves, becomes the model for the highest of all relationships, that with God. This kind of revaluation has a parallel in the theme of being "lowly" (Greek: *tapeinos*). In both cases the aim is to extinguish human pride, particularly in its form as a striving for social prestige. Grasping after public esteem is therefore looked on as the driving force behind conflict and discord—in a word, behind "godlessness." One must address human beings at the nodal point of their social interactions. A slave is, par excellence, one without honor and status. There can be genuine peace only under the condition that all people renounce the striving after influence and honor. There is often too little appreciation for the degree to which Paul tries to put a cap on all forms of "social climbing." Paul does not advocate economic communism, but he certainly promotes a kind of communalism based on shared renunciation of prestige. (c) The standard of evaluation has thus become something nearly inconceivable in status-conscious Hellenistic society, namely, one in which regard is no longer paid to rank of any sort. (d) This radical vision even excludes the dimension of treating one another as "equals." The notion of friendship also no longer suffices as a model for social harmony. Putting the notion of being a "slave" at the center of consideration precludes both of these other options.

Driven by Impulse

Human sexuality is consistently regarded by Paul as being driven by impulse. Thus he speaks of a "lack of self-control" in 1 Cor 7:5; he sees it as a reason for marriage when two people cannot control themselves and are "aflame" (1 Cor 7:9); he speaks of a "virgin" in 1 Cor 7:36 (Greek: *parthenos*). In all of these cases, sexuality is considered under the rubric of lust.

One significant consequence of this perspective is a greatly heightened sensitivity to the danger of trafficking with a prostitute (1 Cor 7:2). It is basically because of this danger that Paul allows for marriage at all; marriage becomes, in effect, a last-ditch effort to avoid sin. The second view is conditioned by the first. Where sexuality is basically seen as driven by impulse, then satisfying the sexual drive by turning to a prostitute is a thought that comes readily to the fore. Put another way, celibacy and promiscuity are the two sides of the same coin—at least where sexuality is not seen in the broader context of personhood. Where the personal dimension is left out of consideration, one and the same basic impulse is at work in both celibacy and promiscuity. In the former case it is under control; in the latter it is not.[16]

Being Unmarried Is Preferable

Paul does allow marriage, but this permission comes at a high price, namely, at the expense of inner unanimity. It is not a sin to marry—this much Paul can concede. Moreover, it is better to be married than to engage in sexual relations with a prostitute. Remaining unmarried amounts to a religious gift, since it directs the gaze of a human being away from the normal state of affairs and toward God. The Christian who remains unmarried is "holy"—a Pharisaic ideal, but in this case enabled by the gift of the Holy Spirit. In other words, Paul is here striving after totality and unity of commitment. Acting on one's sexual impulses directly interferes with this goal. At best, it amounts to a compromise with human weakness.

What Paul Wants to Change

Righteousness

Without doubt Paul perceives the area of sexual relations to be the locus of a whole lot of unrighteousness. Therefore he is careful to issue instructions to men as well as to women (e.g., 1 Cor 7:4, 10-16). Paul speaks with a blunt specificity, directing his remarks to areas about which people are most concerned and where experience shows that mistreatment is especially apt to occur.

Against Autonomy for This Area

Paul is compelled to begin his admonition of the Corinthians with a lengthy exposition on sexuality because the Corinthians obviously thought that sexuality was an area not affected by Christianity. The whole character of the argument in 1 Corinthians 5–7 rests on the fact that Paul must first establish its connection with the elements of Christian faith. Paul at the outset confronts the opinion that issues relating to sexuality are strictly private, and that he therefore has really nothing to say about them. For Paul, the topic of intimate relations is definitely not to be left to the conscience of each individual.

Detachment

Chief among the things that call for liberating detachment, according to 1 Cor 7:29-31, stands the statement that "those who have wives be as though they had none." The list of realities to keep at a distance goes on to include weeping and rejoicing, buying, and dealing with the world. Paul is calling for the ability to bid the world adieu, for nothing worldly is ultimate. Giving priority to God's will takes place more easily under some circumstances than others, and to that end it is necessary when priorities conflict to be able to recognize the one priority that outranks all others. The capacity Paul here hopes to stimulate has, admittedly, something of the "inhumane" about it. On the other hand, its appeal lies in the way it is directed toward what is lasting—twice in the immediate context Paul makes reference to this. Because "the appointed time has grown short" (v. 29a), and already "the present form of this world is passing away" (v. 31b), the power of normal emotions and the lure of amassing goods have been broken. These all play themselves out within the horizon of finite time, but what lies beyond that horizon has now drawn near. Only in such a circumstance is it conceivable to renounce the spouse that one loves, to suppress emotional highs and lows, and to forgo the pleasures that come from participating in the ordinary affairs of life. Intense desire and unimpassioned detachment are, in fact, two sides of the same intimation of finitude. Paul's remarks draw attention to this ambivalence.

All of this again emphasizes that there is nothing "divine" about sexuality. Love abides (1 Corinthians 13), to be sure, but not sexuality. Paul sets a barrier before any effort to mythicize sexual experience.

Objectivity

What has often been noted with regard to Paul's treatment of charismatic phenomena in 1 Corinthians 12–14, namely, the objectivity with which he boldly restores order in a volatile situation, applies also to 1 Corinthians 5–7. What Paul says here cannot fail to have a sobering, even chilling, effect upon sexual expression of any stamp. Paul comes down firmly on the side of sober reason.

Evaluation

For Paul, sexuality is essentially a matter of property rights, and the morality of sexuality is judged from such a perspective. Sexuality is also to be judged from within the "new righteousness" (to speak in the terminology of Paul's letter to the Romans) that has been established between God and human beings. Paul sets the dominating control of reason against any mythicizing or sacralizing of sexuality—although he would prefer all Christians to remain unmarried. Holiness (belonging totally to the Lord) is what matters most. Toward this end, Paul sets up a counterweight to his own emphasis on reason, namely, the claim that God makes on people. God's law has physical consequences; God's law is to be rendered visible even down to the last fiber of human existence.

In sum, whether in the exercise of reason or in the expression of holiness, the claim of the new revelation massively intervenes into human vitality. Even in its most intimate forms of expression, that vitality does not remain as it was before. As is evident not least in the summons to detachment, human vitality has been placed at the disposal of another power. In no other area of life is the consequence of this new claim evidenced more decisively.

Risking and Gaining Life

Whoever lives too cautiously and parsimoniously will soon come to regard life as wanting and eventually as not worth living. Commonsense psychology says so, but one can find much the same thought in words Jesus spoke to his followers when he said, '. . . Those who want to save their life will lose it' (Mark 8:35). Does that not mean that anyone who allows excessive anxiety to permeate the ordinary affairs of daily living will be incapable of experiencing spontaneity, a sense of involvement, and finally even freedom itself?[17]

In the same source one also finds the following remark by Friedrich Schiller: ". . . and if you never risk life, neither will you have ever won life." These comments offer a point of entry in determining the relationship between the proverb "no pain, no gain" and a distinctly biblical psychology.

THE ANCIENT RULE

Almost all ancient parallels to these comments involve military commanders exhorting their troops before battle. An early example is this: "Those who are daring and stand by one another and go aggressively into combat are less likely to die, and they save the people behind them. When men are afraid, however, they lose all their strength" (Tyrtaeus, *Fgm. lyr.* 8). With such words commanders roused their soldiers before battle. Actual experience with the significance of courage and determination here come together with ideological and practical aims. Somewhat closer to the wording of the Bible is the following: "Never let your courage subside, and never retreat in battle, for those who do not retreat in battle but rather expose themselves to death will remain alive; they will acquire a good name and be praised" (Pseudo-Menander 55). In the latter there is an opposition between life and death; both examples refer to war. The link between moral ideals with military images deserves further investigation.

THE MARTYR TRADITION

The Judaism of Hellenistic times conceived of martyrdom as a battle against an adversary.[18] Here we find the point from which the large stock of military and battle metaphors entered the New Testament tradition, for example, the Revelation to John. At first glance it seems that in the situation of martyrdom the ancient rule discussed in the preceding section was passed over. That is the case, however, only so long as the martyr was not posthumously rewarded with resurrection or immortality or repose in the bosom of Abraham. The notion of the martyr's being raised from the dead thus essentially amounts to an application or postmortem activation of the above-mentioned rule. The martyr risks his life and then in fact does gain it as a glorious existence with God. The statement about the Maccabean martyrs in *4 Macc.* 17:11-12 is to be understood in this sense: "Truly it was a divine battle that was fought by them. Virtue had offered the battle prize, and the verdict was that it should go to those who stood firm. The trophy was immortality, life everlasting." The same holds true for *2 Macc.* 7:14: "When we die at the hands of men, it is comforting to us to cherish the hope, granted by God, that we will once again be raised by him." The second text in particular seems to offer the guarantee that God will restore life after it has been lost.

In the theology of martyrdom, then, the proverbial wisdom about risking and gaining life has acquired a transcendent meaning. This is the only condition under which such statements can hold true for martyrs. Obviously, then, the Jewish-Hellenistic interpretation of martyrdom as a battle serves as the bridge to the New Testament's reception of the military rule (above).

NEW TESTAMENT EXAMPLES

In the New Testament there are at least four independent places where the tradition under consideration surfaces:[19] Mark 8:35 (par. Matt 16:25 and Luke 9:23-24),[20] Matt 10:38-39 and its Q parallel in Luke 14:26-27 (reworked to say "hates his life"),[21] Luke 17:33 (from Luke's special section), and John 12:25. Closely related are John 12:24 ("Unless a grain of wheat falls into the earth and dies, it remains just a single grain") and Luke 21:19 ("By your endurance you will gain your souls"). The scope of these statements reveals the significance attached to the fundamental precept. It serves to shed light not only on the fate of Jesus but also on that of the disciples who followed him. Only Luke 17:33 shows some deviation from the usual pattern; here the precept is understood not as referring to martyrdom but as an illustrative exhortation.[22]

THE UNDERLYING STRUCTURE OF THE PHENOMENON

Giving up one's life (dying) as a precondition for new life also occurs in Paul's baptismal theology in Rom 6:2-11. The old person must be crucified and buried with Christ so that there can be new life, life for God and life from God (thus the force of the dative in 6:11), and also resurrection in the end. Moreover, if it is accurate to say that the death of the "sinful body" (6:6) affects all of one's relationships with other human beings,[23] then the proximity of these words to the tradition discussed above becomes especially easy to recognize. Note how in the Q rendition (Matt 10:38-39; Luke 14:26), the comment about losing one's life and finding it again is connected to the motif of hating one's relatives.[24]

The search for comparisons leads to a biblical model of thought and experience according to which it is precisely the renunciation of normal ways of managing life that leads to an unimaginable and incomparable intensification of life.[25] All this happens if such renunciation takes place "before God." The issue, then, is not just renouncing all that one normally worries about but rather an actual interruption of normal ways of proceeding.

All of this is already evident in the Old Testament and early Judaism with regard to sexuality and the engendering of life. Nearness to God, the Holy One and thus the true source of life, entails restrictions on normal sexual practices. All sorts of taboos having to do with fertility and birth, in particular, seem to have their origin here. So, for example, the prohibition against sexual intercourse where the sanctuary is located (*Damascus Document* 12.1) expresses the conviction that there one is in the presence of the source of all fertility and life. Substituting a holy time for a holy place, the prohibition against sexual intercourse on the Sabbath points in the same direction (*Jub.* 50:8). Other parallels include sexual restrictions imposed on high priests and cultic asceticism in general. Similarly, taboos abound both inside and outside Judaism where fecundity itself occupies the center of attention. Consider, for example, the impurity of a woman after the birth of a child and the associated restrictions on her visits to the sanctuary (Lev 12:2-5; *Jub.* 3:9-14). This most likely expresses the notion of a taboo surrounding the time of bringing a child into the world, a taboo that in effect throws up a wall of protection around this dangerous time.[26] The thought is that a woman is endangered after the birth of a child and that her continued ability to bear children depends on keeping her carefully protected following a birth.

It is foolish to regard these taboos as expressions of unenlightened thinking or insufficient appreciation of women. Precisely the opposite is the case. The place where life originates is also a place where one deals directly with God. Therefore it is rightly a place for fear and trembling. Along the same line, everything affected by the origin of life must stand in tension with the cultic area. It is not a low estimation of women that leads to these prohibitions and anxieties about contact with them. Moreover, they certainly have nothing to do with a lack of appreciation for the bringing of new life into the world. On the contrary, ordinary human sexuality and fertility are being treated as not ordinary at all. For all its mundaneness, this dimension of life is threatening and at the same time empowering. All of this is linked to the presence of the Holy One.

In summary,

1. Where life before God (participation in the cultus) is interrupted, it is not because of animosity toward life but for the sake of gaining richer, fuller life.

2. In the Old Testament such suspension affects sexuality, childbirth, behavior around the dead and dying, and the taking in of nourishment (fasting). Its social parameters are expanded in the New Testament (hatred of relatives), and eventually it is expanded to include life itself.[27] Closely corresponding to the particular realities that one gives up "before God"

are those that one gets back from God: the blessing of children, new parents and siblings (Mark 10:30), or eternal life.

3. This curtailment can also be borne for the sake of others (e.g., restrictions on sexual activity of priests for the sake of increased fertility of others; giving up the life of one for the sake of others and their resurrection). Cultic curtailment and vicarious representation, here connected with each another, are two fundamental features of the religions of the ancient Near East. Bringing the notion of vicarious representation into connection with that of disruption or curtailment of cultic life does not mean, however, that the representative would be excluded from the gaining of life.

4. The curtailment takes place "before God," "in the name of God," "before the face of God." Unlike in some wisdom traditions or idealistic or pagan contexts, here the risking of life does not take place with regard to some dark abstraction. Conversely, in this context the image of God is one of life itself, life in its fullness.

5. It is thus to be emphasized that asceticism—indeed, even martyrdom—is not inimical to life but in the highest degree life-affirming. Asceticism and even martyrdom are to be understood as an indirect path to fullness of life.

6. From a purely pragmatic point of view, one might say that gain is the intended outcome of renunciation. But it would be no more than irrelevant polemic to declare that such renunciation is driven by thought of reward or as a way of coercing God. The issue is not one of compelling God to act in a certain way or of calculating how to come out ahead but of doing what is required for genuine newness. Such newness can be understood only as a gift. The same meaning obtains in the above-mentioned suspensions as in cultic contexts, namely, that the ensuing gifts come from God alone. Confession and prayer here flow together. Both are oriented to the fact that God alone is the source of life. Cultic modes of self-denial give symbolic expression to this conviction.

7. This particular tradition of sayings about losing and gaining life serves a distinctive purpose for Christian symbolics. Christians are not simply being lifted out of the present and transposed into the future but are enabled to proceed in such a way that makes their eventual arrival all the more certain. The time of denial, the time of sacrifice, is also a time of hope. This is no exercise in masochism, for only the one who dies will live. Only the one who can reject will acquire; only the one who can share will possess; only the one who can give away will become rich. Only those who abandon themselves will preserve themselves; only those who give up all will acquire everything.

The sayings here discussed reflect the experience that, in the presence of God, life is not acquired directly but only by a detour through its opposite. One is admonished to take a deep breath, to reject all self-pity and self-centeredness. There is another way, a way opposed to immediate gratification. This other way is risky, to be sure, but it also promises a qualitative enhancement of life. The decisive factor is what one understands by "life." In the light of the above, a comment such as the following misses the point entirely: "At its core Christianity is not an ascetic but a therapeutic religion."[28]

Possessions

POSSESSION AND CONVERSION

In New Testament writings the psychology of ownership or possession comes across quite starkly. This can be illustrated with regard to three texts from the Gospel of Mark: the stories of the rich young man (Mark 10:17-22), the poor widow who gave all that she had as an offering (Mark 12:41-44), and the woman who anointed Jesus with three hundred denarii worth of oil, an amount equivalent to the annual wage of a common laborer (Mark 14:3-9). In these stories, both of the women successfully accomplish what the rich young man was incapable of doing.

In all three cases the immediate expression of opening oneself to God is the giving up of possessions, and a distinctive relationship is seen to exist between these two. The practice of giving up one's possessions on converting to Judaism or Christianity is attested in writings of both Hellenistic Judaism and the apocryphal acts of the apostles. By and large, such an act visibly confirms one's solidarity with the new community, somewhat like an admission ticket. This particular aspect is not at play in any of the three Markan texts, however; none of the characters in these stories seeks integration into a group. Perhaps one could say that renunciation of possessions functions as an external sign of the seriousness of an internal conversion. But other indications of conversion are certainly possible, so one must then ask why precisely this one plays such a prominent role. What does the practice of renouncing possessions, at a decisive encounter with God, tell us about the valuation of possessions or of ownership before conversion, or apart from the opening of oneself to God?

A CONCRETIZING OF THE CHIEF COMMANDMENT

One can certainly say that the widow who sacrificed "everything she had" (Mark 12:44) is a paradigm for the fulfilling of the chief commandment, that one should love God with all one's heart and strength. In fact, this commandment was often interpreted by the rabbis in a financial sense ("with all of your strength" means "with all of your fortune").[29] Such an interpretation is clearly built on a kind of experience in which love of God and love of possessions exclude each another.

THE FASCINATION WITH POSSESSIONS

The rich young man goes away downcast (Mark 10:22), since his ties to his possessions prove too strong. Other texts similarly emphasize not the possibility of freely disposing of one's possessions but precisely the opposite. The basic experience underlies Luke 16:13 ("No slave can serve two masters. . . .You cannot serve God and wealth"), which speaks of a voluntary enslavement to riches. The fascination with riches here has nothing to do with what they enable one to do but rather with what *they* do to one. Rather than having one's riches at one's disposal, one is drawn into their service. Possessions possess their possessors. Ownership and worry about possessions come up against a longing for dependence, and herein is the underlying fascination with possessions.

In this case we are dealing with a perversion of the need to be bonded to someone or something. In the case of possessions it is transparent that we have a "lord" without an independent will, a lord who grants nothing and expects nothing. In place of the will of the servant's master stands the peculiar dynamic of possession, namely, a desire for the preservation and propagation of the riches to which one is enslaved. What remains finally is no master at all, only the slave.

THE QUALITY OF THE NEW BONDAGE

We must not overlook the seriousness with which Jesus presses his theme of renunciation of possessions. The dismay with which the disciples react to Jesus' remarks about the camel and the eye of the needle (Mark 10:26) is significant in this regard. Note also how the scene of the poor widow offering her last coin (Mark 12) comes at the conclusion of the public ministry of Jesus, giving it emphasis. Third, Jesus explicitly promises the woman who anoints him that her deed will be mentioned where the gospel is proclaimed (Mark 14:9). There is good reason for this promise, since we are here obviously quite close to core of the proclamation of Jesus. Finally, the teaching about seeking heavenly riches (Matt 6:33) is directly attached to the related comments about having no concern for worldly matters. This gets at the main thrust of the teaching of Jesus as a whole.

The words of Jesus about renouncing worry show how superior is the new bondage of those who have renounced their old bondage to possessions, who have escaped from the lordship of mammon. The renunciation of worry is like an initiation into the service of a new master, one who is a living Other. The rigid dynamic of fixation on possessions is replaced by a new dependency, one characterized by a readiness to take risks. This is now possible because the new Other, unlike possessions, is independent and free. So the renunciation of worry is at the same time an initiation into a new kind of dependency, the essential feature of which is the sovereign freedom of the One on whom this dependency rests.

The twisted dynamic of subjection to possessions is replaced by subjection to an unconstrained Other. It is all somewhat like learning how to fly. Above all, it is a matter of coming to trust God to uphold one in every situation. As difficult to imagine as this might be, it brings us close to an important aspect of the message of Jesus. His arguments that go from the lesser to the greater are essentially just stepping stones leading us to take the decisive step toward true freedom from worry, setting us on the path of complete trust in God. To this end one thing is essential: not knowing the outcome in advance. One must wait on God for everything. One must enter fully into the tension of not knowing. One must allow God freely to bestow whatever he will.

This last aspect reveals the new relationship that is possible between God and human beings, one that could be called the "righteousness" of the kingdom of God. For the call to renounce worry is not a bald, one-sided demand for obedience. It says something about interaction and opens the possibility for God to step in as the bestower. The human being who no longer worries gives God the chance to be revealed, to become manifest once again as Father. In a manner of speaking, God thus gets room to operate; a "space" is created in which God is free to act. It thus becomes possible for God once again to be experienced.

The same sort of courage is here being called for as was demanded of Peter, the courage that enabled him to walk on the water. Freedom with regard to possessions bears a close relationship to what the Gospels mean when they talk about faith (cf. the section "Faith" in chapter 9, above). According to the texts here under consideration, dependence on possessions stands directly in the way of the qualitatively new relationship of trust to which we are summoned by Jesus. Behind these texts stands a distinctly new sort of experience of God.

Vengeance

Several New Testament texts raise the issue of vengeance for Christians or for persecuted but righteous persons to whom injustice has been done. These texts bring up not just ethical questions or the problem of theodicy but also psychological considerations, because nowhere in these texts is any challenge raised against the legitimacy of the desire for revenge. I think here specifically of Luke 18:1-8; Rom 12:19-20; Rev 6:9-11; and Rev 19:11-21. The dominant genres in this material are prayer (Luke 18; Revelation 6) and apocalyptic vision (Revelation 19). Frequently employed in this context is the Greek stem *ekdik-* (to avenge). The following features are especially striking in these texts.

1. Vengeful feelings are not squelched; there is no psychological suppression of the urge for revenge. In fact, according to Rom 12:20, someone who renounces acts of vengeance piles glowing coals on (and thereby brings judgment on) the adversary's head. In any case it would be pointless to pass off these texts as somehow unauthentic or as lamentable pre-Christian relics.

2. As with worry (see chapter 7, above), vengeance is consistently given over to God. This takes place through prayer or in visions. Theologically, this expresses the unique sovereignty of God; psychologically, this "transforms" the particular victimization of the petitioner or the visionary into a mode of the incomparable and inexorable activity of God (cf. Luke 18:8a; Rev 6:10). For human beings to exact revenge is strictly forbidden.

3. From a form-critical perspective, both prayer and visions function in such a way that something immediate and direct takes place in them. Whether in words (prayer) or in images (visions), the oppressed victim is able to reshape his or her oppression and yearning for revenge. In this process the problematic features get taken up and actually become a part of the rescue (redemption). This is so because, through prayer or visionary experience, the victim acquires access to God. The persecuted no longer feels isolated; the victim brings an appeal to the highest court of all.

4. When vengeful feelings are transformed by such a turning to God, the petitioner or the visionary gains certainty that the event in which he or she was injured is but one part of a drama that is hastening toward its end. The threatening devastation will be reversed. In both the possibility and the actuality of addressing everything to God (including vengeful feelings), the victim becomes totally open to God and belongs entirely to God.

5. Despite appearances, through prayer and visionary experience the persecuted are able to see that order prevails in the world. Certainly one must recognize that, for victims, the perception of a just world order (and thereby of God's lordship) has reached a critical point. Prayers and visions of the sort here under consideration seem to function somewhat like the punishing of villains in fairy tales. When they come to that point in the story, readers experience a certain sort of satisfaction—and rightly so. The

genres of apocalyptic vision and petitionary prayer as here envisioned do not intend to arouse sympathy but to awaken a sense of partisanship. Such genres serve the needs of those who feel threatened or vulnerable; they deal with the compensatory righteousness of God and offer emotional (not theoretical or dogmatic!) verification of the same.

Nowadays feelings of revenge have been exiled from the domain of religion. The Psalms that speak of vengeance on enemies are no longer regarded as suitable. It could be the case, however, that this actually amounts to a serious impoverishment of the religious dimension of life. When revenge is excluded from religion, it is likely to crop up in some other dimension of life—one where the divine prohibition against revenge is not in effect. Perhaps the only effective way of dealing with revenge is to carry it to God, in prayer and in the imagery of visions. The reality of such feelings cannot be denied. To overcome them requires the help of God.

On the other hand, some sort of renewal of the practice of public prayer for vengeance is certainly not possible; this would be much too open to political misuse. Moreover, in view of modern society's complicated mechanisms for the proper dispensing of justice, one must wonder exactly what religion, with its vision of an alternative to the ways of the world, could offer. Certainly it would not lie in the area of fine-tuning the connection between acts and consequences but would come from some sort of emphasis on the grace-proffering otherness of God. In view of the incomprehensible depravity of the crime of Auschwitz and other subsequent atrocities, any close connection between religion and the punishment of evildoers (or the rewarding of the good) has been irreparably severed. Finally, because of the contemporary extension of the notion of sin, few martyrs would any longer be in a position to regard their sufferings as totally undeserved. For all that, we in the West must not overlook the nearly incomprehensible sufferings of contemporary Christians in other parts of the globe.

In sum, despite objections of the sort I myself have raised, there remains the suggestion that there needs to be room within Christianity for honest and guilt-free incorporation of the element of vengeance. Suppressing the desire for revenge is not in and of itself a virtue.

Notes

1. Introduction

1. Drewermann, *Tiefenpsychologie und Exegese*, 1:66.

2. Martin, "Eugen Drewermanns 'Strukturen des Bösen,'" 321–32 (329). See also Lohfink and Pesch, *Tiefenpsychologie und keine Exegese*.

3. Theissen, *Psychological Aspects of Pauline Theology*.

4. Note, e.g., the following remark from *Psychological Aspects*, 146: "We must again ask self-critically if we are imposing modern thoughts on Paul. Can an interpretation of this sort be made historically plausible? Does it correspond to analogies?"

5. Cf., e.g., Theissen's own answer, on p. 153 of *Psychological Aspects*, to the question posed in note 4. Note also his reliance upon contemporary modes of psychological theory in comments such as the following: "Christ serves as a learning model for overcoming normatively conditioned anxieties" (p. 226) and "Romans 7 depicts how the once-unconscious conflict with the Law became conscious" (p. 229).

6. For more detailed criticism of Theissen's approach, see my *Exegese und Philosophie*, 186–87, and my *Hermeneutik des Neuen Testaments*, 141–42, 250–51.

7. Cf., e.g., Theissen's recourse to Epictetus (*Psychological Aspects*, 146) who, of course, knew nothing of the "unconscious."

8. On the relation of philosophical anthropology and the modern sciences of human behavior to biblical hermeneutics in general, cf. my *Exegese und Philosophie*, 184–88.

9. This theme is more fully developed in my *Hermeneutik des Neuen Testaments*.

10. On the theme of experience in contemporary hermeneutics, cf. the following: Hinske, *Lebenserfahrung und Philosophie*; Lange, *Erfahrung und die Glaubwürdigkeit des Glaubens*; Logstrup, "Erlebnis und Lehre"; Mostert, "Erfahrung als Kriterium der Theologie"; Ritter, "Theologie und Erfahrung"; idem, *Glaube und Erfahrung*; Schroedter, *Erfahrung und Transzendenz*; Weymann, *Glaube als Lebensvollzug*; Timm, *Zwischenfälle*; see also my *Hermeneutik des Neuen Testaments*.

11. Cf. Colpe's article "Geister," in *RAC* 9 (1976) 615–25 (esp. pp. 624–25).

12. Likewise the return of the Lord is often tied to a specific place—on the strength of Acts 1 to the Mount of Olives. This theme is evident in early Christian apocalyptic works.

13. Even the endeavor to gain insight into the hidden must be restricted to a few, according to Gnosticism or parts of Rabbinic Judaism. Furthermore, this seeking always amounts to an attempt somehow to overcome the reluctance of

truth to let itself become manifest. The very limitations imposed upon those who would gain insight further restricts access to the truth.

14. Thus, in modern understanding the Eucharistic bread is solely a didactic symbol; in itself it has nothing to do with what Jesus truly is or really gives. Or if the decisive feature is a new faith-relationship between my unique soul and God, then any particular narrative about the actual Jesus of history becomes irrelevant; the physical proximity of Jesus is but a narrative illustration of the kerygma. Or an account of a miraculous healing, if taken at face value, would indeed challenge our understanding, but what really matters in such stories is the emphasis on faith. Or it is not really necessary for a believer to attend a service of divine worship, if one's "heart" is in the right place. The actual location of the body ought rightly to be a matter in indifference.

15. On this point cf. also my *Hermeneutik des Neuen Testaments*, 396ff.

16. *Metaphorik und Personifikation der Sünde*, e.g., 150ff.

17. There can be no question of any sympathy on my part with any contemporary school of psychology. In fact, this book arose, at least in part, out of the desire to impede access to the New Testament through any aspect of this contemporary science. At the same time, I readily concede that approaching the New Testament from the standpoint of modern psychology has a certain legitimacy and that it can lead to some interesting insights. As a historian, however, such is not my concern.

18. The question of "implicit axioms" is quite another matter, on which see my essay, "Zur Kritik der Theorie der impliziten Axiome," in Huber, Petzold, and Sundermeier, eds., *Implizite Axiome*, 229–45.

19. *Psychological Aspects*, 96–106. On p. 110 of the same work Theissen attempts to establish that Wisd. 17:11 exhibits the earliest (in Judaism? in this particular writing?) "conception of the unconscious." In the same context (17:3), there is reference to the Egyptians being terrified by apparitions (Greek: *indalmata*); 17:8 speaks expressly of "the sick soul." On the connections here with Hellenistic psychological or psychologizing literature, cf. Reese, *Hellenistic Influence on the Book of Wisdom and Its Consequences*, 21ff., 101–2. Apparitions are as old as humankind itself, and modes of depicting them are widely conventional. Thus the important question becomes the modes of experience and perception which are tied in with reports about apparitions. In my opinion, with regard to Wisdom 17 it makes a big difference indeed whether one chooses to speak, on the one hand, of a "sick soul" or of "fear" (as opposed to "reason") or, on the other hand, to invoke the complex modern notion of the unconscious mind (from which one then goes on to explain other features). My inclination would be to hold strongly to the ancient modes of perception and to compare these texts with others that expressly speak of the "fear" of "sick souls."

20. Mentioned as gifted with "knowledge of the heart" are the following: the Elect One (*1 En.* 49:1-4 and 62); Enoch (*3 En.*11:1-3 and 48[C]:4); Jesus (Luke 2:35, 7:39, 9:47; John 1:46-48, 2:24-25, 4:16-19; *Acts of Thaddaeus* 3; *Clementine Recognitions* 1.33.1 and 3.45.3; *Constantine the Apostle* 2.24.6 and 3.7.8); several apostles (Acts 13:9-10); the early Christian community as a whole (1 Cor 14:25).

21. The pattern of thinking goes like this: As an artist or a craftsman knows precisely what he makes, so also does God as Creator. Consider, for example, the following: (1) "Let no sinner say that he has not sinned. . . . Behold, the Lord

knows all the works of men, their imaginations and their thoughts and their hearts. He has said, 'Let the earth be made' . . . [the One who has] made all things and who searches out hidden things in hidden places, surely he knows your imaginations and what you think in your hearts" (2 Esdras 16:53-54, 62-63); (2) "before you create them you know their deeds for ever and ever" (1QH 1:7); (3) "Before they were formed you knew their works" (CD 2:8); (4) "For he [God] is a searcher of thoughts and desires . . . for his breath is in us" (*1 Clem.* 21:9); (5) "for he alone is the true God and creator of the whole world, examining the hearts of men and knowing everything before it comes to pass, since he is the Creator of all things" (*Acts of Thaddaeus* 8). God as judge also knows the hearts of men; cf. Jer 17:10 and Rev 2:23. As a sharer in the divine light, Jesus knows the hidden things (*Acta Xanthippae et Polyxenae* 28). It is quite possible that the origin of this conception has something to do with the Egyptian sun god.

22. In substantiation of this claim, cf. the following: 1 Chr 28:9 (a "whole heart" is a "willing mind"); *Clementine Recognitions* 1.33.1 (hearts and intentions) and 3.43.3 ("secreta hominum atque arcana"); *2 Bar.* 83:3-4 ("the secret thoughts and everything that is within the innermost members of the human being . . . he will make manifest in the presence of everyone with sharp blame on that day"); *1 En.* 9:5 ("Everything is naked and open before your sight . . ."); *Herm. Man.* 4.3.4 ("the weakness of men"); *Acts of Apollonius* 5 ("all the thoughts of men"); *1 Clem.* 21:9 ("thoughts and desires").

23. Having one's heart be known amounts to being held personally responsible and judicially accountable. The "heart" is what connects the deed to its outworking. The saying of Jesus, "Where your treasure is, there your heart will be also" (Matt 6:21), suggests a heavenly treasure (a storehouse of deeds, a sort of heavenly bank account). An analogy to this New Testament notion is to be found in ancient Egyptian juridical conceptions. It is not the "soul" but rather the "heart" that is liable to be found guilty and punished (personal communication of November 11, 1990, from J. Assmann of Heidelberg).

24. Here the following factors should be noted: (1) the role of Romantic irrationalism in the origin of the theory of the unconscious mind; (2) the consequent inroads of natural science even into the work of "poets"; (3) the significant hermeneutical function of the category of repression within middle-class circles in the nineteenth century. The various theories that link conflict-producing tensions with the unconscious are also revealing when one recalls their origin in the nineteenth century.

25. Here I am pleased to acknowledge the stimulating suggestions I received from a lecture given by Carsten Colpe in the context of the workgroup on the scientific study of religion which met in Heidelberg November 9–11, 1990. The title of his lecture was "Archetyp und Prototyp: Vorschläge zur Bereinigung des Verhältnisses zwischen Tiefenpsychologie und Geschichtswissenschaft."

26. Thus, for example, for any given man, his own mother—the first woman he gets to know—might well become the prototype for all the subsequent women he meets. If this sort of dynamic is seen to apply in general, then we are approaching the notion of "mother" as an archetype.

27. On this point, see also my *Exegese und Philosophie*, 185–88.

28. See my *Hermeneutik des Neuen Testaments*, 317.

29. For example, the role that "boasting" (root: *kaucha-*) plays in Paul's theology illustrates the apostle's awareness of differening dimensions in the psyches of his hearers.

2. Identity and Person

1. On this issue cf. esp. Pannenberg, *Jesus: God and Man*, passim.

2. Of course, one must also go on to ask the related question of what the various mediators between God and world (e.g., wisdom, *logos*, *nous*, archangel, "son" and "daughter" of God, *memra*, *shekinah*, etc.) have to teach us about the understanding and the experience of the structure of the human psyche in biblical times.

3. According to *Jub.* 2:2 and the similitudes in *1 Enoch*, angels have been installed over the various regions of creation, ruling much like modern cabinet secretaries.

4. With regard to these first two criteria, occasionally one encounters the notion that angels have another sort of language (the "tongues of angels"). This, of course, leads to problems of intelligibility. Such problems are not insurmountable, however. Even human beings can acquire or be granted competence in the tongues of angels (1 Cor 13:1). A medieval notion holds that, since they have a "voice," clocks also possess something like a personality. In fact, clocks were sometimes "baptized" by name, and it was believed that they were be capable of rendering petitions unto God. A clock's prayer sometimes appears as an attached inscription, as for example in the frequently attested "O rex gloriae Christe, veni nobis cum pace" (O Christ, king of glory, come to us in peace).

5. Cf. Berger, *Die Weisheitsschrift aus der Kairoer Geniza* 10:19. After enumeration of the five senses (10:18) that are common to all living beings, the following words are found: "Preeminent is the power of speech, which is found only in the human being." According to Philo (*Creation* 69), the chief feature determinative of the human being is "mind" (*nous*, the pinnacle of the soul). In these texts human beings are distinguished from lower creatures, with the capacity for speech setting the human being off from the other creatures (viz., the animals). The relationship between speech and reason becomes evident in the convergence between *logos* and *nous* in the speculation about mediators.

6. On these issues cf. Vollenweider, *Freiheit als neue Schöpfung*, 64–67 ("Vom Ich zum Selbst"). In the context of ancient reflection, the self has a certain freedom over against the individuality of the empirical person.

7. Here it is helpful to recall the current state of form-critical discussion; cf., e.g., Dihle, "Evangelien und die biographische Tradition der Antike," 3–49; see also my *Formgeschichte des Neuen Testaments*, 346ff. "Biography" is not a fixed genre in antiquity. The most common ancient designation of such works is *encomion* (speech of praise). Obviously, there are *encomia* only for important people.

8. The reference in Mark 13:5-6 can hardly be to malicious imposters. More likely the reference is to Christians who apply to themselves labels current in the

christological and baptismal discussions of the day. The four Gospels themselves give evidence of these discussions.

9. Cf. the Pauline conception of Christ as the new Adam in Romans 5 and esp. in 1 Corinthians 15; recall also the typological function of the miracles of Elijah and Elisha in the Synoptic tradition.

10. I am deliberately forgoing any discussion of whether modern psychological disorders (e.g., someone's mistaken belief that he is Napoleon) are somehow distantly related to the New Testament phenomena here under discussion. This issue was already taken up in a whole array of medical treatises around the beginning of the twentieth century, among them the medical dissertation of Albert Schweitzer. It seems to me that the possibilities for fruitfully carrying out such comparative studies are very limited. All that having been said, however, one could at least entertain the notion that certain sorts of experiences are today consigned to the domain of mental illness that in an earlier setting would have been regarded as religiously significant. Identifying oneself with some worthy from the past strikes us as baseless; in biblical antiquity a corresponding claim could well have been regarded as legitimate.

11. Cf. Paul's comments in Rom 7:17, 20 on the consequences of the immanence of sin; sin demands its due and directs behavior.

12. For Paul, to be alive is to be active, either in obedience to or in rebelliousness against the divinely willed order; to be alive is to contend for one's position relative to others in the social order.

13. With reference to the material in Romans 8, see Warner et al., "Geist," in *TRE* 12 (1984) 188, 25ff.

14. To be sure, Simon Magus is also called "the great power" (viz., of God) in Acts 8:10, but in this context he is being regarded (uniquely) as the representative of God.

15. Cf. also synonymous terms based on the root *energ-* and oppositional terms based on the root *asthene-*.

16. Mysticism does not necessarily involve self-extinction, or a melding of the human with the divine, and these features should be kept out of discussion about mysticism as reflected in the New Testament. The New Testament actually speaks of an intensive association with Jesus Christ.

17. Certainly one must ask whether Paul is here speaking out of actual experience or only presenting some theological doctrine. This question is hardly to be answered apart from a thorough consideration of the well-known problems presented by Romans 7 as well. With attention confined strictly to Rom 6:15-23, it certainly appears that Paul actually regards himself as tied up in some sort of bonded service. In these verses he seems to be directing the attention of his readers to his experience. For a fuller appreciation of Paul's understanding of himself as a "slave," passages such as Phil 1:1 would also have to be taken into consideration.

18. To speak further in a Pauline mode, alienation from oneself and from others can finally be overcome only through entering into a trusting relationship with God. Only in allowing God to rule over us as our Lord can we find our real liberation (theonomy, not autonomy). Christian faith is a matter of entering into a radical relationship with the Other, and in this sense it is a kind of slavery.

19. The terms "vicarious" and "substitutionary" are not quite equivalent. The former term involves the notion of authority, deputized from some higher source, to carry out some task or exercise some function; the latter term applies to a situation in which someone simply does something for someone else so that the other person does not have to do it. The distinction comes out quite clearly in the case of John 11:50-52. There Caiaphas means for Jesus' death to be substitutionary but, quite apart from Caiaphas's intent, the death of Jesus also has vicarious quality.

20. Cf. also the query in the *Dies Irae* of Thomas of Celano. "Quem patronum rogaturus?" ("What defender is then to be beseeched?")

21. The line from the *Dies Irae* cited in the previous note amounts to a plea that Jesus show mercy in judgment.

22. It was probably an unintended misunderstanding at the time of the Reformation to carry over the wages-for-work schema into the conceptualization of cultic actions. In any case, this misunderstanding has had far-reaching consequences.

23. I have attempted to interpret the New Testament notions regarding expiation in just this way; cf. my *Gottes einziger Ölbaum,* specifically the section dealing with Rom 3:25-27.

24. In certain regions or sociocultural contexts, the donning of one's "Sunday best" or of some other distinctive costume is still a standard way of expressing one's allegiance to or membership in a certain group. In such cases, however, the garments had better be sparkling clean!

25. In the traditional practice of the distinctive baptismal dress, the church's liturgy has carried over this motif into the realm of cultic symbolism.

26. In our own complex society, we participate in a number of different groups and move in a variety of circles. Ancient society, on the other hand, was characterized by much greater uniformity of social situations. Thus clothing became important as a marker of social differences. Such a setting fostered a close relationship between the felt quality of events and the significance of garments for those involved.

3. Demonic Possession

1. For a good introduction to this area of study, see the following: K. Thraede, "Exorzismus"; F. E. Brenk, "In the Light of the Moon"; E. Schweizer, "Geister (Dämonen)"; C. Zintzen, "Geister (Dämonen)"; O. Böcher, *Christus exorcista*; idem, *Das Neue Testament und die dämonische Mächte.* Important earlier studies include H. Nowack, "Zur Entwicklungsgeschichte des Begriffs Daimon"; P. E. Dion, "Raphael l'exorciste"; C. Bonner, "The Technique of Exorcism."

2. One also needs to ask about the nature of demonology in early Pharisaic Judaism. If it is indeed the case that the Pharisees believed in spirits (Acts 23:8 mentions "spirit" in conjunction with "resurrection" and "angel"), then it is also possible that this reference is to be understood dualistically. Did Jesus differentiate himself from the Pharisees in that his "offensive purity" was based upon a superfluity of the divine spirit? Cf. Matt 12:27-28, and also my article, "Jesus als Pharisäer und frühe Christen als Pharisäer."

3. According to Mark 3:15, next to preaching, the chief aim of the mission of the Twelve is that they might "have authority to expel demons." This is the only theme mentioned in conjunction with the sending out of the disciples in Mark 6:7, while in vv. 12 and 13 of the same chapter exorcism and healing are explicitly mentioned along with preaching. Another Markan theme is recognition of the true identity of Jesus by the demons; their witness is accepted as on a par with the witness of others and, like the witness of others, is subject to the admonition to silence prior to Easter. For the compiler of the Gospel of Mark, only the full array of witnesses—the women who witness the empty tomb on Easter, but also the demons—produces the foundation necessary for belief. Moreover, even the witness of the demons taken alone is in no way regarded as controvertible or unintelligible (cf. Mark 1:24, 34; 3:11-12). The only problem with the witness of the demons is that it is ambiguous (Mark 3:23-27 is thus to be understood).

4. Mark 5:1-20 deals with the issue of "impurity" resulting from contact with pagans (note the mention of the Decapolis), while Mark 9:14-29 takes up the question of the power of the disciples after Easter or in the absence of Jesus. Mark 9:38-41 addresses the issue of the use of Jesus' name outside the circle of the disciples as well as that of legitimate access to Jesus outside the Christian community. Acts 26:18 summarizes the Christian mission per se as a freeing of humankind from the power of Satan.

5. Cf., e.g., the remarks of Cardinal Ratzinger reprinted in *Die Weltwoche* (no. 30, July 25, 1985, in the article by theologian Herbert Haag entitled, "Der Teufel meldet sich aus der Verbannung zurück"): "If there is no Evil One, then evil resides wholly within human beings. Then humankind alone is responsible for the abysmal depths of wickedness, vileness, and cruelty. Then humankind alone must shoulder responsibility for the deaths in the Soviet gulag and the Nazi death camps, and for all the many inhuman acts of torture and torment. But this then forces the question: Can God really have created such a monster as the human being seems to be? No, God cannot have done that, for God is goodness and love. If there is no Satan, then there also can be no God." In response to these remarks by Ratzinger, Haag rightly wonders whether the devil is not being held on to as some sort of scapegoat. Also, with regard to the infamous 1976 exorcism at Klingenberg (diocese of Würzburg), which resulted in the death of the "possessed," cf. J. Mischo and U. J. Niemann, "Die Besessenheit der Anneliese Michel." Finally, objection must be voiced against the effort of some right-wing religious groups to take the reawakened interest in angels and demons—an interest that is as much aesthetic as anything else—and transform it into an attack on the modern state of knowledge in general.

6. Cf. *OTP* 1:949, n. 82 (trans.).

7. The original readers of Mark's Gospel were primarily oriented toward their Palestinian homeland and, despite the military origin of the metaphors used in conjunction with the passages about demons, they apparently did not relate the accounts of Jesus' exorcisms to the theme of Christ's worldwide rule. A different dynamic is at work, however, where the talk shifts to "principalities" and "powers." In 1 Cor 2:8-9 a possible connection is made between Jesus' exorcisms and the worldwide rule of Christ. (In this particular case I am not inclined to think the reference is to demonic powers. In the other passages cited in this paragraph of my

text, however, we are certainly dealing with reference to demonic powers and forces.)

8. Brenk, "In the Light of the Moon."

9. Ibid., 2119f.

10. Ibid., 2111.

11. As the supremely capable exorcist, Jesus has taken upon himself a function traditionally ascribed to the archangel Michael. The ancient view is that a "political" domain is a network of personal relationships; a realm stretches not so much over a particular territory as wherever people become subject to a given ruler. From this it follows that the kingdom of God expands with each exorcism.

12. In the research one continues to find connections being made between "possession" and epilepsy or hysteria; cf. Brenk, "In the Light of the Moon," 2108.

13. See the examples given in ibid., 2113.

14. Virginity works as an especially effective deterrent against demons.

15. Cf. *Religionsgeschichtliches Textbuch zum Neuen Testament*, ed. K. Berger and C. Colpe (NTD Textreihe 1; Göttingen, 1987), p. 32, no. 12; cf. also *b. Hull.* 105b (end) and *b. Pesach* 112b/113a. It must be emphasized that Philo's *That God Is Unchangeable* 138 deals with a word of welcome for the "spirit" rather than a defense against a demon, as wrongly supposed by K. Thraede (note 1, above).

16. On this, cf. my *Einführung in die Formgeschichte*, 153–55 and notes.

17. Cf. the parallel in *Testament of Solomon*: "We fall on account of our weakness, and because we have nothing to assist us we fall like lightning upon the earth" (20:17); also Rev 12:8 ("he [the dragon/Satan] did not prevail").

18. This does not mean that the exorcisms of Jesus therefore had anti-Roman overtones. The military imagery fits with exorcisms as such; the area of activity that supplies the metaphors remains clearly distinct from their usage.

19. The connection the New Testament makes between public order and demonic possession might well produce some insights that are still helpful. An obvious point of application would be with our notion of anxiety. The helplessness many feel today in the face of an imposing array of societal forces triggers a sense of inner chaos. Antiquity, however, was more fearful of insufficiently powerful cohesive forces in society, which in turn led to a fear of destructive powers directed against those outer forces.

20. Ancient pedagogy also saw in all youthful disruptions a defiant will that needed to be broken. This observation alone is enough to make all the more imperative a critical understanding of those New Testament texts that deal with power and its dissolution.

21. "The Rise and Function of the Holy Man in Late Antiquity."

22. The issue of the relationship of the exorcist to the political domain is part of the larger question of the relationship of the "powers, dominions, and thrones" to earthly institutions as such. Despite repeated claims to the contrary, there is no proof that the New Testament really links these invisible powers to the mundane centers of power (e.g., such that the demonic powers stand "behind" the earthly dominions). Paul clearly differentiates between the "rulers" (*archontes*) of this world" (1 Cor 2:8) and the "powers" (*archē*; 1 Cor 15:24). Moreover, the political powers are quite different from, say, the power that is death, according to 1 Cor

15:26. But it is correct to say that the political and military areas of human experience generate the metaphors used to describe the relationship between God and humankind. This can be seen in the fact that, in New Testament demonology, military images abound. A further link occurs in the way those chosen by God are elevated to God's royal court, being permitted to attend God in the inner chambers of the heavenly palace. All such images are also analogous to practices in the world of the Bible. Above all, however, the question of whether the demonic powers are to be understood as themselves metaphors for earthly powers or as superhuman realities envisioned by means of earthly metaphors is to be answered on the basis of whether they are seen as having functions distinctly their own. Only if they were to have no specific functions would we rightly assume that they "rule" only through the ordinary political powers. That, however, is not the case; the various regions of the universe are ruled by obedient angels, and the various peoples of the world all have their own angelic overlords. (Early Judaism reckoned only with Michael as ruler of the world's people.) Beyond that, powers hostile to human beings block access to God, while other angelic beings—including the angel of death—guard the majesty of God. In effect, God entrusts his own majesty to these heavenly powers in order the better to be able to pursue his own predilection for human beings. This is the sense in which I understand Rom 8:31-39 and 1 Cor 15:20-26. In sum, the mundane arena of politics provides the metaphors but is not itself the substance.

23. I am thinking, for example, of experiences suggestive of providential guidance or of being loved by something greater than ourselves. Especially with regard to the message of Jesus, we have an awareness of being granted access to God through prayer or through a sense of being called.

24. Underlying the issue is doubtless the assumption that human (which basically means linguistically articulate) personality is supremely valuable. Therefore, essences that are ultimately inferior to human beings cannot adequately be grasped by means of personal metaphors.

25. A declining respect for the role played by metaphor in religious language can be traced back to A. Jülicher's book on parables. Quite the converse holds true in the most recent thought, however, where the importance of metaphor is once again being recognized (cf., e.g., the work of H. Blumenberg). Naturally, one can ask if a differentiation between a "causal" explanation and a "metaphoric" one is really possible. It may well be the case that the only change has been in the domains of experience which generate the metaphors; antiquity turned to the realm of interpersonal relations, whereas the modern world looks to the workshop.

26. Cf. P. Volz, *Das Dämonische in Jahwe.*

27. The "demonic" side of Yahweh can be experienced in many ways; the following are just some of its more apparent features. The natural phenomena that accompany a theophany evoke an awareness of the uncanny and threatening aspect of the deity; examples of this include the volcanic display at Sinai (Exodus 19) and the earthquakes that threaten to shatter the very foundations of the earth when Yahweh comes to the rescue (Judg 5:4-5; Ps 18:7-8). Proximity to the deity is life-threatening (Exod 19:21—note the warning that the very sight of Yahweh brings death, and see also Exod 33:20); death ensues when Yahweh strides

through the land (Amos 5:17); the very mention of Yahweh's name can prove deadly (Amos 6:8-10). Meddlesome spirits can issue forth from the deity, causing inner turmoil or conflict within a group (1 Sam 16:14-23; Judg 9:23; 1 Kgs 22:22). The deity can fall on individuals in ways that seem totally arbitrary and without recognizable motive; Yahweh nearly kills Moses during a nocturnal encounter (Exod 4:24-26), though timely performance of the rite of circumcision deflects Yahweh from his deadly intent. Another scene of nocturnal encounter is presented in Gen 32:23-33, where once again death is narrowly averted. With texts such as these in mind, it is easy to see how a range of human experiences and emotions can be tied in with the demonic: terror, dread, the feeling of lowliness, anxiety in the face of death. Is it any wonder that primitive apotropaic rites find their way into the texts (Exod 3:5; 4:25)? Even people in the grip of prophetic inspiration could be seen as personifications of the demonic (1 Sam 10:1-13).

28. Cf. my suggestions with regard to Rom 8:38-39 in *Gottes einziger Ölbaum*.

29. Cf. in general the writings of G. Bernanos; in particular, see my *Wie ein Vogel ist das Wort*, 14–15 (which cites texts from Bernanos's *Die Sonne Satans*).

30. The main point is that no necessary tension underlies a combination of playfulness of language and seriousness of purpose. Both poetic speech and playful activity simply have a different sort of relationship with the communicative sign, one that might be called "indirect"— as opposed to the "direct" relationship between signifier and signified in technical proceedings. Certain areas of experience are accessible only through indirect formulation of signs. A certain degree of freedom and of willingness to play along is necessary if one is meaningfully to participate in such communicative gestures. Where technical concerns dominate, this same sort of playful freedom ceases to be appropriate. In other words, indirect modes of communication are simply invitations to exercise a certain degree of communicative freedom.

31. The malaise that afflicts so much of the church these days could well be due to a pervasive urge within the church's leadership for more "rational" management of the ecclesial organization. Where this bureaucratic approach takes hold, human beings simply take their need for metaphoric articulation of religious experience outside the church. This has happened especially in those parts of Protestantism that, from the early nineteenth century, have embraced an idealistic theology.

32. In talking about angels and demons, it is important not to stray too far away from the domain of everyday experiences. Moreover, only certain kinds of experiences are appropriately interpreted as encounters with such "powers." From a biblical perspective, for example, one has an experience of "demons" only where one has a negative experience of weakness or of being hemmed in.

33. One might think of the pluralism of modern society as so many zones within which are preserved distinctive hermeneutical modes. Among such zones are the following: (a) the uneducated and the nonspecialized, with their "irrationality"; (b) the professionally educated, with their commitments to "enlightened" thinking; (c) a "time lag" subculture, the bearers of which hold on to pre-Enlightenment modes of thinking and patterns of living as a result of their not having been accepted into the cultural mainstream. It is within this last-named group that one can still find, for example, genuine credulity regarding demons and exorcisms.

34. On the issue of criteria for discussing the pre-rational legacy of the church, cf. §26 of my *Hermeneutik des Neuen Testaments*. There I argue that reason has an important role to play as a point of orientation around which the nonrational can be considered.

35. Guidelines for such discussion might well include the following: (a) resistance to complete hegemony of rationalism in the church (the nonrational has a necessary place in human life); (b) tolerance of subcultures wherever they exist, even if within our own midst (cf. note 33, above); (c) avoidance of the reciprocal relationship with a certain kind of irrationalism, namely, authoritarianism, into which the de facto rationalistically minded church so often enters; (d) a holistic view of human nature, in both theory and practice; (e) avoiding giving the impression that religion is somehow intrinsically tied in with parapsychology. (So, for example, not every "spirit" is a matter of concern for the church; neither is the church responsible for everything that happened in biblical antiquity any more than it is responsible for everything that happens today.) Entrance into the area of the nonrational could also lead to some unconventional practices. So, for example, one might envision healing services held at certain places other than at the home or home parish of the sick (following the example of medieval pilgrimages), or a greater willingness to draw on the treasury of metaphors found in first-millennium Christian funeral liturgies.

4. Experience of the Body

1. For the particulars, see Bultmann's *Theology*, esp. 1:195–99.

2. Ibid., p. 197.

3. Bultmann regards the external factors (other human beings, world) as of only preliminary significance, or even as a distraction from authentic self-discovery (cf. *Theology*, 1:197–98, where he speaks explicitly of the self's alienation from the body). On the other hand, he also openly refers to a "helping power, which restores the alienated man to himself." However, this power remains external and merely a means to an end. It is precisely such a devaluation of the external features that is here being contested.

4. The "instruments of righteousness" in Rom 6:13 can only be the transformed members of the community; otherwise Paul could only be speaking of spiritual realities such as prayer. Here for the first time Paul ties in the image of weaponry with his notion of a new, or renewed, corporeality.

5. This is how the situation would be described by Bultmann (see note 3, above). But the modern notion of estrangement from one's self and its concomitant notion that one can be restored to one's self are historically out of place when applied to Paul.

6. Cf. Isa 49:3 (God will be glorified through his servant Israel), Mal 1:6 (the slave glorifies his lord), and 1 Chr 17:18 (slaves . . . glorify); note also 1QH 11:33.

7. Paul is operating with a specific notion of proper social ordering. Prostitution is a mode of interaction where no reciprocity exists. Failure to observe the rule of reciprocity is disobedience against God. (The notion of a proper social ordering also forms the basis of Paul's argument in Rom 13:1-2.) This whole line of

thinking in Paul shows how far he has superseded the individual precepts of Torah through a mode of thinking shaped by general principles.

8. Mark 10:11 ("he commits adultery against her") identifies the woman as the one affected by the sin. But it is as a wife, not as an individual, that she is so affected.

9. On the theme of ghosts having no bodies, cf. my *Die Auferstehung des Propheten und die Erhöhung des Menschensohnes*, esp. p. 462, n. 123; p. 476, n. 151.

10. Cf. Gal 3:27-28. Here indeed the underlying notion is something like that of the body as clothing. Could one say that the new body is Christ, and that he then binds us all together into one "body of Christ" (a phrase not used in Galatians)? In this way all differences would be set aside automatically, since it was precisely these differences that characterized the people as individuals outside the body formed by Christ. This new "body of Christ" would then have to be essentially spiritual in nature (cf. v. 14). Likewise, in 1 Cor 12:12-13 becoming one with the body of Christ is a spiritual event. In contrast to the body envisioned in 1 Cor 15:44-51, however, the spiritual body of Galatians 3 and 1 Corinthians 12 would be a present, not a future, reality. However, in neither Galatians 3 nor 1 Corinthians 12 is the talk expressly of the bodies of individual Christians. Does the theme of putting on Christ not go so far as to include the theme of the transformation of our bodies? Certainly it does! In any case, in 2 Cor 4:16-17 Paul is trying to build a bridge between the two images.

5. Interior and Exterior

1. In Matt 23:25, the terms "greed" (Greek: *arpagē*) and "self-indulgence" (Greek: *akrasia*) refer not only to the mood of the Pharisees but also to that which they are doing in secret. Matt 6:2-18 is also important in this context. What is there said to happen "in secret" is not something one does only in the mind and is therefore, by definition, not visible. Rather, what is being spoken of is something one is not to do publicly, so as not to be observed by other people. The admonition about prayer in Matt 6:6 has come to be seen over the course of time as referring specifically to the mood one is to have while praying.

2. The relevant parts of the text in question read as follows: "And he [Jesus] took them [the disciples] with him into the place of purification itself and walked about in the Temple court. And a Pharisaic chief priest, Levi (?) by name, fell in with them and said to the Saviour: Who gave thee leave to tread this place of purification and to look upon these holy utensils without having bathed thyself and even without thy disciples having washed their feet? . . . Then said the Saviour to him: Woe unto you blind that see not! Thou hast bathed thyself in water that is poured out, in which dogs and swine lie night and day, and thou hast washed thyself and hast chafed thine outer skin, which prostitutes also and flute-girls anoint, bathe, chafe and rouge, in order to arouse desire in men, but within they are full of scorpions and of badness of every kind. But I and my disciples, of whom thou sayest that we have not immersed ourselves, have been immersed in the living . . . water which comes down from. . . . But woe unto them that . . ." (cited from Schneemelcher, *New Testament Apocrypha*, 1:93-94).

3. Recall here the traditional polemic against prostitutes in the Jewish wisdom tradition.

4. From a historical perspective one reads these texts correctly only when one recognizes the reproach of hypocrisy as a consequence of and reaction against the Pharisaic endeavor to have piety permeate all aspects of daily living. Every effort of this sort eventually and inevitably calls forth the reproach of hypocrisy.

5. In this reconstruction I draw also on historically oriented studies of a phenomenological sort.

6. Cultic activity has largely been abandoned in the contemporary world, not only because of the danger of mistaking the part for the whole, but also—indeed, even more so—because the symbolic character of cultic activity is no longer understood. Our inability to grasp something as a symbol (as something which points beyond itself to some larger whole) or indeed to appreciate the nature of symbols as such has led to the general inclination of our times to regard only the ethical domain as religiously relevant.

7. Enlightened Hellenistic Judaism, in keeping with Greek philosophy, tended to argue as follows about the cult: The materiality of the cult is not suited to the spirituality of God, especially because of its particularity over against the universality of God. The bourgeois prejudice against cultic concretization on the part of the "enlightened" nineteenth century was also derived from a supposed incompatibility between the material and the spiritual. It is only in our postmodern situation that a renewed relationship to materiality is becoming possible.

8. Cf. also Matt 7:16-18, 20; 12:33-35; and the *Gospel of Thomas*.

9. Cf. Heiligenthal, *Werke als Zeichen*.

10. Cf. Theobald, *Die überströmende Gnade*.

11. Cf. Philo of Alexandria, *On Curses* 168; also 2 Esdras 2:32 ("my springs run over, and my grace will not fail," *OTP* 1:527).

12. Cf. my "Jesus als Pharisäer und frühe Christen als Pharisäer," esp. pp. 238–48. The association between "proactive" purity and Jesus' message of the kingdom of God can be traced back at least as far as Daniel 7, in which the "saints" overcome the powers of this world (vv. 21-22). Working with this notion of purity, Jesus becomes the Holy One who conquers the powers of this world, accomplishing the task assigned in Daniel 7 to the Son of Man. In the same vein, the imposing power of death is overcome in 1 Cor 15:26. (Note how vocabulary from Daniel 7 is used in 1 Cor 15:24).

13. If we do not uncritically blend the Synoptic Gospels with Paul or transpose a Pauline notion of grace into the Gospels, then we can see here a certain analogy between the Gospels and Paul. Paul also regards the status of the Christian as fundamentally determined; for Paul the Christian has already been pronounced righteous, on the basis of faith.

14. Cf. Heiligenthal, *Werke*, p. 244, n. 19.

15. The sentence "give as alms what lies within" could be understood like this: If a person's essence (that which determines his or her fundamental nature) is within that person like a deed-filled treasury, then the challenge is to transfer those hidden deeds to the outside, in the form of a giving of alms.

16. Cf. Berger and Carsten, *Religionsgeschichtliches Textbuch zum Neuen Testament*, pp. 216–17. According to Plato (*Politics* 9.12 [588D–589B]), the human

being has within a "lion," a "man," and a "many-headed beast." The "inner person" is the noblest of these components; according to 589D it is the "divine" element within the human being. What it comes down to for Plato is that "the inner person must be strong." The lion stands for desire. (Note the echo of this theme in v. 7 of the *Gospel of Thomas*: "Blessed is the lion that becomes man when consumed by man; and cursed is the man whom the lion consumes, and the lion becomes man.") According to *Corpus Hermeticum* 13.7, the inner person suffers from the senses; the passions compel the imprisoned inner person to suffer from the senses. Rebirth brings about a change in this state of affairs.

17. It is unclear whether Romans 7 describes the Christian or the pre-Christian status of the human being.

6. Perceptions

1. Since the time of Hermann Gunkel it has been customary to speak of the "eschatological aorist" to represent future acts, but of course this notion has not yet been more carefully investigated. For example, consider the following remarks by H. Schürmann, *Das Lukasevangelium*, 1:71: "The passage speaks of the final act of God as though it had already happened. The prophetic gaze sees the completion of the acts of God already in their modest beginning. . . . Characteristic of the Song of Mary is an interweaving of thanks for personally experienced divine grace and hymnic extolling of God for future acts—acts nonetheless described in the past tense, as though they had already taken place. . . ."

2. On the diverse genres of these hymns, see my *Formgeschichte des Neuen Testaments*, 242.

3. Cf. Bejick, *Basileia*.

4. Cf. Ego, *Im Himmel wie auf Erden*.

5. Cf. *Religionsgeschichtliches Textbuch zum Neuen Testament*, no. 25, pp. 37–38.

6. Cf. Heiligenthal, *Werke als Zeichen*.

7. Early Christian apocalyptic works reckon with the possibility that God can transform years into months, months into days, days into hours, hours into minutes, and minutes into seconds, as in the Pseudo-Johannine Apocalypse (cf. *Apocalypses Apocryphae*, ed. Tischendorf [Leipzig, 1866] chap. 8, p. 76).

8. *OTP* 1:627.

9. With regard to the theme of the acceleration of time, two basic trends can be discerned, depending on their impact on human beings. The first is negative. Here God shortens the span of life as a mode of punishment. This happens to both human beings (Gen 6:3) and animals (the serpent, according to *3 Bar.* 9:7 [following the Greek text]). The cosmic changes envisioned in *1 En.* 80:2ff. also fit in here. The second is positive. The transformation of the seventy years for punishment (Jer 25:11-14) to seventy weeks of years for fulfillment (Dan 9:24) is basic in this regard. Out of the final three and a half "times" of Dan 7:25 there develops, in the Revelation to John, both three and a half "years" (Rev 11:2-3) and three and a half "days" (Rev 11:11). Here the time of distress is being curtailed. Anticipated positively is also the hastening demise of the world according to 2 Esdras 4:26; in 4:34 Ezra is admonished not to out-hasten the Lord! *L.A.B.* speaks of a hastening of the resurrection, *2 Baruch* about a hastening of punishment on the world.

10. I recall with pleasure a conversation with Kurt Erlemann of Heidelberg, who was engaged in a comprehensive investigation of precisely this theme.

11. Recent Protestant hermeneutics, especially since the time of A. von Harnack, has directed overwhelming attention to experience of the personal nearness of God; this is the constant feature of liberal, pietistic, and existential interpretation. The nearness of God can be experienced also in two kinds of sectarian groups: the charismatic movement, with its inclination toward fundamentalism, has picked up on the theme of wondrous divine power, while temporal eschatological expectation is a feature of millenarian sects.

12. Cf. Rev 6:9-10 with its cry, "Sovereign Lord . . . how long will it be before you judge and avenge our blood on the inhabitants of the earth?" Parallels are to be found, notably in Job 24:12, Heb 12:26-29, *1 En.* 9:4—10:3, 47:1-4, 97:5, and also in the widow's plea in Luke 8:1-8 with its special emphasis on the widow's emotions (vv 5-7). The martyr's death suffered by Jesus will thus have had the effect of heightening anticipation of the end. The connection between martyrdom and anticipation of the end is especially apparent in Matt 23:35. (All the righteous blood will come "upon you," and then "Truly, I say to you, all this will come upon this generation.") The import of vv 37-39 is that one is here to be thinking of the death of Jesus.

13. Cf. Schimanowski, *Weisheit und Messias*, 107ff. On Schimanowski's conclusion that the preexistent name of the Messiah is his "person" (p. 308), see chap. 2, above, regarding "person" and "self." The notion of "person" that Schimanowski employs is in need of further clarification.

14. Thus Schimanowski, *Weisheit und Messias*, 308.

15. Ibid., 302.

16. E.g., Col 1:15. Unfortunately, not all the relevant texts which mention a firstborn can be read along the lines of this metaphor. In fact, it is more common for such texts to be speaking of realities that are, strictly speaking, "first-created."

17. In Heb 11:4 (cf. Rev 6:9-10) the "blood" of the martyrs cries out (for revenge). This is a parade example of a notion of the relationship between persons and things that differs from our own. In Heb 12:24 this same ancient mode of perception is at work, in that the "blood" of Jesus is the ultimate cause of the approaching judgment.

18. Cf. my article "Die königlichen Messiastraditionen," 1–44, esp. pp. 3–15; also Lövestam, "Jesus Fils de David," 97–109.

19. Cf. Böcher, *Christus Exorcista.*

20. The main differences have to do with motivation (e.g., in the case of "magic," a desire to work harm) or with the manner in which the "cultic" element is established (e.g., the use of drugs or sacrificial offerings in place of calling upon the name of Jesus). In the best of circumstances, one might say that the principles of *solus Christus* and *sola gratia* managed to penetrate even into the world of magic, establishing a beachhead in this otherwise ungodly domain.

21. Berger, *Hermeneutik*, esp. 391–92, "Zum Verhältnis von Metapher und Vision."

22. Cf. my treatment of Mark 9:2ff. in *Formgeschichte des Neuen Testaments.*

23. To be sure, the telling of parables—indeed, the telling of tales in general—is also associated with particular sociocultural conditions. "Narrative theology" was discovered precisely in those decades of the twentieth century in which this storytelling for the first time really seemed to be threatened with extinction. Thus "narrative theology" gives the impression of being a cultural form whose lifetime is being artificially extended by means of theological intervention.

24. Cf., e.g., the connection between visions and certain stages of life in *1 En.* 83:2 (while undergoing schooling and just before marriage); note also the requirements associated with preparation for heavenly journeys in the Jewish mystical writings.

25. Among us, eidetic perception still exists among children, but this particular mode of perception gets suppressed as children are taught to engage in abstract thinking. In the process of such learning, children lose the ability to perceive in eidetic or visionary ways. This is all a part of what we now call the acculturation process.

26. In similar fashion, spirit-possession is not necessarily a religious phenomenon, and a theologian is hardly thereby a specialist in alternative modes of perception! Precisely through its multiplicity of genres, however, the Bible shows that all human forms of understanding can serve the revelatory purposes of God. This principle makes the fable as important as the proverb, and the anecdote as valuable as the elaborate argument.

27. Where visions are not being regarded as supernatural occurrences, their revelatory character consists in the way they disclose meaningful connections within human experience.

28. With regard to the reappearing of the deceased, cf. *L.A.B.* 64 (the witch of Endor speaking to Saul about Samuel): "You ask me about the ghost. Behold, his countenance is not that of a man. He is clothed in a white garment with a mantle overlying it, and two angels accompany him . . . that I should announce to you that you have already for the second time sinned against God in negligent fashion. . . ." On the possibility of postmortem appearances by prophets, cf. Philo's *On Abraham* 113 (concerning Sarah and her laughter on the occasion of the promise given to her by the three men): "She was granted a different perception of the three strangers, one more worthy, one of prophets or angels who had transformed themselves from their spiritual nature into human form."

29. Cf. my *Die Auferstehung des Propheten*, 573–74.

30. "When Methuselah heard the words of his son [viz., Lamech, to whom had just been born a wonderful, beaming son (Noah) about whom the question had been raised if perhaps the child had been generated by an angel], he came to us at the ends of the earth; for he had heard that I was there. He cried aloud, and I heard his voice and came to him; and I said to him, 'Here I am, why have you come here?' Then he answered me and said, 'On account of a great distress have I come to you. . . . For unto my son Lamech a son has been born. . . . And behold, I have come to you in order that you may make me know the real truth.' Then I, Enoch, answered, saying to him, 'The Lord will surely make new things upon the earth; and I have already seen this matter in a vision and made it known to you. . . . There shall be a great destruction upon the earth. . . . Now make known to your son Lamech. . . .' And when Methuselah had heard the words of his father Enoch—for he revealed everything to him in secret—he returned home and revealed them to him." (*1 En.* 106:8ff., *OTP* 1:86–88)

31. The work of H. E .G. Paulus can serve as an illustration of what to avoid; cf. Burchard, "H. E. G. Paulus," 222–97.

32. Cf. the description of the childlike (mythic) manner of perceiving death in William Wordsworth's poem "We are Seven."

33. As the form-critical parallels attest, Jesus' "presence" with his disciples refers to the charismatic power they experience and attribute to their resurrected Lord; cf. my *Auferstehung des Propheten*, 434–35, n. 29; 505–6, n. 235; 510, n. 244; 513, n. 257; 532, n. 299.

34. Ibid., 183–84.

35. Comparative religiohistorical material can be found in my essay, "Der tra-ditions-geschichtliche Ursprung der *traditio legis*," 104–22, esp. 114ff.; see also my *Einführung in die Formgeschichte*, 95–102 ("Joh 21, das sog. Nachtragskapitel des JohEV"), esp. 99–101.

36. Rau, *Eschatologie*, 476.

37. Cf. my *Auferstehung des Propheten*, 454ff., nn. 92–98.

38. E.g., Philodemus; cf. von Arnim, *Stoicorum veterum fragmenta* 4:152.

39. Artemidorus is perhaps an exception; cf. section 1.1 of his *Oneirocriticon*, ed. R. A. Pack (Leipzig, 1963).

40. The "magical" aspects of later sacramental theology also have their origin here.

41. In a way, the origin of the Johannine "I am [+ metaphor]" predications can be understood in a similar fashion.

42. Because in Jesus—human like us—one nonetheless encounters mythic power, reality is transformed such that it becomes a series of brief epiphanic moments (wonders, transfigurations, etc.). Against this background one can also better understand how appropriate it is that the Gospels are broken up into dis-crete pericopes, that there is no consistent narrative strand running throughout.

43. Here one thinks, for example, of how the story of Jesus' walking on the water is linked with his miraculous feeding of the multitude (in both the Synop-tics and John). Recall also the statement about Jesus as the mediator of creation in 1 Cor 8:6, as well as the many other "Christologies in a nutshell" scattered throughout 1 Corinthians. All of this points to widespread usage of christological formulas already at the very early stages of Christian tradition.

44. As I see it, we are here dealing with a basic form-critical issue. Briefly put, the genre of the epideictic encomium exerts a sort of intrinsic pressure in the direction of maximizing statements.

45. The kinds of doubts that arise in connection with miracle stories are them-selves culturally conditioned; recall the comments on historicity and facticity in the first part of this chapter.

46. The first loop of the spiral would then lie in early Jewish expectations regarding the Messiah and other divine emissaries. In my judgment the christo-logical spiral thus did not begin with the Easter experience; it began earlier. To be sure, the Easter event is the loop of the spiral that determines the twist of all the others.

47. Attention to the powers that determine time is shown, e.g., in the synchro-nisms in Luke 2:1-2 and 3:1-2.

48. Here note should be taken of the high degree to which the Sabbath liturgy from Qumran and the tractates of the *Hekalot* literature mediate experiences of proper ordering. Likewise Revelation, which of all the apocalypses is most strongly oriented toward the liturgical (cf. the so-called hymns in the heavenly realm), is at the same time the most thoroughly structured.

49. In Jesus' estimation she gave "her whole life." The wordplay involving the Greek term *bios* ("life" but also "livelihood") is certainly intended.

50. The sum of "three hundred denarii" mentioned in the Markan account corresponds to a full year's wages for an ordinary laborer of that time.

51. The nature of the connection of Mary Magdalene with both the crucifixion of Jesus and the Easter event is illustrative at this point. Her special relationship to Jesus is shown by her physical proximity during these fateful moments. The different sort of relationship the male disciples have with Jesus is shown by their greater physical distance.

52. On this particular nuance to the theme of love in the New Testament, cf. my *Wie ein Vogel ist das Wort*, 211–12.

53. *Pace* Lührmann, *Das Markusevangelium*: "[E]ven that event, incorporated into the account of the passion of Jesus, fits into the Gospel as a sign of how near the kingdom of God approaches in the words of Jesus" (p. 233). But one must ask why it is just this act that is supposed to convey such a message. In my judgment, Lührmann's interpretation moves on much too high a level of theological abstraction.

54. Cf. the still irreplaceable material collected by Bousset in his *Die Himmelsreise der Seele*, esp. 136–69, 229–73.

55. Cf. Werner et al., "Geist," in *TRE* 12:179–80.

56. This holds true even though ancient representations of the dead already show a certain tendency toward psychologizing; on this cf. Reese, *Hellenistic Influence*, 101f.

57. Cf. the assertions in the *Apocalypse of Sophon* (Coptic); Steindorff, 170.

58. Rau points out a connection between "visions" and insights garnered from the "heavenly tablets" (*Kosmologie*, 345–53). With regard to the issue at hand, note especially Rau's observations on pp. 497f., comments that coincide with mine. Rau also correctly characterizes as dubiously apologetic the hypotheses of Wegenast, *Das Verständnis der Tradition*. In Judaism the connection between vision and the passing on of tradition shows up especially in the way that the Enoch-tradition was handed down. (The recipients of the tradition sleep alongside the books while also in the presence of the tradents, so that in this way the Lord can pass the tradition on to his own.)

59. Cf., e.g., the summarizing article by Wolter, "Gewissen II," in *TRE* 13:213–18.

60. Seneca: "Fortune frees many from punishment, but none from fear (*metus*). Why is this so, if not because there has been implanted in us an abhorrence of behavior which nature has condemned? Thus one can never count on being able to remain hidden, even if one is hiding. Conscience exposes one to oneself and convicts (*coarguit*) one. The fate of the guilty is to tremble (*trepidare*)" (*Epistulae* 97.16).

61. Polybius: "There are no witnesses more terrifying, no accusers more frightening, than the conscience that resides within each person's breast" (18.43).

62. In my reading of 1 Pet 3:21, I am expanding the explicitly stated material in two directions, both of which seem to me to flow quite effortlessly from the tradition lying behind this verse: (1) sitting at the right hand of God designates holding the office of advocate, and (2) the powers and authorities that have been reduced to an inferior position previously functioned as accusers.

63. There is yet another illustrative point of comparison between 1 Peter and Hebrews. According to Heb 9:24 (cf. 7:25), it is the task of the glorified one to intercede (as advocate) on behalf of his own. This strikes me as an obvious parallel to the function of Jesus who sits at the right hand of God in 1 Pet 3:22.

64. Already in Cremer (*Lexicon*, 386) the following remark occurs: "in forensic usage, connected with *eperotan*, in the sense of requesting a judicial decision or determination, as also in the Codex Justinian. . . ." The same source suggests that, where the term occurs in inscriptions, it is to be translated "in keeping with resolutions or decrees of the Senate" or "carrying the overtone of official consent." Cremer goes on to say that Dan 4:14 (in Theodotion's Greek version) [= 4:17 Eng.] is also to be interpreted from this angle. Surprisingly, Cremer then goes to great lengths to disallow a juridical interpretation at 1 Pet 3:21! In the same vein H. Greeven (*ThW* 2:685–86) suggests the meaning "judgment, decision" for the *eperotema* in Dan 4:14 (Septuagint), and he then offers additional attestations of the term. Greeven expressly notes that reading *eperotema* in the sense of "appeal" finds no support in the Greek of the LXX. (Cf. also N. Clausen-Bagge, *Eperotema*.) In light of the foregoing, I find it hard to understand why theologians still try to isolate the language of 1 Peter from contact with the juridical sphere—especially since Paul's fondness for juridical language is so widely recognized. To me it seems obvious that Jesus' intervention before God is being imagined as equivalent to a judicial finding in the Roman senate. Baptism is then simply the manifestation of that decision.

65. When one today speaks of "internalized norms" in conjunction with the conscience, one means something only roughly similar to what was meant in antiquity. What the ancient conscience internalized was not so much the norms as the structure of the social system.

66. Philo of Alexandria: "This person that lives in the soul of each one of us appears sometimes as lord and king, sometimes as judge, and sometimes as a distributor of prizes in the contests of life. At other times this person takes on the roll of a witness or an accuser, invisibly convicting us from within and not allowing us to open our mouths in defense. Instead, this person takes us captive, bridling us and restraining with the reins of conscience the otherwise impudent running on of the tongue" (*That the Worse Attacks the Better* 23). The commentaries on this passage in Philo also refer to the above-cited passage from Polybius (n. 61).

67. Wolter deserves credit for having established that this is the clear sense of 1 Cor 10:29b; cf. his article "Gewissen," in *TRE* 13:215. In that text Paul in fact defends the freedom of the strong to eat the disputed food (Wolter: vv. 25 and 27 are a "warrant to eat"). Not so easy to clarify is the question whether Paul is here still (or once again) referring to the conscience of the weak who are mentioned in chapter 8 (so Wolter) or to the conscience of pagan meal companions, who in turn are pointing out that the meat has come from animals sacrificed to idols. (In their own consciences the pagans are convinced of the special significance of the flesh of animals sacrificed to idols and, taking this fact into account, the Christian is not to eat of it.)

68. Faltin, "Brücke in eine unbekannte Zeit," 48.

69. In applying the message contained in statements about death as a cessation of communion with God, it is important to emphasize what becomes possible

through a living faith in the resurrection. Death then is not utter abandonment by God, but rather the prelude to God's subsequent renewal of communion.

70. "With whom shall I take refuge, or what shall I speak, I the virgin and an orphan and desolate and abandoned and hated? All people have come to hate me, and on top of those my father and my mother, because I, too, have come to hate their gods and have destroyed them, and caused them to be trampled underfoot by men" (11:3–4), *OTP* 2:218; cf. 12:3: "And I am now an orphan and desolate. . . ."

71. Cf. ibid.: "my lips have become like a potsherd, and my face has fallen" (13:9), and "Lord, bless this virgin, and renew her by your spirit" (8:10).

72. In an age such as ours, when infant baptism is widely practiced, it is difficult to speak of baptism as an experience of dying. Nonetheless it is important, indeed necessary, to advance some critical observations from our consideration of Pauline baptism. For example, an understanding of baptism shaped by historical-psychological considerations could help break through the familiar baptismal slogans by emphasizing the broader societal dimensions of being Christian. It could also contribute to a critical revaluing of societal constraints through emphasis on the heightened obligations which Christianity imposes.

73. As is evident already in the thinking of John the Baptist, the "others" who will replace "the Jews" include women (especially prostitutes), tax collectors, Samaritans, and Gentiles.

74. Such nonparticipation is indeed very risky and abrasive to the sentiments of others. This can already be seen in the struggle of *Jubilees* against mixed marriages and in the battle of *2 Maccabees* and *4 Maccabees* against the compulsory measures undertaken to force violation of the dietary laws. The same dangers are to be associated with the freedoms demanded in 1 Cor 7:29-31, with the attitude toward virginity exhibited in Matt 19:12, and with the embargo against trade with Christians known from Revelation. The effect of all such refusals to follow conventional practices tends to be underestimated by intellectuals, whose addiction to the conceptual aspect leads them to dismiss "mere" customs and conventions. One would do better here to trust in the wisdom of the books of Maccabees; it is in mundane acts, not grandiose theories, that issues are decided.

7. Emotions

1. Cf. *Who Is the Heir?* 24.28.29; *On Flight and Finding* 6; *On the Life of Moses* 2.169.

2. Cf. *Heir* 19.28. Surprisingly, in the Pauline corpus this particular verbal root is lacking all the way up to 2 Cor 3:12 (where it is better taken, however, in the sense of "open, unveiled") and 1 Thess 2:2 ("take courage").

3. Bultmann, *Second Letter*, ad rem.

4. The human will is conceived of by Paul not as a feeling but as a stimulus to action. As is obvious from Rom 7:15-25 (note the parallelism between the power of recognition in v. 15 and the mind in v. 25!), Paul understands the will as rational.

5. Cf. my *Formgeschichte des Neuen Testaments*, 130ff. (§40).

6. It is peculiar that Paul, who presents himself as one who has died to self, nonetheless also stands out (not only in 2 Corinthians but elsewhere as well) as a distinct individual to a degree unprecedented elsewhere in early Christianity. Here the familiar reciprocity between giving up/losing oneself and attaining/finding oneself could be operative (cf. "Risking and Gaining Life," in chapter 10, below).

7. Note the frequent references to *pneuma* in Acts 6–8 and the scriptural interpretation of Stephen in Acts 7. Similar things are reported of Apollos, who has an affinity with the Stephen-group (cf. Acts 18:24-25).

8. The revelatory pattern here displayed shows that the secrets of God are not ipso facto irrational. Instead, they are shaped by the circles of people who surround the recipient of the revelation.

9. Cf. Rom 8:6; note the important parallels in Berger, *Die Weisheitschrift aus der Kairoer Geniza*, 14:4-8.

10. In this way the Law was forced into the situation where it had to condemn human beings. Setting up the universal dominion of death, then, was an intrinsic component of the "plan" of sin; cf. Rom 7:7-11.

11. From now on the "desires" have to do with the carrying out of all the functions necessary to living; it is no longer just a matter of dealing with various sorts of appetites.

12. As a Pharisee, it is hardly accidental that Paul saw a close connection between desire and sin. Making precisely such a connection is a trademark of Pharisaic radicality, since it allows the very roots of evil to become visible (so to speak) and thus more effectively combated.

13. Trans. Burchard in *OTP* 2:214.

14. Cf. 1QS 10:16: "I will bless him for his exceeding wonderful deeds at the beginning of fear and dread and in the abode of distress and desolation" (trans. Vermes, *The Complete Dead Sea Scrolls in English*, 113]). In 1QS 1:16-17. much the same is said with reference to Belial (Satan).

15. A "heavenly man" appears, and "Aseneth was filled with great fear, and all of her limbs trembled."

16. In 2 Cor 5:12-15 the issue at hand is "pride" and the real nature of the social prestige that attaches to the individual (esp. that of the one who brings the message of salvation). Paul points out that all Christians have died "to themselves" and hence are now freed from the necessity of being concerned about their own persons. Therefore in 5:13 he identifies the two poles to which his pride now attaches itself: God and the community. Just as in Phil 2:12-13 so also here the ability so to disregard oneself is grounded in an act of God: in 2 Corinthians 5 in the death of Jesus, and in Philippians 2 in the immediate assistance of God in the works of faith.

17. Many of the commentaries employ the notion of synergy in their discussion of Phil 2:12-13 (cf., e.g., Gnilka, *The Epistle to the Philippians*), but I see the problem attached to these verses in a different light. I think the issue is one of pastoral psychology. That is to say, Paul's remarks here do not deal with some notion of enhancing human activity by means of divine assistance (or vice versa). Paul instead is trying to instruct his readers on how the Christian community is to be motivated.

18. In Romans 11 Paul is admonishing Gentile Christians; in 2 Cor 5:11 the issue is a moral defense of his own apostolate; in Phil 2:12-13 the focus is on the fundamental readiness of the community to obey. For Paul, each of these issues is as important as the others; all have equally to do with governance of the church.

19. Luther's *Small Catechism* therefore maintains the two in partial synonymy: "We should so fear and love God that . . ." (in exposition of each of the Ten Commandments).

20. Occult practice emphasizes trafficking with the uncanny. To me, it seems this is essentially a substitute for the fact that God has lost all uncanniness. One price we pay for the rationalizing and ethicizing of Christianity is renewed fascination with the occult.

21. Cf. my *Die Auferstehung des Propheten*, 433, n. 22 (on "fear not"). Also the summons to take courage (n. 23) presupposes that fear/anxiety can be overcome.

22. According to *Acta Ioannis* (ibid., 397, n. 543), the disciples of John rejoice as they find the grave of their master empty, seek his corpse without success, and then recall the words of Jesus as found in John 21:23b (i.e., that John has been raptured).

23. By way of contrast to Luke 24:41, cf. *L.A.B.* 42.5 ("Manue did not believe his wife, confused by sadness"); in this case, sadness is contrasted with joy.

24. In particular, with its frequent and significant use of the Greek stem *phaneroun* (to make manifest/visible), 2 Corinthians strikes me as providing evidence of Pauline confidence. Here we see how Paul can accuse his opponents of timidity while he himself marches boldly forward without concern for his safety (e.g., 2 Cor 11:23-30; also compare 3:12 with 7:4).

25. The Bauer-Arndt-Gingrich-Danker lexicon includes the following among its translations of *parrhesia*: "outspokenness, frankness, plainness of speech that conceals nothing and passes over nothing"; "openness to the public"; "courage, confidence, boldness, fearlessness (esp. in the presence of persons of high rank)"; "joyousness, confidence (in relation to God)."

26. "Someone will say that I am now summoning the slaves to freedom and ousting the masters from their position because I have said they should respect their masters rather than fear them. 'How so?' says such a person. 'Should they show respect as dependents, as visitors?' Someone who speaks like this forgets that what suffices for God is not too little for a master. Who would be respected is also loved; love can not mix with fear ("non potest amor cum timore misceri"). Thus you act most rightly, I think, when you do not want to be feared by your slaves . . ." (*Epistulae Morales* 47.18–19).

27. This comment is not to be taken as maintaining that no instances of contrast between fear and love are to be found before the first century c.e.; one needs to no more than glance at Wettstein to see that is not so. Neither is this comment to be taken as questioning the fundamental proposition of the phenomenological study of religion, namely, that there is always a *mysterium tremendum* accompanying the *mysterium fascinosum*. All I am saying is that, over against anxiety/fear, love alone is regarded as truly fitting.

28. Mary is never a judge; she always stands for pure love and charity. Some Mariological developments probably stem from the very human desire for a saving Christology in the face of an overgrown dogmatics.

29. Cf. also my article "Unfehlbare Offenbarung: Petrus in der gnostischen und apokalyptischen Offenbarungsliteratur," with particular reference to the Ethiopic *Apocalypse of Peter* (text: *ROC* 5 [1910] 425–39) and its admonition, "Reveal it to no one other than the wise and the knowing." Sinners are not to know of the mercy of God but are to be left in danger of being cut off from the possibility of remorse and repentance. The mass of humanity should rather live in fear of divine judgment, terrified by the threat of chastisement. Similarly, in the Ethiopic *Apocalypse of Schenute*, one reads as follows: "Unveil it not for the crowd, that this speech not give them hope, and that they not desist from regret in their lives" (text: *ZDMG* 67 [1913] 217).

30. This comment does not ignore the fact that, even here and now, many accept the prevailing systems of order from the outset and therefore still hold fast to the older perceptions of perversity.

31. It is quite possible to imagine that the readers of Revelation had only recently and superficially become Christians and, precisely as such, were receptive to Hellenistic melodrama. In falling back on imagery drawn from Jewish apocalyptic, the writer was able to get his point across all the more sharply.

32. Modern pastoral conversations tend to be strongly biographically stamped. In Revelation one finds precisely the opposite: generalized descriptions of experience within a specific (historical-theological) framework.

33. The sort of psychological reading in mind here has nothing to do with suppositions about the young man's feelings or the associations that come to his mind—and certainly even less about those of Jesus or the disciples during the course of this conversation. I am interested instead in the nature of the signals put out for the reader, in his or her own situation. Keeping in mind all that is known about antiquity, at what point would an ancient reader feel touched within the psyche? Does the particular course of action in this little narrative also pay any attention to the situation of the people for whom it was told? Is the narrative actually intended for these people, and are they able to recognize themselves within it? At what point in the story are they supposed to be moved?

34. Falling to the knees (v. 17), the prudent teacher's rejecting excessive honor (v. 18), and the teacher's compassion (v. 21) are all part of the tradition attached to instructional situations; none of these features is directed explicitly to the situation of the reader.

35. This interpretation of Mark 10:27 is supported by close analogies found in Philo (*Spec. Laws* 1.282, on purifying the contaminated soul) and *Theophilus ad Autolycum* 2.13, 2–4 (on the creative activity of God). The major theme in both is that God can do what for human beings would be impossible.

36. Father and mother are left behind (10:29). In the new community, however, one gets only a new mother, not a new father—undoubtedly because there God is the "Father." In general, Matt 23:9 offers a good parallel to this. The important point is that, on earth (viz., in the Christian community), the function of the earthly father is left unfilled. Among other things, this fact testifies to the institutional power of the father in a patriarchal society. Precisely because his role is the decisive one, in the new community of Christians it is altered—or reserved for God. Here we find additional evidence that in the early church the need arose to think in fresh ways.

37. "To worry about someone" implies being ready to offer concrete assistance to that person; "to worry about something" includes the notion of engaging in some specific kind of action in the future.

38. There is debate about the unity of 2 Corinthians. In my treatment of the material, I do not bother with the various suggestions for dividing it up. But I do regard the approach I take here as offering, among other things, a new kind of argument in favor of the unity of this epistle. I think that the sorts of questions I raise open new avenues of approach to this old problem.

39. I can also find no reason for supposing that the opponents were promoting some sort of "Judaized" gospel. Nowhere in 2 Corinthians 3, where one might expect it, does one find mention of "the Law"; neither is there any reference to circumcision.

40. The love of Christ compels Paul to act as he does, and therefore his actions take on a form that imitates Christ himself, namely, as someone who is totally "there" for the other.

41. I read 2 Cor 11:9-12 as follows: "And while I was with you and was in need, I became a burden to no one; for my brothers, who came from Macedonia, helped me out of my need. And in every relationship I comported myself such that I did not become a burden to you, and I will continue to act in the same way. Thus the truth of Christ is surely in me; this particular boast of mine should not be silenced in the region of Achaia. Why? Perhaps because I do not love you? God knows I do! What I am doing, however, I will continue to do, so that I might take away the occasion of those who seek an occasion against me that would allow them to praise themselves for standing at the same level as we do."

42. Obviously as a substitute for accepting support for himself, in 2 Corinthians 8–9 Paul returns to the topic of the collection for the Jerusalem church, a concern that has in the meantime become dormant in Corinth. If the Corinthians are indeed willing to expend resources in connection with Paul, then please let them do so in the form of that collection. This opens up a compromise position.

43. Paul regards his refusal of support as grounds for heightened respect, but for the Corinthians that is perhaps not the case.

44. It is an error for scholarly research on 2 Corinthians to assume that Paul condemns any and all sorts of boasting. It would be more correct to say, in view of 2 Cor 10:17, that Paul feels ambivalent about boasting. Generally it is bad, but there is nothing objectionable in boasting of the Lord and the Lord's judgments.

45. Special attention should be directed to 2 Cor 12:14-16; v. 16b is obviously ironic. [The author reads v. 16 thus: "Well now, I myself did not become a burden to you; but as a master of cunning I took you in by guile"—trans.]

46. Lang, *Die Briefe an die Korinther*, 353.

47. Cf. also Marshall, *Enmity in Corinth*.

48. 2 Cor 5:2 speaks of the "heavenly dwelling" that is to be put on, while v. 4 contrasts the current state of being burdened ("in this tent") with the future state of being better attired; in Rom 8:23 the "redemption of our bodies" is awaited.

49. Cf., e.g., *The Works of Philo*, trans. Yonge, 74–75.

50. Cf. Rom 7:24, a verse that shows how the "groaning" of chap. 8 could have been verbalized. Form critically, there is a good parallel in Philo, *Alleg. Interp.* 3.211: "Oh we miserable ones! How long have we wandered around in the illness

of misunderstanding, afflicted by foolishness and wanton striving!" In the case of Philo, we are dealing with an outcry of remorse. With Paul, we are dealing with a lament over the consequences of sin.

51. This word, attested only in Hellenistic texts, means "tense or anxious waiting"; cf. Wilckens, *Der Brief an der Römer*, on Rom 8:19.

52. This is clearly the sense in Luke 21:28 ("Stand up and raise your heads . . ."), and also in Acts 3:19-20 ("times of refreshing"); contrast the imagery in Luke 21:26 (fainting).

53. As should be clear in 2:1-3, the community and Paul alike experience both joy and sadness in their mutual relationship.

54. Cf. Windisch, *Der zweite Korintherbrief*, 79, ad loc.: "At first glance 2:2 has an egotistic ring to it. Somewhat surprisingly, the person of Paul and his need for joy stands front and center. Paul's motive seems to be to take care of himself, not the Corinthians; his greatest desire seems to be to get joy from the others, not to bring joy to them. The strong emphasis on Paul's personal interest, however, can satisfactorily be explained by the fact that the church he established at Corinth was one of his most important. This community lay especially close to his heart. Thus Paul, with an effluence of his own love, wants to awaken the community's love for him—cf. 11:2, 11."

55. Paul employs a topos familiar in the rhetorical strategy of antiquity. Note, for example, the following comment: "But I will show you a few things, not as a teacher but as one of yourselves, in which you shall rejoice at this present time" (*Barn.* 1:8). Two features of this remark correspond to 2 Cor 1:24: (a) the writer sets himself on the same level as his readers, and (b) the reference to joy.

56. "Paul would destroy the very font of his joy were he to plunge the community into sorrow" (Lang, *Die Briefe an die Korinther*, 261).

57. The old observation that Johannine Christology has deep correspondences with the Pauline notion of apostleship here finds some confirmation. Love goes out from the Johannine Christ (John 15:9-10) just as it goes from Paul toward the community (2 Cor 2:4). Joy is the manifestation and the goal of this love. Particularly striking is the correspondence between 2 Cor 2:3b ("that my joy would be the joy of all of you") and John 15:11 ("that my joy might be in you and that your joy might be complete"). Joy is thus something of a continuum upon which both partners stand, though to be sure it starts from Christ or from the apostle.

58. The *perissoterōs* ("overflowing" or "abundantly rich") of 2 Cor 2:4, which Paul certainly does not use accidentally, also fits into the context of eschatological fullness. But there is no distinctively psychological nuance to this term.

59. The theme of seeing Jesus again refers either to the encounter of the disciples with the resurrected Jesus ("The disciples rejoiced when they saw the Lord," John 20:20b) or to the presence of the Exalted One or to the coming of the Paraclete or the *parousia* of Jesus. Probably this ambiguity is deliberate. The only certainty is that the disciples do not remain alone and abandoned.

60. Honi the Circle-Drawer first successfully prays for rain, then with equal success for the cessation of rain. This leads to his being compared to a child who demands of his father that he be bathed, first in warm water, then in cool water. Subsequently he demands, in sequence, hazelnuts, almonds, pears, and pomegranates. Jewish tradition sees Honi as a charismatic scribe. A (male) "child of the

household" would be equivalent to a "son of God." Cf. *b. Ta'anith* 23a; the text is reprinted with commentary in *Religionsgeschichtliches Textbuch zum Neuen Testament*, pp. 48–49, no. 44.

61. Nearly the same is said in 1 Pet 4:12-14.

62. "Favored by God are those who suffer, for the glory of the Lord rests on the one upon whom suffering comes" (*Sifre Deuteronomy* 6:5; cf. Strack-Billerbeck, 3:243).

63. "And while Isaiah was being sawed in half, he did not cry out, or weep, but his mouth spoke with the Holy Spirit until he was sawed in two" (*Mart. Isa.* 5:14, *OTP* 2:163; cf. *Martyrdom of Perpetua and Felicitas* 1:4; Acts 7:55). Note also *NumR* 15:20 on Num 11:16: "the elders and overseers who have given themselves up in order to be punished (vicariously) for them (the people as a whole) in Egypt on account of the work with the bricks . . . from this you learn that all who give themselves up for Israel are worthy of honor, greatness, and the Holy Spirit . . . similar to Moses" (on this passage cf. Schäfer, *Die Vorstellung vom heiligen Geist*, 130). On the theme of the Holy Spirit's "resting" on someone, note also Num 11:25 and the further instances cited by Schäfer, p. 159.

64. "Rejoice in the suffering which you now suffer! . . . Prepare yourselves for that which lies prepared for you, and make yourselves ready for the reward which is set aside for you" (*2 Bar.* 52:5-7).

65. The motif of divine aid in juridical situations can be traced back to ancient wisdom literature; cf. Werner et al., "Geist, Geistesgaben," in *TRE* 12:182.

66. The "testament" genre frequently exhibits the theme of being filled with the Holy Spirit (of prophecy); on occasion, a whole unit is taken up with Spirit-inspired prophecies about the future. Note the function of the Holy Spirit as reflected in the words of Paul in Acts 20:23. On the theme of the glory of God when a significant individual is facing death (e.g., Moses), consider the following from Pseudo-Philo, *L.A.B.*: when Moses received the announcement of his impending demise, "he was filled with understanding and his appearance became glorious, and he died in glory according to the word of the Lord (19:16—cf. "I will glorify you" in v. 12). The vision at the hour of death sometimes focuses on earlier martyrs or righteous individuals (as in the vision of the "Son of Man" in Acts 7:55-56), who might then greet the "newcomer" (cf. *4 Macc.* 18:23 and also entry 135 in *Religionsgeschichtliches Textbuch zum Neuen Testament*). Concerning joy at the hour of death, note the following: Baruch is already sitting in a grave, but he sees the figs in the basket of Abimelech, well preserved after seventy years, and he says, "There is one God, who vouchsafes reward to his saints. Prepare yourself, my heart; rejoice and be joyful in your tent. I mean, in your house of flesh. For your sadness will be transformed (*metastrophe*) into joy. You have no sin! Breathe freely, my pure faith; believe that you will live" (*Par. Jer.* 6:3; the miracle of the figs functions in the same way here as does the resurrection of Jesus in 1 Pet 1:3). A similar scene appears in *T. Levi* 18, when Isaac reaches the hour of his death: "And Isaac saw the Father of us all and blessed us and rejoiced" (v. 12, cod. e). Some near parallels can also be found in the pagan literature of the time; note, e.g., the "divinare morientes" of Cicero (1.30.64).

67. First Peter emphasizes both of these aspects. It would be a "private" form of suffering if one were to suffer as an evildoer. Moreover, the Christian faith is

not a personal opinion but a reality foretold by the prophets (1 Pet 1:10-12), and the Christian community is a royal priesthood and a distinctly new people (1 Pet 2:1-10).

68. Cf. Cyprian's *Agraphon* (*Aleat* 3): "nolite contristare spiritum sanctum, qui in vobis est, et nolite extinguere lumen, quod in vobis effulsit" (Do not wish to sadden the holy spirit who is in you, and wish not to extinguish the light which shines in you). Cf. esp. *Herm. Mand.* 10, where the following comments appear: (a) The doubter is sad, but this grieves the Spirit (10:2). (b) The sisters of sadness are doubt and sudden anger, and the deeds which follow from these also grieve the spirit (10:4). (c) The Holy Spirit from above is expressly described as "joyous." One who grieves this Spirit acts contrary to the divine law. Joyousness, on the other hand, calls forth the favor (*charis*) of God, effects good, and despises sadness. Above all, however, the prayer of a sad person no longer has the power to ascend to the throne of God. Such a prayer is no longer pure; it is like wine mixed with vinegar. Even sadness is a "spirit," but it is the wickedest spirit of all. This latter spirit literally drives away the Holy Spirit (10:1, 2). See also *T. Dan*: "If you lose something by your own action or otherwise, do not be sorrowful, for grief arouses anger as well as deceit" (4:6)

69. On this cf. v. Arnim, *Stoicorum veterum fragmenta* I, no. 211; also Philo, *Decalogue* 144 and *Corpus Hermeticum* 6.1 ("Sorrow is an aspect of wickedness").

70. Cf. the following from *Herm. Mand.* 5:2–3: "Patience . . . in you is a forceful and capable power . . . happy, joyous, without worry, it praises the Lord at all times, does not become intense, but remains calm and gentle under all circumstances."

71. This *pathos* is to be distinguished from the sorrow that, as a prelude to repentance, draws salvation in its wake. On the whole issue of *pathos*, cf. Haas, *De geest bewaren.*

72. Older analogies are actually only Isa 63:10 (MT: "grieved"; LXX: "provoked his Holy Spirit") and *Jub.* 25:1 (embitter the soul). Also in Eph 4:30-31 "bitterness" is set in opposition to joy. On the notion of grieving the Spirit (but not explicitly the "Holy" Spirit), cf. also 2 Sam 13:21 (LXX); Tob 4:3 (*S*).

73. "Let us be zealous to accomplish every good work with energy and readiness. For the Creator and Master of the universe himself rejoices in his works. . . . Let us observe that all the righteous have been adorned with good works; and the Lord himself adorned himself with good works and rejoiced in them. Since we therefore have this example, let us follow his will without delay; with our whole strength let us work the work of righteousness" (*1 Clem.* 33:1b-2, 7-8).

74. Because of the way it links emotionality and ritual, the Old Testament offers the better texts to peruse in conjunction with this point. For what follows I must also acknowledge, with thanks, two seminar works I suggested but which were worked out by two of my former students: A. F. Nehls, "Untersuchungen zum semantischen Feld von LYPE und LYPEIN," and H. Dase, "Trauer und ihre Bewaltigung bei Johannes und im Hebräerbrief."

75. Cf. Hardmeier, *Texttheorie und biblische Exegese.*

76. Cf. Isa 15:2-3; 32:11ff. (tremble, shutter, undress, expose oneself, put sackcloth upon one's loins); note also 1 Esd 8:71 (LXX) and Sir 38:17.

77. Cf. Strack-Billerbeck 4/1, Excursus 23 (Ancient Jewish Acts of Charity,

Section F: Burial of the Dead, pp. 578ff.). Note also esp. *Aboth de Rabbi Nathan* 14 (5b), on the sorrow of R. Johanan b. Zakkai over his son. (R. Johanan is not consoled by having his attention shifted to other matters, but rather through praise of his son to the effect that he had read the Torah and the Mishnah, and that he had departed the world without sin.)

78. On this point cf. my *Formgeschichte des Neuen Testaments*, 79–80.

79. Ehrlich, *Die Kultsymbolik im Alten Testament*, 117.

80. Cf., e.g., Epictetus, *Discourse* 3.13.11: The emperor can grant only external peace, but the philosopher offers another kind. The philosopher says, "When you heed me, you people—wherever you are, or whatever you might be doing—you cease to be troubled, you are not angry, you are not constrained, you are not hindered, you live without passion and in freedom from all things." Also: "Pay attention to yourself in everything, that you need not remain hidden when you . . . are beside yourself with sorrow or become furious through anger . . ." (*Sentences of Moschion* 1).

81. Cf., e.g., the LXX of Esth 1:12 ("The king became grieved and angered"); the order is reversed in *S*. Note also *Bar.* 4:8-9 (grieved—anger—sorrow) and Eph 4:26-31.

82. Irenaeus of Lyon, *Against the Heresies* 1.4.1-2 (*Ante-Nicene Fathers*, volume 1).

8. Suffering

1. On the whole the letter is pitched in such a way that the community should not come to see its isolation and antagonism vis-à-vis the surrounding community as an occasion for religious and cultural accommodation.

2. Two related questions: (1) To what extent did the persecutions of the early Christians (esp. martyrdoms) further the development of gnosis? (2) Did not the measures directed against the Gnostics themselves have the same effect?

3. Here are important differences between 1 Peter and the writings of Paul, for Paul regularly speaks of the holy or the righteous, and for him the issue is often one of life or death.

4. Cf. my *Formgeschichte des Neuen Testaments*, 193.

5. "Enjoy yourselves in the suffering which you suffer now. For why do you look for the decline of your enemies? Prepare your souls for that which is kept for you, and make ready your souls for the reward which is preserved for you." Cf. 78:6: "Therefore, if you think about the things you have suffered now for your own good so that you may not be condemned at the end and be tormented, you shall receive hope which lasts forever" (*OTP* 1:639, 648). *2 Bar.* 52:6 and 1 Pet 1:4-6 show strikingly close correspondence, particularly with regard to the theme of the reward that already stands prepared.

6. In my *Auferstehung des Propheten*, 514–16, n. 259, I show that there is a close and widely attested structural correspondence between the phenomenon of the absence of the master (because of rapture or death) and the bestowing of the spirit on his disciples who remain behind. What this means is that the disciples, without their master, are in an orphanlike situation, something that is ipso facto diffi-

cult. Ecstatic experience of the master's spirit opens up important access to him. As a rule, such experiences occur only after the master has departed from the earth. Then the question would arise, How does the situation of the "orphans" relate to that of the oppressed minority? From the Farewell Discourses in the Gospel of John, one can see that the two situations are closely related. One would then be led to ask whether this is generally the case elsewhere.

9. Religion

1. According to Heb 11:13, the gist of a confession of faith can be that one recognizes oneself as a stranger and an alien on earth. Faith can be articulated in terms such as these.

2. It would also be good in the area of personal relationships if one makes allowance for different phases rather than judging everything by the characteristics of the initial phase. Each phase has its distinctive strengths and weaknesses.

3. Emphasis is to be placed on the element of "should." The challenge for faith to produce works, which is regarded as obvious by Paul (cf. Gal 5:6b), rightly forms a barrier against the temptation to let faith rest content as no more than a blessed inner certainty.

4. I speak generally here at the outset of the practices and gestures of faith; later on I will use terms more authentic to the New Testament itself.

5. An example of a moralistic-pedagogic interpretation: Jesus praises people for their faith because his real concern is to help them advance in faith, carrying it far beyond the specific instance at hand. Here faith would amount to a person's fundamental stance toward Jesus, but it would have no causal significance for the miracle per se. From this point of view, the miracle is a gift on the part of Jesus to help people find salvation *through* faith.

6. The following is from a meditation I once gave on Luke 17:6:

> The issue here is not whether one believes certain things but has to do with faith as power. We much too quickly think the church demands that we believe something—statements or doctrines. But that is by no means the crucial issue. Faith is actually a power rather than a matter of intellectual assent. Unlike other types of power, however, here it does not matter how much one has but only that one has some of it. Jesus describes this power as the creative power of God. Only God can do something like order a tree to uproot itself and be replanted in the sea! Taken at face value, this would be crazy. But Jesus is talking about a kind of playfulness, the spontaneous joy and uplifting sense of freedom of those who have real faith.

7. This theme is obvious in Matt 8:10 and Luke 7:9; it also permeates the Pauline theology.

8. On this point, cf. Berger, *Die Weisheitschrift aus der Kairoer Geniza* 4:8 ("for even a little faith is righteousness"). This is another analogy which shows wisdom writings as more closely allied to early Christianity than are other expressions of the Judaism of antiquity.

9. Logion 48 of the *Gospel of Thomas* reads: "Jesus said, 'If two persons make peace with each other in one house, they will say to the mountain, "Tumble!" And it will tumble.'" Logion 106 has Jesus say, "When you make two into one, you will become sons of man, and when you say, 'Mountain, tumble,' it will tumble." In the (Syrian) *Didaskalia* we read, "When two come together into one and say to this mountain, 'Lift yourself up and throw yourself into the ocean,' it will happen" (Achelis-Fleming, 345). Cf. also Mark 11:25 (forgive one another—prayer will be heard, because God has forgiven); Matt 5:23-24 (be reconciled with one's brother—the offering is significant); 1 Pet 3:7 (honor the wife as a fellow heir—prayer will be heard). Notice how, in the latter instances, success of cultic actions occupies the same place, functionally speaking, as do the miraculous deeds in the former instances. The same presuppositions are operative in both.

10. There are still other indications of this "principle of disproportionality." So, for example, the least among the brothers is significant in Matthew 25, just as are the smallest and most ordinary acts according to Mark 9. This structural principle is operative in a number of places.

11. Jesus does not actually proceed in the manner indicated by the centurion. The "faith" of the centurion is presented as a faith in Jesus' stipulations. Jesus accepts this faith, letting it stand as it is, but then does not follow the course of action prescribed by the centurion.

12. Both faith and the majesty of Christ are interpreted by means of visually striking metaphors in 2 Cor 3:18—4:6. Here the focus is not on opposition to the crucified one but on the contrast between God and world (cf. 2 Cor 4:4).

13. Mark 4:40-41 (par. Luke 8:25); Mark 5:36 (par. Luke 8:50); Matt 14:26-33; Heb 11:23, 27; 1 Cor 2:3, 5.

14. The mythic mode of presentation serves not only to make the invisible narratively visible, but it also exhibits the sovereign power of God as a force that cuts through ordinary experiences of power.

15. The so-called failure of the disciples to understand (esp. in the Gospel of Mark) has often been noted. This motif is hardly just an ingenuous way of making a contrast. It is much more an indication of why it was necessary, fundamentally, to connect the contents of a Gospel (in the present case, Mark) with the teachings of Jesus. Structuring a Gospel in this way necessarily sets it up against whatever teachings might be making the rounds in the name of one or more of the disciples themselves.

16. Nowhere in Paul can one find clear reference to perverted will. Even if one could, one would still then have to ask from whence it came. Paul has nothing specific to say on that score.

17. As I see it, it is in keeping with the hortatory nature of Romans as a whole that Paul proffers, along with the Christian (instead of just the Jewish) way of acting, also the spiritual (in place of just the fleshly) way. Moreover, he does it such that the Jewish way is not simply identical to the fleshly way.

18. Cf. the description of conflict in Gal 5:17-18, 6:8.

19. I owe thanks here to insights gleaned from conversation with my colleague at Heidelberg, Chr. Burchard. It should also be noted that we are not here dealing with categories of modern psychology but with a part of ordinary experience.

20. Krates, fifth century B.C.E., comedy (Kock, p. 44); Nikostratos, fourth century B.C.E., comedy (Kock, p. 32).

21. On this point cf. W. C. van Unnik, "'Alles is dir möglich,'" 27–36. According to this, the text consists of the elements of address, praise, and petition.

22. Thus, e.g., Pesch, *Das Markusevangelium*, 2:390.

23. Psalm 40:8, "I delight to do your will, O my God; your law is written within my heart"; Ps 103:21, "Praise the Lord, . . . his ministers that do his will"; Ps 143:10, "Teach me to do your will. . . ."

24. On the "regard" paid to lowliness, cf. *1 Clem.* 55:1: Esther fasted and abased herself and mollified the Lord, "who saw the humiliation of her soul and saved the people."

25. It can very well be that even in this act of submission the christological secret is being maintained, since as elsewhere the witnesses to this event are the three disciples. If that is so, then we have here a connection to the theme of watchfulness evident in Mark 13. (Both chapters are farewell discourses!) Not only that, but there could be an intentional contrast between the majesty of the coming Son of Man in chapter 13 and the self-abasement of the Son of God here in chapter 14. This would yield a relationship between the two christological titles at the end of the Gospel of Mark, which is a reversal of their relationship in chapters 8 and 9.

26. The "because" clause in Jas 1:10 thus cannot be intended in a causal sense. Rather, this clause is the content, the actual confession, of one who is abasing himself. In a sense, then, what we have here is a prayer being placed on the lips of a rich person.

27. Cf., e.g., *1 Clem.* 53:2; 55:6; *Herm. Vis.* 3.10.6 ("Every prayer needs humility: fast therefore, and you shall receive what you ask from the Lord").

28. Colossians 2:18, 23, with its reference to the worshiping of angels on the part of the writer's opponents, can be at least partly understood in conjunction with this tradition of fasting. In any case, the worship of angels takes place in self-abasement; striking in v. 18 is the puzzling use of the word "wanting" (Greek: *thelon*). Comparison with Mark 14:36 casts some light on this issue. Whoever humbles himself in a certain sense circumvents his own will; he fundamentally renounces his own inclinations. Verse 23 then follows up with (oblique) reference to fasting.

29. On this cf. part 4 of my article "Gebet" in *TRE* 12:47–60, esp. lines 30–36 on p. 51 (with regard to Rom 15:30, "striving with God").

30. Philo, *De Iona* 30: "Let us now pray, dear friends, to God, the Lord of the universe! Since no law can hinder the power of our prayer, we will try to move the Lord of the Law through prayer. . . . We do not wrestle with the will of any other, since all depends on the will of the king."

31. On the theme of prayer ascending to God, cf. Rev 8:3-4 and Acts 10:4; also *L.A.B.* 50.4 ("let my prayer ascend . . ."); *1 En.* 9:10; 47:1-2. Note especially *Herm. Mand.* 10:3 ("Whoever is sad grieves the Spirit, for the prayer of such a one has no power to ascend to the altar of God, since it is without spirit.") If sadness (the spirit of sadness) drives out (in a quasi-exorcistic fashion) the spirit that is, in essence, joy, then it only follows as a matter of course that prayer cannot ascend to God. For further similarities between prayer and sacrifice, cf. "Gebet" in *TRE* 12: 53, lines 10–15, 16–31.

32. This maxim is used in a christological context in John 3:13. I regard it as widely applicable.

33. Cf. part 4 of my article "Gebet," in *TRE* 12:49–50.

34. I here approach an understanding of pastoral care along the lines of what in antiquity fit within the context of the genre known as the diatribe/*dialexis*. For more details, cf. my "Hellenistische Gattungen im Neuen Testament." Other sources include Rabbow, *Antike Schriften über Seelenheilung und Seelenleitung*; ibid., *Seelenführung*; Hadot, *Seneca*.

35. A literary model for this sort of language might have been provided by *1 Macc.* 5:65 (first a conquering and a tearing down of fortified places, then a taking captive of the inhabitants).

36. Cf. Rom 6:23, where the imagery has to do with the mercenary in relation to death.

10. Behavior

1. *OTP*, 2:218.

2. Cf. Hengel, *The Charismatic Leader and His Followers*.

3. In *On Drunkenness* 67–70, Philo interprets this passage as referring to cutting away irrational portions of the soul, and in *On Flight and Finding* 90–91 as referring to suppressing the body for the sake of the soul. Later the church fathers will explain the New Testament passages along similar lines.

4. Cf. Deut 13:7-10 [English: 6-9]; note how Philo moderates the statement: "such a one should be punished as a public and common enemy" (*Spec. Laws* 1.316). Philo also expands the list of nearby persons to include "one who seems to be well-intentioned."

5. Cf. Berger, *Die Weisheitsschrift aus der Kairoer Geniza*, 220–24.

6. Perhaps it is the case that figurative language necessarily starts out from conventional estimations; this seems to follow from the structure of arguments which proceed from a lesser reality to a greater reality, as in the case of Luke 11:11-13. In such a situation, no criticism of the "lesser," from which the argument proceeds, is possible. In an admonition, however, the speaker is looking at matters from another direction.

7. The closest biblical analogy to this concept of the new community is to be found in the traditions about the relationship between Elijah and Elisha, to which an obvious link exists with the accounts of Jesus' calling of his disciples (compare 1 Kgs 19:19-21 with Mark 1:19-21 and 2:14). Also in the case of Elijah's prophetic summons of Elisha, the call takes the form of breaking off prior family relationships. Might one say that, in contrast to the narrative about Joseph and Aseneth, discussed earlier, the point of agreement between the Elijah/Elisha tradition and the material about Jesus and his disciples consists in the connection between a learner and his teacher? On the other hand, does not Aseneth's connection to Joseph also exhibit elements of a teacher-student relationship? One feature, at least, stands out: Unlike in the Elijah/Elisha tradition, with Jesus there is express mention of hatred—which is how the inner, or psychological, aspect of the new relationship gets conceptualized.

8. Cf. also *Did.* 2:7 and *Barn.* 19:5 ("Love your neighbor more than your own life").

9. *Exegesis on the Soul* (135) renders Luke 14:26 as follows: "If one does not hate his soul, he cannot follow me. For the beginning of salvation is repentance. Therefore John came . . . and proclaimed the baptism of repentance."

10. Cf. Clement, *Strom.* 7.79.5.

11. Any ethic based on a principle of reward is also supposed to be rejected by "enlightened" citizens. This follows from a view of human beings, not only as too eager to act out of self-interest, but also as having their integrity threatened by their dependence on a paycheck. Religion is supposed to stand aloof from such concerns; from religion one expects something in the way of a "higher" confirmation of human dignity. The writers of the Gospels, however, speak quite unabashedly of "wages." They can do so because, in their view, we are not in charge; we are slaves who must wait on God for everything. If we start from the recognition that we are totally dependent upon God, then we see that we are not in a position to "earn" anything.

12. From this perspective, radical evil is all that does not follow from a universal principle of reason. Universal reason is the court of final appeal, and its judgments are self-evident.

13. Cf. Catullus: "Ille mi par esse deo videtur . . ."; the enchanted lover experiences erotic fascination as a divinizing power.

14. In 1 Corinthians 1–4 Paul chiefly discusses the problem of apostolic authority. Only starting with 5:1 does he take up specific issues dealing with the behavior of the community.

15. A similar dynamic is at work where Paul speaks of the human relationship to God in terms of "righteousness"—a term equally applicable to interhuman relationships (cf. Rom 13:7-8).

16. When one finds in Jewish writings contemporary with the New Testament comments to the effect that "whoring" is the greatest temptation faced by scribes and by the "wise" (4Q186), this more likely indicates something about the social and personal constraints attached to these particular professions.

17. Niemann, "Priesterliche Realutopien," 107.

18. On this cf. esp. von Henten, *Die Entstehung der jüdischen Martyrologie*.

19. General characteristics of the Christian versions of the tradition include an antithetically parallel structure and references to "life" as well as to the "losing" of life.

20. One characteristic of this tradition's reception in the Gospels outside of Luke's special material is some connection, in the immediate context, with the theme of "following." Distinctive traits of Mark's rendition are references to "saving," "desiring," and "on account of me."

21. Characteristic of the Q rendition is combination with the motif of the necessary hatred of relatives. John 12:25 also speaks of "loving" and "hating," but the reference is to one's own life.

22. The meaning of Luke 17:33 is that "on that day" one should be concerned neither about one's possessions nor about one's life. All of the normal concerns no longer matter. The worries of the individual person no longer can have any influence on what happens. Now the only chance one has consists in presenting oneself for judgment. In this sense, all that counts anymore is a "rush to the head of the line." (By contrast, consider the story of Lot's wife.)

23. Recall here chap. 4 and the section "Death" in chap. 6, above.

24. New Testament scholars will find in this yet another interesting parallel between Paul and the traditions in Q.

25. Perhaps there is at least a partial analogy between the dynamics of the psyche and the life of plants. In pruning trees growth is trimmed (life is cut back) for the sake of a richer harvest. Might we not say that something similar takes place in the development of human beings? (People can "grow" in response to painful experiences.) Admittedly, however, there are limits to such analogies.

26. Corresponding narratives include stories about the infertility of the wives of the patriarchs. Their very difficulties in bringing children into the world served as the precondition for the direct and propitious intervention of God.

27. Luke 14:26 explicitly shows hatred of relatives being brought into conjunction with hatred of one's own life. Given what we have said about the matrix of such ideas, that is no longer hard to understand.

28. Biser, "Mehr Einheit durch das Wort," 22, col. 1.

29. On this point cf. Gerhardsson, "The Hermeneutic Program in Matthew 22:37-40," 129–50.

Bibliography

Arnim, Hans Friedrich August von. *Stoicorum veterum fragmenta.* 4 vols. Leipzig: Teubner, 1903–24.

Bejick, Urte. *Basileia: Königsherrschaft Gottes im religionsgeschichtlichen Umfeld des Neuen Testaments.* TANZ. Tübingen: Francke, 1991.

Berger, Klaus. *Die Auferstehung des Propheten und die Erhöhung des Menschensohnes: Traditionsgeschichtl. Unters. zur Deutung d. Geschickes Jesu in Frühchristl. Texten.* SUNT 13. Göttingen: Vandenhoeck & Ruprecht, 1976.

———. *Einführung in die Formgeschichte.* UTB 1444. Tübingen: Francke, 1987.

———. *Exegese und Philosophie.* SBS 123/124. Stuttgart: Katholisches Bibelwerk, 1986.

———. *Formgeschichte des Neuen Testaments.* Heidelberg: Quelle & Meyer, 1984.

———. "Gebet." In *TRE* 12 (1984) 47–60.

———. *Gottes einziger Ölbaum: Betrachtungen zum Römerbrief.* Stuttgart: Quell, 1990.

———. "Hellenistische Gattungen im Neuen Testament." In *ANRW* 2/25.2:1124–32.

———. *Hermeneutik des Neuen Testaments.* Gütersloh: Gütersloher, 1988.

———. "Jesus als Pharisäer und frühe Christen als Pharisäer." *NovT* 30 (1988) 231–62.

———. "Die königlichen Messiastraditionen des Neuen Testaments." *NTS* 20 (1973) 1–44.

———. "Der traditionsgeschichtliche Urspruing der *traditio legis.*" *VigChr* 27 (1973) 104–22.

———. "Unfehlbare Offenbarung: Petrus in der gnostischen und apokalyptischen Offenbarungsliteratur." In *Kontinuität und Einheit: Für Franz Mussner,* 261–305. Ed. Paul-Gerhard Müller und Werner Stenger. Freiberg: Herder, 1981.

———. *Die Weisheitsschrift aus der Kairoer Geniza: Erstedition, Kommentar und Übersetzung.* TANZ 1. Tübingen: Francke, 1989.

———. *Wie ein Vogel ist das Wort: Wirklichkeit des Menschen und Parteilichkeit des Herzens nach Texten der Bibel.* Stuttgart: Quell, 1987.

Berger, Klaus, and Carsten Colpe. *Religionsgeschichtliches Textbuch zum Neuen Testament.* TNT 1. Göttingen: Vandenhoeck & Ruprecht, 1987.

Biser, E. "Mehr Einheit durch das Wort." In *Rheinischer Merkur/Christ und Welt* 5 (Feb. 1, 1991) 22, col. 1.

Böcher, Otto. *Christus Exorcista: Dämonismus und Taufe im Neuen Testament.* BWANT 96. Stuttgart: Kohlhammer, 1972.

———. *Das Neue Testament und die dämonische Mächte.* SBS 58. Stuttgart: Katholisches Bibelwerk, 1972.

Bonner, Campbell. "The Technique of Exorcism." *HTR* 36 (1943) 39–51.

Bousset, Wilhelm. *Die Himmelsreise der Seele.* Libelli 71. Darmstadt: Wissenschaftliche Buchgesellschaft, 1961 (=ARW 4, 1901).

Brenk, Frederick E. "In the Light of the Moon: Demonology in the Early Imperial Period." In *ANRW* 2/16.3 (1986) 2068–2145.

Brown, Peter. "The Rise and Function of the Holy Man in Late Antiquity." *JRS* 81 (1971) 80–101.

Bultmann, Rudolf. *The Second Letter to the Corinthians.* Trans. R. A. Harrisville Jr. Minneapolis: Augsburg, 1985. German ed. 1970.

———. *Theology of the New Testament.* 2 vols. Trans. Kendrick Grobel. New York: Scribner, 1951–55.

Burchard, Christoph. "H. E. G. Paulus in Heidelberg, 1811–1851." In *Semper Apertus* 2:222–97. Ed. Wilhelm Doerr. Berlin: Springer, 1986.

Charlesworth, James H., ed. *Old Testament Pseudepigrapha.* 2 vols. Garden City, N.Y.: Doubleday, 1983–85.

Colpe, Carsten. "Geister." In *RAC* 9 (1976) 615–25.

Cremer, Hermann. *Biblico-Theological Lexicon of New Testament Greek.* 3rd ed. Edinburgh: T. & T. Clark, 1883.

Dase, H. "Trauer und ihre Bewaltigung bei Johannes und im Hebräerbrief." Dissertation: University of Heidelberg, 1989.

Dihle, Albrecht. "Evangelien und die biographische Tradition der Antike." *ZThK* 80 (1983) 3–49.

Dion, Paul-Eugène. "Raphael l'exorciste." *Bib* 57 (1976) 399–413.

Drewermann, Eugen. *Tiefenpsychologie und Exegese.* 2 vols. Freiburg: Olten, 1984–85.

Ego, Beate. *Im Himmel wie auf Erden: Studien zum Verhältnis von himmlischer und irdischer Welt im rabbinischen Judentum.* WUNT 2/34. Tübingen: Mohr/Siebeck, 1989.

Ehrlich, Ernst Ludwig. *Die Kultsymbolik im Alten Testament und im nachbiblischen Judentum.* Symbolik der Religionen 3. Stuttgart: Hiersemann, 1959.

Faltin, Th. "Brücke in eine unbekannte Zeit." *Die Zeit* 43 (Oct. 9, 1990) 48.

Gerhardsson, Birger. "The Hermeneutic Program in Matthew 22:37-40." In *Jews, Greeks and Christians: Religious Cultures in Late Antiquity: Essays in Honor of William David Davies*, 129–50. Ed. Robert Hammerton-Kelly and Robin Scroggs. SJLA 21. Leiden: Brill, 1976.

Gnilka, Joachim. *The Epistle to the Philippians.* NTSR 17. New York: Herder and Herder, 1971.

Haas, C. *De Geest Bewaren: Achtergrond en Functie van de Pneumatologie in de Paraenese van de Pastor van Hermas.* The Hague: Boekencentrum, 1985.

Hadot, Ilsetraut. *Seneca und die griechisch-römische Tradition der Seelenleitung.* QSGP 13. Berlin: de Gruyter, 1969.

Hardmeier, Christof. *Texttheorie und biblische Exegese: Zur rhetor. Funktion d. Trauermetaphorik in d. Prophetie.* BET 79. Munich: Kaiser, 1978.

Heiligenthal, Roman. *Werke als Zeichen: Untersuchungen zur Bedeutung der menschlichen Taten im Frühjudentum, Neuen Testament und Frühchristentum.* WUNT 2/9. Tübingen: Mohr/Siebeck, 1983.

Hengel, Martin. *The Charismatic Leader and His Followers.* Trans. James Greig. New York: Crossroad, 1981. German ed. 1968.

Henten, J. W. von, ed. *Die Entstehung der jüdischen Martyrologie*. StPB 38. Leiden: Brill, 1989.

Lang, Friedrich. *Die Briefe an die Korinther*. NTD. Göttingen: Vandenhoeck & Ruprecht, 1986.

Layton, Bentley. *The Gnostic Scriptures*. ABRL. Garden City, N.Y.: Doubleday, 1987.

Lohfink, Gerhard, and Rudolf Pesch, *Tiefenpsychologie und keine Exegese: Eine Auseindersetzung mit Eugen Drewermann*. SBS 129. Stuttgart: Calwer, 1987.

Lövestam, Evald. "Jesus Fils de David chez les Synoptiques." *StTh* 28 (1974) 97–109.

Lührmann, Dieter. *Das Markusevangelium*. HNT 3. Tübingen: Mohr/Siebeck, 1987.

Marshall, Peter. *Enmity in Corinth: Social Conventions in Paul's Relations with the Corinthians*. WUNT 2/23. Tübingen: Mohr/Siebeck, 1987.

Martin, G. M. "Eugen Drewermanns 'Strukturen des Bösen' als Ausgangspunkt eines umstrittenen theologischen Denkweges." *ThLZ* 115 (1990) 321–29.

Mischo, Johannes, and Ulrich J. Niemann. "Die Bessenheit der Anneliese Michel (Klingenberg) in interdisziplinärer Sicht." *Zeitschrift für Parapsychologie und Grenzgebiete der Psychologie* 25 (1983) 129–93.

Nehls, A. F. "Untersuchungen zum semantischen Feld von LYPE und LYPEIN in Septuaginta und Neuem Testament." Dissertation: University of Heidelberg, 1989.

Niemann, Ulrich. "Priesterliche Realutopien: Erfahrungen und Überlegungen zum heutigen Leben in geistlichen Berufen aus der Sicht psychosomatischer Anthropologie." In *Priester Heute: Anfragen, Aufgaben, Anregungen*, 90–133. Ed. Karl Hillenbrand. Würzburg: Echter, 1990.

Nowack, H. "Zur Entwicklungsgeschichte des Begriffs Daimon: Eine Untersuchung epigraphischer Zeugnisse vom 5. Jh. v. Chr. bis zum 5 Jh. n. Chr." Dissertation, University of Bonn, 1960.

Pannenberg, Wolfhart. *Jesus: God and Man*. 2nd ed. Trans. Lewis L. Wilkins and Duane A. Priebe. Philadelphia: Westminster, 1977. 5th German ed. 1976.

Pesch, Rudolf. *Das Markusevangelium*. HTKNT. 2 vols. Freiburg: Herder, 1976–77.

Rabbow, Paul. *Antike Schriften über Seelenheilung und Seelenleitung, auf ihre Quellen untersucht*. Vol. 1: *Die Therapie des Zorns*. Leipzig: Teubner, 1914.

———. *Seelenführung: Methodik der Exerzitien in der Antike*. Munich: Kösel, 1954.

Rau, Eckhard. "Eschatologie, Kosmologie und die Lehrautorität Henochs: Traditions- und formgeschichtliche Untersuchungen zum äth. Henochbuch und zu verwandten Schriften." Dissertation, University of Hamburg, 1974.

Reese, James M. *Hellenistic Influence on the Book of Wisdom and Its Consequences*. AnBib 41. Rome: Biblical Institute Press, 1970.

Röhser, Günter. *Metaphorik und Personifikation der Sünde: Antike Sündenvorstellungen und paulinische Hamartia*. WUNT 2/25. Tübingen: Mohr/Siebeck, 1987.

Schäfer, Peter. *Die Vorstellung vom heiligen Geist in der rabbinischen Literatur*. SANT 28. Munich: Kösel, 1972.

Schimanowski, Gottfried. *Weisheit und Messias: Die jüdischen Voraussetzungen der urchristlichen Präexistenzchristologie*. WUNT 2/17. Tübingen: Mohr/Siebeck, 1985.

Schneemelcher, Wilhelm. *New Testament Apocrypha.* 2 vols. Trans. A. J. B. Higgins. Ed. R. McL. Wilson. Philadelphia: Westminster, 1963–65.

Schürmann, Heinz. *Das Lukasevangelium.* Vol. 1. HTKNT 3/1. Freiburg: Herder, 1969.

Schweizer, Eduard. "Geister (Dämonen)." In *RAC* 9 (1975) 688–99.

Theissen, Gerd. *Psychological Aspects of Pauline Theology.* Trans. John P. Galvin. Philadelphia: Fortress Press, 1987. German ed. 1983.

Theobald, Michael. *Die überströmende Gnade: Studien zu einem paulinischen Motivfeld.* FzB 22. Würzburg: Echter, 1982.

Thraede, Klaus. "Exorzismus." In *RAC* 7 (1969) 44–117.

Unnik, W. C. van. "'Alles is dir möglich' (Mk 14,36)." In *Verborum Veritas: Festschrift für Gustav Stählin z. 70. Geburtstag,* 27–36. Ed. Otto Böcher and Klaus Haacker. Wuppertal: Brockhaus, 1970.

Vermes, Geza. *The Complete Dead Sea Scrolls in English.* New York: Penguin, 1998.

Vollenwieder, Samuel. *Freiheit als neue Schöpfung: Eine Untersuchung zur Eleutheria bei Paulus und in seiner Umwelt.* FRLANT 147. Göttingen: Vandenhoeck & Ruprecht, 1989.

Volz, Paul. *Das Dämonische in Jahwe.* Sammlung gemeinverständlicher Vorträge und Schriften aus dem Gebiet der Theologie und Religionsgeschichte 110. Tübingen: Mohr/Siebeck, 1924.

Wegenast, Klaus. *Das Verständnis der Tradition bei Paulus und in den Deuteropaulinen.* WMANT 8. Neukirchen-Vluyn: Neukirchen, 1962.

Werner, H., et al. "Geist, Geistesgaben." In *TRE* 12 (1984) 182

Wilckens, Ulrich. *Der Brief an die Römer.* 3 vols. Neukirchen-Vluyn: Neukirchener, 1978–82.

Windisch, Hans. *Der zweite Korintherbrief.* KEK 6. Göttingen: Vandenhoeck & Ruprecht, 1924. Reprinted 1970.

Wolter, Michael. "Gewissen II." In *TRE* 13 (1984) 213–18.

Yonge, C. D., trans. *The Works of Philo.* Peabody, Mass.: Hendrickson, 1993.

Zintzen, C. "Geister (Dämonen): Hellenistische und kaiserzeitliche Philosophie." In *RAC* 9 (1975) 640–68.

Index